# Robert E. Lee
# and His High Command

## Gary W. Gallagher, Ph.D.

THE
GREAT
COURSES

PUBLISHED BY:

THE GREAT COURSES
Corporate Headquarters
4840 Westfields Boulevard, Suite 500
Chantilly, Virginia 20151-2299
Phone: 1-800-832-2412
Fax: 703-378-3819
www.thegreatcourses.com

# Gary W. Gallagher, Ph.D.

Professor of History of the American Civil War, University of Virginia

Gary W. Gallagher is the John L. Nau Professor in the History of the American Civil War at the University of Virginia. Before coming to UVA, he was Professor of History at Pennsylvania State University—University Park flagship campus. He graduated from Adams State College of Colorado and earned both his master's degree and doctorate in history from the University of Texas at Austin. His research and teaching focus are on the era of the Civil War and Reconstruction.

Recognized as one of the top historians of the Civil War, Dr. Gallagher is a prolific author. His books include *The Confederate War*, *Lee and His Generals in War and Memory*, *Stephen Dodson Ramseur: Lee's Gallant General*, and *The Myth of the Lost Cause and Civil War History* (co-edited with Alan T. Nolan). He has also co-authored and edited numerous works on individual battles and campaigns, including Antietam, Fredericksburg, Chancellorsville, Gettysburg, Wilderness, Spotsylvania, and the 1864 Shenandoah Valley campaign and published more than eight dozen articles in scholarly journals and popular historical magazines. Virtually all his books have been History Book Club selections.

Dr. Gallagher has received numerous awards for his research and writing, including the Lincoln Prize (1998—shared with three other authors), the Fletcher Pratt Award for the best nonfiction book on the Civil War (1999), the Laney Prize for the best book on the Civil War (1998), and the William Woods Hassler Award for contributions to Civil War studies (1998). Additionally, Professor Gallagher serves as editor of two book series for the University of North Carolina Press (*Civil War America* and *Military Campaigns of the Civil War*). He has appeared regularly on the Arts and Entertainment Network's series *Civil War Journal* and has participated in other television projects. Active in historic preservation, Professor Gallagher was president of the Association for Preservation of Civil War Sites from 1987 through mid-1994, has served on the Board of Directors of the Civil War Trust, and on numerous occasions, has testified before Congress on battlefield preservation.

# Table of Contents
# Robert E. Lee and His High Command

# Table of Contents
## Robert E. Lee and His High Command

# Robert E. Lee and His High Command

**Scope:**

This course examines Robert E. Lee and the high command of the Army of Northern Virginia. The lectures engage such questions as why Lee and his army are central to an understanding of the Civil War, how their operations influenced the Northern and Southern home fronts, why Lee was so successful as a field commander, and what kinds of officers flourished and failed under his leadership. A principal goal is to explain how and why Lee and the Army of Northern Virginia came to be the most important national institution in the Confederacy. The course explores the careers of Lee and 13 other generals in detail, assessing their contributions to famous military campaigns, highlighting their strengths and weaknesses as officers, and seeking to create a descriptive and analytical portrait of a storied army's high command. The course departs from its biographical approach with four topical lectures, including one devoted to the ways in which former Confederate generals wrote about their wartime experiences.

Lee receives the fullest attention, with four lectures on his generalship. His three most successful infantry corps commanders—Thomas J. "Stonewall" Jackson, James Longstreet, and Jubal A. Early—are each the subject of two lectures, and the other 10 generals are either covered in one lecture or share a lecture with another officer. The 14 generals were chosen for their importance and as representatives of types; for example, army commanders Joseph E. Johnston and P. G. T. Beauregard offer revealing contrasts to Lee, and a quartet of younger men—John B. Gordon, Robert E. Rodes, Stephen Dodson Ramseur, and Edward Porter Alexander—serve as case studies of how officers with very different military backgrounds rose through the ranks to positions of considerable authority.

The course breaks down into seven sections of unequal length. The first lecture sets the stage by placing Lee and his army in the larger context of the war. The next four lectures explore Lee's generalship, with the last of them examining whether Lee should be considered an old-fashioned general caught up in a modern mid-19th-century conflict. The six lectures on Jackson, Longstreet, and Early come next, followed by a quartet on James E. B. "Jeb" Stuart, Ambrose Powell Hill, Richard S. Ewell, and John Bell Hood. Stuart ably commanded Lee's cavalry for most of the war, neither Hill nor Ewell distinguished himself as a corps commander, and Hood left the army as a superior division commander who would fail at higher levels of responsibility in Georgia and Tennessee. Lectures Sixteen and Seventeen break the biographical pattern. The first looks at Lee's ability to make hard decisions regarding personnel and the second at the impact of combat attrition on the high command. Lectures Eighteen through Twenty-One shift the spotlight to the four young officers: Rodes, a graduate of the Virginia Military Institute; Ramseur, a West Pointer from the class of 1860; Gordon, a lawyer with no formal military training; and Alexander, another West Point graduate who, unlike any of the other generals examined in the course, made his principal reputation as an artillerist. Failure of different types forms a strong thread in Lectures Twenty-Two and Twenty-Three, the first of which covers Johnston and Beauregard and the second, John Bankhead Magruder and George E. Pickett. The final lecture explores how postwar writings, especially those of Jubal Early, John B. Gordon, and others of the Lost Cause school of interpretation, helped shape popular perceptions of Lee and several of his most famous lieutenants.

# Lecture One
# Lee and the Army of Northern Virginia

**Scope:**    Robert E. Lee and his Army of Northern Virginia occupied a central position in Confederate and Civil War history. Myriad connections linked the battlefield and the civilian sector during the conflict, and no military force wielded greater influence on the respective home fronts than Lee's command. Citizens in the United States came to view it as the principal stumbling block to restoring the Union, while Confederates invested increasingly more emotional capital in it as their best hope for winning independence. The Confederate people looked to Lee and his army much as colonists had looked to George Washington and the Continental Army during the American Revolution. Long before the end of the war, Lee and his army, rather than Jefferson Davis and the Confederate Congress, had become the most important national institution in the Confederacy. The surrender of Lee's army, at a time when scores of thousands of Southern soldiers remained under arms elsewhere, understandably signaled the end of the war to most observers, North and South. Lee and his subordinate commanders had played a hugely important role in the war that renders them worthy of continuing investigation.

## Outline

I.    Robert E. Lee and the Army of Northern Virginia occupy a central position in Confederate and Civil War history.

    **A.**   It is important to understand how the home front and the battlefield influenced each other.

        **1.**   Civilian morale depended in large measure on news from the battle fronts.

        **2.**   Civilian expectations in two democracies at war often affected military planning.

        **3.**   Much writing about the Civil War has neglected to examine ties between the military and nonmilitary spheres of the conflict.

    **B.**   No military force on either side wielded more influence on the respective home fronts than Lee's Army of Northern Virginia.

    **1.** Lee's army was the only Confederate force to win a series of major victories.

    **2.** Citizens of the United States saw Lee and his army as the greatest threat to restoration of the Union.

**II.** Lee and his army became the most important national institution in the Confederacy.

    **A.** Confederate citizens came to expect success from the Army of Northern Virginia.

        **1.** Operations between late June 1862 and mid-June 1863 elevated Lee and his army to a special position.

        **2.** Lee and his army were more important in terms of Confederate morale than Jefferson Davis and the Confederate government.

    **B.** Lee and his army functioned in the Confederacy much as George Washington and the Continental Army had for the colonists during the American Revolution.

**III.** Belief in Lee's army sustained widespread Confederate optimism long past the point often considered the turning point of the war.

    **A.** Many historians and other writers have identified the summer of 1863 as the moment when the eventual victory of the United States was assured.

        **1.** Lee's defeat at Gettysburg is often portrayed as a watershed.

        **2.** Ulysses S. Grant's victory at Vicksburg is described as a similarly pivotal success for the United States.

    **B.** Confederate morale did not suffer a critical blow in the summer of 1863.

        **1.** Faith in Lee's ability to sustain the war effort remained high among Confederates.

        **2.** U.S. morale bottomed out in the summer of 1864.

**IV.** Lee's surrender marked the end of the war for most observers, North and South.

    **A.** The fact that thousands of other Confederate soldiers remained under arms was less important than Lee's surrender.

    **B.** The response to Lee's surrender underscored the unique position he and his army had occupied.

**V.** It is highly unlikely that the war could have lasted four years without the presence of Lee and his army.

**Essential Reading:**

Gallagher, *The Confederate War*, chapter 3.

———, *Lee and His Generals in War and Memory*, chapter 1.

McMurry, *Two Great Rebel Armies*, chapters 1, 8, 9.

**Supplementary Reading:**

Connelly and Jones, *The Politics of Command.*

Freeman, *Lee's Lieutenants.*

**Questions to Consider:**

1. How long would the war have lasted if Lee had not taken control of the Army of Northern Virginia?
2. Was it a sign of weakness in the Confederacy that Lee's army loomed so large in the national psyche?

# Lecture One—Transcript
# Lee and the Army of Northern Virginia

This course examines Robert E. Lee and the high command of the Army of Northern Virginia. In twenty-four lectures we will engage such questions as why Lee and his army are central to an understanding of the Civil War, how their operations influence the Northern and Southern home fronts, why Lee was so successful as a field commander, and what kinds of officers flourished and what kinds failed under his style of leadership. Our principle goal is to examine how and why Lee and the Army of Northern Virginia came to be the most important national institution in the Confederacy. The course will explore the careers of Lee and 13 other generals in detail, assessing their contributions to famous military campaigns, highlighting their strengths and weaknesses as officers, and seeking to create a descriptive and analytical portrait of a storied army's top leadership. The course will depart from its biographical approach with four topical lectures, including one devoted to the ways in which former Confederate generals wrote about their wartime experiences—a body of writings that remains very important today.

Lee will receive the fullest attention with four lectures on his generalship. His three most successful infantry core commanders, Stonewall Jackson, James Longstreet and Jubal Early, will each be the subject of two lectures, and the other ten generals either will be covered in one lecture or will share a lecture with another officer.

I selected the fourteen generals for their importance, and in some cases as representative types. For example, army commanders Joseph E. Johnston and P. G. T. Beauregard offer a revealing contrast to Lee, and a quartet of younger men—John B. Gordon, Robert E. Rodes, Steven Dodson Ramseur, and Edward Porter Alexander—provide case studies of how officers with very different military backgrounds rose through the ranks to positions of considerable authority.

The course breaks down into seven sections of unequal length. The first lecture sets the stage by placing Lee and his army within the larger context of the war. The next four lectures explore Lee's generalship, the last of those four examining whether Lee should be considered an old-fashioned general caught up in a modern type of mid-19th century conflict.

The six lectures on Jackson, Longstreet and Early come next, followed by a quartet on Jeb Stuart, A.P. Hill, Richard S. Ewell, and John Bell Hood. Stuart ably commanded Lee's cavalry for most of the war. Neither Hill nor Ewell, who had done very well as division commanders, distinguished himself as core commander, and Hood left Lee's army as a superior division commander who would fail at higher levels of responsibility in Georgia and Tennessee.

The next two lectures, numbers sixteen and seventeen, break the biographical pattern. The first looks at Lee's ability to make hard decisions regarding personnel—many historians believe he couldn't make such decisions, I disagree with that. The second of these two examines the impact of combat attrition on the army's high command.

Lectures Eighteen through Twenty-One shift the spotlight to the four young officers: Rodes, a graduate of the Virginia Military Institute; Ramseur, a West Pointer from the class of 1860; Gordon, a lawyer with no formal military training before the war; and Alexander, another West Point graduate who, unlike any of the other the generals were going to look at, made his principle reputation as an artillerist.

Failure of different types forms a strong thread in lectures Twenty-Two and Twenty-Three, the first of which covers Johnston and Beauregard, and the second John Bankhead Magruder and George E. Pickett. The final lecture explores how post-war writings, especially those of Jubal Early, John Gordon, and others who wrote in the Lost Cause school of interpretation, helped shape popular perceptions of Lee and several of this most famous lieutenants.

Let's begin with an overview. Lee and the Army of Northern Virginia occupied a central position in Confederate and Civil War history. A myriad of connections linked the battlefield and the civilian sector during the conflict, and no military force on either side, no other military force, wielded a greater influence on the respective home fronts than did Lee and his command. Citizens in the United States came to view Lee and his army as the principle stumbling block to restoring the Union; and Confederates invested increasingly more emotional capital in Lee and his army as their best hope for establishing the independence of their slave-holding republic.

The Confederate people looked to Lee and his army as much as the colonists had looked to George Washington and the Continental Army during the American Revolution. Long before the end of the war, Lee and his army, rather than Jefferson Davis and the Confederate government, had become the most important national institution in the Confederacy. The surrender of Lee's army, at a time when scores of thousands of

Confederates remained under arms elsewhere, understandably signaled the end of the war to most observers North and South. Lee and his subordinate commanders had played a hugely important role in the war that renders them worthy of continuing investigation.

Lee and his army occupy a central position in the history of the Confederacy and, in a broader sense, in the history of the Civil War. Civilian morale depended on, in large measure, both in the United States and the Confederacy, on the activities of the armies in the field. Civilians very eagerly followed the activities of the armies. They got most of their information from newspapers. They either subscribed to them or they passed them around—the newspaper was the principal source of information, but they also got a lot of information from letters written home by soldiers in the armies, and as they received this information and as they processed it, morale went up and down, big shifts of morale, in fairly short times, often.

There's a sense on the part of many people that morale was linear during the Civil War. People often begin their consideration of the conflict at Appomattox with knowledge of the United States' victory, and they work backwards from that point trying to find what went wrong with the Confederate war effort, and there's a sense from that approach to the war that there is a pretty straight line going from the beginning of the war to Appomattox, with morale declining on the Confederate side and rising on the side of the United States. That simply wasn't the case. There were great shifts of morale, many spikes on both sides, almost always in direct response to what people are learning about the activities of their respective armies on the battlefield. It's always a mistake to begin at the end of a story, of any historical story, and read backward trying to understand what is going on. It's far more important to read forward through the story, and in terms of the army's events and military events on civilian morale, that is especially important during the Civil War. You have to follow events forward and see how the people on each side reacted to the unfolding news.

Civilian expectations in these two democracies at war often affected military planning, could affect the choice of commanders. Both Abraham Lincoln and Jefferson Davis appointed a number of political figures to generalships because it served certain constituencies. Lincoln appointed Nathaniel P. Banks and John C. Fremont and Benjamin Franklin Butler and others, not because he thought they were great generals, but because he was serving constituencies behind the lines. Jefferson Davis did the same thing. In Robert E. Lee's army, two prominent Georgia politicians, Robert

Toombs and Howard Cobb held positions as general officers because of their political importance, not because of their military gifts.

The civilian expectations also could affect strategic planning. Early on the Confederacy followed what some historians have called a "cordon offense." That is trying to defend every part of the Confederate national territory because the people demanded it. The people in Arkansas wanted Confederate forces protecting them, so did the people in Virginia, so did the people in every other Confederate state, and, at first, the government tried to do that. In the end, or long before the end, Davis and his advisors realized that they couldn't protect everything and they shifted to a strategic posture that is often called either the "offensive defensive" or the "defensive offensive," which consisted of congregating the bulk of national military resources in large field armies and having them try to protect certain areas. Mobile field armies that would meet major United States threats. Don't defend everyplace, concentrate your resources, stand on the broad defensive but try to find moments at which to launch counter blows against the United States forces that were making their way into the South. But civilian expectations played a role here, too, in the strategic planning.

Much of the writing about the civil war does not focus on these connections between the home front and the battlefield. There's a great divide in much Civil War writing, which tends to either focus either entirely on military topic or to focus on entirely civilian topics. Academic historians tend not to be interested in military affairs, so they write about the non-military dimensions of the war. Non-academic historians tend to focus on the military dimensions of the war, and they have created a great literature in terms of its size on the individual campaigns and generals and how officers reacted on different battlefields. They've looked at the tactical minutia of almost every major and many minor battles during the Civil War. But these two parts of the literature often don't intersect in any significant way, which is a mistake because in order to understand the war, in order to understand how it unfolded and why it unfolded the way it did, we have to understand the reciprocal influences between the home front and the battlefield. Lee's army is a perfect vehicle for us to try to understand that, all the ways in which what happened on the military front influenced events behind the lines, and vice versa. As I said earlier, no military force on either side wielded greater influence in this regard than Lee, than the Army of Northern Virginia.

Lee's army was the only Confederate force that ever really won victories. The story of Confederate military affairs, except for Lee and his army, is largely a story of failure. Out in the western theater, the great theater between the Appalachian Mountains and the Mississippi River and beyond, is a theater where almost nothing good happens for the Confederacy. All the great battles in the west with one exception, the battle of Chickamauga in September 1863, all the other great battles were failures for the Confederacy. The whole strategic landscape in many ways is filled with failure for the Confederacy except for events in Virginia, the Virginia-Maryland-Pennsylvania theater where Lee and his army operated. That is where the Confederate people could find some good news. Now much of the rest of the story of the war was negative for the Confederates, so they tended to focus on Lee and his army, they tended to look at where the good news was coming from, and they came to invest more of their emotional capital in the army that gave them victories rather than the armies that did not give them victories.

On the other side of the Potomac River, citizens of the United States understandably saw Lee and his army as the greatest threat to the restoration of the Union. This is the army that's defeating United States forces, especially the most famous and the largest of the United States armies, the Army of the Potomac. There are two great moments of peril in 1862 and 1863 for the United States, two moments in which events seemed to be trending towards Confederate success. One came in the summer and autumn of 1862 after Lee's victories at the Seven Days around Richmond, and then at Second Manassas, or Bull Run, these took place in late June/early July and in late August, then Lee moved across the Potomac River into Maryland. That was a period of great crisis for the United States, because so much bad is happening to United States forces here in the eastern theater.

The second moment of great crisis came the following spring, and again Lee's army is at the center of this. Lee won a victory at Fredericksburg, Virginia in December of 1862, and then followed up with his most dazzling victory at Chancellorsville in May of 1863. It's a period, again, of great peril for the United States, and the key to drooping morale behind the lines in the United States was what Lee and his army were accomplishing in the Virginia theater.

Lee, of course, followed up these twin victories at Fredericksburg and at Chancellorsville with his second movement across the Potomac River in the form of his Pennsylvania campaign in the summer of 1863, the campaign that ended at Gettysburg. People behind the lines in the United States followed these events very closely, and became very much concerned about the way the war was going because Lee won these pairs of victories in the summer and autumn of 1862, and then again in the winter and spring of 1863. He is the real problem for them. Their armies are doing well in the west, the armies of the United States, but they cannot seem to find anyone, Lincoln and his advisors cannot seem to find anyone who can cope with Lee and the Army of Northern Virginia.

Lee loomed even larger, he and his army, because of where they operated. They operated in the eastern theater, the theater made up of Virginia and Maryland and Pennsylvania. There was more attention paid to the eastern theater than the western theater at the time. Many historians don't like this, and they argue that too much attention has been accorded to Lee and his army, more attention should be given to Grant and Sherman and Thomas and the United States commanders who won all those successes in the western theater, in effect, won the war in the western theater, say many modern historians. Why all this focus on Lee? Well, the answer is because people at the time focused on Lee. The great centers of population were in the east then. The great daily newspapers with the largest circulations were in New York and Philadelphia and Boston and Washington and Baltimore. The majority of the men who fought for the United States fought in the eastern theater. The majority of the men lived in this most populous part of the United States. The two capitals, of course, were in the eastern theater, just a hundred miles apart—Washington and Richmond. The most famous armies were there, the Army of the Potomac and the Army of Northern Virginia. This is where many people looked to see, this eastern theater, where many people looked to try to determine who was winning the war.

Certainly those who viewed our war from abroad, from London and from Paris, focused almost exclusively on the eastern theater. They determined how the war was going by how things were unfolding in the eastern theater. How was Lee's army doing? How was the Army of the Potomac doing? Depending on what the answer to that was, leaders in Paris and London would make their conclusions about what the likely outcome of the war would be. All of these factors come together to make the activities of Lee and his army loom especially large both in the Confederacy and in the Union.

As the war unfolded, certainly by the mid-point of the war, I believe, by the summer of 1863, Lee and his Army of Northern Virginia had become the most important national institution in the Confederacy. Confederate citizens had come to expect success, as I said earlier, from the Army of Northern Virginia. They were focusing on the one part of the military landscape where they received good news, where they heard about the Seven Days, where they heard about Second Manassas, where they heard about Fredericksburg, and

Chancellorsville. That year especially cemented in the minds, the year between the Seven Days in June of 1862 and the battle at Chancellorsville in May of 1863, that year, that eleven months more properly, was a time when the people of the Confederacy cemented in their thoughts about their military posture that Lee and his army were the key. What Lee and his army did was going to shape, more than any other factor, how the war would go. That critical year continued to wield influence all through the rest of the war. The hopes and the belief in the army forged between the Seven Days and Chancellorsville continued to promote a very strong sense that Lee and his army would prevail all through the rest of the war.

There is a residual effect that is very important. Lee and his army became more important than Davis and the Confederate government. There aren't all of the political controversies associated with Lee and his army. You can just look at them as a positive national institution; Davis and his government was much more complex, much more wrangling going on among the Confederate people about what Davis and his government were doing. Lee and his army, as I said in my opening, came to occupy a position much like George Washington and the Continental Army did during the American Revolution. They came to embody the Confederacy in many ways. People looked to the army, not to Richmond, to judge the state of their experiment in nation building.

Let me just read a couple of quotations that suggest the stature of Lee and his army. One is from early 1864, when a soldier from a Louisiana regiment wrote home about his experience during a furlough in the state of Georgia. He'd been away from the army, to Georgia, and then had gone back to the army. He said, "I never had the most distant idea of the honors that our army had gained until I visited Georgia. The mere name of being one of the Army of Northern Virginia is sufficient to pass one into the best circles of society down in Georgia."

Another soldier, this one in a Georgia infantry unit, voiced a sentiment pervasive inside and outside the army. "The Army of Northern Virginia," this soldier wrote in September of 1864, "The Army of Northern Virginia alone is the last hope of the South. It will sooner or later, by its own unaided power, win the independence of the Confederacy."

A Confederate brigadier named Clement Evans voiced a very common sentiment in tying Lee and George Washington together more explicitly. He wrote in early 1864, "General Robert E. Lee is regarded by his army as nearest approaching the character of the great and good Washington than any man living. He's the only man living in whom they would unreservedly trust all power for the preservation of their independence."

The belief in Lee and his army that grew in that first year in 1862 and 1863, and then continued through the rest of the war, sustained widespread Confederate optimism long past the point often considered the great dividing line of the war. Most historians, or many historians, both academic and non-academic, point to the summer of 1863 as the moment when the war turned decisively in favor of the United States. The victories at Gettysburg, Meade's victory over Lee there, and U. S. Grant's capture of Vicksburg, and the Federal power, subsequent control over all of the Mississippi River—those events mark the point at which Confederate success was no longer possible argue many historians, professional and non-professional. After the summer of 1863, there is an inexorable slide toward Appomattox, many have stated. It's not a question of whether the United States is going to win, whether the Confederacy is going to lose, it's just a question of how long it's going to take. That's the dividing line, the summer of '63. I think that is not correct. I think that, again, that's a question of reading backward from Appomattox. Gettysburg does not loom as large at the time as it does to us now.

Vicksburg was a disaster, no way to dress that up if you are looking at it from a Confederate perspective. The South lost an army and soon lost control of the Mississippi River. Gettysburg was much different. There were mixed reports. The first day had been a great victory for the Confederates. It was not perceived, Gettysburg was not perceived, as a disaster that pointed toward eventual Confederate defeat.

It wasn't viewed that way in the United States either. Abraham Lincoln is the easiest place to go to find someone who tells us, or should tell us, not to view Gettysburg as the great turning point in the war. Lincoln wrote a letter in the wake of Gettysburg to George Gordon Meade, his army commander. He wrote it, he poured out his thoughts in it, and then he didn't send it to Meade, he wisely didn't send it to Meade, but this is what he wrote to Meade, "I do not believe you appreciate the magnitude of the misfortune involved in Lee's escape [Lee's escape back to Virginia from Pennsylvania]. He was within your easy grasp, and to have closed upon him would, in connection with our other late successes," wrote Lincoln, that is at Vicksburg and on the Mississippi River, "would have ended the war. As it is," concluded a bitterly disappointed president, "the war will be prolonged indefinitely. Your golden opportunity is gone, and I am distressed immeasurably because of it."

Lincoln didn't think Gettysburg marked the beginning of the end of the war, and neither did others at the time. It is important for us to remember that. There is still a very strong belief in Lee, very strong belief in Lee across the South, and that belief continued in a way that makes it clear that many people in the Confederacy didn't consider Gettysburg a real defeat at all for Lee because they continue to talk about Lee after Gettysburg as a general who had never been defeated, and who probably never would be defeated. They talk about him that way in late 1863. They talk about him that way in early 1864. There's an abiding faith among most Confederates both within the Army of Northern Virginia, in other armies of the Confederacy, and among the civilian population across the South, an abiding faith in Lee's abilities to sustain the war, to continue the Confederate national resistance in a way that eventually could, or even likely, would bring success. That belief in Lee, I believe, continues because of the great victories he had achieved during his first year in command, and those are extremely important.

A woman named Catherine Ann Devereux Edmondston kept a diary. It's the best-published diary, North or South, by any woman from the Civil War. I think she lived in eastern South Carolina. She wrote in the summer of '64 about Lee, "What a position does he occupy—the idol, the point of trust, of confidence and repose of thousands. How nobly has he won the confidence, the admiration, of the nation."

A young artillerist in Lee's army in the summer of '64 said that he wanted Lee to have more power in the Confederacy. He thought Lee was the key to such an extent that, as he put it, "I should like to see him as king, or dictator. He's one of the few great men who ever lived who could be trusted in such a position."

Confederate morale and belief, I think, in Lee remained high. In that grinding summer of 1864, the Overland campaign between Lee and Grant, where casualties were enormous, even within a Civil War context, we'll talk more about this in subsequent lectures, but at the same time morale in the United States bottomed out. The darkest period of the war in many ways for the United States is June and July and August of 1864. Abraham Lincoln in August wrote his famous Blind Memorandum, made his cabinet members sign it, in which he said the Republicans were not going to be reelected, and if the United States was going to win the war it would have to win the war before the Democratic administration took office in 1865. Lincoln was very pessimistic. There was a great pessimism across the North, much of it tied to the fact that Ulysses S. Grant, having gone from the western theater to the eastern theater to confront Lee because the civilians in the United States demanded it—another example of civilian wishes having an effect on where generals went. Grant had not been able to defeat Lee. People in the United States believed they finally had someone who could defeat Lee. When that didn't happen morale dropped behind the lines in the United States. Gettysburg was a distant memory by the summer of 1864. No one in the United States, in the summer of 1864, would have said, "Yes, things don't look great right now. Grant hasn't been able to get into Richmond or defeat Lee, but Gettysburg was the turning point and we know we're going to win." Again, read forward in the evidence and you'll get a better sense of the ebb and flow of sentiment behind the lines.

One of the best indications of just how important Lee and his army became to the Confederacy comes at Appomattox. When Lee surrendered about thirty thousand men at Appomattox, far more than thirty thousand men remained under arms elsewhere in the Confederacy, and yet Lee's surrender marked the end of the war in the view of almost everyone—in the United States, in the Confederacy, and abroad. Once Lee's army had surrendered, that is it. The Confederacy is dead; the United States triumphed in the view of almost everyone. That is the attitude people take because of the importance of Lee and his army, because Lee and his army had become the leading national institution in the Confederacy. The death of the Army of Northern Virginia removed the Confederate people's most cherish rallying point, and for most of them effectively marked the demise of their nation.

Across the Confederacy, soldiers and civilians reacted with dismay. "My last hope died within me when General Lee surrendered," wrote an officer serving out in the trans-Mississippi theater. He wrote this to his father in May of 1865. This man was still under arms, he hadn't surrendered, but Lee's demise marked the end of the war for him.

A woman named Sara Strickler Fife, a Virginian, wrote on April 11 in her diary. She had just learned about Lee's surrender. On April 11, 1865 she wrote, "I cannot keep off the terrible feeling that I am standing at the deathbed of the dearest thing on earth to me." A young Floridian received news of Lee's, or reacted to news of Lee's surrender in very similar fashion. She wrote, "General Lee has surrendered the Army of Northern Virginia. Oh how I wish we were all dead. It's as if the very earth had crumbled beneath our feet."

Very common reactions across the Confederacy, very common, and reactions across the United States were very similar. Lee and his army had come to occupy this tremendously important position in the minds of people on both sides. Some measure of his success on the battlefield that many in the United States army wrote, the Army of the Potomac that was there at Appomattox that compelled the Army of Northern Virginia, a number of those soldiers reacted in a sort of dazed fashion. They wrote home and said, in effect, I can't believe the war is over. We've been fighting Lee for all of these years." One man, a New Englander, wrote in a very evocative passage, that he had a sense that he would be fighting Lee all of his life, and that Lee was like a ghost who haunted children. It was hard for this man to put into words to his sister why he wasn't more jubilant about Appomattox. He had written a letter to her earlier, a sort of muted letter, and she had written back and said, "Well, why aren't you happier? You've won the war, why aren't you jubilant?" And he explained it to her that way. He couldn't really believe that Lee had been defeated. He in many ways had thought that Lee never would be defeated.

I think it's highly unlikely that the war could have lasted four years without the presence of Lee and the Army of Northern Virginia. I'm going to flesh this point out more in subsequent lectures, but Lee and his army are critical. The great moment in this regard is the Seven Days' campaign in June and early July 1862. That is a point at which the war was going so badly for the Confederacy, before Lee took command of the Army of Northern Virginia, when Joseph E. Johnston was wounded in the battle of Seven Pines at the end of May 1862. Things were going so badly for the Confederacy both in the western theater and in the eastern theater that United States victory seemed almost certain. I don't believe in counter-factual history, I think it is a waste of time for the most part, so I'll indulge in some here and say that I think that the Confederacy would have lost the war in the summer of 1862 if Robert E. Lee had not taken command of the Army of Northern Virginia and turned the strategic situation around. Once he did that, the war was prolonged, was prolonged in a way that, for one thing, allowed emancipation to be put on the table. A war ending without Lee and what his army did after 1862 would have almost restored the United States to the status quo antebellum. Once Lee got in command and the war began to lengthen, it took on a much more revolutionary character, and that is another reason that it is well worth our time to explore the campaigns of Lee and his army and their impact on the Confederacy and on the Civil War.

# Lecture Two
# The Making of a Confederate General

**Scope:** Robert E. Lee's military career prior to his taking command of the Army of Northern Virginia afforded a range of experiences and highlighted disparate talents that would influence his role as the Confederacy's most famous field commander. He compiled a remarkable record at West Point, worked in important engineering projects in the 1830s, and distinguished himself in the war with Mexico as the most celebrated member of General Winfield Scott's talented staff. As a reform-minded superintendent at West Point in the 1850s and, later, as the officer who oversaw the mustering of Virginia's state forces early in the Civil War, Lee honed skills that would make him a superior army administrator. His engineering training had given him a grasp of the importance of fortifications, knowledge he put to good use when, in late 1861, Jefferson Davis assigned him to head a department along the south Atlantic coast. That service, together with an earlier, largely unsuccessful, stint in the mountainous regions of western Virginia, raised doubts among the Confederate people about Lee's aggressiveness and overall military capacity. By the spring of 1862, many newspapers, citizens, and soldiers who had applauded Lee's decision to cast his fortunes with the Confederacy in April 1861 derided him as "Granny Lee" and an "old stick-in-the-mud." Many would not have predicted success when he assumed charge of the army defending Richmond on June 1, 1862.

# Outline

**I.** Robert E. Lee had a varied career as a soldier before the Civil War.

    **A.** He compiled a distinguished record at West Point and graduated second in his class.

    **B.** He worked on important engineering projects as a junior officer.

    **C.** He served on Winfield Scott's staff during the war with Mexico.

        **1.** His skills as an engineer and a reconnaissance officer contributed to several U.S. victories in Winfield Scott's campaign from Vera Cruz to Mexico City.

        **2.** Scott developed a high opinion of Lee.

       **3.**   Lee earned three brevets for gallantry.

   **D.**  Lee was a successful superintendent at West Point. Many of his cadets would later serve under him as generals.

   **E.**  Lee's only experience as a field officer came with the Second Cavalry in Texas in the 1850s.

**II.**  Lee oversaw the mustering of Virginia's state forces in the wake of secession in the spring of 1861.

   **A.**  He proved to be an able administrator in Richmond.

   **B.**  This duty denied him a field command, unlike many of his friends and colleagues.

**III.**  Lee's first year as a Confederate general yielded mixed results. He ranked third in seniority among full Confederate generals.

   **A.**  Confederates initially hailed his decision to join the new Southern republic.

   **B.**  He mounted an ineffective defense of western Virginia in the summer and autumn of 1861.

       **1.**   He commanded in a region of difficult terrain.
       **2.**   Many of his subordinates were poor soldiers.
       **3.**   He sought to implement overly complex strategic plans.
       **4.**   He was widely considered a failure when he left western Virginia in October 1861.

   **C.**  Able service along the south Atlantic coast in the winter of 1861–1862 did not restore his diminished reputation.

       **1.**   He improved the defensive situation in this theater.
       **2.**   His call for fortifications, together with a lack of battlefield success, promoted a belief that he was a timid officer. He was even called "Granny Lee."

**IV.**  He completed his first year as a Confederate general as Jefferson Davis's principal military adviser.

   **A.**  Davis valued Lee's opinion. Lee argued for a national conscription act, which was adopted in 1862.

   **B.**  Lee would have preferred field command—and his luck soon changed.

**V.**  Lee's first great opportunity came in June 1862.

**A.** Joseph E. Johnston's wounding at the battle of Seven Pines or Fair Oaks (May 31, 1862) left the army defending Richmond without a commander.

**B.** Davis's selection of Lee to replace Johnston provoked mixed reaction.

    **1.** Many Confederates predicted that Lee would be a passive army commander poorly fitted to defend the capital.

    **2.** Some Confederates had retained a high opinion of Lee and predicted success for him.

**C.** Lee confronted a critical strategic situation that would largely decide the fate of the Confederacy in the summer of 1862.

**Essential Reading:**

Gallagher, *Lee and His Generals in War and Memory*, chapter 1.

Thomas, *Robert E. Lee: A Biography*, chapters 15–18.

**Supplementary Reading:**

Freeman, *R. E. Lee: A Biography*, vol. 1; vol. 2, chapters 1–10.

Harsh, *Confederate Tide Rising: Robert E. Lee and the Making of Southern Strategy, 1861–1862*, chapters 1–2.

**Questions to Consider:**

**1.** What does the fluctuation in Lee's reputation in 1861–1862 indicate about the relationship between Confederate civilians and their military leaders?

**2.** Could a defensive specialist have turned the strategic tide for the Confederacy in the summer of 1862?

# Lecture Two—Transcript
# The Making of a Confederate General

Our second lecture will turn the spotlight on Robert E. Lee. We'll discuss his career down to the point at which at took command of the Army of Northern Virginia. His military career prior to taking that position as the head of the army that he would make famous, and would in turn make him famous, afforded a range of experiences, and highlighted disparate talents that would influence his role as the Confederacy's most famous field commander. He compiled a remarkable record at West Point, worked on important engineering projects in the 1830s, and distinguished himself in the war with Mexico as the most celebrated member of General Winfield Scott's talented staff. As a reform minded superintendent at West Point in the 1850s, and later as the officer who oversaw the mustering of Virginia's state forces early in the Civil War, Lee honed his skills that would make him a superior army administrator. His engineering training had given him a grasp of the importance of fortifications, knowledge he put to good use when in late 1861 President Jefferson Davis assigned him to head a department along the south Atlantic coast. That service, together with an earlier and largely unsuccessful stint in the mountainous regions of western Virginia, raised doubts among the Confederate people about Lee's aggressiveness and overall military capacity. By the spring of 1862, many newspapers, citizens and soldiers who had applauded Lee's decision to cast his fortunes with the Confederacy in April of 1861 derided him as "Granny Lee," or an "old stick-in-the-mud." Many would have not predicted success when he assumed charge of the army in charge of defending Richmond on June 1, 1862.

Lee had a varied career as a soldier before the Civil War. Let's talk a little bit about his background. He came out of one of the most prominent families in the United States, a family that had made enormous contributions to the history of both the colonies and of the nation founded with the Constitution in 1787. His mother was Ann Carter Lee, of the famous Carter family in Virginia. His father was Henry Lee. Two of Lee's relatives signed the Declaration of Independence. His father served as governor of Virginia. His father was a famous soldier during the American Revolution who led cavalries under George Washington. It was Lee's father who, in his eulogy to Washington, said that Washington had been first among all Americans in the hearts and minds both in war and peace of his countrymen. He was a very prominent actor on the Virginia stage, was Henry Lee (Light Horse Harry Lee, as he had been called during the American Revolution) for many years. He was also a man who was given to speculation and who amassed enormous debts.

Lee was born in 1807 at Stratford Hall, one of the Lee ancestral homes out on the Northern Neck, and his father lost that house when Lee was a young boy. The family moved to Alexandria. Lee's father was briefly put into debtor's prison and left the family when Lee was still young. Lee never saw him again. He grew up really under the influence of his mother more than his father, and I believe Lee's father worked a powerful influence on his son. Lee reacted to both his father's positive and negative characteristics. His father was an audacious soldier, a man willing to take risks, aggressive. Lee certainly, I think, modeled himself in part on that. But he also was very careful to exercise self-control. Self-control meant everything to R. E. Lee through almost all of his life, and I believe that, I'm not a psychologist and so this is worth what it's worth, but I think that his insistence on self-control was partly in response to his father's woeful mismanagement of the family's resources and other ways in which Henry Lee didn't exercise self-control.

The family had so little money that Lee's only options for an education as a young man lay at West Point, where he would get a free education. The family had wonderful connections. They called on those connections for Lee to get an appointment to the United States Military Academy, and he compiled a distinguished record there. He graduated second in his class. It was a class that included his friend Joseph Eggleston Johnston, about whom we'll talk a good deal more in the course of this class. One class ahead of him was Jefferson Davis.

Lee held the highest position that a cadet could hold while he was at West Point. He impressed many of the other cadets there, graduated without any demerits. So did several others in that class, Lee wasn't the only one, but he was a cadet who looked like a soldier, who did very well in his class work. It was basically an engineering school then, West Point was, the greatest engineering school in the United States down through the mid-point of the $19^{th}$ century. It basically trained engineers. It didn't teach much about how to command troops in battle, it didn't teach much about strategy and tactics, but it taught a great deal of math and physics and engineering, and Lee excelled in those things. The top ranked cadets got to select the part of the service they would go in, the top ones almost always went into the engineers, and Lee was one who went into the engineers upon his graduation in the class of 1828.

He was a striking figure, as I said. He was just under six feet tall, he was very handsome, everyone commented on that throughout most of his life actually. He weighed about one hundred and seventy pounds, larger than average in other words for his time. His nickname, and I think it wasn't entirely an appreciative nickname on the part of his fellow cadets, was the Marble Model. I think many of them thought he was almost too perfect, always trying to do everything just right, not one of the boys in any real sense of the word. One of his classmates later recalled how Lee had looked at West Point, and this might be partly colored by the fact that when this man wrote this Lee had become a very famous figure, but this classmate wrote this, "His personal appearance surpassed in manly beauty that of any other cadet in the corps. Though firm in his position and perfectly erect, he had none of the stiffness so often assumed by men who affect to be very strict in their ideas of what is military. His limbs, beautiful and symmetrical, looked as if they had come from the turning lathe, his step was elastic as if he spurned the ground upon which he trod." Well, that's a little bit overdone, but there's a great deal of evidence that suggests that Lee did stand out, he was simply a striking figure, even as a young man.

He worked on important engineering projects as a junior officer in the 1830s. He worked on Fort Pulaski, an installation that guarded Savannah, Georgia. He worked at St. Louis, the Mississippi River threatened to change course in the 1830s and leave St. Louis as no longer a great river port. Lee was one of the principle engineers who worked at St. Louis to make sure that the Mississippi kept flowing past St. Louis, so that St. Louis could continue to thrive as a river city. He was promoted to captain in 1838. Promotion was very slow in the peacetime army of the United States. Many years often went by in between promotions. Lee was promoted to captain in 1838.

In 1831, he married Mary Anne Randolph Custis, who was the daughter of Martha Washington's grandson, George Washington Park Custis. This gave Lee a great tie to George Washington. Most of the Washington relics were in the Custis home, Arlington, overlooking the Potomac River. Washington was Lee's absolute model, both as a man and as a soldier in many ways. He'd looked to him throughout his life, and this marriage that connected him to Arlington and to Washington, I think, cemented in many people's minds during the Civil War a connection that seemed apparent even to some people even before the war, this connection between Lee and George Washington became a familial connection as well as one of a young man idolizing an earlier hero.

Lee's first real military action took place during the war with Mexico. He served on Winfield Scott's staff. Winfield Scott was the greatest soldier of his age. Even the duke of Wellington called him that once he saw what Scott had done in Mexico. Wellington, with his ego, said that Scott was the greatest soldier of the ages. Certainly the greatest American soldier the first half of the 19<sup>th</sup> century, and Lee served on his staff. Scott had an inner circle in Mexico that he called his "little cabinet" and Lee was part of that inner circle that was the little cabinet. Scott forged one of the great military campaigns in United States history, the campaign that went from Vera Cruz to Mexico City, a campaign in which his army was always outnumbered, and a campaign in which he never lost a battle, Scott did not. At one point he even abandoned his supply lines, set all kinds of precedents in terms of how to operate in the midst of hostile territory with a smaller force and aiming toward a great city and it's capture. Mexico City, one of the great cities of the western hemisphere at that point, and Scott's little army, which numbered only about ten thousand men for much of the campaign, in the end, took that capital city. It was a remarkable campaign in 1847, and Robert E. Lee played a crucial role in this campaign. He did not command men in the field, he was not a field commander, he did not command men in combat, he was a staff officer, but as a staff officer he did a number of very useful things, and came to the attention of almost every major United States officer during the war. He placed artillery batteries at Vera Cruz, he conducted reconnaissance before the battle at Cerro Gordo, which was a key battle that allowed Scott's army to get out of the malaria low-lands and onto the high ground where it would be safer and so they could proceed on to Mexico City, he crossed a very treacherous lava field called the Pedregal before the battle of Contreras-Churubusco, outside Mexico City. He crossed it twice, in fact, ground that no one thought that anyone would cross, and he helped place guns again before the battle of Chapultepec at the final phase of the fighting at Mexico City.

Scott developed an extremely high opinion of Lee in the course of this campaign, and Lee learned a number of lessons from Scott. He learned that audacity—doing the unexpected—can often yield results. Scott did that again and again in this campaign. He learned, again and again did Lee, that turning movements can be used very effectively. Scott used turning movements, flanking movements, on more than one occasion to great success, but Scott also used frontal assaults when he had to and Lee saw those frontal assaults succeed in Mexico. He saw you can both be direct and indirect, and Lee also learned that numbers don't always dictate who wins. He knew, the American knew, that every Mexican army they faced from

Vera Cruz to Mexico City outnumbered their American opponent, and yet the American opponent triumphed again and again. That is something well worth keeping in mind within a Confederate context if you're Lee, because you're always going to be outnumbered as a Confederate commander as well. It was a great training period for Lee, a great training period learning under this great soldier, Winfield Scott, and there's a reciprocal process of impressing one another going on here—Scott being impressed with Lee and Lee being impressed with Scott. Scott time and again praised Lee when he talked about Lee's trip across the Pedregal; Scott said it was "the greatest feat of physical and moral courage performed by any individual during the entire campaign from Vera Cruz to Mexico City."

Another of the United States generals, a man named Persifor Smith, in his official report wrote this about Lee, he said "his reconnaissances, though pushed far beyond the bounds of prudence, were conducted with so much skill that their fruits were of the utmost value, the soundness of his judgment and personal daring being equally conspicuous." Another officer serving in Mexico said this about Scott, he said that the American commander came away from Mexico with "an almost idolatrous fancy for Lee, whose military genius he estimated far above that of any other officer in the army."

So, Mexico was a crucial element in Lee's development as a soldier. It's his first series of tests in the field, and he passes them spectacularly, and impresses everyone that it would behoove him to impress. After the war, he served as superintendent of West Point in the early and mid 1850s. He was a very effective educator here. He installed a five-year course to replace the old four-year course at West Point. A number of the soldiers who would later fight under Lee as Confederate generals were cadets at West Point while he was there. Jeb Stuart was there, John Bell Hood was there, Edward Porter Alexander was there as a young cadet under Lee's superintendency, those three among the men that we will discuss later in this class. Lee didn't especially like the work at West Point, he didn't especially like being behind a desk and running an educational institution, but he did a very good job of it.

His only experience as a field officer in command of soldiers in the field before the Civil War came with his work with the Second Cavalry Regiment on the Texas frontier in the late 1850s. The Second Cavalry was one of two cavalry regiments created in the 1850s at Jefferson Davis's recommendation. Davis was the secretary of war under Franklin Pierce, and Davis pushed for these regiments, the First Cavalry and the Second Cavalry.

A number of very famous Civil War officers served as officers in these regiments, Albert Sydney Johnston, who would be a leading general in the Confederacy, commanded—he was the colonel, of the Second Cavalry, Lee was lieutenant colonel of the Second Cavalry, and he spend a good deal of time in Texas in really boring duty. He left a diary from the time, and reading the diary just gives a very strong sense of how frustrating much of this service in Texas was. A lot of it consisted of pursuing groups of Comanche warriors, whom the American soldiers never caught up with, never even saw really, just back and forth chasing across the trackless Texas wastelands, from Lee's point of view, and a lot of court martial duty as well, neither one very satisfying. But this was Lee's only field service before the war.

The Secession Crisis presented Lee with a great dilemma. He had been a United States military officer his entire adult life. He was promoted to colonel of the First Cavalry in March of 1861. He accepted that promotion. But Virginia secedes in mid-April and Lee in the end decided to go with his native state, decided he could not stay in the United States Army, despite the fact that the command of the major United States Army gathering outside of Washington to deal with the seceding states, a command of that force was offered to Lee just before Lee left the United States service. Montgomery Blair and Winfield Scott both talked to Lee about taking command of it, Lee in the end decided he couldn't. He had a very emotional parting with Winfield Scott; he hated to leave Winfield Scott. Scott was also a Virginian, a Virginian who was staying loyal to the United States, but Lee did, in the end, leave.

He was made major general of Virginia state forces, and he worked hard to muster the manpower of the state of Virginia. Forty thousand of them or so brought into uniform while Lee was the head of the state forces. He saw to the setting up of camps of instruction, an improvement of fortifications in the state, all of which, as he was doing that from Richmond, denied him a field command. What he really wanted was a field command, but he was in this desk job in Richmond while others were getting field commands. His friend, an exact contemporary, Joseph Johnston was given command of a force in the lower Shenandoah Valley; P. G. T. Beauregard was given command of a Confederate force near Manassas; and those are the two officers who oversaw the first great Confederate victory of the war on July 21, 1861—the battle of First Bull Run or First Manassas. Lee wished he had been there, but he very generously sent a letter of heartfelt praise to his friend Johnston saying that he was so happy Johnston had done so well, he wasn't surprised that Johnston had done well, but he was very happy for him.

Lee's first year as a Confederate general yielded mixed results. He left the Virginia state service and became a Confederate brigadier general in the summer of 1861, and then was promoted to full general, that is what we would call a four-star general, that same summer. He ranked third among the Confederate full generals. Samuel Cooper, who was, in essence a paper pusher, was the ranking Confederate general, Albert Sydney Johnston was second, and Lee was third. Lee's friend Joseph Johnston was fourth, which caused great anguish for Johnston, as we will see later in this course. Lee's first year—mixed results. Many people were very happy that he'd come to the Confederacy. They knew how highly Scott thought of him, and they thought they had landed, the Confederates had landed, the greatest prize in terms of officers. They had Lee and were extremely happy about it, but they saw their high expectations diminish tremendously over the next several months. They diminished because of Lee's service in western Virginia and later along the south Atlantic coast. He mounted an ineffective defense of western Virginia in the summer and autumn of 1861. He was sent out to that area on July 28 by Jefferson Davis, and it was a very difficult situation—mountainous terrain, scattered forces throughout it, and a group of subordinates who were very troublesome, including two political generals, two of the kinds of generals we talked about last time who came into uniform not because they were good soldiers. They were Henry A. Wise and John B. Floyd, two Virginia politicians who loathed one another, wouldn't cooperate, gave Lee headaches. Another general named W. W. Loring resented Lee's being assigned to this command; Loring thought he should have it. So Lee has this difficult command situation.

He also planned very complex ways to get at the Federals, and in the end he simply couldn't achieve the coordination: the weather, the terrain, the quality of his subordinates, and the complexity of his plans all ended largely in failure, and he left western Virginia in late October, left an area that not that far down the road would break away from the state of Virginia and become West Virginia. That is a measure of how difficult that area would have been to manage in a way that would help the Confederacy. It was out of the Confederacy just a few months hence.

Lee added very little to his reputation in his service along the south Atlantic coast in the winter of 1861–62. He was sent to Charleston in late 1861 by Davis to try to coordinate about a three hundred mile stretch of the south Atlantic coast, to coordinate the defense of that area, and he actually did a good job. He put fortifications and obstructions along the rivers. He set up mobile forces who could move from one threatened point to another along the coast. He used his engineering skills in this work and did a good job, but he didn't fight any battles. And by telling his men to dig in he sent a message both to them and to the people behind the lines of the Confederacy that he wasn't aggressive, that he wasn't going to go out and try to smite the enemy, he was just going to dig in and wait for the Federals to come to him, and that was not the kind of leadership most of the Confederate people, especially at this time of the war, wanted. They wanted someone who would smash things up, and Lee acquired a couple of pejorative nicknames during this part of his career, the "King of Spades" because he had men dig so much, "Granny Lee" was another one. "Granny" was applied to a number of Civil War generals, and I can promise you it was not something you would want to be called if you were a general; it had all kinds of negative connotations. The bottom line is although Lee did a good job here, he got no credit for it and, in fact, his stock dropped even more across the Confederacy.

He completed his first year as a Confederate general as Jefferson Davis's principle military advisor. He was summoned back to Richmond in early March 1862 for a desk job, another desk job. Davis described Lee's duties as "to manage the conduct of military operations in the armies of the Confederacy." That's a grand description. In fact, Davis was managing the military operations of the armies of the Confederacy, Lee was a trusted advisor but he didn't have any real power here. He had power if he and Davis got along and Davis agreed with what he wanted to do. Davis didn't really want a general-in-chief; he acted as his own general-in-chief for most of the war. He and Lee got along well, that's important. Lee was a very perceptive military politician, and he read Jefferson Davis very well. He knew that Davis didn't like people to argue with him. He knew that Davis liked to get a lot of information, always wanted to know what was going on, and Lee was very careful through all the rest of his military career to observe these qualities of Davis to make sure that he gave Davis all the information he needed, to make sure that he sort of stroked Davis's ego, which is what Lee did. He got along with him, but Lee himself was frustrated during this period because he would have rather been in the field. He did a good job; he did a very good job. He wrote Mrs. Lee, however, that he saw neither pleasure nor advantage in the duties he would be undertaking. Having said that, he worked very hard to bring a strong national character to the Confederate defense.

He supported a national focus rather than a local focus. He insisted that resources would have to be mustered in a national context, not try to defend local areas. The most important thing he did was argue for a national conscription act. Now, that doesn't sound so radical to us, but it was very radical within a mid-19th century American context. There had never been a national draft, there had never been a government that compelled national military service from all of its military-aged citizenry, white citizenry, and that is what Lee argued for. "We had volunteers early in 1861," said Lee, "Many of them are due to get out of the army, we need to keep them in the army and get everybody else into the army. So, let's extend the terms of service. Those men who volunteered in good faith for twelve months service back in May of 1861, let's now extend their service to three years, and let's make everybody else of military age subject to this national draft." Highly controversial. The men who volunteered for a year believed they had been betrayed. The biggest spike of desertion of the entire war comes right here in the spring of 1862 in the Confederacy, the biggest spike until the very end of the war. But Lee knew that this was an essential step that the Confederacy had to take if it was going to keep its armies in the field, and he was very influential in pushing it through. One of his staff officers named Charles Marshall was very important in drafting this legislation. It is such a change in attitude on the part of the government. It's important for us to keep this in mind, just how radical of a step this was. The government wasn't just saying we would like your support in this effort, the government was saying you will support this effort by carrying a musket, a tremendous change. The United States wouldn't take this step for another year, and it would be equally controversial when the United States did it.

Lee also planned in a strategic sense. He was the architect of Stonewall Jackson's Shenandoah Valley campaign, for example, we'll talk more about that later; an effort to prevent troops in the Alleghenies and the Shenandoah Valley, United States troops, from being brought to the army that was approaching Richmond, the army under George B. McClellan. He also concentrated forces from other parts of the strategic chessboard outside Richmond, brought Joseph E. Johnston down from northern Virginia, brought other troops to face this large army. The Army of the Potomac, under George B. McClellan, was advancing up the Virginia peninsula from New York and James Rivers toward Richmond.

He's very effective at all of this. He's doing an excellent job at all of this. Looking at the strategic picture, moving forces around, trying to get the most out of the sources the Confederacy had, trying to see that there was a national focus to the Confederate war effort. It's all solid service, but it's not the kind of service Lee wants. He does not want to go to an office every day in Richmond. He wants to be in the field. He wants to be doing what Joseph Johnston is doing. He wants to be doing what P. G. T. Beauregard is doing. But, as luck would have it, he simply was not in a position to get that kind of job as events unfolded.

He did get his first rate opportunity in early June 1862, and he got the opportunity because his friend, Joe Johnston, who was a frequently wounded soldier, wounded in Mexico, wounded in the Civil War, he was wounded, and quite seriously wounded, shell fragments and minié balls in the chest and limbs at the battle of Seven Pines or Fair Oaks on May 31, 1862. Johnston had retreated all the way up the peninsula to Richmond, that's what he did very well, Johnston, and he was doing it very well—I'm using that sarcastically, here in April and May of 1862, had retreated to within about five miles of Richmond, and then had attacked George B. McClellan on May 31, and in that first big battle of the peninsula campaign Joseph Johnston was wounded. A disabling wound that left the army defending Richmond without a commander, and this is, I believe, one of the great watersheds of the war. It helped set up a campaign, the Seven Days' campaign, that, in my view, is more important than Gettysburg in terms of its long-term impact on the war because Jefferson Davis has to find someone to stand in for Joe Johnston and he looks around and decides that person should be Robert E. Lee. Robert E. Lee should be given this field command of this most important of Confederate forces, the one that would be defending the national capital. When many Confederates found out about this they were chagrined. They thought not Lee, don't put Lee in charge of this army. Lee from western Virginia? Lee from the south Atlantic coast? He hasn't done anything. We had such high hopes for him and those hopes didn't turn out. We need an aggressive soldier commanding this army outside Richmond and Robert E. Lee is not that man. This is an example of a truly spectacular miscalculation on the part of many people who were viewing Lee's appointment to command this army.

I mentioned Cate Edmondston, quoted her, in fact, in my opening first lecture, the diarist from North Carolina. She became a tremendous admirer and advocate of Lee, as that quotation I read suggested, but here in early June of 1862, she was not happy to hear that Lee had been appointed. She wrote in her diary, "I don't much like him. He falls back too much. He failed in western Virginia owing, it was said, to the weather. He's done little in the eyes of outsiders in North Carolina. His nickname last summer was

'Old Stick-in-the-Mud.' There's enough mud now in and about our lines, pray God he may not fulfill the whole of his name."

Another officer who served on Lee's staff wrote, "Some of the newspapers, particularly the *Richmond Examiner*, pitched into the general with extraordinary virulence, evidently trying to break him down with the troops and to force the president to remove him. The paper argued that henceforth the army never would be allowed to fight because all Lee was interested in doing was digging in."

Some Confederates expressed more optimism about Lee's appointment, but there's a very strong strain of doubt when he's named to command the force outside Richmond. It is an army he will rename, he'll christen it the Army of Northern Virginia, but when he takes command there's a sense that my God, we have somebody in charge here, a quite pervasive sense, there's someone in charge here who's probably not going to be aggressive. When Lee stepped into a critical strategic situation, one that without exaggeration we could say would decide the fate, at least the short-term and medium/long-term fate of the Confederacy. Next time, we will turn to Lee's actions right after he was put in command and see what a remarkable change in situation his first steps brought.

# Lecture Three
## Lee's Year of Fabled Victories

**Scope:** Lee's first year in command of the Army of Northern Virginia catapulted him to a position of unequaled fame and popularity in the Confederacy. He immediately demonstrated his innate aggressiveness during the Seven Days' battles, during which he blunted George B. McClellan's powerful drive against Richmond in June–July 1862. Following the Seven Days, which stood as one of the war's great watersheds in terms of impact on the broad strategic situation, Lee maintained the offensive by marching northward and winning a follow-up victory at Second Manassas or Bull Run in late August. His movement into Maryland in September marked the culmination of a seismic strategic reorientation that saw the focus of the war in Virginia shift from the outskirts of Richmond to the Potomac frontier. The invasion of Maryland ended at Antietam, where McClellan forced Lee to retreat to Virginia. Subsequent victories at Fredericksburg in mid-December 1862 and at Chancellorsville in early May 1863 completed the process by which Lee assumed center stage in the Confederate war effort. Chancellorsville also marked the final act in a year-long drama that witnessed a remarkable bonding between Lee and the soldiers in his army. Despite many difficult times over the next two years, that bond remained powerful and helps explain why the army retained its ability to mount a formidable opposition to the U.S. forces arrayed against it.

## Outline

I. Lee's performance during the Seven Days' campaign set up the rest of his Confederate career.

    A. Confederate prospects were poor on June 1, 1862.

        1. Defeats elsewhere gave greater importance to operations outside Richmond.

        2. Joseph E. Johnston's retreating had hurt Confederate morale.

    B. Lee's aggressiveness during the Seven Days turned the strategic tide. Fought from June 26 (Mechanicsville) through July 1

(Malvern Hill), the campaign established a new standard for bloodletting in the eastern theater.

    **1.** George B. McClellan retreated from Richmond.

    **2.** Confederate civilian morale shot upward.

    **3.** The Seven Days must be reckoned one of the military watersheds of the Civil War.

**II.** Lee maintained strategic momentum through the summer and autumn of 1862.

    **A.** He reorganized the army following the Seven Days.

        **1.** He eased several officers out of the army, including J. B. Magruder.

        **2.** He gave James Longstreet and Stonewall Jackson command of the right and left wings, respectively, eventually called *corps*.

    **B.** The campaign of Second Bull Run or Manassas in late August reoriented the war from Richmond to the Potomac frontier.

    **C.** Lee invaded Maryland in the wake of Second Manassas.

        **1.** He planned the campaign with logistics and politics in mind: to remove the war from Virginia, to influence the Northern elections, and to attract volunteers in Maryland.

        **2.** The campaign revealed that Lee had pushed his army to the limit.

        **3.** The battle of Antietam (September 17, 1862) brought an end to Lee's strategic offensive when he was forced to withdraw.

    **D.** The Maryland campaign marked the end of a remarkable 15-week period for Lee. During this time, the Army of Northern Virginia suffered some 50,000 battle casualties.

        **1.** The Confederate people gained ever greater faith in Lee and his army.

        **2.** Lee was in the process of making the army his own.

**III.** The winter and spring of 1862–1863 completed the process by which Lee and his army gained ascendancy among Confederate institutions.

    **A.** The battle of Fredericksburg in December 1862 marked an easy defensive victory.

    **B.** The Chancellorsville campaign of April–May 1863 provided Lee with his most striking battlefield success.

1. He overcame huge odds—almost two to one against him—and crushed Joseph Hooker by taking the initiative on May 2 and 3.
2. He and his soldiers gained unshakable belief in one another.
3. The Confederate people drew sustenance from a remarkable victory, even though Stonewall Jackson was shot down by his own men.

IV. The campaigns of June 1862–June 1863 created a national expectation of success for Lee and his army that lasted for the rest of the war.

    A. Many historians have argued that Lee's aggressive battles in 1862–1863 hurt Confederate chances for independence.
        1. They cost the Confederacy precious manpower—70,000 casualties during the 12-month period.
        2. They never delivered a knockout blow to a U.S. army.

    B. Such arguments focus too narrowly on casualties and fail to take into account Lee's impact on national morale.

## Essential Reading:

Gallagher, *The Confederate War*, chapter 3.

———, *Lee and His Army in Confederate History*, chapters 1–2.

———, ed., *Lee the Soldier*, essays by Castel, Connelly, Davis, Freeman, Hartwig, Gallagher, Krick, Nolan, Reardon, and Roland.

## Supplementary Reading:

Freeman, *R. E. Lee: A Biography*, vol. 2, chapters 11–35.

Harsh, *Confederate Tide Rising: Robert E. Lee and the Making of Southern Strategy, 1861–1862*, chapters 3–6.

———, *Taken at the Flood: Robert E. Lee and Confederate Strategy in the Maryland Campaign of 1862.*

Nolan, *Lee Considered*, chapter 4.

Thomas, *Robert E. Lee: A Biography*, chapters 18–22.

## Questions to Consider:

1. Could Lee have followed a successful nonaggressive strategic blueprint in the summer and autumn of 1862?

**2.** Was there any strategy that would have conserved Confederate manpower *and* met public expectations?

# Lecture Three—Transcript
## Lee's Year of Fabled Victories

We left off last time with the wounding of Joseph E. Johnston at Seven Pines on May 31, 1862, which opened the way for Lee to assume his first major field command as a Confederate general. Lee's first year at the helm of what he christened the Army of Northern Virginia catapulted him to a position of unequaled fame and popularity in the Confederacy. He immediately demonstrated his innate aggressiveness during the Seven Days' battles, during which he blunted George B. McClellan's powerful drive against Richmond in June and July 1862. Following the Seven Days, which stood as one of the war's great watersheds in terms of impact on the broad strategic situation, Lee maintained the offensive by marching northward and winning a follow-up victory at Second Manassas or Bull Run at the end of August.

His movement into Maryland in September marked the culmination of a seismic, strategic reorientation that saw the focus of the war in Virginia in the eastern theater shift from the outskirts of Richmond to the Potomac frontier—to go back, in other words, to where it had been at the outset of the war. The invasion of Maryland ended at Antietam where McClellan forced Lee to retreat to Virginia. Subsequent victories at Fredericksburg in mid-December 1862, and at Chancellorsville in early May of 1863, completed the process by which Lee assumed center stage in the Confederate war effort. Chancellorsville also marked the final act in a year-long drama that had witnessed a remarkable bonding between Lee and the soldiers in his army. Despite many difficult times over the next two years, that bond remained powerful, and helps explain how the army retained its ability to mount a formidable opposition to the United States forces arrayed against it.

Let's start with Lee at the Seven Days, a campaign that really set up the rest of his Confederate career. Confederate prospects were very poor on June 1, 1882, when Lee took command. Very poor almost anywhere you looked on the strategic landscape. Out west, Confederate forces had suffered an unbroken string of reverses. They had lost Forts Henry and Donelson at the battle of Shiloh; they'd lost the city of New Orleans, which was the largest city in the Confederacy; Memphis would very soon fall. The crucial railroad crossroads at Corinth was just about to fall. Huge stretches of Tennessee had gone to United States control and would never return to the Confederacy—

nothing but very bad news out west, and not any good news, really, in terms of the major armies in Virginia either. George B. McClellan's army had made its way very slowly up the Virginia peninsula, had gone through Williamsburg, Yorktown, and was now within five miles of the Confederate capital. Another major United States army lay at Fredericksburg, just fifty miles to the north of Richmond. The only good news for the Confederacy in this whole period, the only really good news, had come in the Shenandoah Valley where Thomas J. Jackson, Stonewall Jackson, had won some little victories that gave hope to some people in the Confederacy. But what was going on in the Valley was not nearly as important and what was going on outside Richmond, and what was going on outside Richmond was that the biggest United States army in the field was closing in on the Confederacy's capital. So, it's a very, very perilous situation for the Confederates in the military sense when Robert E. Lee took command.

You also have the added problem, in terms of morale in the Confederacy, of the recently enacted conscription act in the Confederacy, which had come in the spring of 1862, and I said last time had been very controversial. Controversial behind the lines and prompting a number of desertions among men in the army who had volunteered for a year initially and then had the rules changed on them by the Confederate Congress. Not very much positive anywhere in this picture if you're trying to find good news from a Confederate perspective.

All of this bad news in theaters outside of Virginia added even greater importance to what Lee and the Army of Northern Virginia would do in Richmond. It already was going to be important because it's in the eastern theater where so many people look anyway, but all that bad news makes it even more important. Lee was dealing with a situation here in Virginia that had been made quite serious by Joseph E. Johnston's retreating. Johnston had retreated and retreated without really fighting a battle, and many people across the Confederacy had become disenchanted with him before he was wounded. They thought he gave up too much ground too easily. They wanted their army to fight. They wanted their army to reach out and strike the enemy rather than just sitting back and waiting for the United States armies to do something to them.

Lee broke that pattern completely once he took command of the army. His aggressiveness during the Seven Days turned the strategic tide. He took about three weeks to get his army into condition to launch his offensive blows. He spent most of the first three-and-a-half weeks of June doing that, and then he struck in a campaign that came to be called the Seven Days' campaign, a campaign that included several major battles. The campaign opened on the 26<sup>th</sup> of June with the battle of Mechanicsville, the battle of Gaines's Mill followed the next day, on the 27<sup>th</sup>. Subsequent fighting at Savage's Station, at Glendale, and finally at Malvern Hill on July 1, 1862, brought a new standard of bloodletting to the eastern theater. Shiloh had done it in the west; Seven Days had done it in the east. Throughout this campaign Lee was trying to strike the Army of the Potomac, trying to catch McClellan's army at a disadvantage so that a powerful, telling blow could be delivered against the Army of the Potomac.

The story of the Seven Days is the Confederates attacking, Federals fending them off, McClellan retreated southward across the peninsula to a safe position along the James River where the strength, the size of this army and the power of the United States Navy, which controlled the James River, would make him safe from what the Confederates were trying to do to him. The real story here is McClellan had been on the offense; McClellan had been on the strategic offensive in Virginia moving ever closer to the Confederate capital. Lee seized that initiative from McClellan and McClellan allowed him to do it in the Seven Days' battles. Lee took the initiative and Lee began to dictate the action. That would be a hallmark of his generalship for the rest of the war. He sometimes took spectacular risks in order to take that advantage. He took that advantage in the Seven Days and he never relinquished it. In the end, McClellan retreated—he didn't really have to. McClellan, however, was not a good match for Lee in terms of his ability as a field commander, and McClellan retreated south along the James River to Harrison's Landing and sort of hunkered down there for the rest of July.

The effect of this campaign was electric across the Confederacy. Here at last was good news from a major Confederate army. After all of this dismal news across so much of the Confederacy, here was a general who had delivered a victory, and not just any kind of victory, it's precisely the type of victory the Confederate people wanted. It was an aggressive offensive victory. Here was a general who went out to find the enemy, sought out a battle, didn't just wait. This may not make sense to many of us as we look back. We might think that the Confederacy should have fought the war mainly on the defensive, conserve manpower, and so forth, but here is an instance of where civilian expectations loomed very large. It's not just what the army does, but how it does it that will create the greatest effect on the home front, and Lee achieved that greatest effect during the Seven Days, not only winning a victory, but winning a victory behind a victory that meant most to the Confederate people. He saved the capital. He vanquished the United States Army and sent it retreating along the James River where it would be under cover of the United States Navy.

The Seven Days must, in any assessment of important campaigns of the Civil War, be reckoned, as I said last time, a watershed. In many ways—in terms of scale, that's one way; I alluded to the fact that it brought this big scale war to the eastern theater. Shiloh did that in the west; there were more Americans shot at Shiloh on April 6 and 7, 1862 than in all of the wars fought in America, in North America, by what we would call Americans now—the Colonial Wars, the Revolutionary War, and so forth, more shot at Shiloh in two days than in all the other wars put together down to that time. Well, there were about 25,000 casualties at Shiloh. At Seven Days there are 36,000 casualties—20,000 Confederate casualties and 16,000 United States casualties. The armies are huge, more than 100,000 in McClellan's army, and Lee fought the Seven Days with the largest army the Confederacy ever put into the field, between 85,000–90,000. This isn't David against Goliath, not a huge United States army against a poor little, poorly provisioned Confederate army. This is two heavyweights fighting each other in the Seven Days and extracting an enormous toll from one another.

Tactically, Lee did not achieve anything really remarkable. It's a fumbling effort on his part in many ways. He has a cumbersome sub-command structure, which we'll talk about in a minute. But the point is he never did get good coordination from his army in any of these battles, and in the end he launched pretty unimaginative frontal assaults at Malvern Hill, which cost 5,000 Confederate casualties to no purpose. It was not a tactical masterpiece, but that didn't matter to the Confederate people, it didn't matter in the broader picture. What mattered was Richmond was safe, McClellan was retreating, and it had been an aggressive victory, and it re-oriented the war in Virginia. Now it's not: Is the capital going to fall any day? It's: What will Lee do next? The threat to the capital seemed to diminish enormously. The Confederate people absolutely loved what had happened. It's their first really big victory since First Manassas, which had been July 21, 1861. Here we're almost a year later before there's another major victory in the Virginia theater, and that helps push Lee absolutely to center stage. All of those doubts about whether he would be aggressive or not fall away very quickly, very quickly indeed. It seems that he was not what many people were afraid he would be when he took command of the army—that is, a timid, defensive-minded general. He's been the antithesis of that once he's in command of the Army of Northern

Virginia, and he maintained the strategic momentum in the wake of his victory in the Seven Days.

He reorganized the army right after the Seven Days' battles. He had had a group of division commanders—let me talk just very briefly about how armies were built during the Civil War so that when I allude to different kinds of units we'll all be on the same page. The basic building block is a *company*, a hundred men on paper, often raised in the same area. You'd go in with friends and neighbors and so forth. Ten of those companies created a *regiment*. That's a thousand men on paper. Usually four regiments would create a *brigade*. Two or more brigades would create a *division*. Two or more divisions, later in the war, would create a *corps*. There were already corps in the United States but not in the Confederate army at the time of the Seven Days. The largest unit is a division, so Lee has this collection of division commanders (they're all major generals) he was trying to coordinate during the Seven Days. Well, he moves very quickly after the battle of the Seven Days to get rid of people who do not suit what he considers the right style of generalship.

He is going to create a culture in the Army of Northern Virginia. Every army has a culture with certain characteristics in its high command and Lee sets about creating his kind of culture in the Army of Northern Virginia. He wants officers who will be aggressive, who are offensively inclined, who want to go out and smash things, who want to pursue the enemy and inflict the greatest possible damage, to harass an opponent who's on the ropes, to deliver a knock-out blow, if possible. Those are the kind of men Lee wants, men with the killer instinct. It's a very different culture than the kind that George B. McClellan created in the Army of the Potomac, which was a culture much more given to playing it safe, trying to avoid losses rather than achieving big victories, trying to cover all the bases, not trying to risk too much. Lee wants a very different kind of culture, and he gets rid of a bunch of division commanders in the wake of the Seven Days who don't fit his model—John Bankhead Magruder, Benjamin Huger, Theophilus Holmes, W. H. C. Whiting, G. W. Smith—they're all gone.

He divides the army into two wings, Lee does, two wings. These are two bigger sub-categories now with divisions grouped within them. They will eventually become corps; right now he calls them wings. He gives the Right Wing to James Longstreet and he gives the Left Wing to Stonewall Jackson. So he now has his two best subordinates each commanding half of the infantry in the army. He considered Longstreet the more reliable of those two subordinates at this stage of the war. We'll discuss Jackson and Longstreet a little bit later.

The first campaign where this new structure was put into operation was the campaign of Second Manassas or Bull Run, which played out in August. The United States had fielded another army in Virginia, in north central Virginia, under an officer named John Pope. McClellan sits down outside Richmond with the Army of the Potomac. John Pope's new Army of Virginia begins to operate in the area between Warrenton and Culpepper, north central and central Virginia, and Lee has these two threats to deal with now.

He sends Jackson to confront Pope, initially, and once Lee is sure that McClellan is not going to be a threat to Richmond any more (McClellan is recalled to Washington), Lee reunites the army and the reunited army defeats John Pope's army in the battle of Second Bull Run, Second Manassas, at the end of August 1862. Lee planned the campaign in a daring sense. Jackson made a very famous flank march to get around Pope's right flank, and in the end, hard fighting and a major assault delivered by Longstreet at Second Manassas on August 30 swept the Federals from the field. Lee, then, was poised all the way in northern Virginia, back to where the first great battle of the war had been fought, he's poised there having won a second victory in a row.

The question is: What does he do next? He wanted to maintain the momentum. He never wanted to relinquish the momentum, never wanted to relinquish the initiative, so he could either stay where he was, or he could try to continue going forward, and in the end he decided to cross the Potomac River into Maryland.

He was pushing his army really past the limits in doing this. His army was not in good shape after Second Manassas. There had been enormous casualties, a great deal of marching. The army was worn out. It had overstressed its logistical capacity. It's an army on the edge when Lee decides to cross the Potomac River, but he decides to go anyway because he believes that the risks of not going forward are greater than those in going forward.

He has a number of goals in mind. He has a huge logistical goal in mind: to get the war out of Virginia so farmers will have a respite from the presence of the armies. Lee wants to gather food and fodder from the countryside in Maryland, and eventually maybe from Pennsylvania. He wants to influence the Northern elections that are coming up in November, the off-year elections of 1862, and he thinks if he moves into Maryland that thousands of Marylanders will flock to the Confederate colors. He believed that

Maryland was ripe to join the Confederacy. Many Confederates believed that. They didn't really understand what was going on in Maryland, and especially didn't understand that the part of Maryland they were moving into, western Maryland, had relatively few slaveholders and was very unlikely to embrace this Confederate army very warmly. But Lee went across the river, and it very quickly became clear that he had pushed his army absolutely to the point where it really couldn't continue to function well. He estimated that between a third and a half of the men dropped out of the ranks as the Maryland campaign unfolded. Lee admitted that in correspondence with Jefferson Davis.

They were straggling, there was desertion, men worn out, men didn't have shoes—it was an army literally falling apart. So when the climactic part of the campaign comes at the battle of Antietam on September 17, Lee can only muster 30,000–35,000 men on that battlefield. He crossed the Potomac with about 55,000. Thirty to thirty-five thousand fight at Antietam. Remember there were 85,000–90,000 during the Seven Days' battles, the outset of the Seven Days' battles. This army has been fought to a nub, and it fights at Antietam—the bloodiest single day in the United States history. It is, in terms of Lee's behavior and day at Antietam, when he exercised very hands-on leadership, present all over the battlefield, trying to deal with this crisis and then that crisis. He used every available soldier, every soldier who was actually there, and managed to hang on by the narrowest of margins, but he withdrew back to Virginia after the battle of Antietam. It's probably a battle he shouldn't have fought. He had asked too much of this army, an army that really wasn't even his yet. He's still just sort of a caretaker. He's only been in command for about fourteen weeks.

He falls back to Virginia and ends what we should look at, what I believe we should look at, as this sprawling campaign that began at the Seven Days and closes with the retreat from Antietam. It's one huge campaign fought in three acts: the initial act—the Seven Days; the middle act—the campaign of Second Manassas; and the final act—the movement into Maryland and eventually the retreat from Maryland. It is a bloody exercise for the Confederate army. If anybody wondered about Lee and his aggressiveness, they could count the casualties during this fifteen-week run that he just put in. Twenty thousand at the Seven Days, 10,000 at Second Manassas, 10,000 at Antietam, and another miscellaneous 10,000 at other actions. There are 50,000 battle casualties in the Army of Northern Virginia during Lee's initial stint in command, 50,000. It's an enormous butcher's bill that Lee extracts, and the return is this series of aggressive successes and movements that thrills the Confederate people. The Confederate people do not count the casualties so much as they look at the result. They see the war as back to the Potomac front here, they see this list of victories, they see the United States army not even in Virginia any more, at the end of this fifteen weeks, and they respond with very great praise, for the most part, of R. E. Lee.

Lee during this period was in the process of making the army his own, setting his culture up among his subordinate officers, winning the loyalty of soldiers, giving them victories that would make them look to him with confidence and demonstrating that his hallmark as a commander is going to be an unwillingness to be passive in the face of the United States movements in Virginia. He'll do almost anything, as I said earlier, to dictate the action rather than simply to respond. Many in the Confederacy noted how rapidly Lee's reputation changed. Those doubts just before the Seven Days are pretty much swept away by this phase of the war. This phase of the war works a great change in Lee's reputation in the Confederacy.

Following the Maryland campaign, Lee changed the wing structure of the army, where Longstreet and Jackson command wings, to a two corps structure. The Confederate Congress had okayed a three-star rank in the Confederate army, a lieutenant general's rank, which is what you needed to command a corps, so Lee changed the wings to corps. Otherwise the structure stays the same, Longstreet commands the first, Stonewall Jackson commands the second of these two corps.

They fight their first battle with this structure at Fredericksburg in December 1862. Another Union commander on the field, this is Ambrose Burnside, he had replaced George B. McClellan. It's a very easy defensive victory for Lee. Lee's army occupied high ground on the west side of the Rappahannock River, the Federals crossed the river and then attacked uphill in a really sickening display of foolhardy frontal assaults on the afternoon of December 13, 1862. It was a very easy defensive victory for Lee and the Army of Northern Virginia.

The army was back up to about 75,000 in strength at Fredericksburg, inflicts 12,500 on the Federals at Fredericksburg. Lee's army suffers about 5,000 casualties. It's a great humiliation for the United States. It sends ripples of happiness across the Confederacy. One woman, a woman named Mary Jones, wrote a letter about this battle when she heard about the result of Fredericksburg. She said, "I have not the words to express the emotions I feel for this single success." In turning to Lee specifically, Jones said, "The head of our army is a noble son of Virginia and worthy of the intimate relation in which he stands connected with our immortal Washington. What confidence his wisdom, his integrity and valor and undoubted piety inspire." One of the many instances that people tie Lee to Washington.

Abraham Lincoln, on the other hand, when he heard about Fredericksburg, not only that it's a defeat, but this sort of senseless butchery of the United States soldiers that attacked up that high ground at Fredericksburg, Lincoln was quoted by one standing near him at one point as saying, "If there's a worse place than hell, I'm in it." Another victory for Lee; another failure in the eastern theater for the Federals, and an even greater defeat just around the corner. The Chancellorsville campaign of April and May 1863 provided Lee with his most striking battlefield success.

He overcame huge odds. James Longstreet and half of the First Corps was away in south side Virginia because logistics had been so poor that Lee couldn't provision his whole army in one place. Lee had 60,000–64,000 men defeat yet another Federal commander, Joseph Hooker, who had about 130,000—it's two-to-one odds at Chancellorsville. Hooker opens with a great move, gets around Lee's left flank, but rather than retreating or responding as Hooker expected, Lee and Stonewall Jackson seize the initiative. Lee divided his army in the course of the Chancellorsville campaign three times in the face of the Federals, took the tactical initiative, and in the end won another victory. It was the victory that involved the most famous flanking attack of the war, Jackson's flanking attack on May 2, 1863. A battle that had very hard fighting, especially on May 3, but a battle than in the end sent the Army of the Potomac, the proud Army of the Potomac, retreating back across the Rappahannock River—yet, another failure in Virginia. Yet another example of Lee's taking the initiative; he began on the defensive, found a way to take the initiative, and, in the end, won. He shouldn't have won this battle; Hooker should have won the battle. Time and again Hooker was in a position to win the battle, but it's a perfect example of one commander being overawed by another commander. Everything was on Hooker's side. If the roles had been reversed, if Lee had commanded Hooker's army and Hooker Lee's army, I believe Lee would have smashed Hooker. As it was Hooker, in effect, who allowed Lee to get away with this audacious behavior, which resulted in another victory.

Another victory. It cost the Confederacy Jackson, who was shot down by his own men on the evening of May 2, but it's still a great victory, another bloody victory—13,000 Confederate casualties nearly, about 17,000 Union casualties. In other words, a much higher proportion of Lee's army is killed or wounded or captured at Chancellorsville than of Hooker's army, but it's a victory seemingly against the odds. Again, with a large aggressive component that thrills Confederates behind the lines. Here Lee is doing again what they want their generals to do. I know that I'm hammering this point hard, but we can't overstate it. Lee's generalship suits the temper and expectations of the Confederate people almost exactly, and that is extremely important in a democracy at war. He is a perfect fit. His behavior and the expectations of the people he and his army are representing in the field.

There was an epiphany, a special epiphany, for both Lee and his men on May 3 at Chancellorsville. There are always these moments when something important happens. On the morning of May 3, after very heavy fighting, two parts of Lee's army had divided. The men fought their way together. Enormously costly fighting on the morning of May 3, as heavy as any of the days at Gettysburg for example; they fought together in this wilderness of Spotsylvania, this forest, they came into a clearing where Hooker had had his headquarters. Hooker had retreated. The headquarters was on fire, the woods were on fire around this clearing, and the two wings of Lee's army emerged into the clearing and reunited. Just as the wings of the army came together, Lee rode into the midst of his men. There was an enormous and spontaneous outburst of emotion on the part of the soldiers— shouting and brandishing their muskets and throwing their hats. Lee stood there amidst the men taking in this scene and understanding that they had through very hard fighting given him a victory, and they understood that he, somehow, had put them into a position to achieve this victory against the odds. It cemented, I believe, the bond between Lee and his men. He came away from there believing his infantry could do anything, we'll talk about what that meant at Gettysburg, and I think the men came away believing that whatever Lee asked them to do they could do.

A Georgian shortly after this time said this about Lee, he said, "Wherever he leads we will follow, whatever he says to do can and must be done. Language is inadequate to convey the idea of the supreme confidence this army reposes in its great and good leader."

The impact of Chancellorsville: Confederate morale goes up; Abraham Lincoln anguished again. Yet, again, Lincoln has put his big army into the field with high expectations, and they are defeated. An anguished Lincoln responded when he realized that Hooker had failed, he said, "My God, my God, what will the country say?" Well, what the country said, what the United States said, was, "We've lost again. Our army has lost again to Lee and his army. What is going on in Virginia? What will it take to achieve a victory in the eastern theater? What will it take?"

The *Lynchburg Virginian*, a newspaper in Lynchburg, Virginia, observed just a few days after Chancellorsville, "The central figure of this war is beyond all question that of Robert E. Lee. Lee is the exponent of southern power of command." Here at the end of this initial year in command, again, not quite a year, but almost a year, the Seven Days to Chancellorsville, Lee has gone from a man who raised enormous doubts among many people in the Confederacy to someone who has become the most important person in the Confederacy. More important for Jefferson Davis—he and his army having won another victory.

Many historians believe that Lee's victories were too bloody, he piled up too many casualties, he, in effect, hurt the Confederacy's chances to win independence, and there's no way of getting around how bloody Lee's victories were. We've talked about the 50,000 casualties—another 13,000 at Chancellorsville, 12,000 at Fredericksburg, that's another 25,000—75,000 battle casualties during this period that we're talking about in an army that numbered 85,000–90,000 when he first took command. He is the bloodiest commander on either side during the war. If you don't want to get shot, you don't want to be in Robert E. Lee's army, because your chance will be the best of getting shot if you're in that army among all the armies on either side. What historians overlook, I think, by narrowly concentrating on casualties, is the effect that these victories, these bloody victories, had both on the civilian population in the United States and the civilian population in the Confederacy. Lee is wielding tremendous influence and he is shaping the war in a way that gives the Confederacy a chance for success by depressing Northern morale to the point that the Northern people might just say enough, it's just not worth it, it's too big a task to try to subdue these Rebels. The bloodiest of all the battles lay just ahead, and we'll turn to that and the rest of Lee's career next time.

# Lecture Four
# Lee from Gettysburg to Appomattox

**Scope:**  Lee and his army continued to carry the hopes of the Confederacy
on their bayonets through the remainder of the war. Just as they
supplied the only positive counterpoint to Southern defeats in
other geographic theaters in 1862 and early 1863, so, too, did their
campaigns in 1864 provide hope to the Confederacy. Even the
costly defeat at Gettysburg in July 1863 did little to tarnish Lee's
reputation or that of his army. Lee's epic confrontation with
Ulysses S. Grant during the Overland campaign of May–June 1864
left both armies reeling from horrendous casualties, and the
ensuing nine-month siege of Petersburg and Richmond brought a
new kind of grinding attrition to the conflict. Lee worked hard to
maintain an effective command structure as subordinates failed or
fell victim to wounds. Through it all, he remained vastly popular
with both soldiers and civilians in the Confederacy. His surrender
to Grant at Appomattox on April 9, 1865, stood as the practical
end of the war—the moment when the one indispensable national
institution in the Confederacy ceased to exist.

## Outline

I.  The Gettysburg campaign brought to an end Lee's major strategic
initiatives.
   A. Lee invaded Pennsylvania with logistical and political goals in
   mind.
      1. He successfully provisioned his army in the United States and
      gave northern Virginia's farmers a respite from war.
      2. He hoped to exploit the political divisiveness in the United
      States, which centered on such subjects as emancipation and
      conscription.
   B. Defeat at Gettysburg ended the campaign sooner than Lee had
   planned.
      1. The first day's battle was a Confederate offensive success.
      2. Lee insisted on continuing the tactical offensive on the second
      and third days of battle.

      **3.** The Confederates retreated from Gettysburg after the war's bloodiest three days.

  **C.** Gettysburg was a Confederate defeat but not a catastrophe.

      **1.** Casualties were ghastly. At least 23,000 were killed, wounded, and captured, what amounted to roughly a third of Lee's army.

      **2.** Lee failed to influence U.S. politics.

      **3.** He gained a logistical bounty, siphoning Union goods and animals out of Pennsylvania to be used for the Confederate cause.

      **4.** The Virginia theater was quiet for the next 10 months.

  **D.** Gettysburg had little effect on Lee's reputation among his men or in the Confederacy.

**II.** The confrontation between Lee and Grant in 1864–1865 brought a new kind of war to Virginia.

  **A.** The Overland campaign of May–June 1864 set a chilling standard for casualties.

  **B.** Battles such as the Wilderness and Spotsylvania exacted a huge toll but offered no clearcut winner or loser. Grant lost 18,000 and Lee, 12,000 men at each battle. And still more battles were to come.

  **C.** Lee's subordinate command structure fractured.

  **D.** The armies that settled into the siege of Petersburg in June 1864 had been bled nearly beyond recognition.

  **E.** Confederate faith in Lee remained high, while many in the United States became critical of Grant.

**III.** Nine months of siege at Richmond and Petersburg set the stage for U.S. triumph.

  **A.** Lee wrestled with problems of supply and manpower.

  **B.** He sought to mount a few tactical offensives in the midst of the siege.

  **C.** The turning of his western flank at Five Forks in April 1865 proved decisive.

**IV.** The Appomattox campaign ended Lee's career as a Confederate general and foreclosed any option for Southern independence.

**A.** Grant frustrated Lee's efforts to break free of U.S. pursuit and join Joseph E. Johnston in North Carolina.

**B.** The surrender at Appomattox set the tone for future Confederate surrenders.
   1. Lee vetoed guerrilla war as an option.
   2. He embraced Grant's generous terms, which even allowed Confederates to keep their horses.

**C.** The surrender of the Army of Northern Virginia removed what most Confederates looked to as their most important national institution.
   1. Lee towered above other Confederate leaders.
   2. Further national resistance seemed futile.

## Essential Reading:

Gallagher, *The Confederate War*, chapter 3.

———, *Lee and His Army in Confederate History*, chapters 3–4.

———, *Lee and His Generals in War and Memory*, chapters 3–4.

———, ed., *Lee the Soldier*, essays by Alexander, Connelly, Freeman, Gallagher, Nolan, Roland, and Trudeau.

## Supplementary Reading:

Freeman, *R. E. Lee: A Biography*, vol. 3; vol. 4, chapters 1–11.

Nolan, *Lee Considered*, chapter 4.

Thomas, *Robert E. Lee: A Biography*, chapters 23–29.

## Questions to Consider:

1. Have historians paid too much attention to Gettysburg?
2. Are problems relating to logistics the most important factor in assessing Lee's military operations?

# Lecture Four—Transcript
## Lee from Gettysburg to Appomattox

In our last lecture we left Lee in his moment of triumph at Chancellorsville. In this lecture we'll follow him on to war's end at Appomattox. After Chancellorsville, Lee and his army continued to carry the hopes of the Confederacy on their bayonets, and did so throughout the remainder of the war. Just as they supplied the only positive counterpoint to Southern defeats in other geographic theaters in 1862 and 1863, early 1863, so also did their campaigns in 1864 provide hope to the Confederacy. Even the costly defeat at Gettysburg in July of 1863 did little to tarnish Lee's reputation or that of his army. Lee's epic confrontation with Ulysses S. Grant during the Overland campaign of May and June 1864 left both armies reeling from horrendous casualties. The ensuing nine-month siege of Petersburg and Richmond brought a new kind of grinding attrition to the conflict.

Lee worked hard to maintain an effective command structure. His subordinates failed or fell victim to wounds. Through it all, he remained vastly popular with both soldiers and civilians in the Confederacy. His surrender to Grant at Appomattox on April 9, 1865 stood as the practical end of the war, the moment when the one indispensable national institution in the Confederacy ceased to exist.

The most famous of Lee's campaigns was, of course, Gettysburg. The campaign that has gotten, by far, the most attention from both people who write about his campaigns and those who read about his campaigns. And that campaign into Pennsylvania in June and July 1863 also brought to an end Lee's major strategic initiatives. Never again would he cross the Potomac River, he would not have the same kind of impact across the Potomac after July of 1863 that he managed to have twice in his career down to that point.

Lee invaded Pennsylvania with logistical and political goals in mind, and logistics probably loomed largest. The war had been very hard on the agricultural capacity of the state of Virginia. A British observer passing though the region between, or just not far north of Charlottesville along the eastern slope of the Blue Ridge Mountains in June of 1863 commented that, "The region upon the eastern slope of the mountains was completely cleaned out. The presence of the armies for more than a year had left many acres almost uncultivated, and no animals are grazing where there used to be hundreds. All fences have been destroyed and numberless farms burnt. The chimneys alone left standing." This man concluded this is in a diary, "It is difficult to depict and impossible to exaggerate the sufferings which this part of Virginia have undergone."

Not just that part of Virginia, that was a part of Virginia where there hadn't even been a battle. The war had been very hard on the logistical capacity of Virginia, and Lee hoped to get north of the Potomac River and gather food and fodder from the lush Pennsylvania countryside. His army had come out of the winter of '62–'63 in very weakened condition, and this would be a chance both to let agriculture recover in Virginia and to pull food, fodder, animals—whatever his army could use, from the Pennsylvania farmers.

He also hoped that a movement north of the Potomac would exploit political divisiveness that he knew was present in the United States. He read newspapers assiduously. People on both sides did. They read the other side's newspapers, that was an excellent source of information about what was going on behind the lines in your opponent's camp, and Lee knew that in the spring of 1863 there were enormous political debates in the United States.

Once centered on emancipation. Lincoln's Emancipation Proclamation had taken effect on July 1, 1863 and it was very controversial in the North. Millions of Democrats in the North were adamantly against the emancipation, they did not want to fight a war to free black people. They were willing to fight a war to restore the Union; they were not willing to risk their lives to free African-Americans. So, this is a very hot issue in the United States.

A second very hot issue was conscription. The Lincoln government turned to conscription in the spring of 1863. It was the first national conscription act, the first national draft, in United States history. A year later than the Confederates had done it, but now the United States has done it because their manpower was running short as well. That's also highly controversial. Those two issues are going to come together, emancipation and the draft, in the riots in New York City in mid-July 1863. The worst urban riots in the United States history are going to have dimensions related to both antipathy for the emancipation and antipathy for the draft. Gold prices were fluctuating on Wall Street. The Copperheads, the anti-war element of the Democratic Party reached apogee during the spring of 1863—Lee was aware of all these things and he believed that the presence of his army north of the Potomac would aggravate the situation, the political situation, for Abraham Lincoln and his government. So, he hoped both to get food and fodder and to aggravate this situation for Lincoln, and the campaign went well initially. He spread his army across a good part of southern Pennsylvania, one piece of it got all the way to the Susquehanna River near Harrisburg. But Jeb Stuart, the cavalry commander in the army, wasn't doing his job very well, we'll talk more about that later, and in the end Lee found out that the Army of the Potomac was pursuing rather rapidly, under yet another commander, George Gordon Meade, and Lee pulled his army together hoping not to fight a battle until it was all in one piece. But a battle came on before the army was united into one piece near the crossroads town of Gettysburg in Adams County, Pennsylvania.

It was a meeting engagement that very rapidly escalated into a major fight. Lee arrived on the battlefield the first of the three days of fighting. He hadn't wanted a general battle but he saw that luck was favoring the Confederates, the Confederates happened to be coming onto the field in a way that gave them an advantage, and so he sought to press the advantage, and at the end of the first day's fighting he had won one of the great tactical victories for all of the war for the Army of Northern Virginia. Two Union corps pretty much destroyed on July 1, 1863, the Federals hunkering down on a good piece of high ground and hoping the rest of their army would come up and retrieve the situation. So, a great victory on July 1. The question is: What do you do on July2?

Lee had a number of options. He had decided to maintain the tactical offensive, probably the most controversial decision of his career, to continue the tactical offensive after July 1 at Gettysburg. He continued it on the 2$^{nd}$, and again on the 3$^{rd}$. James Longstreet, his senior and most trusted subordinate disagreed with this course. He thought that the Confederates should try to get the Federals to attack them. Lee's safest play probably would have been to just stay where he was after the first day's fighting and compel Federals to attack him, which they almost certainly would have had to do because it was simply intolerable, from Lincoln's perspective, from the Republican perspective in the United States, to have the largest Rebel army in Pennsylvania. The onus was on George Gordon Meade and the Army of the Potomac to throw Lee out of Pennsylvania. And Lee could have gone to the defensive, but he thought otherwise. He always believed in momentum and morale. He knew morale in his army was sky high, momentum generated on July 1 made him think he could continue and deliver the kind of knock-out blow he always hoped to deliver. This is Lee's aggressiveness coming to the fore, his desire always to inflict the greatest possible damage. The result was heavy Confederate attacks on July 2, and then again on July 3, the famous Pickett-Pettigrew assault on July 3. We all know the outcome—the Confederates came close on July 2, but in the end they lost this battle and suffered enormous casualties. Lee retreated from Gettysburg on July 4, the same day Ulysses S. Grant accepted the surrender of the citadel at Vicksburg on the Mississippi River. People behind the lines in the United States read a great deal into this—two victories on July 4, on Independence Day. It seemed to be that God had stepped in and said, "Let's favor the United States."

At any rate, Lee retreated, and he has been heavily criticized over many generations for his decisions at Gettysburg, the decision, as I said, to continue the tactical offensive when he might have gone onto the defensive and saved some of his losses. He immediately, this was one of his hallmarks as a commander, in the wake of the Pickett-Pettigrew assault he literally rode out among the men who were retreating from cemetery ridge and took responsibility on the spot. He said, "All of this is my fault, this is all my fault, now let's try to rally and retrieve the situation." Grant shared that quality of Lee's; Grant never pointed the finger at anybody else, he never looked for a scapegoat when something didn't go right. Grant would step up and take responsibility and say, "Well, now what are we going to do?" That's exactly what Lee did at Gettysburg and at other places, "Well, all right, I ordered this and it didn't work. It's my fault. Now what are we going to do?" What he did was disengage from the Federals and conduct a really masterly retreat from Gettysburg to the Potomac River and eventually across the river. Meade followed but not very aggressively, and I cut Meade slack there. He was the brand new man and he had just been through this enormous battle, but at any rate Lee got back across the Potomac River intact. The question is: What was the effect of this extremely bloody battle?

Many have said it marked, I've talked about this before, that this marked the great turning point in the war, Gettysburg and Vicksburg together—it's all over for the Confederacy, but, you know, I disagree with that. It clearly was a Confederate defeat, of course it was, and casualties were ghastly. Lee took 75,000 men into Pennsylvania. At least 23,000 and perhaps as many as 28,000 of them were killed, wounded, or captured at Gettysburg—23,000 to 28,000 of his 75,000. That is, perhaps, more than a third of the entire army. He did lose a third of his generals, 52 general officers went with the army across the Potomac River— 17 of them were killed or wounded or captured in the course of this campaign.

Lee also failed in some of his goals. He didn't influence the political situation in the United States. The Copperheads lost steam after the spring and early summer of 1863. Lee's retreat was a boon to the Lincoln administration even though, as we've seen, Lincoln was terribly disappointed in Meade for not pressing his advantage against Lee when Lee started to retreat. But, nonetheless, Lee did not influence politics in the North.

He did, however, do splendidly in terms of logistics. From the moment the Confederates crossed the Pennsylvania border until they crossed back into Virginia they were siphoning materials out of the Pennsylvania countryside. Tens of thousands of horses and mules and cattle and swine and sheep, uncounted tons of fodder, anything of use to the Confederate war effort was on its way back to Virginia as soon as the Confederates crossed the river. When Lee prepared to retreat, his trains, that is, his wagon trains that accompanied the army, these are all the trains, with supplies, with wounded, with all of the things that needed to go back to Virginia. They stretched for more than fifty miles, fifty miles of wagon trains had to be gotten back to the Potomac and across the river. Lee probably pulled enough material out of the Pennsylvania countryside not only to subsist his army for a month and more the five weeks that it was out of Virginia, but probably for another six weeks beyond that. It doesn't sound like much, but more than two months is an enormous amount of materials. So, the campaign in that regard was a tremendous success, a tremendous success that helped relieve the enormous logistical problems that Lee had.

It also ended major fighting in the theater for almost ten months. There wouldn't be any until Grant crossed the Rapidan and Rappahannock Rivers in early May 1864 that there would be another major battle in the Virginia theater.

How do we reckon the plusses and minuses of Gettysburg? It was tremendously costly. The army was never as large again as it was when it crossed the Potomac going into Pennsylvania. Edward Porter Alexander, one of our subjects in this class, who was also the most perceptive writer about Confederate military affairs among all the participants who wrote, Edward Porter Alexander said this about Lee at Gettysburg, he was quite harsh on Lee, he said, "Perhaps in taking the aggressive at all at Gettysburg in 1863 and certainly in the place and dispositions for the assault on the third day," that is Pickett's charge, "I think it will undoubtedly be held that Lee unnecessarily took the most desperate chances and the bloodiest road." I think it's hard to disagree with that.

On the other hand, the logistical component was so important to Lee that in retrospect Lee said that he didn't think the campaign was a complete failure.

Most historians have said that Lee couldn't have meant that, he couldn't possibly have meant that. He wrote after the battle that his army had "behaved nobly and cheerfully, and though it did not win a victory it conquered a success." Now, that is Lee's language, and he told another officer, "Sir, we did whip them at Gettysburg and it will be seen for the next six months that that army, the Army of the Potomac, would be as quiet as a sucking dove." There Lee touched on the two points that did show some advantage in this campaign—the Army of the Potomac was "as quiet as a sucking dove" for many months, and logistically Lee had gained a great deal, but he also suffered a shattering tactical defeat at Gettysburg and one that ravaged all levels of command in his army and cost him priceless veteran soldiers.

What was the impact at the time? I've alluded to this earlier, not nearly what we think it should have been. It wasn't perceived as a disaster in the Confederacy. It was perceived as a big, bloody battle that wasn't an overall success, except on the first day. But no one knew that it would be the biggest battle of the war; we know that now. No one knew that it would be the last time Lee went north; we know that now. They didn't know the things we know about Gettysburg now that make it seem to us to be so important. It was a big battle. It wasn't a grand success. It had very little effect on the reputation of either Lee or his army. It was bloody, it was not a victory, but it did not point the way to ultimate Confederate defeat in the minds of most Confederates. For most Confederate people Lee remained a general in whom they had tremendous faith. As many of them said again and again and again, I'll quote one man from May of 1864, this is an officer serving way out along the Mississippi River, he's getting mixed reports about what's happening between Grant and Lee in the first phase of the Overland campaign, and he wrote, "I believe nothing one way or the other until further word is received, but I continue to have complete faith in General Lee, who has never been known to suffer defeat, and who probably never will." That, months after Gettysburg.

So, it's quiet for many months after Gettysburg. A little maneuvering in the fall and winter of '63, but the next real confrontation comes when the best soldier in the United States arrived in the Virginia theater. When Ulysses S. Grant comes east, comes east because the American people, the people in the United States, demanded that he come east—don't run the war from the west. His friend Sherman, Grant's friend Sherman, said, "Grant, don't go to the east. That's where Washington and all those politicians are. They'll get in your way all the time. Stay with me out here in the west and run the war via the telegraph." Grant would have preferred that, but he knew that public opinion demanded that he go to the east and so he did. Here you have, finally, the two greatest soldiers of the war coming together on what would prove to be the bloodiest series of battlefields of the war in the Overland campaign.

The Overland campaign would set a chilling new standard for slaughter, even in this enormously bloody war. There simply was nothing like it before during the war, nothing like it before in United States history. The old pattern had been you fight a big battle, like Antietam for example. When's the next big battle? Antietam's in September, it isn't until mid-December until the next battle. After Fredericksburg, when's the next big battle in the east? You go from December '62 to May of '63. In the Overland campaign, it is pretty much incessant fighting, daily casualties punctuated by enormous bloodlettings, with no respite for the soldiers on either side. There had been nothing like it before, constant action, and it took an enormous toll. In battles such as the Wilderness on May 5 and 6; Spotsylvania, which began on May 8 and continued for a couple of weeks, there were no real winners or losers—it was hard to tell what was actually happening. But what wasn't hard to tell was how bloody these battles were. Grant lost 18,000 men at the Wilderness, a one day respite, he lost 18,000 more at Spotsylvania, the next battle. Lee lost 12,000 in each of those battles. Just in those two battles, the first two battles of the Overland campaign, in other words, you have 60,000 casualties, just in the beginning, and ahead lay the fighting along the North Anna River, Cold Harbor, and then the early skirmishing outside Petersburg and the early fighting outside Petersburg.

This is a kind of action no one had been prepared for, and it has an enormous effect behind the lines, especially in the United States, especially because Grant was not only suffering these casualties, these endless casualties, but he wasn't capturing Richmond. It seemed that Lee was anticipating everything Grant wanted to do. And when Grant ordered the bloody frontal assaults at Cold Harbor, which came to nothing and seemed almost as senseless as Burnside's had at Fredericksburg back in December 1862, public opinion in the North, some of it, especially the Democrats in the North who opposed the Lincoln administration (of course, 45% of the voters in the United States are Democrats during the war), much of the Democratic press and many of the Democrats in the North turned on Grant and began to call him a butcher—somebody who didn't value the lives of his soldiers, who wasn't achieving anything but was wracking up these unacceptable levels of casualties. There's nothing comparable on the Confederate side about Lee. I believe that is a function of this willingness to let Lee pile up casualties because he accomplished so much good the first year that he was in command. I think the residual effect of that is still present during the Overland campaign between Grant and Lee. The United States population doesn't cut Grant as much slack as the Confederate people cut Lee during the bloody series of battles during the Overland campaign.

The armies eventually settled into a siege at Petersburg in June 1864, but not before the command structure of the Army of Northern Virginia had been shattered. At the outset of the campaign Lee has four principle subordinates, three corps commanders—he's reshaped the corps command after Stonewall Jackson died, he went from the two corps model with Longstreet and Jackson as the corps commanders, to a three corps model, Longstreet kept the First Corps; Richard Ewell, one of our subjects later, got the Second Corps; and A. P. Hill, another one of our subjects got the Third Corps. That's the structure at Gettysburg; it's still the structure during the Overland campaign. Jeb Stuart remains in command of the cavalry. Those are the four principle subordinates. Within the first month of the Overland campaign, Longstreet was severely wounded in the Wilderness, Jeb Stuart was killed in action just outside Richmond, Richard Ewell proved so inept as a corps commander that Lee eased him out of the army, and A. P. Hill was sick so much that Lee couldn't count on him at all. All four of his principle subordinates failed in one way or another, either through wounds, failed to do their duties either through wounds, or simply because they weren't up to their job, and Lee found himself behaving in a different way. He took on a number of the functions of the corps commanders as well as those of being army commander. It put a greater stress on him; it's not the way to run an army. It is not the way to run an army, but it simply increased his load and showed that attrition was taking such a toll that the army was not going to be up to the kinds of things they had done before.

Neither would the Army of the Potomac. By the time the two armies reached Petersburg, and the siege began at Petersburg, each had been bled nearly beyond recognition. Grant's causalities: between 60,000–65,000 between May the 5th and June the 18th when the siege began at Petersburg. Another 18,000 U.S. soldiers left because their three-year enlistments had run out. That's 78,000 men who were either casualties or left the army on Grant's part.

Lee lost at least 35,000. His proportion is even higher. He began the campaign with 60,000–65,000 men. Grant had about 130,000 men. Lee's rate of loss is even higher than Grant's. In the army, so many capable company-grade officers (2nd lieutenants, lieutenants, and captains) and field grade officers (majors, lieutenant colonels, colonels, and generals) had been killed, or wounded, or captured that the army simply didn't have the capability. Together with the loss of all the veteran soldiers, these aren't armies that can do what they could do before. They are different armies by the time they get to Petersburg. They are different armies, and they're going to go into a very different kind of war, a very different kind of war.

The nine-month siege of Richmond and Petersburg set the stage for eventual United States triumph, and Lee had foreseen this. This was Lee's greatest fear—one reason he had always been so adamantly against simply standing on the defensive was because his greatest fear was a siege. Every siege in the war ended the same way, every major siege, and that is with the capitulation of the Confederate army, including the siege of Petersburg, which will end with the capitulation of Lee's army. Lee told Jubal Early, a principle subordinate, again, one of ours that we will look at, in June of 1864, in the midst of the Overland campaign, he said, "We must destroy this army of Grant's before he gets to the James River. If he gets there it will become a siege, and then it will become a mere question of time." And that's exactly what happened.

It was a long siege, it lasted nine months, from mid-June 1864 down until the first of April 1865, but it is a siege that went just the way that Lee knew it would. During this long period Lee wrestled with problems of manpower and logistics. He mounted a few tactical offensives in the midst of the siege, the major one he really opened a second front in Virginia, a second Valley campaign, much like the one Jackson had carried out in the spring and early summer of '62. Jubal Early was sent to the Valley with many of Jackson's old troops in June of '64 and he remained in the Valley until mid-October, major action continued until mid-October, and much of it offensive action. That's one way in which Lee tried to maintain some kind of initiative during this period. He also launched an almost pathetic final tactical offensive at Fort Stedman in late March 1865. But really it was a matter of time once the siege began. Grant continually extending the lines around Petersburg, eventually they stretched for fifty miles, these earthworks, very significant earthworks around the cities, and Lee simply, when it was all finished, could not match all of this.

The decisive last moment came at Five Forks on April 1, 1865 when part of Grant's army under Philip Sheridan got all the way around Lee's right flank, broke the right flank, and compelled Lee to abandon the Richmond and Petersburg lines. By that time, the 1st of April 1865, Lee had been functioning for a while as general-in-chief of the Confederate armies; that's what Grant was in the United States army; it's what Winfield Scott had been, George McClellan, and others. Davis, as I said earlier, had been reluctant to have a general-in-chief, he sort of functioned as his own general-in-chief in many ways, but public opinion in the Confederacy had become so strident in this regard that Davis was forced to allow creation of that post in the Confederacy and make Lee the general-in-chief. That happened on February 6, 1865. It was too little too late, but even though it was too little too late from our perspective, people at the time responded, again, with an affirmation of how much they believed in Lee. One Kentucky born officer typified this sentiment when he wrote that "this naming of Lee to be general-in-chief has inspired our country with more hope, courage and confidence than it has had for a year or two."

Well, that was too optimistic because there really wasn't anything Lee could do by that point, but it was as general-in-chief that he presided over the retreat toward Appomattox. He abandoned Richmond and Petersburg. He hoped to get far enough west to outdistance his pursuing Federal opponent under Grant, and then turn south and link up with his old friend Joseph Johnston in the Carolinas who was facing William Tecumseh Sherman there. Lee hoped that together he and Johnston could deal with the Federal opponents in turn, first Sherman, then Grant. But Grant's pursuit, Grant's such an able soldier, had such good subordinates, they gave Lee no respite. They hounded Lee westward, Lee's army staggered westward, probably 60,000 Confederates left Richmond and Petersburg, left the lines, half the armies disappeared over the next week—captured, killed or wounded. There was one major battle, not really a major battle, but one debacle on the way at Sailor's Creek April 6 where thousands of Confederates were captured, including one of Lee's sons, George Washington Custis Lee, who was a major general, had been an aide to Jefferson Davis. Thousands were captured there; Lee witnessed much of this debacle at Sailor's Creek. He turned back and looked at it unfolding below him and said, "My God, has this army been dissolved?"

The army went on to Appomattox, where three days later, having vetoed the idea of a guerrilla war, several people brought this up, "Should we just take to the hills, disband, and continue the resistance that way?" Lee said, "No." His attitude very clearly was we took our best shot at this, we did everything we could, they've won, and now we're going to abide by their terms. And that is how the war ended. They were really Lincoln's terms. Lincoln had told Sherman and Grant in a meeting just before this that he wanted an easy peace, and that is what Grant offered at Appomattox. There would be no mass arrests, no executions, no shipping of Confederate soldiers to prison camps in the North. Lee's soldiers would simply sign a parole promising not to fight again. Grant sent some rations to Lee's army. When he found out that Confederate cavalrymen had to buy their own horses, the government didn't supply them; he said they could keep their horses. They were very lenient terms, amazingly lenient considering the kind of war this was. The astronomical cost in a material and human sense for the United States not to have a more retributive peace than did come. Grant and Lee at Appomattox set that pattern, Grant carrying out Lincoln's wishes here.

The surrender of the Army of Northern Virginia removed what most Confederates looked to, as I've said repeatedly, as their most important national institution. This was it, there's no use fighting anymore. Lee and his army are gone. As one Georgia woman wrote in her diary, "Everybody feels ready to give up hope," this was after she heard about Appomattox, "it's useless to struggle longer. It seems to be the common cry and the poor wounded men go hobbling about the streets with despair on their faces."

Further national resistance did seem futile to people in the Confederacy. People rejoiced in the North, the war was over. There would be more surrenders, a number of other surrenders across the Confederacy, but this was the end of the war. More than once Lee's generalship had brought the Confederacy to the verge of independence, inspiring its people to resist long past the point of which they otherwise might have conceded their inability to overcome United States power. Lee and his army had served as their nation's chief hope during the war. After Appomattox, in the writings we'll talk about later, the Lost Cause writings of former Confederates, Lee and his army also stood as the defeated white South's primary symbol of striving in a struggle that had ended in shattering defeat.

# Lecture Five
# Was Lee an Old-Fashioned General?

**Scope:** Robert E. Lee often appears in writings about the Civil War as a throwback to an earlier style of warfare. Typically contrasted with Grant and William Tecumseh Sherman, who almost always are described as forward-looking practitioners of modern war that engulfed whole societies, Lee seems a quaint remnant from a localist, chivalric past. Many writers, both friendly and hostile to Lee, have suggested that he failed to understand that industrial production, mass railroad transportation, and vast application of national resources were necessary to wage a modern mid-19th-century conflict between two democratic societies. Common notions about him insist that he lacked national vision, thought only about Virginia, failed to understand the connections between politics and military affairs, blindly pursued set-piece battlefield victories without thinking of how each battle fit in the broader sweep of the war, and even failed to grasp the importance of technological advances in weaponry that made frontal assaults a thing of the past. In fact, Lee was an able practitioner of modern warfare in an 1860s context. He understood the connection between politics and military planning in a democratic republic, called for the subordination of state and local interests to national needs, and pursued a military strategy calculated to destroy the civilian North's will to continue the fight. His ultimate failure should not obscure his clear comprehension of the type of conflict in which he and other Civil War generals found themselves engaged.

## Outline

I.  Lee is often described as an old-fashioned general in a modern war.

    **A.** Some admirers portray him as a chivalric anachronism.

        **1.** They describe him as noble, even likening him to King Arthur.

        **2.** They contrast him to such soldiers as Grant and William Tecumseh Sherman.

**B.** Many critics argue that he did not understand a modern 19th-century war.

   **1.** He was a localist who concentrated on Virginia and failed to take in the whole strategic picture.

   **2.** He failed to understand that mobilization of national resources was crucial to victory.

   **3.** He concentrated on winning set-piece tactical victories with no understanding of the importance of politics and public morale.

   **4.** He failed to understand that modern rifled weaponry made aggressive tactics a thing of the past.

**C.** There is irony in the fact that both admirers and critics of Lee have nurtured the idea of him as a backward-looking general.

**II.** Lee, in fact, was an able practitioner of modern war in a mid-19th-century context.

**A.** He was an ardent Confederate nationalist rather than a localist.

   **1.** He called for nearly complete national mobilization.

   **a.** He supported conscription.

   **b.** He supported impressment of resources, including using slaves in the war effort. He later argued to put slaves in the army by promising them their freedom.

   **2.** He advised Southern governors to subordinate their state interests to Confederate interests.

**B.** He had an excellent understanding of the importance of politics and national morale.

   **1.** He knew better than most of his modern critics the effect his battles had on people behind the lines in the United States and the Confederacy.

   **2.** He argued from the outset of the war that civilian morale would be crucial to determining which side won.

**C.** He understood the impact of technology on the battlefield. He fully understood the power of rifled weaponry.

**D.** He formulated an admittedly risky strategy calculated to undermine morale in the United States before Confederate resources were exhausted. He calculated that only big victories would win the day—and his army suffered for it in the way of casualties.

**III.** Lee's ultimate failure should not be taken as evidence that he did not understand what type of war should be fought to achieve Confederate independence.

### Essential Reading:

Gallagher, *Lee and His Army in Confederate History*, chapter 5.

### Supplementary Reading:

Gallagher, ed., *Lee the Soldier*, essays by Connelly, Freeman, Gallagher, Nolan, and Roland.

McWhiney and Jamieson, *Attack and Die: Civil War Military Tactics and the Southern Heritage*, chapter 1.

### Questions to Consider:

1. Is there a satisfactory definition of *modern* in assessing Lee's generalship?
2. Does counting casualties to measure generalship obscure as much as it reveals?

# Lecture Five—Transcript
## Was Lee an Old-Fashioned General?

We traced the end of Lee's Confederate career in our last lecture, now we're going to move away from the chronological sequence to consider the question: Was Lee an old-fashioned general in a modern war, a modern war within the context of the mid-19$^{th}$ century?

Lee often does appear in writings about the Civil War as a throwback to an earlier kind of warfare. He's typically contrasted with Grant and William Tecumseh Sherman in this regard. Grant and Sherman are usually portrayed as forward-looking practitioners of modern war that engulfed entire societies. Lee seems a quaint remnant from a localist chivalric past. Many writers, both friendly and hostile to Lee, have suggested that he failed to understand that industrial production, mass railroad transportation, and the vast application of national resources were necessary to wage a modern 19$^{th}$-century conflict between two democratic societies. Common notions about him insist that he lacked national vision, that he thought only about his home state of Virginia, that he failed to understand the connections between politics and military affairs, that he blindly pursued set-piece battlefield victories without thinking about how each battle fit within the broader sweep of the war, and that he even failed to grasp the importance of technological advances within weaponry that made frontal assaults a thing of the past.

In fact, Lee was an able practitioner of modern warfare within an 1860s context. He did understand the connection between politics and military planning in a democratic republic. He called for the subordination of state and local interests to the national needs, and he pursued a military strategy calculated to destroy the civilian North's will to continue the fight. His ultimate failure should not obscure his clear comprehension of the type of conflict in which he and other Civil War generals found themselves engaged.

Lee is often described as an old-fashioned fellow, a man looking backward, his gaze to the back, to the early-19$^{th}$ century or even to a more medieval model of fighting than his late war opponents, especially U. S. Grant. Some admirers portray him, these are admirers of Lee, people who think by their portrayal they're adding to Lee's luster, some of these admirers portray him as a chivalric anachronism. They love to describe him using terms such as noble, chivalry. They call him a Christian knight, they liken him to King

Arthur and his soldiers to the Knights of the Round Table; I'll read a quotation in just a minute. All of this seems to take Lee out of his own time and put him in an earlier time, an earlier time when machines and railroads and steam power didn't make that much difference, where the human being accounted for more.

The leader that could form a patriarchal bond with his soldiers was the leader who would triumph, not the leader who simply had more of everything. A couple of speeches delivered at the dedication of major statues to Lee will give a flavor of how some of these admirers would describe him. One, delivered by a man named John Warwick Daniel, who had served as a staff member for Jubal Early during the Civil War, and later was a United States senator from Virginia, he spoke at the unveiling of the statue to Lee at Washington and Lee University, the recumbent statue. Daniel observed, this is in 1883, "Lee and his men formed the fellowship as noble as that which bound the Knights of the Round Table to Arthur."

In an address in Richmond, delivered by another former officer, this man named Archer Anderson, to the big statue on Monument Avenue, Anderson described Lee as "the grave and courteous commander, heir of all the knightly graces of the cavaliers." He added, "Let this monument stand as a memorial of personal honor that never brooked a stain of knightly valor without thought of self." Knightly and chivalry and backward looking and stainless honor, all of these are terms that come up again and again and again with Lee, and all of them look to a distance past, to a model in the past, that really has very little to do with what was going on in the American Civil War. These all suggest that Lee is sort of a man stuck out of his time, and these are comments from people who admired Lee.

Now there are also a lot of people very critical of Lee and his generalship who portray him as an anachronism, someone who isn't in touch with the kind of warfare that is engulfing the United States and the Confederacy during the Civil War. Many of these critics came later, and many of them have been academic historians. They say that Lee didn't understand the kind of war that he was involved in, not that his character was such that he simply stood outside of it, they say they didn't understand it. He didn't know what kind of war he was involved in, and therefore he didn't know how to fight it. They argue that he is a localist; he is a Virginian, a Virginian, a Virginian. He never really becomes a Confederate nationalist, they say. He only wants to protect Virginia. His strategic thinking stops at the borders of Virginia. All he ever does is ask for more things to help protect his native state of Virginia. He never can get beyond that, he can never get beyond his background, the background of his ancestors who were so prominent in Virginia politics, and so forth. He can't even see beyond the Appalachian Mountains. One historian, one prominent historian named Thomas L. Connelly has gone so far to argue that Lee didn't even understand the geographical features of the United States beyond the Appalachians. He just was sort of a great void out there. All he knew was Virginia.

One of the most influential historians in this regard was named T. Harry Williams, a giant in Civil War historiography in the 1940s and '50s and '60s and down into the '70s. He wrote a very influential essay titled *The Military Leadership of North and South* in which he offered a multiply faceted critique of Lee as an old-fashioned soldier of very restricted vision. I'll quote him: "For his preoccupation for the war in Virginia Lee is not to be criticized," stated a patronizing Williams, "he was a product of his culture, and that culture, permeated in its every part by the spirit of localism dictated that his outlook on the war should be local." Williams went on to argue that Lee was "in many respects not a modern minded general. Most tellingly he failed to grasp the vital relationship between war and state craft." Williams then said, "If you want a modern model, look at Grant. Grant understood the model of public opinion and shaped his campaigns with that in mind." Williams said it was "this ability of Grant's to grasp the political nature of modern war that marks him as the first of the great modern generals." Grant, the modern general; Lee the backward looking old-fashioned localist who just didn't get it.

He didn't understand, say many of his critics, that mobilization of national resources was critical to victory. You had to mobilize everything because modern war, say these critics, pits societies against one another, not just armies somehow detached from those societies that meet in a chessboard situation on battlefields. That's how Lee thought of it, they say. He's on a chessboard—he has his man and his opponent has his man and you're maneuvering to try to get the advantage on that spot with no sense of how activities on the battlefield radiate out to influence the societies on each side. Lee just didn't get it, he doesn't get the larger framework of the war; Grant did, say many of these critics, and that is one of the great differences between them. Lee just can't get beyond the idea that if he can just win the next battle, just win the next battle, it's all about winning battles, say his critics, not what those tactical successes can be translated into. The impact of democratic pressures were simply beyond him, simply beyond him. He is this very limited soldier in that regard, although a very able one in a restricted way, no one denies that, but they say that he can't make the vital connections that modern warriors can make. He cannot make the connections between politics on the one hand and military activities on the other. He doesn't get those connections, and therefore he is not the best man to be running your armies.

Beyond that, say some of his critics, he didn't even understand that modern rifled weaponry made aggressive tactics a thing of the past. You can't have frontal assaults anymore, argue these critics, because the defenders have muskets that will shoot 250 to 300 yards, rather than the 100 yards that the old smooth bore muskets would fire. That's simply too much ground to cover, too much killing ground to cover, with a frontal assault. You've got to come up with another way to do that, they argue. How do we know that? Look at Gaines's Mill—50,000 Confederates attack there in the course of the fighting on June 27, 1862. Look at Malvern Hill, attacks up a grade against a very well positioned Union enemy that littered the ground with Confederate corpses, killed, and also many wounded Confederates to no purpose, and especially look at the third day at Gettysburg. How could anyone who understood the killing power of rifled weaponry order the Pickett-Pettigrew assault, ask Lee's critics?

I think there is a good deal of irony in the fact that both admirers of Lee, especially from the 19th century, and many 20th century critics of Lee have come together for very different reasons and with very different purposes to contribute to this portrait of Lee as an old-fashioned general, as a man caught out of his time. He didn't really function as someone in the 1860s might be expected to function. That's a very interesting portrait of Lee, and I think it is absolutely wrong. I think that Lee was, in fact, a very able, a very gifted practitioner of modern war within a mid-19th-century context.

Let's look at the notion that he was a localist first off. I already talked about this some. It's just absolutely not right. I don't see how you can read what he wrote during the war and conclude that he was a localist. First to last, once the war got going, he was as ardent a Confederate nationalist as there is. He stood right along Jefferson Davis in that regard, arrayed against those who argued for states' rights and individual rights and individual liberties and didn't want a central government trampling on those things—Lee was absolutely against them, absolutely calling for the subordination of both the individual and the local, in a political sense, to the national needs. Now, that isn't to say he didn't love Virginia, he certainly did, and his decision to join the Confederacy, his decision to resign his commission from the United States Army, certainly was driven by his loyalty to Virginia.

He also was loyal to the South, however. He is often portrayed as being anti-slavery; he was not anti-slavery. He had very conventional views about slavery for one of his time and place and class. He's from the very top of the aristocratic slave-holding structure of the South, and he had views that would be very typical of that class. He often said that he hoped slavery would end, but then he would say, "But humans shouldn't do anything to try to end it. God would end slavery in time." Well, slavery could go on forever in that kind of context. Lee is not anti-slavery; he is not anti-slavery though he is often portrayed as anti-slavery.

He believed in Southern society as well as in Virginia society. He, as almost everyone, had a hierarchy of loyalties. He is loyal to Virginia, he is loyal to the South before the war, and then during the Confederacy he is loyal to the Confederacy. All of our loyalties shift at different times. Some percolate to the top sometimes and others at others. Lee is a Virginian, probably preeminently, when he decides to resign from the United States army. Once he puts on a Confederate uniform he becomes a Confederate. That is his most important loyalty, and his behavior absolutely underscores that. He is a Confederate nationalist, and he calls for, as I've alluded to before, almost complete national mobilization. He understands that will be necessary when you are a nation of five-and-a-half million white people and three-and-a-half million black people, most of them slaves on the Confederate side, arrayed against a nation of nearly twenty-two million white people. The disparity there is such, believed Lee, that you have to mobilize, you have to get the most you can out of your resources. The only way to do that is to compel people in many instances to make the sacrifices to support the war in the ways necessary to maintain the effort.

His support for conscription of all white males of military age is one way that he argued in favor of that. He also argued that slaves should be brought to the war effort and they should be impressed, as it was said during the war. Many slave owners didn't want their slaves used in support of the war effort, didn't want the government to come in and say we are going to use your slaves this way. Lee said that if you employed more slaves in support of the war effort, that would free up white men to carry muskets. He wanted all the white guys carrying muskets and fighting, and one way to do that was to make the most of slave labor in supporting the war effort.

He also, in the end, argued for putting black men in the Confederate army. He said we've got to do that. This isn't because he had some grand scheme of liberating black men in the Confederacy, he said, "Listen, the United States is putting black men in uniform," (put 200,000 in uniform, as we all know, before the end of the war). "They're going to use black soldiers against us, we should use black soldiers if we can. So, put slaves in the army," said Lee. "But, in order to get them to fight you have to promise them something," he said, "you have to free any black man who fights in the Confederate army, you have to free his family, and you have to guarantee that they can live in the South, rather than being forced to leave at the end of the war." This was a huge debate in the winter of 1864–65. Lee's stepping into the debate eventually pushed it in the direction of congress, the Confederate Congress, saying they would put slaves into the Confederate army, but the Confederate Congress didn't go as far as Lee wanted to go. They didn't say they would free all black men who went into the Confederate army, never mind their families or that they could live where they wanted to. My point is, Lee is willing to take this extreme position, this is a Confederacy founded allegedly on states' rights and a belief in a slave-holding system, and in the course of fighting the war Lee says, "Forget states' rights, the nation has to dominate, and, if necessary, we're going to free slaves in order to win the Confederate independence." I don't know how you can go beyond that in terms of being a Confederate nationalist. It would be very hard to do, in my belief.

He also said, "Whatever else we need we should be able to get." As he put it very famously in one instance, "If it requires all the meat in the country to support the army, it should be had. If the army needs meat that means the people behind the lines don't get meat, that's too bad for the people behind the lines." Lee was saying we have to have mobilization of resources. He told Southern governors on more than one occasion, "I don't want to hear," he said it in a nicer way, "I don't want to hear about what you need for your state, I want to hear about what your state is going to do to support the national war effort."

He had an excellent understanding of the importance of politics and national morale both. He knew better than most of his modern critics the effects that his battles had on people behind the lines in the United States and in the Confederacy. He was intensely aware of this, intensely aware of the fact that what his army did had repercussions. He was attuned to that throughout the war. He wrote Mrs. Lee a letter in the spring of 1863, for example. This is mid-April, when, as we've talked about before, so many things were percolating in the North: opposition to conscription, opposition to emancipation, the Copperheads were riding high, the gold prices were fluctuating, things seemed to be on the verge of coming apart behind the lines in the North, and Lee wrote to his wife, "I do not think our enemies are so confident of success as they used to be. If we are successful this year, " he meant we, the Army of Northern Virginia, "next fall there will be a great change of public opinion in the North. The Republicans will be destroyed, and I think the friends of peace will become so strong as the next administration will go in on that basis. We have only, therefore, to resist manfully." Well, the friends of peace are the Copperheads. He is thinking politically, he is thinking connections between the home front and the battlefield here very much so. He knew first hand the direct connection between what happened on the battlefield and how people viewed the way the war was going, and his experience in the Seven Days' campaign taught him that. He knew that he was heavily criticized in the newspapers before he began to exercise control of the Army of Northern Virginia. He knew how many people believed he was not the right man for the job, and he also knew that as soon as he fought an aggressive, successful campaign at Richmond his stock went soaring in the Confederacy. He saw very directly and personally that relationship between what happened on the battlefield and what perceptions were behind the lines.

He also understood that the outcome of the war would be decided by which civilian population remained hitched to the effort longest. He knew that it wasn't just a question of moving chess pieces on a military board. He knew that the key was behind the lines because these were democratic societies at war. It's a question of which people will make the requisite sacrifices in order to stay the course. Civilian morale would be the critical factor, not just what happened on the battlefield. But, of course, he knew that there was a real connection between the two. He wrote to his son, one of his sons, about this early in the conflict. His son Custis, the one that was captured, I mentioned him last time, was captured at Sailor's Creek, George Washington Custis Lee, he wrote to Custis that in a protracted conflict the Northern people's attitude toward the war was crucial. He knew that the North did have too many resources and too much manpower for the Confederacy absolutely to defeat the United States. There is no chance that Confederate armies are going to put the United States under their heal and compel the kind of peace the Confederacy wants. Lee's army is not going to capture Washington; he never even considered that. There's no chance that the great Northern cities are going to fall, that Confederate armies are going to rampage across New York state and into New England the way that, in the end, United States armies went across any part of the Confederacy they wanted to go across. That is not going to happen, but it doesn't have to happen.

It's easier for the Confederacy to win its war than it is for the United States to win its war. For the United States to emerge triumphant, it has to compel the wayward Southern states to come back into the Union, it has to defeat its armies, it has to take the war to the Confederacy, it has to occupy the areas in the end, it has to meet this very difficult standard of subduing a large foe, a numerous foe, in a huge area. The Confederacy doesn't have to do that. All the Confederacy has to do, a tie's as good as a win for the Confederacy, all the Confederacy has to do is to convince the Northern people that the war is too costly. It's costing too many lives; it's costing too much materiel treasure to force these damned Rebels back. Let them go. If you can just get the Northern people to say, "A pox on the South; let them go. Let them go. We'll be fine without them," that's all you have to do. Lee believed the way to do that is to defeat their famous armies in ways that hurt morale behind the lines. That's all you have to do.

Back to his son Custis in early 1863, he had nothing to arrest the enemy's power except a revolution among their people, a revolution that would erode Union commitment prosecuting the war. "And," said Lee, "only systematic" that's his word, not mine, "military success would affect such a revolution." He did his best to provide that systematic Confederate success. We've seen that he was on the road to doing it twice, the Seven Days and Second Manassas, that run came to an end with the Maryland campaign. Fredericksburg and Chancellorsville, that run came to an end with the Gettysburg campaign. But, he understands the road to Confederate success here, and he lays it out to his son here early in 1863.

The idea that he didn't understand the impact of technology on the battlefield is just...I don't see how anyone can argue that. Here's a man that fought on Mexican War battlefields dominated by smooth bore shoulder weapons and who presided over battles in which rifled weaponry was dominant. Lee understood the difference, that doesn't mean he's never going to launch frontal assaults. Everybody launches frontal assaults during the Civil War. U. S. Grant launched frontal assaults at Cold Harbor, massive ones. William Tecumseh Sherman launched frontal assaults at Kennesaw Mountain. Joseph Johnston launched frontal assaults at Seven Pines. Everybody launches frontal assaults; even George B. McClellan launched frontal assaults at the battle of Antietam. Everybody does it, everybody does it, but you don't read that U. S. Grant didn't understand about technology because he launched frontal assaults at Cold Harbor. It's part of this mosaic of factors that make Lee seem out of step with the kind of war he's in. He understands the power of rifled weaponry. He also understands and also believed that in some instances frontal assaults work. He saw them work. They worked at Chancellorsville on May 3, 1863; not only frontal assaults, but frontal assaults against entrenched numerically superior Federal units. It worked at Chancellorsville on May 3. This is something that almost all Civil War commanders did at some point, Lee certainly understood the impact of that weaponry, he just at certain times decided that a frontal assault was the way to go.

He also took in the whole strategic landscape. This is another one of the arguments that perhaps in a superficial way seems right. He did ask for more things for his army, of course he did, what army commander doesn't? Every army commander wants more for his army. No one says, "Well I can get by with one hundred cannons, why don't you give fifty cannons to Braxton Bragg's army out west and see how they do with them." That's not how it works. You ask for as much as you can get. He did, as did all army commanders. He did want to focus resources on the eastern theater, but not because he couldn't see beyond the eastern theater, it was absolutely because he could see beyond the eastern theater. He could see Confederate failures everywhere beyond the eastern theater, and he reached the very reasonable conclusion, from my point of view, that it made sense to give him as much as possible to do his job. He knew that he was in the arena that included Richmond. Richmond was incredibly important not just in terms of its being the Confederate capital, it was the industrial center of the Confederacy. The Tredegar Works in Richmond was the most important iron facility in all of the Confederacy. Richmond included 40% of all of the industrial capacity in all of the Confederacy at the outset of the war. Richmond's important industrially, politically, and in terms of morale and psychology. He understood all of that.

He also understood he commanded the best army in the Confederacy. His army won victories; no other army won victories. He knew that he had the best subordinate commanders in the Confederacy for most of the war. There's no Stonewall Jackson anywhere else. There's no James Longstreet anywhere else. He knows that he has the best army and many of the best lieutenants defending the most important place in the Confederacy. He also knew how much attention people on both sides put on the war of Virginia. Knowing all of those things, and knowing one more thing, which was absolutely obvious to him, and that was that he was the best general in the Confederacy—Lee has an ego, he has a real ego. He is not confused about who the best general in the Confederacy is. Put all those factors together: I'm the best general with the best army in the most important theater, maybe I should get as many resources as possible. Maybe that will give our national effort its best chance of achieving success. That is why he wanted more for his army, not because he didn't understand what was going on elsewhere in the Confederacy. He understood very well what was going on elsewhere.

Bringing all these factors together, Lee put together an undeniably risky strategy, a strategy calculated to undermine morale in the United States and keep it boosted in the Confederacy before Confederate resources were exhausted. He was in a race against the clock. What it takes to win, he reasoned, is the big kind of victories that will lower morale in the United States, defeat the armies that come against me, and, of course, that's always the most famous army, the biggest army, the Army of the Potomac. Beat that army as often as possible to persuade the Northern people to stop this war. That's what I have to do. Of course, to beat the Army of the Potomac takes a lot of men, in terms of casualties, and his casualties are horrific throughout almost all of the war, as we've talked about before. It is a very bloody business being in Robert E. Lee's army. So, I've got to win the kind of victories that will prop up our morale and depress Northern morale, and in doing that I am bleeding the strength from the Confederate pool of white military aged manpower. I know I can't really smash them, I know I can't capture their cities, but maybe if I can win enough of these victories, reasoned Lee, we will emerge triumphant. In the meantime we have to muster every ounce of national strength, human and materiel, in order to maintain this race.

Lee didn't manage to do that in the end. We know what happened— Appomattox happens in the end. Appomattox happens and he becomes one of the great losers in all of United States history. How can you be a bigger loser than Robert E. Lee? You lose your entire army. You surrender your entire army to your opponent, and in doing so, you essentially end the life of the nation that you and your army have been fighting in the name of. They had become so important to the nation that when they're gone, as we've seen, that's the end of the nation. How can you be a bigger loser than that?

Well, let's grant that Lee is one of the biggest losers in the United States history, that doesn't mean that he was pursuing the wrong strategy, that doesn't mean that he doesn't understand what kind of war he was engaged in. It was a war that could have gone either way, and Lee is the only factor in the Confederacy that ever really imperiled the United States in a serious way in the course of this war—summer and autumn of '62, spring and early summer of '63, summer of '64, as we have seen. It just so happens that the United States had a brilliant man sitting in the White House that was determined and who finally found a general who was the match for his determination and ability in Ulysses S. Grant, but even that pair, even that pair, reached a very great crisis in the summer of 1864, in July and August of 1864, and what turned it around? Again, it is the battlefield. It's William Tecumseh Sherman capturing Atlanta. It's Philip Henry Sheridan leading United States forces to victory in the Shenandoah Valley. They reelected Lincoln and the Republicans, and that reelection guarantees the war will be prosecuted to a successful conclusion for the United States.

Those are factors beyond Lee's control, but those factors should not cast into a shadow his, I think, quite extraordinary grasp of the best way for the Confederacy to try to win its independence. He is an able practitioner of modern war within that mid-19$^{th}$ century context. I, in my view, think there is no question about that.

All right, that is enough about Lee, in a direct way anyway. We've spent four lectures on him, and now it's time, I'll begin with our next lecture, to turn to his subordinate command in the history of the Army of Northern Virginia. We will begin with the obvious candidate, we'll start with Stonewall Jackson.

# Lecture Six
# The Making of the Mighty "Stonewall" Jackson

**Scope:** With this lecture, we shift the focus from Lee to his most famous subordinate. Thomas Jonathan Jackson entered the Civil War as an obscure teacher at the Virginia Military Institute in Lexington, Virginia, and within two years, crafted a record on the battlefield that won him renown as Lee's "right arm," a bugaboo to Northern opponents, and perhaps the Confederacy's leading military idol. Jackson overcame a poor educational background to do quite well at West Point, won a measure of distinction as an artillerist in the war with Mexico, and finished his prewar years as a professor at V.M.I. Apart from his service in Mexico, Jackson's antebellum life seldom rose above the mediocre and was characterized by an inflexibility, lack of imagination, and predilection to quarrel with fellow officers that seemingly augured ill for success as a general. The Civil War provided a stage on which he rose to each challenge. He did well in July 1861 at the battle of First Manassas, where his brigade held a key position and he won his famous nickname. The 1862 Shenandoah Valley campaign offered a grander stage, and Jackson made the most of it with a display of audacity and strength of purpose that yielded a series of small victories against an array of modestly gifted opponents. The Confederate people paid scant attention to the fact that Jackson's tactical efforts in the Valley lacked distinction; his victories came at a time when Southern fortunes sagged almost everywhere else and caused widespread rejoicing across the Confederacy. Jackson went into the Valley campaign as an officer with a solid record and a superior nickname and emerged from it as the Confederacy's preeminent military hero.

## Outline

I. Jackson's pre-Civil War career included some high spots but offered scant evidence of future military renown.

    **A.** He overcame a poor initial education to do quite well at West Point (1846) and graduated 17$^{th}$ out of 59 cadets.

    **B.** He earned modest fame and brevets for gallantry as an artillerist with Winfield Scott's invading U.S. Army in Mexico.

    **C.** He left the U.S. Army to teach at the Virginia Military Institute in 1851–1861.

    **D.** Jackson's antebellum activities foreshadowed some of his traits as a Confederate general.

        **1.** He quarreled with fellow officers in the U.S. Army.

        **2.** His teaching at V.M.I. underscored his inflexibility; for example, his pedagogy included reciting texts from memory.

        **3.** After flirting with Catholicism in Mexico, he became a devout Presbyterian who saw God's hand in all events.

**II.** The battle of First Manassas on July 21, 1861, gave Jackson his first opportunity for fame.

    **A.** His brigade occupied a key position as the Confederate army was crumbling under U.S. offensive pressure.

        **1.** Jackson kept his head and stood firm on Henry House Hill.

        **2.** His brigade helped stem the Northern tide and set up a Confederate counteroffensive.

    **B.** Jackson emerged from First Manassas with plaudits from many quarters and the Civil War's best nickname.

**III.** The Shenandoah Valley campaign of March–June 1862 catapulted Jackson to the front rank of Confederate military idols.

    **A.** The campaign took place at a time of sagging Confederate morale.

        **1.** Confederate forces west of the Appalachians had suffered a string of defeats.

        **2.** George B. McClellan's Army of the Potomac was closing in on Richmond.

        **3.** Robert E. Lee charged Jackson with preventing U.S. troops in the Valley from reinforcing McClellan at Richmond.

    **B.** Jackson won success in the Valley against a group of mediocre Federal opponents, among them Nathaniel Banks, John C. Frémont, and Irvin McDowell.

        **1.** He crafted victories at McDowell, Front Royal, First Winchester, Cross Keys, and Port Republic over the course of one month.

        **a.** The battles were fought on a modest scale—total U.S. casualties were estimated at 5,500; the South lost about half that many.

        **b.** The Federal high command lacked unified direction.

    **2.** Jackson displayed daring and decisiveness strategically.

    **3.** His tactical performances lacked distinction, but in the end, he won.

    **4.** He achieved the goals assigned to him by Robert E. Lee.

**C.** The impact of the campaign was enormous, despite the scale of the fighting.

    **1.** Confederates welcomed news from the Valley after months of military defeat.

    **2.** People in the United States saw Jackson as a gifted Rebel general to be feared.

## Essential Reading:

Freeman, *Lee's Lieutenants*, vol. 1, chapters 21–29.

Gallagher, *Lee and His Generals in War and Memory*, chapter 5.

## Supplementary Reading:

Robertson, *Stonewall Jackson: The Man, the Soldier, the Legend*, chapters 1–15.

Vandiver, *Mighty Stonewall*, chapters 1–12.

## Questions to Consider:

**1.** Has Jackson's Valley campaign been blown out of proportion?

**2.** How important was timing in the trajectory of Jackson's fame?

# Lecture Six—Transcript
## The Making of the Mighty "Stonewall" Jackson

With this lecture we shift our focus from Robert E. Lee to his most famous subordinate. Thomas Jonathan Jackson entered the Civil War as an obscure teacher at the Virginia Military Institute (VMI) in Lexington, Virginia, and within two years crafted a record on the battlefield that won him renown as Lee's "right arm," and made him a bugaboo to Northern opponents, and perhaps the Confederacy's leading military idol. Jackson overcame a poor educational background to do quite well at West Point. He won a measure of distinction as an artillerist during the war with Mexico, and he finished his prewar years as a professor at VMI Apart from his service in Mexico, Jackson's antebellum life seldom rose above the mediocre and was characterized by an inflexibility, lack of imagination, and predilection to quarrel with fellow officers that seemingly augured ill for success as a general.

The Civil War provided a stage on which he rose to every challenge, however. He did very well in July 1861 at the battle of First Manassas, where his brigade held a key position and where he won his famous nickname, "Stonewall." The 1862 Shenandoah Valley campaign offered a grander stage, and Jackson made the most of it with a display of audacity and strength of purpose that yielded a series of small victories against an array of modestly gifted opponents. The Confederate people paid scant attention to the fact that Jackson's tactical efforts in the Valley lacked imagination. His victories came at a time when Southern people's fortunes sagged in every other direction and those victories in the Valley caused widespread rejoicing across the Confederacy. Jackson went into the Shenandoah Valley campaign in 1862 as an officer with a solid record and a superior nickname, he emerged from that campaign as the Confederacy's preeminent military idol.

Jackson was born in 1825 in what is now West Virginia, it was then western Virginia, near Clarksburg. He had a quite difficult youth. His father died when he was young and his mother was too poor really to rear him, so he grew up under the care of an uncle. He worked very hard as a young man. As I said earlier, he wasn't given the advantage of a good education. It was a very mediocre education. He, nonetheless, won an appointment to West Point, and there he worked very hard. He began near the bottom of his class, he improved every year, and he ended up graduating 17th out of 59 cadets in the class of 1846. George Pickett was in that same class, graduated dead last in that class. George B. McClellan was also in Stonewall Jackson's class, McClellan ranked second in that famous class of 1846. That class contributed a very large number of generals to both sides during the Civil War.

What Jackson demonstrated above all at West Point was a dogged quality, a sense of purpose, an ability to focus on a task at hand that was really quite remarkable. He was made fun of when he first got there; he seemed to be a hick, sort of a backwoods bumpkin to many of the sophisticated cadets in his class, including George B. McClellan. He wasn't well prepared, in mathematics especially. That was the key to succeeding at West Point, math and physics and the other engineering related disciplines that the cadets had to master. Very few people would have predicted much success for him at West Point, but by sheer hard work he came to improve dramatically and to impress many of his fellow cadets. A couple of them said that they really believed that had the course been a five-years course instead of a four-years course Jackson probably would have ranked near the very top of this famous class.

He went to the war with Mexico, as did so many of the younger officers of his generation, and there he did well. He was an artillerist. He had ranked high enough in the class at West Point to go into the artillery. The best cadets went into the engineers, but artillery was not far below engineering as a preferred branch of the service for the cadets at West Point. He did well fighting under Winfield Scott in the campaign from Vera Cruz to Mexico City. He was a lieutenant in the First Artillery. He won a brevet to captain for his service at Contreras and Churubusco, and a brevet to major for Chapultepec—remember the brevet ranks were sort of honorary ranks that noted distinctive service in the field, but it wasn't a permanent rank, it was an honorary rank, but nonetheless much coveted, and these two brevets for Jackson show that he had done well in Mexico.

He didn't stay in the army very long after the war, however. He got out in 1851, partly because of a quarrel with another officer—we'll talk about that more in a minute, but he accepted a position to teach at the Virginia Military Institute. A relatively new institution, it had been founded in the late 1830s. He was hired there to teach physics and artillery tactics. So, off he went to Lexington at the outset of the decade of the 1850s. He proved to be an exceedingly boring teacher at the Virginia Military Institute. The cadets fastened a number of cruel nicknames on him. They called him Tom Fool Jackson, as much as anything else. They called him Old Blue Light, you often read that description of him, that nickname for him, during the

Civil War, and it's often said that it was because his blue eyes flashed in battle and such and such thing. That's not what it meant at all. It referred to his Presbyterianism and it was not a positive nickname as far as the cadets were concerned at VMI Old Blue Light, Tom Fool: he was not one of the popular professors at VMI.

Jackson's antebellum activities foreshadowed some of his traits as a Confederate general, some of the negative traits, really, that he would show as a Confederate general. He quarreled frequently in the antebellum years with colleagues in the army and with colleagues at VMI. He especially quarreled when he was posted to Florida, Fort Meade, Florida, in the 1840s with a colleague named French. Jackson was the subordinate; French the superior on this post. Jackson accused French of various things including a dalliance with a servant girl. French responded in kind, and it became a very nasty and prolonged exchange of accusations and defenses of both of the officers, both French and Jackson. It proved exasperating to their superiors who tried to calm this thing down. In the end this was one of the factors that led Jackson to leave the army. He was very certain of his positions, always fancied that he had taken the high ground in these kinds of arguments, and wouldn't give in terms of conceding that there might be something to the other person's side.

While he was at VMI. he was a problem at times for the superintendent, Superintendent Smith, at VMI, who had done a lot to help Jackson, but nonetheless Jackson quarreled and disagreed with him. Jackson just showed this tendency to stand on principle, as he would have put it, in his relationships with both superiors and peers, and it was a trait that we will see carried forward in his dealings with his subordinates during the Civil War.

His teaching at VMI underscored his inflexibility. He was famous for getting into situations in the classroom where if a student would ask a question, Jackson wouldn't respond to the question. His lecturing consisted of memorizing the textbook and then stating the textbook's text verbatim to his class. If someone asked him a question in class, he would merely go back to the beginning and start again and read through the text, not read through, but read the text from memory again. He didn't really respond to questions, just started over and did the lesson again. You can imagine how boring that must have been to students in class, and sometimes students would ask him questions just to get him to back and start over again. They toyed with him in that regard.

He had a hand in the expulsion of a number of students at VMI, again, standing on principle, following the rules to the absolute letter. He was very punctilious in that regard, again, a trait he would show as a Confederate general.

He was widely known as an eccentric in Lexington, Virginia, eccentric both in his notions about health and his physical well being, and eccentric in other ways. He founded a Sunday school for black children, for example, in Lexington. Very unusual, very unusual—that set him apart, certainly, from most of his white peers of the era. He had all these ideas about his health that were strange. He thought that if he ate pepper it weakened one of his legs, not both of his legs, but one of his legs. He often held his right hand up in the air. During the Civil War, soldiers always thought that that was because he was invoking the blessing of the Lord, but no, it was because he thought there was a disequilibrium of blood in his body and if he held up his right hand it would establish equilibrium of the blood throughout his body. He would never let his back touch the back of a chair because he said it jumbled his organs. There were lots of these notions that he had about his health. He was very interested in hydrotherapy during the 1850s, all kinds of water cures.

He didn't look like a soldier. The students at VMI commented on that as well. He was about six feet tall, considerably taller than average for the mid-19$^{th}$ century. He weighed about one hundred and seventy pounds. He had enormous feet, size fourteen feet, brown hair, blue eyes that were his most distinctive feature. His eyes caught the attention of many people, but he sort of slouched. He didn't have a military bearing, he just—he looked awkward, he wasn't a graceful man either on the ground or in the saddle, he was not a graceful rider. He did not look like the model of a soldier. Together with his eccentricities and his poor teaching and his tendency to quarrel with people, Jackson offered in many ways an odd and even unlovely picture to those around him in Lexington, although he fit into the community in other ways quite well.

He became a devout Presbyterian while he was in Lexington. He saw God's hand in all events. He hadn't been religious early in his life. While he was in Mexico he had been attracted to the Catholic Church, he liked the ritual, he loved some of the cathedrals in Mexico, he learned Spanish—became quite fluent in Spanish, while he was in Mexico and thought seriously about becoming a Catholic. But in the end, after sampling different religions, he decided to become a Presbyterian, and he became the most fervent of Calvinists. That became the great organizing feature of his life, once he became a Christian, that is what he believed was by far the most important element of his life, strongly, strongly committed to the Presbyterian Church. He was married twice, his first wife died. Both of his wives were the daughters of Presbyterian clerics, and Jackson really ordered his life around the principles he drew from his Presbyterian religion.

He offered his services to the Confederacy immediately upon the outbreak of the Civil War, and he found himself at the battle of First Manassas in July of 1861, July 21, 1861. That was his first opportunity to do well on a battlefield and he absolutely made the most of it. The story of First Manassas or Bull Run is well known in the history of the Civil War. Two green armies are there just about thirty miles outside Washington D.C. Both commanders, Irvin McDowell on the United States side, and Gustave Toutant Beauregard, about whom we'll talk more later, on the Confederate side, having the same battle plan, each wanting to turn the other's left flank. McDowell struck first, turned Beauregard's left flank and the Confederates were in a rather desperate position as the battle unfolded on the 21st of July. They needed a unit that would make a stand, and Stonewall Jackson's brigade, Jackson was a brigadier general at this stage of the war, Jackson's brigade did make a stand on a piece of ground called Henry House Hill. They helped stem the tide of Northern success in the morning, and when the battle began to go the Confederate's way, participated to a degree in the pursuit of the Federal army. Jackson wanted to pursue the Federal army very strongly. He argued for trying to put together a striking force of 10,000 men or so and pushing on toward Washington D.C. The Confederate high command, Jefferson Davis even was on the battlefield there near the end, decided that a pursuit was not possible, but Jackson's aggressiveness, which would become a hallmark of his generalship as a Confederate officer, his aggressiveness stood out at First Manassas. He showed he could both defend a position and then showed that he had a killer instinct. Once the Federals were in retreat he wanted to do everything possible to turn that retreat into the worst situation for the United States and the best for the Confederates.

Jackson emerged from First Manassas with plaudits from many quarters and perhaps most important he emerged with the war's best nickname. He has the best nickname of any Civil War general, probably the best nickname of any military officer in United States history. It came from a moment of crisis on the battlefield when an officer from South Carolina named Barnard Bee, surveying the situation, knowing that the Confederate line had not been holding earlier in the day, looked out toward Henry Hill, looked to where Jackson's command, his brigade, was posted, and hollered out as his

South Carolina soldiers looked, "There stands Jackson like a stone wall, rally on the Virginians." Now, there was debate later whether Bee meant that in a positive or negative way. Some say that Barnard Bee wanted Jackson to move and to come to Bee's aid, and therefore he was being sarcastic when he said, "There stands Jackson like a stone wall." He shouldn't have been standing like a stone wall, he should have been moving. But the consensus was that he meant it in a positive way. Whether he meant it that way or not doesn't matter because it was perceived as a great compliment. Jackson standing firmly, helping to save the day for the Confederate forces at First Manassas, and now he had this nickname. Jackson always said that the nickname didn't belong to him; it belonged to his brigade, the Stonewall Brigade. In truth it was fastened on both of them. The Stonewall Brigade was, for the remainder of the war, known as the Stonewall Brigade, but Jackson, of course, was known as Stonewall Jackson as well. That is a tremendous advantage to a soldier to have a good nickname. We say earlier that Robert E. Lee, one of his nicknames early in the war was Granny Lee. Granny was fastened to a number of soldiers and it hurt them. Lee overcame it. Many of those called Granny did not overcome it. Jackson is on the other end of the scale here with this wonderful nickname coming out of his first major battle of the American Civil War.

There's a long period of quiet in the eastern theater, in the Virginia theater, after the battle of First Manassas. The rest of the year went by, 1861, without major action, and it isn't until the spring of 1862 that action really heats up in the eastern theater again, and it's when that action heated up that Stonewall Jackson would have his first great opportunity to distinguish himself. That opportunity would come in the Shenandoah Valley. The Shenandoah Valley campaign of March through June of 1862 was a campaign that catapulted Jackson to the very front rank of Confederate military idols. In fact, made him, although not the senior officer in the Confederacy, there are a number of officers that are full generals, Robert E. Lee among them, Joseph Johnston, and others, he's not senior in rank but he is the most famous, he is the most idolized, of the Confederacy's generals at the end of the Shenandoah Valley campaign. It's a campaign that has been much exaggerated over the years. As Jackson became more and more famous, the Valley campaign loomed larger and larger and larger in accounts of the war. You often read that Jackson, with 15,000–17,000 men, confronted and then defeated 60,000 United States soldiers during the Shenandoah Valley campaign. Well, there were never anything like 60,000 United States soldiers present in the Shenandoah Valley during this campaign. There were 60,000 in the area, but Jackson didn't defeat all of them. He tied down a lot of them. My point is that this campaign has been exaggerated over the years, but even allowing for that, it is a very important campaign for a number of reasons, not least of which that it propels Jackson to such preeminence in the Confederacy and sets the stage for the rest of his career.

The campaign took place, we talked about this in relation to the Seven Days already, the campaign took place at a time when the Confederacy's fortunes seemed about as low as they could be. Coming into the spring and early summer of 1862, the Confederacy had suffered reverse after reverse after reverse in the western theater—Forts Henry and Donelson and Shiloh and the loss of New Orleans, and so forth. The world is falling to pieces in the western theater for the Confederacy, and there's no good news in the eastern theater either because there are large United States armies menacing Virginia from various directions. George B. McClellan would plant, eventually, his 100,000-man Army of the Potomac on the Lower Peninsula, and move, the peninsula between the James and York Rivers, and move slowly up that peninsula toward Richmond. Irvin McDowell, who had commanded the Federal army at First Manassas commanded another 30,000–40,000 United States soldiers at Fredericksburg. Nathaniel Prentice Banks more than 20,000 in the lower Shenandoah Valley. In Valley terminology lower means northern, upper means southern, because the Valley higher in its southern reaches and drops down to the Potomac River. So, if you travel north in the Shenandoah Valley you're going down the Valley. You've going from the Upper Valley to the Lower Valley, which is the part along the Potomac River finally. There is a United States army under Nathaniel Banks in the Lower Valley, and another United States force under John C. Frémont in the Alleghenies. These four major forces are ready to be brought to bear on the war in Virginia. Not much good news anywhere for the Confederacy, and a sense of real dread on the part of many in the Confederacy both in Virginia and outside Virginia.

Robert E. Lee, as we've seen, was functioning during this period of the war as Jefferson Davis's principle military advisor, and one thing he had to deal with was how to cope with these various United States threats to Confederate forces in Virginia, and part of his plan, part of his strategic plan, involved the Shenandoah Valley and Stonewall Jackson. He wanted Jackson, who initially had about 5,000 men under his command, he (Lee) proposed reinforcing Jackson to about 17,000 men and having him operating in the Valley in such a way as to prevent the deployment of the United States forces under Nathaniel P. Banks and John C. Frémont to prevent them from being deployed to reinforce George B. McClellan who was approaching Richmond. In other words, Lee wanted to keep the immediate threat to Richmond as small as possible, and one way to do that was to keep these Union forces that were in the Alleghenies and in the Valley there. Don't let them come east. That is what he wanted Stonewall Jackson to do. Those were Jackson's orders; they were vague orders, broad orders. These are the goals I want you to accomplish, said Lee. He left the execution of those orders to Jackson, and this is where Jackson would show his greatest strength as an officer. Jackson could take a set of general instructions and he could execute them using his own imagination, his own strength of will, and his own audacious military personality to achieve the goals set before him. That is precisely what he did in the Valley.

Now, he didn't face first-rate opponents in the Valley. There was a group, really, of mediocre United States commanders. Nathaniel Prentice Banks was a politician from Massachusetts. He had his commission and his command because he was an important politician. John C. Frémont, another politician, he was a soldier, a famous explorer from the antebellum years, but also the Republican party's first candidate for president back in 1856. Neither of them was a great field commander. Irvin McDowell, who'd lost the battle of First Bull Run, he's another of those who would face Jackson. A man named Robert Milroy was another, a man named James Shields another. None of those is a name that rings through Civil War military history. Jackson, in other words, is fortunate in his opponents in the Valley. He's also fortunate in that there is no unified command on the United States side in the Valley. These forces are scattered. They give him the opportunity to strike piecemeal at his opponents. That doesn't mean that it was an easy campaign. It's still a brilliant campaign on Jackson's part, but there are factors that militate in his favor. Having said that: mediocre opponents, divided United States military posture, nonetheless Jackson put together a fabulous campaign.

He crafted victories at McDowell, Front Royal, First Winchester, Cross Keys and Port Republic—five victories put together over the course of just about exactly a month. The opening salvo of the campaign came in March, in late March, in 1862, when Jackson made a foray toward a Federal force near Winchester, fought the first battle of Kernstown. The United States forces were being withdrawn from the Valley at that point. Jackson's movement caused the Lincoln administration to keep forces in the Valley. That's what Lee wanted. The forces stay in the Valley, Jackson is reinforced, and the campaign proper began in early May when Jackson took a piece of his command out west from Staunton, Virginia, into the Alleghenies, and knocked back the advance element of Frémont's army in the battle of McDowell fought on May 8. Jackson then returned to the Shenandoah Valley and marched northward, down the Valley, across the Massanutten Range that divides the Shenandoah Valley proper for about fifty miles, between Harrisonburg and Front Royal on the north. He gobbled up a little Union garrison, about a thousand men, at Front Royal on May 23, defeated Banks in the battle of First Winchester two days later, marched all the way to the Potomac River, did Jackson, clear to the environs of Harper's Ferry, then withdrew southward, up the Valley and fought another pair of battles on June 8 and June 9 at Cross Keys, where he defeated part of Frémont's pursuing force, and Fort Republic where he defeated part of McDowell's force that had been trying to track him down that part of the Shenandoah Valley.

It was quite a performance—in the course of a month these five victories. They're not big battles, they're very modest battles, but each one a victory and news of each flashing across the Confederacy and lifting morale as news that Jackson had won again and again and again came. They're very small battles. The total United States casualties in this entire campaign only amount to about 5,500 men, many of them prisoners. Jackson's casualties total about 2,750. Within the range of Civil War battles, these are very modest. Some of them are really sort of big skirmishes rather than battles, but the impact is large nonetheless, largely because of the timing. They come at a time when the Confederacy needs good news and Jackson gives them that good news. They're not tactical masterpieces, not a one of these battles is. He fumbled at McDowell, Jackson did, even though he outnumbered his opponent. He fumbled again, really, at Fort Republic although he outnumbered his opponent again there. But in the end, he won, and he accomplished not only what Lee wanted him to accomplish, tying down Banks, tying down Frémont, he also prevented the Lincoln administration from sending McDowell's force at Fredericksburg to reinforce McClellan. McClellan was very happy about this. It didn't matter. He didn't get the reinforcements he wanted, and he didn't get them because of what Stonewall Jackson had done in the Shenandoah Valley. A very successful campaign strategically, a campaign that accomplished everything, everything, that Lee had wanted it to accomplish. Jackson had been aggressive, hard hitting, he'd moved very rapidly. Part of his army had marched more than forty miles in one day in the course of the campaign. His soldiers acquired the nickname Jackson's Foot Cavalry in the course of this campaign. He pushed them hard, he drove them, he made them do things that they really didn't think they could do. He got the absolute best performance possible out of his infantry in the Shenandoah Valley, and his reputation went up with each part of this campaign.

The Confederate people welcomed news from the Valley, welcomed it as they would welcome rain at the end of a long drought. Here at last was good news to fasten on after all of this bad news coming from every place else. The *Charleston Daily Courier* in mid-June 1862 employed some wonderful hyperbolic language in saying, "We invite attention to the following summer of the achievements of General Thomas J. Jackson, Stonewall. With a handful of citizen soldiers but partially drilled and poorly armed and equipped, he has in little more than sixty days marched over five hundred miles, fought about twelve battles, five of which were pitched battles, defeated four generals, routed four armies, captured millions of dollars worth of stores, and killed, wounded, and secured as prisoners almost as many of the enemy as he had soldiers under his command. These are startling assertions, but they are literally true." Well, they are literally not true, many of them, but that's beside the point. This is the news that people got behind the lines, and they heaped praise on Stonewall Jackson as a result.

There is a legend, really, that Jackson had panicked Abraham Lincoln and that Lincoln had become so frightened for the safety of Washington that he took a number of steps to try to keep Jackson out of Washington that really hurt McClellan below Richmond. Lincoln wasn't panicked by Stonewall Jackson. Lincoln really saw Jackson's movements in the Valley as an opportunity to swoop down to bring together the larger Union forces in the vicinity and crush Jackson. He couldn't get his generals to accomplish that. Lincoln wasn't panicked, but Secretary of War Edward Stanton was. He did do a number of things that suggest Jackson completely upset his equilibrium, and although the Northern people weren't panicked, the newspaper accounts weren't panicky in their coverage of Jackson's operation in the North, but what they did do was give great credit to Jackson, described him as a very able soldier and a very worthy opponent.

So Jackson's stock is going up behind the lines in the United States even as it is going up behind the lines in the Confederacy. It is a situation where one campaign carried out over a month really works a revolution in the reputation of a soldier. This makes Stonewall Jackson as a Civil War soldier, absolutely makes him if not absolutely at center stage, nearly at center stage in the Confederacy. It's a campaign, the casualties modest as I said, once we get to the Seven Days, that enormous bloodletting outside Richmond, we'll see a battle, just one of those Seven Days' battles,

Gaines's Mill, on the 27th of June, there are more casualties at Gaines's Mill in one day than in the whole month on both sides of the Shenandoah Valley campaign, but, then again, that doesn't really matter. It's not the scale of the loss, it's the timing, it's the manner in which Jackson carries out this campaign. Again, I talked about this in regard to Robert E. Lee's style of generalship, Jackson's style of generalship in the Shenandoah Valley is just what the Confederate people want. It's aggressive, it's forward moving, it's taking the war to the enemy, and it is producing victories. At the close of the 1862 Valley campaign, as Jackson began to march his little army of the Valley over toward Richmond to reinforce Lee, he was the leading hero of the Confederacy, and seemingly poised to step into the very front rank of officers in the Confederate army. We'll see what happened in the Seven Days, which came as a surprise to many, in our next lecture.

# Lecture Seven
## Stonewall Jackson as Lee's "Right Arm"

**Scope:** The 11 months between the close of the 1862 Valley campaign and Jackson's death following the battle of Chancellorsville coincided with the greatest period of success for the Army of Northern Virginia. Lee and Jackson formed a legendary partnership, with Lee developing strategic plans that often placed Jackson in the role of a semi-independent commander. Jackson headed Lee's Left Wing in the summer of 1862 and, following a reorganization of the army the ensuing autumn, the Second Corps. Although Jackson never displayed tactical brilliance, his swift marches and ability to place his soldiers where Lee wanted them helped set the stage for a series of striking victories. He was less successful as a military politician, an area in which Lee excelled. Because he often was at odds with one or more of his subordinates, Jackson almost certainly lacked the managerial skills to command an army. Lee exploited his dour lieutenant's strengths, giving him the crucial maneuvering tasks during the campaigns of Second Manassas, Antietam, and Chancellorsville. A somewhat fumbling tactical performance at Fredericksburg in December 1862 took nothing away from Jackson's overall record of accomplishment. Wounded by some of his own soldiers on May 2 at Chancellorsville, as he sought to maintain momentum generated by the war's most famous flank attack, he died eight days later. Lee and the Confederacy mourned his loss, and no one stepped up to fill his place during the final two years of the war.

## Outline

I.   Jackson and Robert E. Lee forged a legendary partnership during the period June 1862–May 1863.

    **A.** The partnership got off to a rocky start during the Seven Days.

        **1.** Jackson was late or lethargic at the battles of Mechanicsville, Gaines's Mill, and White Oak Swamp.

        **2.** Overall Confederate success masked Jackson's failings.

        **3.** Lee came away from the Seven Days with some doubts about Jackson.

**B.** The campaigns of Second Manassas and Antietam showed Jackson at his best in semi-independent command.
  **1.** He carried out a famous flanking march at Second Manassas.
  **2.** He captured Harpers Ferry during the 1862 Maryland campaign, then rejoined Lee at Antietam.

**C.** He anchored Lee's right at the battle of Fredericksburg in December 1862.

**D.** He made the most famous flank march of the war at Chancellorsville on May 2, 1863, shattering the 11$^{th}$ Corps of the Army of the Potomac. Later, he was accidentally wounded by one of his own units.

**II.** Jackson's strategic maneuvers often outshone his tactical accomplishments.

**A.** Lee played to Jackson's strengths in this regard at Second Manassas, in Maryland in 1862, and at Chancellorsville.

**B.** Jackson's tactical performances often left much to be desired.
  **1.** He fumbled repeatedly at the Seven Days.
  **2.** He barely won victories against smaller Union forces at McDowell, Port Republic, and Cedar Mountain.
  **3.** The Federals temporarily broke his line at Fredericksburg.

**III.** Jackson had reached his level of competency as a soldier.

**A.** He was an excellent subordinate to Lee.

**B.** He lacked the political skills necessary to command an army.
  **1.** He quarreled with and often arrested subordinates.
  **2.** He was too secretive, confiding very little to subordinates, which often led to confusion.

**IV.** Jackson's death delivered a major blow to the Confederate military effort.

**A.** Lee never found a replacement of equal skill.

**B.** Jackson's style of generalship had suited the Confederate people.
  **1.** He was aggressive, which proved a spur to civilian morale.
  **2.** He won victories, and some of them were exaggerated.

**C.** Jackson's compelling personality had added to his legendary status.
  **1.** His eccentricities attracted attention.

2. His deep religious belief inspired many Confederates.

V. Jackson must be reckoned Lee's greatest lieutenant. Even Abraham Lincoln paid tribute to him as a worthy opponent.

### Essential Reading:

Freeman, *Lee's Lieutenants*, vol. 1, chapters 30–32, 42; vol. 2, chapters 1–2, 5–7, 12–13, 15–17, 19, 21, 30–33, 36–37.

Gallagher, *Lee and His Generals in War and Memory*, chapter 5.

### Supplementary Reading:

Robertson, *Stonewall Jackson: The Man, the Soldier, the Legend*, chapters 16–25.

Vandiver, *Mighty Stonewall*, chapters 13–19.

### Questions to Consider:

1. What did Jackson really accomplish at Chancellorsville?

2. How should we assess Jackson's and Lee's relative contributions to Confederate military history during 1862–1863?

# Lecture Seven—Transcript
## Stonewall Jackson as Lee's "Right Arm"

At the close of our last lecture we left Stonewall Jackson at the wake of his success in the Shenandoah Valley. Now we'll follow him through the remainder of his Confederate career.

The eleven months between the close of the 1862 Valley campaign and Jackson's death following the battle of Chancellorsville coincided with the greatest period of success for the Army of Northern Virginia. Lee and Jackson formed a legendary partnership, with Lee developing strategic plans that often placed Jackson in the role of a semi-independent commander. Jackson headed Lee's Left Wing in the summer of 1862 and later, following a reorganization of the army the ensuing autumn, he led the Second Corps. Although Jackson never displayed tactical brilliance, his swift marches and ability to place his soldiers where Lee wanted them helped set the stage for a series of striking victories. He was less successful as a military politician, an area in which Lee excelled. Because he often was at odds with one or more of his subordinates, Jackson almost certainly lacked the managerial skills to command an army. He had reached his level of competency at the corps stratum of command. Lee exploited his dour lieutenant's strengths, giving him the crucial maneuvering tasks during the campaigns of Second Manassas, Antietam, and Chancellorsville. A somewhat fumbling tactical performance at Fredericksburg in December 1862 took nothing away from Jackson's overall record of accomplishment. Wounded by some of his own soldiers on May 2 at Chancellorsville, as he sought to maintain momentum generated by the war's most famous flank attack, Jackson died eight days later. Lee and the Confederacy mourned his loss, and no one stepped up to fill his place during the final two years of the war.

Jackson and Robert E. Lee forged a legendary partnership during the period June 1862 to May 1863. Their's is the second most important partnership of the Civil War. The most important one is Ulysses S. Grant and William Tecumseh Sherman. Theirs is more important really because they operated on a broader stage, a stage that spread across the entire strategic landscape really, opposed to Lee's and Jackson's which was restricted to the eastern theater. But it is a great partnership, and one that yielded tremendous dividends for the Confederacy. But it wasn't a partnership that got off to a great start. It got off to a rocky start during the Seven Days. Jackson went into that campaign as he marched from the Shenandoah Valley to the environs at Richmond to reinforce Lee's army outside Richmond, he marched to those battlefields that would be known as the Seven Days battlefields as a more famous soldier than Lee. He was the man to whom most people in the Confederacy would have looked for good news on the battlefield. He was popular, he was famous, but he failed tremendously in the sequence of events that began to unfold, beginning with the battle of Mechanicsville on June 26 and continued on to the battle of Malvern Hill on July 1, that week of fighting that made up the Seven Days.

Lee, of course, expecting great things from Jackson, expecting great things from this officer who had done so well in the Shenandoah Valley, gave Jackson important roles in each of the battles planned for the Seven Days. He was supposed to come in on the Federal flank at Mechanicsville. He never showed up, never got to the battlefield, and the battle went on without him. He was late at the battle of Gaines's Mill on June 27. The battle of White Oaks Swamp, also called Glendale and Frayser's Farm, on June 30, Jackson literally fell asleep on the battlefield. More than one witness attests to this. Now, he was exhausted, he'd been getting very little sleep for the last week or so, exhausted, that probably explains it, but many soldiers in the army were exhausted. It's just incredible that Stonewall Jackson, in the midst of this critical operation outside the Confederate capital, fell asleep, very lethargic, not responding to the situation. That's his worst day, on the 30th, at White Oaks Swamp. He played a modest role on the last day at Malvern Hill. Overall, his performance in the Seven Days must be reckoned a tremendous disappointment for Robert E. Lee and for the Confederacy. Lee won in spite of Stonewall Jackson during the Seven Days, not because of anything that Stonewall Jackson did. But timing once again helped Jackson, just as timing, this thirst for good news, had helped so much in terms of making the Confederate people look up to him because of what he did in the Shenandoah Valley, his victories couldn't have come at a better time, so also did it help him when he didn't do well in the Seven Days. It's an overall victory; Jackson's failings don't stand out because the overall result is so positive to the Confederacy. Jackson's performance sort of gets lost in the story of the Seven Days. Lee came away from the Seven Days, however, with some doubts about Stonewall Jackson. Lee didn't think Jackson was his best subordinate, I don't think, in the wake of the Seven Days. I think Lee believed that James Longstreet was. He did have some doubts about Jackson, but nothing really came of it.

Edward Porter Alexander, again, whom we'll look at later and as I've said before was such an astute critic and analyst of Confederate military operations, was very hard on Jackson during the Seven Days, and he admired Jackson greatly. Alexander wrote, "General Lee's best hopes and plans were upset and miscarried, and he was prevented from completely destroying and capturing McClellan's whole army, and all its stores and artillery, by the incredible slackness and delay and hanging back which characterized General Jackson's performance of his part of the work." Very hard on Jackson. Walter Taylor, of Lee's staff, wrote after the war that there had been unhappiness at Confederate headquarters with Jackson's performance during the Seven Days, but Taylor wrote, "Nothing was said of it in a general way, although there was quiet talk of it at the time because we were so elated at raising the siege at Richmond and there was no disposition to find fault." This is an example of Lee's political astuteness. He knew how important to the Confederate war effort Stonewall Jackson was. He knew that Jackson was this great military presence for the Confederate people, and he knew that it would be very counter-productive to raise questions about Jackson's performance during the Seven Days. Lee wasn't against getting rid of people he didn't think had done well at the Seven Days. John Bankhead Magruder, we've talked about this before, left. Benjamin Huger left, Theophilus Holmes left, others—they're gone from the army, Lee gets rid of them. He does not do anything about Jackson, although I believe in his own mind he did mark down the number of things that were quite questionable about Jackson's performance.

Jackson rebounded very quickly, however, and in the next pair of campaigns, the campaigns of Second Manassas and Antietam, or Maryland, the Maryland campaign of the autumn of 1862, Jackson performed extremely well. He redeemed himself in Lee's mind, and he added to his reputation in the view of the Confederate people. Now there is the new army structure that we talked about before. There had been all of these division commanders under Lee during the Seven Days. He reorganized the army into two wings after the Seven Days, the Right Wing he gave to James Longstreet, the Left Wing he gave to Stonewall Jackson. Lee figured out early on what the real strengths of these two principle subordinates were. He knew that Jackson did very well in semi-independent command. He still admired what Jackson had done in the Shenandoah Valley, he knew that Jackson had moved with great confidence and great effect in the Valley, and for the rest of this partnership between Lee and Jackson, Lee would allow Jackson to function that way in any situation that called for a piece of the army operating semi-independently.

In the campaign that ended up in the victory at Second Manassas, Jackson was deployed away from Richmond to deal with the threat of John Pope's Army of Virginia, which we talked about before. McClellan still has the Army of the Potomac menacing Richmond, but this new army is put together, an army made up largely of the units that Jackson had faced in the 1862 Shenandoah Valley campaign, Banks's men, Frémont's men, McDowell's men—those forces are put under John Pope and Jackson is sent to deal with John Pope in early August. He won a victory at Cedar Mountain on August 9 against a piece of Pope's army, and then as Lee began to march the rest of the army to join Jackson, as McClellan was being called back to Washington, at that juncture Jackson carried out one of the great flanking marches, great flanking marches of the war. He marched in extremely rapid fashion, pushing his men very hard up and around John Pope's right flank and descended on Pope's rear at the great depot as Manassas Junction. That was the principle staging area for the supply element for Pope's Army of Virginia and Stonewall Jackson captured it in late August. He burned an enormous quantity of stores; he carried off what he could carry off. It has been one of the most spectacular marches of the entire war. Lee eventually brought up the rest of the army, Longstreet's wing joined Jackson, and won the battle of Second Manassas. During the battle itself Jackson operated mostly on the defensive. He mounted a stalwart defense on August 29 as Longstreet got into position for a devastating attack against Pope's army on the 30$^{th}$. So, Jackson showed both the ability to march rapidly in a semi-independent way during this campaign; he also showed he could fight well as a defensive fighter on the battlefield at Second Manassas.

During the Maryland campaign that followed hard on the heels of Second Manassas Lee made a decision while the army was gathered at Frederick, Maryland, early in the campaign, Lee made the decision to divide his army. He believed he had to capture Harpers Ferry in the course of this action north of the Potomac River, and he selected Jackson for that semi-independent component of the campaign. Jackson had set off with more than half the army, Jackson did capture Harpers Ferry, and then marched the bulk of his men on to rejoin Lee and the rest of the army on the battlefield near Sharpsburg for the bloodiest day of the war in the battle of Antietam on September 17. Jackson did a good job at Antietam, no question about it. He was everywhere on his end of the line and helped hold off a very powerful attack by McClellan's Army of the Potomac through that day that seemed endless to the vastly outnumbered Confederate defenders.

So, in these two campaigns, Second Manassas or Bull Run and the Maryland campaign which culminated in the horrible fight at Antietam, Stonewall Jackson met every test that Lee had in mind for him, and the memories of the Seven Days, of Jackson's failures in the Seven Days, began to recede. When Lee reorganized the army formally in the aftermath of the Maryland campaign, when the two wings were turned into the two corps, when Longstreet and Jackson were promoted to the new rank, the newly authorized rank, of three-star general, of lieutenant general, Lee gave Jackson, as I said earlier, his Second Corps, that would be his corps in people's minds for the rest of the war. He now had the Second Corps. But in recommending Longstreet and Jackson for promotion from major general to lieutenant general you can still see that Lee had had some doubts about Jackson. In recommending Longstreet he just put his name in forward, we'll talk more about that a little bit later, but with Jackson, Lee believed that it was important to explain why he was being put forward. He wrote to Jefferson Davis, "My opinion of the merits of General Jackson has been greatly enhanced during this expedition." That is the Maryland campaign. "He is true, honest, and brave, has a single eye to the good of the service and spares no exertion to accomplish his object." Lee's opinion had been greatly enhanced. Greatly enhanced, I believe, since the opinion he formed during Jackson's lackluster performance in the Seven Days' battles outside Richmond.

Lee and Jackson's partnership reached apogee in the Chancellorsville campaign in early May 1863. It's Lee's most famous battle, his most brilliant tactical victory, carried out against the very longest of odds, and Jackson once again is at the heart of this. What Jackson had shown in his grand marching at Second Manassas, in his marching during the Maryland campaign, was that he could be very aggressive operating in semi-independent command. That, of course, is what Lee liked. He hadn't been so aggressive in the battle of Fredericksburg back in December 1862, not early on. The only breakthrough the Federals achieved at the battle of Fredericksburg is at Jackson's end of the line because Jackson had drawn his line poorly in one regard, but after the breakthrough Jackson's soldiers had counter-attacked, and then Jackson had sought a way to get at the Federals, to get at Fredericksburg. It proved to be impossible because the powerful United States artillery along the Rappahannock River, the high ground across the river, prevented him from any kind of counter-attack, but Jackson wanted to get at them. He proposed a couple of quite daring but really—they would be in some ways even fool hardy attempts, they would have been very costly attempts, but I think Lee appreciated that Jackson wanted to strike the opponents. Jackson fit in in that regard, I've talked about this a good deal, we'll talk about it more, he fit into the kind of military culture that Lee tried to promote among the commanders in the Army of Northern Virginia, this military culture that was always trying to exploit any weakness in any opponent, always trying to follow up even the smallest success with some kind of pursuit, with some kind of blow, that would inflict greater damage. Jackson had wanted to do that at Fredericksburg, but he couldn't really do it because the circumstances were not in place that would allow it.

At Chancellorsville, however, his aggressiveness was put on full parade. Hooker got around Lee's left flank, as we've talked about, at Chancellorsville. Hooker expected the Confederates to just hunker down in a defensive position or retreat, but instead both Lee and Jackson took the battle to Hooker, and Jackson was in the vanguard. Jackson marched out on May 1 from Fredericksburg, struck the Federals, and then that night, on the night of May 1, he and Lee sat down and tried to figure out how to inflict a greater blow against the Federals. What they decided on was a very daring flanking movement, a movement that would allow Jackson to take his entire corps around the right flank of the Army of the Potomac. Lee would, with two divisions, keep an eye on the bulk of Hooker's forces, and the next day, on May 2, that is what Jackson did. It's the most famous flank attack of the war. It's the most famous flanking march of the war. About a ten-mile march—Jackson took his 28,000–29,000 men of the Second Corps around Hooker's right flank and late in the day on the 2nd of May, delivered a flank attack that shattered one United States military corps, the 11th Corps of the Army of the Potomac.

It was late in the day, there wasn't a lot of daylight left, the lines became confused, the units intermingled, the attack lost steam, and Jackson rode out that night and tried to find a way to keep the momentum going. He rode out in between the lines of the two armies and was accidentally fired upon by one of his own units, he and his little cavalcade. He was wounded, hit by three bullets. His arm was amputated; his left arm was amputated that night at a field hospital. He seemed to be getting better for a while, but then died on May 10 of complications arising from his wounds. He had been shot down in the midst of doing what he always tried to do—keep the momentum going, find a way, find a way to inflict greater harm on the enemy. This collaboration at Chancellorsville was Lee and Jackson at their zenith, and the Confederate people celebrated it enormously during the war, and after the war in a number of very famous Lost Cause engravings that showed Lee and Jackson together. This is the partnership that defined the spirit and success of the Army of Northern Virginia, Lee and his right arm, Jackson. As Lee said in a note to Jackson, "You've lost your left arm, but I have lost my right." Lee was very cast down at the death of Jackson. We'll talk a little more about that in just a minute.

So, Jackson's gone, how do we assess him as a soldier? Well, he's not a great tactician. That is absolutely clear. His strategic maneuvers often outshone his tactical accomplishments. He was great at getting where his command needed to be, often through prodigious marching, pushing his men to their absolute limits as he did in the Valley, as he did during the Second Manassas campaign, as he did at Chancellorsville. He was brilliant at that. Lee says do X, get in a position to do X, and Jackson would get his men into a position to do that. But once on the battlefield he wasn't brilliant, not ever, in the course of the entire war, and a number of times he was far less than brilliant. We've seen in the Seven Days that he did not do well tactically on any of the battlefields. He barely won victories against smaller Union forces at McDowell, at Port Republic, and at Cedar Mountain, and he wasn't opposing brilliant generals. At McDowell he fought a general named Robert Schenck; at Port Republic a general named E. B. Tyler; and at Cedar Mountain, Nathaniel Prentice Banks, a man who managed to lose battles in nearly every theater of the war in the course of his service. Those were the kinds of officers Jackson was facing in these places, and he always outnumbered them in these instances, and yet he barely won victories. He did win victories, but he barely won victories. He is not distinguished tactically. His tactical preparations at Fredericksburg were such, as I suggested earlier, that they permitted, these dispositions did, permitted the Federals to achieve their only breakthrough on that battlefield. George Gordon Meade, who would command the Army of the Potomac at Gettysburg, gained lodgment on Jackson's lines at Fredericksburg that required counter-attacks in order to reestablish the Confederate situation there. The only bad element in the Confederate drama at Gettysburg is down on Jackson's end of the line.

So, in all of these performances we can pick nits with Jackson's tactical skills. He simply is not a great tactician, nor do I believe that he was equipped to move up to higher commands. You often read that it's a shame the Confederacy didn't give Jackson an army. Why not make Jackson an army commander? Why not let him command an army out west instead of someone like Braxton Bragg, who didn't seem to be very successful on battlefields in the western theater? I believe there are a couple of reasons why Jackson was not promoted. One was he was too important to Robert E.

Lee. Here where you have an almost perfect partnership, why break that up? But beyond that, I do not believe that Jackson possessed the political skills, the military political skills, the managerial skills, the personnel skills, to manage an army. He was an excellent subordinate. Lee would say do X, he would do it. He said at one point that he would follow Lee blindfolded, and I think that was true. He did his utmost to carry out whatever orders he received from R. E. Lee. He didn't question them, he didn't say, "Gosh, these really don't make sense" or "These really seem too complicated." He would be given a mission and he would try to carry it out. So, he's a very good subordinate, he didn't question Lee. He would show initiative. He would do the very best with what he had; he didn't always demand more resources. He would do the best with what he had and he would show imagination in doing it. So as a subordinate he is just right; as a corps commander functioning under Robert E. Lee he is very, very effective. He, for example, could find a situation on a battlefield that was a little different from what he and Lee might have envisioned and he could adjust on the spot. He wasn't rigid in that regard. At Chancellorsville the original plan for the flank attack was for his army to go around to a road called the Plank Road and attack along the Plank Road against Hooker's right flank. When he got out to the Plank Road he received intelligence that suggested it would be better to move on to the next road, which was called the Orange Turnpike. It was getting late in the day, the original plan had been to go along the Plank Road, but Jackson adjusted on the fly—he moved on, he made the decision to move on to the Turnpike, and the attack was much more successful because of that.

So, in these respects he is very good as a subordinate to Lee, but he did not have the political skills necessary to go up to that next rung. As he had in the old army and at VMI, he quarreled with, and during the Civil War often arrested subordinates, even important ones. He had A. P. Hill arrested during the Maryland campaign. He and Hill quarreled about marching orders. Hill was very sensitive to personal slights, Jackson very punctilious, as I've said before. I've used that word twice now but he was, very punctilious about having the absolute letter of his orders carried out and have people not deviate at all from those orders. He and Hill got crossways with each other, and the quarrel between them went on and on. Lee tried to intervene and get them both to step aside. Two of his division commanders were under arrest during the Maryland campaign at one point. Earlier, in the wake of the battle of Kernstown, he had preferred charges against a brigadier general named Richard B. Garnett. Garnett had actually done very well on the battlefield, but Jackson thought he retreated when he shouldn't have retreated, and he leveled charges against him, charges that almost everyone in the army, even those who really liked Jackson, believed were unfair, but Jackson wouldn't drop it. He was pressing forward toward a court martial of Garnett even at the time of his death

So, his reaction often is to arrest somebody, or prefer charges against them, rather than talking with them, trying to bring them along, trying to reason with them. That's not the kind of behavior you want in an army commander, and the response of some of his lieutenants who were the objects of these decisions or behaviors on Jackson's part could be quite extreme. A. P. Hill, for example, complained to Jeb Stuart about Jackson at one point and described him as "that crazy old Presbyterian fool." Said he didn't want to take orders from him anymore. Richard Ewell, in the Shenandoah Valley campaign, had also said that he thought Jackson was crazy because Jackson seemed to engage in behaviors that didn't make sense in terms of promoting the greater good of the Confederate cause. The term "crazy" comes up in a number of instances regarding Jackson.

Jackson was also very secretive, very secretive. He wouldn't tell his subordinates what he was up to. He would tell them what to do, but didn't give them the context in which to understand how what they were doing fit into a broader plan, and it often led to confusion, it often led to incorrect moves on the part of his subordinates because Jackson simply hadn't brought them on board with what was going on. This caused a problem as well more than once. It caused a problem with Ewell again in the Shenandoah Valley; he couldn't understand why Jackson was having him march away from the arena of action, for example, at one point. Jackson had a reason, but he didn't tell Ewell what the reason was, and that caused a problem. Edward Porter Alexander wrote at one point, "It seems to me that General Jackson, at times, was something of a martinet." And I think that that was certainly true. He was a martinet. He wanted things done precisely his way, and he didn't think that subordinates necessarily had to know why, know the context; he just wanted them to do it. I've told you to do it, now do it. If they didn't do it exactly the way he wanted it done he tended to arrest them or prefer charges against them. That is not the kind of behavior you want in an army commander.

So, he reached the level of competency, I think, at which he best functioned. We don't have a great lost opportunity having the Confederacy make Jackson an army commander. His death delivered a major blow to the Confederate military effort. Lee never found a replacement of Jackson's caliber. Some men seemed promising in that regard, we'll talk about two of them later in the course—Richard S. Ewell and A. P. Hill, both seemed very promising, neither came within shouting distance of Jackson's level of performance. The only one who came close was Jubal Early, and he, in some ways, was as effective as Jackson in semi-independent command, but in other ways he fell far short of the standard that Jackson has set. Lee never found a replacement for Jackson, never.

Jackson's style of generalship had suited the Confederate people perfectly. In terms of impact on morale behind the lines, no one who followed Jackson came even close to creating the belief in victory and the sense of possible triumph that people had when they thought about Stonewall Jackson. He was aggressive, just what Lee wanted in a lieutenant, just what Lee wanted in that culture. He was aggressive, he seemed to be inflicting damage on the enemy, and the Confederate people loved it. Even in little actions, even when small triumphs were blown out of proportion, they were blown out of proportion for this reason, because people believed Jackson was doing more than he actually was doing. There was a little after shock to the battle of Antietam. At Shepherdstown, Virginia, on the 19th of September, 1862, a division of the Army of the Potomac crossed the river and they were pushed back by elements of Jackson's command, and this little battle of Shepherdstown got enormous coverage across the Confederacy, and the coverage always had as its main theme that Jackson had just slaughtered the Federals in this battle. As always, Stonewall Jackson had slaughtered the enemy. Let me read from the diary of a woman in Fredericksburg, Virginia, who employed typical overstatement here. She said, "On the 19th a division of the enemy crossed over to Shepherdstown. Jackson captured or killed the whole of them. The Potomac was dammed up with their bodies." The Potomac was dammed up with their bodies—it would take a lot of bodies to dam up the Potomac River, but this treatment of the little action at Shepherdstown appeared in newspapers and diaries across the South. Jackson killing so many of the enemy that the Potomac River was filled with their corpses—that is the impact that Jackson's operations had behind the lines in the Confederacy. He won victories large and small, he always carried the war to the enemy, he promised success. His behavior, his actions promised success.

I think his compelling personality also added to his legendary status, his eccentricities. I don't think we like our heroes to be just like we are. I think it's nice if our heroes are a little different, and Jackson, believe me, was different. Very strange character, very strange character, and people, even in the midst of the war, believed that. This isn't just a retrospective view. A

British visitor to the Confederacy noted in May of 1863, after Jackson's death, the stories of Jackson's many peculiarities. He wrote in his diary, "I heard many anecdotes about the late Stonewall Jackson. When he left the U.S. service he was under the impression that one of his legs was shorter than the other, and afterwards his idea was that he only perspired on one side of his body, and that it was necessary to keep the arm and leg of the other side in constant motion in order to preserve circulation." I think the Confederate people liked those stories; they loved the stories of Jackson's religiosity. They wanted, many of them, they wanted their heroes to be on the right side with God, and they believed that Jackson was. He was compared to Joshua, the Confederate Joshua, the Confederate Cromwell; it was comforting to many people in the Confederacy that Jackson was an open and avowed believer.

He has to be reckoned as Lee's greatest lieutenant, there's no question about that. There was deep mourning when news of his loss spread across the Confederacy. Lee wrote to the army, "I desire to pay tribute of my admiration to the matchless energy and skill that marked the last act of General Jackson's life. He formed a worthy conclusion that long series of splendid achievements which won for him the lasting love and gratitude of his country." Lee was right on target there. Even Abraham Lincoln paid tribute to Stonewall Jackson after his death, and said that he thought he'd been in many ways a good man. Jackson, a major figure in the eyes of the Northern people, a worthy opponent, an opponent they wished weren't there, but still they treated him as a worthy opponent. There's not going to be anyone to take his place, as I've said. The man who came closest in the Army of Northern Virginia was James Longstreet, and we will talk about him next time.

# Lecture Eight
# James Longstreet's Road to Prominence

**Scope:** James Longstreet stood next to Jackson as one of Lee's two premier lieutenants. A West Pointer who spent his entire prewar career in the U.S. Army, Longstreet served under Winfield Scott in the war with Mexico and ended the antebellum period as a staff officer. He entered Confederate service at the war's outset and, as the title of his post-Civil War memoirs stated, fought, literally, from First Manassas to Appomattox. Longstreet's first 15 months in command included successes and failures. His soldiers did well at Blackburn's Ford, a preliminary clash before First Manassas, but he added nothing to his reputation at the battle of Seven Pines or Fair Oaks in May–June 1862. In the aftermath of Seven Pines, he joined Joseph E. Johnston, the army's commander, in trying to divert attention from their own failings. The Seven Days' battles, Longstreet's first under Lee, showed his military gifts at their best. Indomitable in combat and able to deliver powerful offensive blows, he impressed Lee, who called him "the staff of my right hand," and was soon given charge of the army's Right Wing, later denominated the First Corps. Always Lee's senior subordinate, Longstreet, known as "Old Pete" among his soldiers, fought well at Second Manassas, Antietam, and Fredericksburg. Lee's fondness for Longstreet was unquestioned, and at the end of the day at Antietam, the commanding general greeted his lieutenant warmly as "my old war horse." At the war's midpoint in May 1863, with Jackson removed from the scene, Longstreet stood unchallenged as Lee's most important subordinate and the Confederacy's best corps commander.

## Outline

I.  Longstreet compiled a competent but unspectacular pre-Civil War record in the U.S. Army.

    **A.** He graduated near the bottom of his West Point class in 1842, thus receiving an infantry appointment.

    **B.** He earned a pair of brevets for gallantry during the war with Mexico.

        **1.** He fought with the 8$^{th}$ Infantry and was promoted to first lieutenant.

        **2.** He was wounded at Chapultepec while fighting with Winfield Scott.

    **C.** He finished the antebellum period as a paymaster at the rank of major.

**II.** Longstreet participated in several early military operations in Virginia.

    **A.** He served during the campaign of First Manassas as a brigadier general.

        **1.** His soldiers fought at Blackburn's Ford on July 18, 1861, where he showed his typical fearlessness in combat.

        **2.** His command missed the main fighting at Manassas on July 21.

    **B.** Longstreet performed poorly at Seven Pines or Fair Oaks in late May 1862.

        **1.** He joined his commander, Joseph Johnston, in trying to divert attention from their mistakes.

        **2.** His actions caused no serious harm to his reputation.

    **C.** He fought effectively during the Seven Days' battles.

        **1.** He demonstrated his ability to deliver powerful offensive tactical blows.

        **2.** He impressed Robert E. Lee, who was looking for an able offensive tactical fighter.

        **3.** He became Lee's senior subordinate in the aftermath of the Seven Days.

**III.** Longstreet commanded Lee's Right Wing, then the First Corps through the remainder of 1862.

    **A.** His soldiers mounted an impressive tactical offensive at Second Manassas on August 30, using 30,000 Confederate troops.

    **B.** He stood at Lee's side through most of the Maryland campaign.

        **1.** He offered hands-on leadership during the battle of Antietam.

        **2.** Lee greeted him warmly after the battle as "my old war horse."

    **C.** He oversaw the Confederate defense of high ground at Fredericksburg on December 13.

**IV.** Longstreet stood as Lee's principal lieutenant and the Confederacy's best corps commander on the eve of the Gettysburg campaign.

    **A.** He missed the battle of Chancellorsville while conducting operations near Suffolk, Virginia.

        **1.** This episode demonstrated that Longstreet possessed little flair for independent command.

        **2.** Longstreet nonetheless believed he had the talent for higher responsibility.

    **B.** Stonewall Jackson's death in early May left Longstreet with no peer among Lee's subordinates.

    **C.** Longstreet and Lee had developed a close relationship.

        **1.** Lee understood Longstreet's strengths—a good administrator and commander—and he used him to his best effect.

        **2.** Lee liked Longstreet.

        **3.** Longstreet admired Lee but probably considered Joseph E. Johnston a better commander.

## Essential Reading:

Freeman, *Lee's Lieutenants*, vol. 1, chapters 17, 32, 34–36, 43; vol. 2, chapters 7–9, 15–17, 20–22, 29.

Gallagher, *Lee and His Generals in War and Memory*, chapter 7.

## Supplementary Reading:

Longstreet, *From Manassas to Appomattox*, chapters 1–14.

Piston, *Lee's Tarnished Lieutenant: James Longstreet and His Place in Southern History*, chapters 1–2.

Wert, *General James Longstreet: The Confederacy's Most Controversial Soldier*, chapters 1–11.

## Questions to Consider:

**1.** Did Longstreet's record justify his position as Lee's senior subordinate from the Seven Days forward?

**2.** Was Longstreet fortunate to serve under Lee?

# Lecture Eight—Transcript
## James Longstreet's Road to Prominence

We now begin a two-lecture look at the man who functioned throughout Lee's tenure at the head of the Army of Northern Virginia as his senior subordinate, and that was James Longstreet. Longstreet stood next to Stonewall Jackson throughout as one of Lee's two premier lieutenants. He was a West Pointer who spent his entire prewar career in the United States Army. He served under Winfield Scott in the war with Mexico, as so many of the men we'll look at did, and he ended the antebellum period as a staff officer. He entered Confederate service at the war's outset and literally, as the title of his post-Civil War memoirs stated, fought from Manassas to Appomattox. Longstreet's first fifteen months in command included successes and failures. His soldiers did well at Blackburn's Ford, a preliminary clash before the battle of First Manassas, but he added nothing to his reputation in the battle of Seven Pines or Fair Oaks on May 31 and June 1, 1862. In the aftermath of Seven Pines, he joined Joseph E. Johnston, the army's commander, in trying to divert attention from their own failings. The Seven Days' battles, Longstreet's first under Lee, showed his military gifts at their best. Indomitable in combat and able to deliver powerful offensive blows, he impressed Lee, who called him "the staff of my right hand." After the Seven Days, Longstreet was soon given charge of the army's Right Wing, later denominated the First Corps. Always Lee's senior subordinate, Longstreet, who was known as "Old Pete" by his soldiers, fought well at Second Manassas, Antietam, and Fredericksburg. Lee's fondness for Longstreet was unquestioned, and at the end of the day at Antietam the commanding general greeted his lieutenant warmly as "my old war horse." At the war's mid-point in May 1863, with Stonewall Jackson removed from the scene, Longstreet stood unchallenged as Lee's most important subordinate and the Confederacy's best corps commander.

Longstreet compiled a competent but unspectacular pre-Civil War record in the United States Army. He was born in South Carolina, the Edgefield District of South Carolina, but spent most of his boyhood in Georgia, and was really more associated with Georgia than with any other state. Like Jackson, Longstreet lost his father when he was a young man, and like Jackson he was sent to live with an uncle, but in Longstreet's case it was a famous uncle, the local colorist Augustus Baldwin Longstreet. He went to West Point from Alabama. Georgia's slots at West Point were full, and the family managed to garner an appointment for young James from Alabama. There he graduated near the bottom of the West Point class of 1842. He was 54th of 62 members of that class, which meant that he went into the infantry. If you end up that low in a class, you're probably going to be in the infantry. Other cadets there during Longstreet's time at West Point included Richard S. Ewell, William Tecumseh Sherman, and William Stark Rosecrans. Sherman and Rosecrans would be United States army commanders during the Civil War, and for a time Rosecrans and Longstreet were roommates at West Point.

Longstreet fought in Mexico. He fought under Winfield Scott during the campaign from Vera Cruz to Mexico City. He was a second lieutenant at the outset of the war, promoted to first lieutenant in February of 1847. He fought for a while under Zachary Taylor in northern Mexico, and then went with Scott in Scott's famous campaign. He was wounded in the battle of Chapultepec outside Mexico City. Just like Thomas Jonathan Jackson, Longstreet won two brevets for gallantry in Mexico, brevetted to captain for Contreras and Churubusco, and brevetted to major for the fighting at El Molino del Rey, which was just before the battle of Chapultepec.

Longstreet finished the antebellum period as a paymaster in the United States Army, at the rank of major. He'd been promoted to captain in the 8th Infantry in December 1852; the promotion to major came in July 1858, but that's a staff position, not a line position, and therefore not the kind of work that would lead to a great glory should another war come. Longstreet decided to take the safer and bit more ruminative path by going for the majority of staff rather than staying as captain of the line.

He was very close to U. S. Grant before the war. He and Grant were great friends through all of their lives, really. Their friendship continued very strongly into the post war years. We'll talk a little about that much later in the course when we talk about the Myth of the Lost Cause. He married Julia Dent, Grant's cousin, Grant's wife's cousin, a woman named Maria de Louisa Garland. Now that brought him and Grant even closer together, and they, throughout the antebellum years, and I think even through the war years, had very fond thoughts of each other. His friendship with Grant would prove to be a problem late in his life among former Confederates who held that as a very strong mark against him.

Once the war came Longstreet moved into Confederate service very soon and he participated in several early military operations in Virginia. His entire service was in Virginia. During the campaign of First Manassas he was a brigadier general, one of the early brigadier generals in the Confederacy. He was commissioned on June 17, 1861. He commanded the 4<sup>th</sup> Brigade of P. G. T. Beauregard's Army of the Potomac, the Confederate army early in the war was called the Army of the Potomac, not for very long, but it was. Later that would be the name, of course, of the most famous United States army in the eastern theater.

His soldiers fought at Blackburn's Ford on July 18, 1861, and there Longstreet demonstrated great personal courage. That would be one of his hallmarks as a soldier; he was absolutely fearless in combat. He showed that again and again, and at every level of his rank during the Civil War. He also handled his men very well under fire; he was very cool under fire. Innumerable witnesses commented on this, whether he was commanding a brigade or a division, or later a corps, combat did not seem to bring any kind of disequilibreum in Longstreet. If anything it caused him to focus more clearly on the task at hand, and he was absolutely unflappable in the midst of artillery fire and musketry and so forth. Beauregard praised Longstreet profusely in his report of the campaign of First Manassas. It's a very long document, one of the longest battle reports written by anybody on either side in the course of the war. Beauregard was effusive in his praise of many people; Longstreet was one of them, praising Longstreet for the work at Blackburn's Ford.

In the actual battle of Manassas, Longstreet and his brigade were outside the mainstream of the fighting, although late in the day Longstreet had been ordered to engage in a pursuit and was getting his brigade ready to do so, wanted to follow up the victory, in the end he was ordered not to do so, but not a big role in the actual battle of First Manassas for him. But still, a good early indication that he had some talent, and an indication of aggressiveness in the wake of the major fighting at First Manassas, when he was told that he wasn't going to be able to engage in the pursuit, several witnesses said that he took his hat off, flung it to the ground, and exploded with an oath, said, "Retreat, hell, the Federal army has broken to pieces." We should be going after them was the implication here and he was unhappy that his command was not allowed to. During a period after First Manassas he impressed a number of his officers as well, both with his ability to drill large units, regiments always drill when there are slack times in the campaigning, some officers even drill entire brigades. Longstreet engaged in division drills. Very few officers did that. He had a sense that it was important to try to have larger units practice, so to speak, so that on the battlefield they would be able to perform, and he proved very adept on battlefields in crisis at maneuvering large bodies of men very effectively. Part of that came from his training regimen that he had.

He also impressed his officers with his approach to how you should behave in battle. Again, this showed a key side of his military personality, his unflappability. One officer wrote, this is from the period after First Manassas, he said, "Longstreet very often tells his officers as well as his men whenever they begin to talk of our retreating or being defeated that it is nonsensical to have any such idea, for in every battle somebody is bound to run, and that if they will only stand their ground long enough, like men, the enemy will certainly run." That is an attitude Longstreet took on battlefields, and he tried to inculcate that notion among his men as well.

So, he does well at First Manassas. His next major battle is Seven Pines, and there he didn't do well at all. As I said, he and Johnston conspired after that battle to place blame for the inept Confederate performance upon others, especially on Benjamin Huger. Johnston had issued verbal orders there, the orders were not clear, units got on the wrong roads, Longstreet got on a road that he initially wasn't supposed to get on, blocked other units, and in the end it was a very awkward performance against George B. McClellan's army. An effort on the part of the Confederates to strike a smaller part of the Army of the Potomac that came to very little, to a large degree because of Johnston's flawed orders and because of Longstreet's performance. Longstreet showed an element of his personality here, his military personality, that was not at all attractive, and that was, unlike Lee, he did look for scapegoats when things didn't go well. He was willing to point the finger at others. Oh, it didn't go well, it's not my fault, it's someone else's fault. At Seven Pines he and Johnston agreed that it was Huger's fault that things did not go well. It hadn't really been Huger's fault.

Longstreet should have been promoted to major general back in October of 1861. He had impressed not only Johnston back then, but also Beauregard. Both Beauregard and Johnston asked that Longstreet be made their senior subordinate in the commands that they led in the autumn and winter of 1861 and 1862, but there were men senior in rank, in date of rank, to Longstreet, and there was no way to finesse that at that point in the war. Longstreet wasn't able to move up in the hierarchy under either Beauregard or Johnston, although each of those officers considered him able enough to hold that position, and he didn't get it officially.

He first fought under Robert E. Lee during the Seven Days' campaign. Lee had a fairly high opinion of him going into that campaign, he had a much higher opinion of him coming out of it. Longstreet did very well during the battles outside Richmond in late June and early July 1862. He demonstrated his ability to deliver very powerful offensive tactical blows that would become one of his hallmarks as a soldier. If you want to mass your soldiers on a battlefield and have them strike the enemy with the greatest potential power, put Longstreet in charge of that effort and you likely will have a good result. He launched assaults of this sort during the Seven Days at Gaines's Mill on June 27, and again at Glendale, or Frayser's Farm on June 30. He proved himself capable of pulling large bodies of men together and applying their strength very effectively, and this impressed Robert E. Lee a great deal.

Lee, again, is looking for this kind of behavior in his subordinates. Longstreet has a reputation, we'll talk about this later, as a defensive fighter, someone who really preferred to be on the defensive, but, in fact, he was one of the most able tactical offensive fighters that Lee developed among his subordinate commanders during the Civil War. That was one of his great strengths. Lee first saw that in action during the Seven Days, and it really did appeal to him as part of Longstreet's military personality. Lee, like Beauregard, and Joseph E. Johnston before him, wanted Longstreet to be his senior lieutenant, wanted to make Longstreet number two in the hierarchy of command in the Army of Northern Virginia. Unlike Johnston and Beauregard, Lee managed to accomplish that by getting rid of everybody that was senior to Longstreet in the subordinate command of the army. We've talked about this several times already, part of the reason that Lee got rid of a number of division commanders after the Seven Days was he didn't think they were up to their jobs, but he also wanted to clear the way for the men he thought were better. Longstreet is the most important of those men. So, out of the army go the men who outrank James Longstreet: John Bankhead Magruder, Benjamin Huger, Theophilus Holmes, G. W. Smith. They all ranked Longstreet; they are all gone from the Army of Northern Virginia in the wake of the Seven Days, and James Longstreet is cleared to become Lee's senior subordinate.

Lee had said of Longstreet in early June, and this is before he saw him in action during the Seven Days, he said, "Longstreet is a capital soldier. His recommendations hither to have been good, and I have confidence in him." He had even more confidence, as I said, after the Seven Days. He described Longstreet as the "staff in my right hand" during the fighting outside Richmond in June and July 1862. Now, that's a great contrast to how Lee would have described the fighting of Stonewall Jackson during that campaign. Coming out of the Seven Days, I don't think that there's much doubt that Lee believed that Longstreet was at least the equal, and perhaps the superior, of Stonewall Jackson as a subordinate within the Army of Northern Virginia.

Longstreet commanded Lee's Right Wing, and then the First Corps of the Army of Northern Virginia throughout the remainder of 1862. We've talked about the reorganization—you go from the clumsy group of division subordinates to the Right and Left Wings of the army. Longstreet is given the Right Wing. There are five divisions in the Right Wing of the Army of Northern Virginia; there are three divisions in Stonewall Jackson's Left Wing. One of those is the biggest in the army, A. P. Hill's, but still, Longstreet commands a bit more than half of the strength, the infantry strength, in the Army of Northern Virginia. His soldiers mounted an impressive tactical offensive at the battle of Second Manassas on August 30. This is, perhaps, Longstreet's very best performance in this regard during the war.

Jackson, as we've seen, conducted the famous flank march to get behind Pope's army and to draw Pope's attention to Manassas Junction, then Lee and Longstreet and the rest of the Army of Northern Virginia came up to the battlefield. They arrived on the battlefield, spent August 29 getting in position, and on August 30, as Pope was still focusing on Jackson's men and delivering attacks against Jackson's defensive position at Second Manassas, Longstreet brought the power of his wing of the army against Pope's left flank. It's one of the grand assaults of the war. Thirty thousand Confederates are involved in this attack, and Longstreet gets them going in less than half an hour. It's a really remarkable performance to bring that many men into action in that short of time in a major battlefield is something that no other officer in Lee's army managed to accomplish in the entire war. That afternoon of August 30 shows James Longstreet with his ability to manage large numbers of men in the midst of combat, focus the power of those many thousands of men, and bring that power to bear at the weakest point in the enemy's line. The assaults were enormously successful, Pope's army withdrew from the battlefield, retreated to Washington D.C. It was very costly on Longstreet's part. It's interesting that most accounts of the battle of Second Manassas focus on Stonewall Jackson, what a resolute defense his men put up against Pope, but, in fact, James Longstreet's wing of the army suffered more casualties in about four hours than Stonewall Jackson's had suffered in their several days of action at Second Manassas. It's a key part of the battle and one that was very, very productive, very well managed, and showed again that here is James Longstreet, a soldier who, in a tactical situation, can be very effective on the aggressive.

During the Maryland campaign, Longstreet stood by Lee's side virtually at every step of the way. While Jackson went off to Harpers Ferry, Lee and Longstreet were together. During the fighting at Antietam on September 17, Longstreet was absolutely magnificent in the views of his soldiers. He was suffering from a slight disability there, he couldn't ride his horse very well, but he moved back and forth along the lines, he shifted strength from his end of the line to help Jackson, whose wing was pushed to the limit more than once at Antietam. At one point Longstreet even held horses for some members of his staff while they helped serve a cannon on the battlefield—it was that desperate of a day for the Confederacy that you have a wing commander holding the horses of his staff who are helping gunners in a battery that has lost a lot of its men.

Lee worried about Longstreet at Antietam. He didn't seem right after the battle for a while, he was afraid that Longstreet had been hurt, and when Longstreet did join Lee after the battle, Lee, in one of the rare instances where he showed emotion, this was absolutely out of character for Lee, Lee stepped over to Longstreet, actually placed his hands on his shoulder, or at least touched his shoulders it seemed, that's a wildly friendly gesture for Lee, and said, "Here's Longstreet, here's my old war horse, from the field he's done so much to save." That attaches a second nickname to Longstreet, most of the men called him "Old Pete" but then he's known as Lee's "old war horse" after this. It's a very affectionate gesture on Lee's part, there's nothing equivalent with Jackson. There's only one other person that Lee ever gave an affectionate nickname to and that's Jubal Early, we'll talk about that a little bit later.

Lee and Longstreet liked one another. Lee appreciated Longstreet's capabilities as a soldier, but he also liked him. Many of the Confederates writing after the war who were unhappy with the fact that Longstreet became a Republican and criticized Lee and was friends with U. S. Grant, they tried to present a picture of Longstreet as a slow marcher, someone Lee didn't really trust, someone that Lee camped with while the army was campaigning because he believed he had to keep a close eye on Longstreet or Longstreet wouldn't do a good job. That is simply not true. Longstreet was a good marcher. He kept his command well in hand, he moved it efficiently both on long marches and on battlefields, and Lee camped close to Longstreet because he liked him, because they got along as men, and I think that because Longstreet's headquarters was a lot more convivial place than Stonewall Jackson's. No one would want to hang around with Stonewall Jackson, it would have been a very awkward, quiet headquarters, I would think, with Jackson not talking to anybody, sort of lost in his own thoughts, and not drinking and not playing poker and probably not smoking cigars or doing anything else that staff officers and soldiers like to do. All of those things went on at James Longstreet's headquarters. Lee had a very gregarious element of his personality, he enjoyed people enjoying themselves, and I think it was simply a more pleasant place to be with James Longstreet than it was with Stonewall Jackson. Lee admired Jackson, he valued Jackson, but I don't think he liked Jackson in the way that he liked James Longstreet. They had a very, very close relationship, I think, in that regard.

In the reorganization after Antietam, when Longstreet got the First Corps, Lee sent his name forward to Jefferson Davis with absolutely no embellishment. Lee, in effect, is telling Davis, "I need two lieutenant generals to command these wings in my army. I want James Longstreet to command one, and I want Stonewall Jackson" and then he gave the qualifications and explanations for Jackson that I mentioned earlier in the course. He gave no qualifications, no explanations for Longstreet, which suggests to me that Lee thought it was evident that Longstreet deserved to have this lieutenant generalship to command one of the corps in the army. I think that he stood very, very high in Lee's estimation there, and Lee saw no reason to embellish this recommendation that he be promoted. So he is promoted, and he is the senior lieutenant general, then in the Army of Northern Virginia and, of course, would remain so for the remainder of the war. He oversaw the Confederate defense of high ground at the battle of Fredericksburg on December 13, 1862. That's a battlefield, this grand natural amphitheater at Fredericksburg with high ground on the left bank of the Rappahannock River and high ground on the right bank. The Confederates arrayed on that high ground on the right bank west of the old colonial city of Fredericksburg, the Federals coming off the high ground, Stafford Heights, east of the Rappahannock, and then attacking up the Confederate position on Marye's Heights and other high ground west of town. Longstreet commanded those lines on the high ground just west of town. He was in a very good mood that day. He knew he had a strong position. Units in support of the units in front, lots of artillery on the high ground. He knew that it was a position that would be very hard to take on the part of the Federals, and his soldiers slaughtered the attacking soldiers in the United States units that advanced against them through that long afternoon, that long winter's afternoon on December 13, 1862. At one point

Longstreet told Lee, who wondered whether he would be able to hold the position, he said, "Give me enough ammunition, give me enough of everything I need, no one will get to my lines," and no one did. Not a single Union soldier reached the Confederate lines through that long afternoon, and probably eight thousand plus of them were shot down in the front of Longstreet's position. It's an easy defensive victory for the Confederates, and it's a victory that many later writers would say showed what Longstreet really preferred, and what he was really good at, was the defensive, that he understood how powerful rifled weaponry was. He knew that attacks didn't really work anymore. He knew that the army should act on the defensive.

Well, he was good on the defensive, he did do a good job at Fredericksburg in that regard, but he also, long before then, had demonstrated that he also could deliver powerful offensive blows, as we've seen at Gaines's Mill, at Glendale, at Second Manassas. He could do both; he was both a good defensive fighter that appreciated a strong defensive position and a very good offensive fighter in a tactical situation.

Longstreet stood as Lee's principle lieutenant and the Confederacy's best corps commander on the eve of the Gettysburg campaign. He didn't participate in the battle of Chancellorsville. Lee had deployed Longstreet and half of his corps, two divisions of his corps, John Bell Hood's division and George E. Pickett's division, to the south side of Virginia, down near Suffolk. They had gone down in that direction to accomplish several goals. There were actually a range of things that Lee wanted Longstreet to accomplish. He was to protect Richmond from any Federal advance from that direction. He was to guard the railroads that led into the capital from that direction and were vital supply lines. But most important he was to collect fodder and other provisions. It had been such a hard winter that Lee couldn't really keep his whole army together and provision them effectively, and so he sent Longstreet to the south side on a sort of grand foraging effort in the spring of 1863, and Longstreet missed Chancellorsville. It's a period of semi-independent command for Longstreet. It showed some success, but also underscored that Longstreet really didn't have much flair for this kind of operation. He was really best working under Lee.

He did gather a great deal in the way of supplies, but he also mounted an ineffective siege of the city of Suffolk and generally did not distinguish himself in this independent command. It's not an abject failure, it's just he didn't show great promise in this regard for Longstreet. Longstreet, however, did believe that he did have the aptitude for higher command. He really believes that firmly. He probably could command an army, I think. He was an ambitious man. I think that he was somewhat jealous of Stonewall Jackson through much of his career. Jackson's always getting these semi-independent assignments, Jackson makes the famous march at Second Manassas, Jackson had done so well at the Shenandoah Valley on his own. I think that there's a good deal of professional rivalry between the two, on Longstreet's part, not on Jackson's, I don't think. I don't think that this is a problem on Jackson's radar screen, but I think it is on Longstreet's, and especially because Jackson got so much attention in the Confederate press. Longstreet's the senior of the two, he's the senior subordinate, he knows that, but Jackson is the one that got more ink in the newspapers than he did, and I think that rankled Longstreet some. I think that Longstreet thought he was better at semi-independent command than he really was.

Lee, I think, understood perfectly what his real strengths were, Longstreet's, just as he understood what Jackson's real strengths were, and he used each man to the best effect in that regard. He knew better than Longstreet, I think, where Longstreet should be and what Longstreet should be doing. But the removal of Jackson after the battle of Chancellorsville left Longstreet with no peer among Lee's subordinates. He no longer has to be jealous of Jackson, Jackson's not there anymore. He is the principle subordinate in the Army of Northern Virginia, and there he is, he and Lee, with their close relationship, with their history of success. I talked last time about what a great partnership Lee and Jackson had forged, well, Lee and Longstreet had forged a very good partnership as well, beginning in the Seven Days. Lee had seen Longstreet again and again do just what he wanted him to do. When he needed something on a particular battlefield, when he needed a powerful blow at Second Manassas, when he needed a stalwart defense during the Maryland campaign, he could look to Longstreet with great confidence that Longstreet would deliver it. The fact that Longstreet thought he was better than he was at semi-independent command really didn't matter because Lee knew what he was good at. Longstreet was a great manager of his corps, he was very good with logistics, he was a very good administrator, he was a very good marcher. He would bring his command to a battlefield in tremendous shape, cohesive, ready to go into action.

Those are traits that are very unusual at this level of command. It's hard to find someone who can command a corps both effectively on a battlefield and administrate that corps very effectively when you are not in action, and Lee knew that James Longstreet could do those things. He knew that

Longstreet had put together a very good staff, he commanded respect among his subordinates, he commanded respect among his soldiers. The soldiers looked to Longstreet with great affection, the soldiers in his corps, great affection. The soldiers in Jackson's corps had had affection for him, but also a sort of awe. I mean, they loved being a part of a really successful corps, but in some ways I think there is warmer, almost familial bond between Longstreet and his soldiers than there was between Jackson and his soldiers, a very, very good relationship here that Lee understood. Also the very, very close relationship that I've talked about between Lee and James Longstreet as men. Still Longstreet was restive as you move through the spring of 1862 and the summer of 1862, and he was part of what some historians call a "western concentration bloc" (bloc without a "k") that thought that it might be well for the Confederacy to deploy more strength to the western theater, to take strength from the Virginia theater and either reinforce Bragg's army in the Tennessee theater, or John C. Pemberton's army defending Vicksburg.

What Longstreet really thought would be a good idea was to put his friend Joseph E. Johnston in charge in the west, and make him, Longstreet, a key subordinate of Johnston's. As much as Longstreet liked Lee, and I think respected Lee, he was even closer to Joseph Johnston. I think Joseph Johnston was his ideal as an army commander, and he envisioned the two of them fighting in the west, thought that that would be a good idea. That wasn't going to happen. The strength was going to stay in the east, and the next campaign would be the one that would have the most impact on Longstreet's post-war reputation, an impact that was decidedly not positive among former Confederates. That would be the Gettysburg campaign, and next time we'll look at that and the remainder of James Longstreet's Confederate career.

# Lecture Nine
## Longstreet's Later Confederate Career

**Scope:**  The last two years of Longstreet's Confederate career included more negative than positive experiences. He and Lee differed about how to fight the battle of Gettysburg in July 1863, with Longstreet arguing for a more defensive posture and Lee insisting on an aggressive one. Longstreet did not "lose" the battle, but at times, he dragged his feet. Deployed to the western theater in the late summer of 1863, he helped win the battle of Chickamauga. After a series of quarrels with General Braxton Bragg, who commanded the Confederate Army of Tennessee, Longstreet conducted a remarkably mismanaged siege of Knoxville, Tennessee, during which he ordered unimaginative frontal attacks, preferred charges against key subordinates, and conclusively showed his unfitness for army command. Back with the Army of Northern Virginia in April 1864, he fought brilliantly at the battle of the Wilderness on May 6. A severe wound, delivered by fire from one of his own regiments just a short distance from the spot where Jackson had been similarly struck down at Chancellorsville, caused Longstreet to miss the rest of the Overland campaign. He rejoined the army in October, remaining at his post through Appomattox, where he helped oversee the final surrender of the army. At the time of surrender, none of Lee's senior subordinates could claim longer or better service, and none stood higher in Lee's estimation.

## Outline

I.  Longstreet's conduct at Gettysburg has generated enormous debate.

   A.  Lost Cause writers and many others have accused him of insubordination that brought Confederate defeat.

   B.  His defenders have insisted that he knew better than Lee how to fight the battle.

   C.  His actions on July 1–3, 1863, include positive and negative elements.

      1.  He properly stated his views on how to fight the battle when asked by Lee.

**2.** He clearly disagreed with Lee's decision to pursue the tactical offensive on July 2.

    **a.** He took a great deal of time to get his divisions into position to attack on July 2.

    **b.** He dissembled when he claimed to have no authority to improvise on the ground.

    **c.** His divisions fought exceedingly well in the Wheat Field, the Peach Orchard, Devil's Den, and Little Round Top once they went into action.

**3.** He opposed the Pickett-Pettigrew assault on July 3 but carried out his orders diligently.

**II.** Longstreet spent an unhappy period in Georgia and Tennessee between September 1863 and April 1864.

  **A.** His initial enthusiasm for reinforcing Confederate forces in the west wilted after a short time under Braxton Bragg in the Army of Tennessee.

    **1.** His divisions played a key role in the victory at Chickamauga.

    **2.** Longstreet left Bragg's army during the siege of Chattanooga.

  **B.** He conducted a remarkably ineffective siege of Knoxville in November–December 1863.

    **1.** He ordered an unimaginative attack against Union Fort Sanders on November 29.

    **2.** He quarreled with key subordinates after the siege.

**III.** Longstreet returned to Virginia in April 1864 and served the rest of the war under Lee.

  **A.** He fought brilliantly at the battle of the Wilderness on May 6.

    **1.** He stopped a major Union assault that seemed certain to break Lee's army.

    **2.** He launched a successful flank attack.

    **3.** He was badly wounded by fire from some of his own soldiers.

  **B.** He rejoined the army after recuperating from his wounds and participated in the siege of Richmond and Petersburg.

  **C.** He was at Lee's side from Petersburg to Appomattox.

**IV.** Was Longstreet a modern soldier who understood better than Lee the power of the tactical defensive?

A. Historians who support this view point to Longstreet's actions at Fredericksburg and Gettysburg.

B. Michael Shaara's novel *The Killer Angels* and the film *Gettysburg* support this interpretation of Longstreet.

C. Longstreet's behavior at Knoxville and elsewhere suggests that he was not far-seeing as a tactician.

D. His record stands on its own merits as that of a gifted 19th-century soldier.

## Essential Reading:

Freeman, *Lee's Lieutenants*, vol. 3, chapters 3, 7–8, 12–13, 16–18, 26–27.

Gallagher, *Lee and His Generals in War and Memory*, chapter 7.

Krick, *The Smoothbore Volley That Doomed the Confederacy*, chapters 3–4.

## Supplementary Reading:

Longstreet, *From Manassas to Appomattox*, chapters 15–44.

Piston, *Lee's Tarnished Lieutenant: James Longstreet and His Place in Southern History*, chapters 4–5.

Wert, *General James Longstreet: The Confederacy's Most Controversial Soldier*, chapters 12–20.

## Questions to Consider:

1. What is a fair assessment of Longstreet's conduct at Gettysburg?

2. What might explain recent efforts to portray Longstreet as a modern soldier whose grasp of tactics was superior to Lee's?

# Lecture Nine—Transcript
## Longstreet's Later Confederate Career

Our second lecture on James Longstreet will examine the last two years of his Confederate career, a period that included more negative than positive experiences. He and Lee differed about how to fight the battle of Gettysburg in July 1863, with Longstreet arguing for a more defensive posture and Lee insisting on an aggressive one. Longstreet did not "lose" the battle, but at times he dragged his feet. Deployed to the western theater in the late summer of 1863, he helped win the battle of Chickamauga, the only great victory in all the war for the Confederate armies in the western theater. After a series of quarrels with General Braxton Bragg, who commanded the Confederate Army of Tennessee, Longstreet conducted a remarkably mismanaged siege of Knoxville, Tennessee, during which he ordered unimaginative frontal assaults, preferred charges against key subordinates, and conclusively showed his unfitness for army command. Back with the Army of Northern Virginia in April 1864, he fought brilliantly at the battle of the Wilderness on May 6. A severe wound, delivered by fire from one of his own regiments just a short distance from the spot where Jackson had been similarly struck down at Chancellorsville, caused Longstreet to miss the rest of the Overland campaign between Grant and Lee. He rejoined the army in October 1864, remaining at his post through Appomattox, where he helped oversee the final surrender of the Army of Northern Virginia. At the time of surrender, none of Lee's senior subordinates could claim longer or better service, and none stood higher in Lee's estimation.

Longstreet's conduct at Gettysburg has generated enormous debate. It's by far the most controversial element of his career as a Confederate soldier. Lost Cause writers, that is, former Confederates that wrote in the Lost Cause tradition in the decades after the Civil War, made Longstreet a special target in their attempts to absolve Lee of blame for the defeat at Gettysburg. We'll talk more about his in the last lecture of the course when we examine the Lost Cause more directly, but a few comments about it are appropriate here.

The Lost Cause writers said that Lee had a good plan at Gettysburg, a plan that would have worked had it not been for James Longstreet's behavior, especially his behavior on July 2, the second day of the battle. They claimed that Lee had issued a sunrise attack order, as they called it. Longstreet was supposed to attack at sunrise, and the fact that he didn't attack until about four o'clock in the afternoon on July 2, claimed the Lost Cause writers, cost Lee the battle. If only Longstreet had been in place when Lee wanted him to be in place, the Confederates would have won the battle. They also accused, these writers, they accused Longstreet of dragging his feet on July 3 at Gettysburg. Well, many writers picked up these arguments later, many writers in the 20th century, and Longstreet has come down as a very controversial figure because of this treatment of his part of the battle of Gettysburg.

Well, there was no sunrise attack order on July 2, Longstreet himself proved that by having a bunch of Lee's former staff officers testify to that effect in the late-19th century, but that didn't have much of an effect. The problem for Longstreet had nothing to do with what had happened in the war, these kinds of criticisms didn't arise during the war, they came after the war, and the problem was that Longstreet, after the war, became a Republican when almost all of the white South was Democratic. He also accepted positions from his friend Ulysses S. Grant, who was president of the United States in the late 1860s and early 1870s. He criticized Robert E. Lee in print, he became a Catholic, he did all kinds of things that former Confederates weren't supposed to do, and he invited these attacks on his wartime career. That is what was really going on with much of the Gettysburg controversy, but the net effect was that James Longstreet's reputation dropped in many quarters in the South, and subsequently among many students of the Civil War in all parts of the United States.

Longstreet's defenders said, "Listen, Longstreet knew better than Lee what should have happened at Gettysburg. Lee's the problem here. Lee insisted on attacking. Lee bled his army to death at Gettysburg. Longstreet knew best. Longstreet said, 'Don't attack the Federals after July 1. Let them attack us. Let's work around their left flank, let's interpose our army between the Army of the Potomac and Washington and make them attack us.'" Well, that's easier said than done, to disengage, to get around the Army of the Potomac, and make them attack. But, the point is, Longstreet's defenders said, "That's a better idea" than the one Lee had at Gettysburg. The Confederates lost the battle of Gettysburg, they said, not because of Longstreet, but because of Lee.

Longstreet's actions on July 1, 2, and 3, 1863 include positive and negative dimensions. He did some things well and other things less well. Some have criticized him for disagreeing so strongly with Lee. They met on July 1 and met again on July 2 to talk about what should happen in the battle. Lee asked for Longstreet's opinion, so Longstreet should have given Lee his opinions, that's his job as senior subordinate in the army. He wasn't stepping out of bounds in telling Lee that he thought the army should do something other than what Lee wanted the army to do. I don't think Longstreet should be faulted at all for that. He should have made known his views, he did, that's his role as the senior subordinate. He clearly disagreed with what Lee wanted to do, that was not lost on Lee, that was not lost on the men around them. Their staff officers knew it as well. One of Jackson's staff officers was a man, a Georgian, named Gilbert Moxley Sorrell, a very literate, bright guy who wrote one of the best and most revealing memoirs written by any of the Confederates after the war. Sorrell was a man who admired Longstreet, was always loyal to Longstreet, but he, in writing about Gettysburg, made clear how tense the relationship between Lee and Longstreet got in these conversations at Gettysburg. Sorrell wrote, "Longstreet didn't want to fight on the ground or on the plan adopted by the general-in-chief [that is Lee]. As Longstreet was not to be made willing, and Lee refused to change, or could not change, Longstreet failed to conceal some anger. There was apparent apathy in his movements. They lacked the fire and point of his usual bearing on the battlefield. His plans may have been better than Lee's, but it was too late to alter them with the troops ready to open fire on either side."

I think Sorrell's comments are right on point. Longstreet should have disagreed with Lee if he wanted to, but once Lee decided what the army was going to do, it was Longstreet's job as the subordinate, as the corps commander, to do his very best in carrying out those orders, and on July 2 that meant getting his corps into position, or two-thirds of it, John Bell Hood's division and Lafayette McLaws's division, George Pickett's division wasn't up yet, to get those two divisions into position to attack the Union left flank as soon as possible, and Longstreet did not do that. He dragged his feet on July 2, took a great deal of time to get his divisions into position to attack. He insisted on waiting for the very last brigade in his attacking column, that of Evander Law, to come up before he even began the rest of his troops on their march. That was not a subordinate acting in good faith to carry out his chief's plans. Longstreet took a great deal of time, he counter-marched, a long counter-march at one time, he finally got into position about 3:30, four o'clock in the afternoon. Most of the day was gone, no daylight savings time, of course, it would get dark between 7:30 and 8:00. He's not into position to begin the battle until there are fewer than four hours of daylight left in the day. So, should he have disagreed with Lee and made known his views? Yes. Was he a subordinate acting in good faith to the best of his ability on the rest of July 2? No, not in getting his command into position to attack.

Once he got his command into position to attack, he got his divisions in place, one of his division commanders, John Bell Hood, said that he thought it would be a good idea if they marched just a little bit farther and got all the way around the Federal left. It became clear that when Longstreet got down to the positions along the Emmitsburg Road, positions opposite the Peach Orchard and Devil's Den and Little Round Top, that the Union line extended farther south than Lee had thought. "Let's move all the way around", said Hood, and Longstreet said, "No. We have to do what General Lee wants." Well, he was dissembling in that regard. He knew that he had the authority, as the corps commander on the scene, who knew things that Lee didn't know, to adjust. We saw how Stonewall Jackson did that at Chancellorsville. The original thought was to attack along the Plank Road, but Jackson went on to the Turnpike when it became clear that that would work better. Longstreet had the authority to do that on the second day at Gettysburg, he chose not to do so. I think he was making a point. Lee said, "To do this, we're going to do it." Lee's wrong, we're going to do just what Lee said to do. Hood attacked under protest. We'll talk a little more about his when we discuss John Bell Hood later in the course.

Once his divisions went into action on the second day at Gettysburg, Longstreet was at his best. These two divisions numbered about 15,000 men, attacked more than twenty thousand Federals on the afternoon of July 2, and inflicted higher casualties than they sustained. It was a remarkable piece of fighting, of aggressive, defensive fighting for these two Confederate divisions at the Peach Orchard, at the Wheat Field, Little Round Top, Devil's Den. All that fighting is carried on by these two Confederate divisions, and it was a really quite astonishing performance for the two divisions. Once Longstreet got going he did very well, very well indeed.

Longstreet moved along the line, came under fire, exposed himself to danger, as he always did, during the action on July 2. He became himself once the shooting started, in a sense, but down to that point on July 2, I don't believe he was being a good subordinate.

Now, on the 3rd of July, the question becomes again: Do we still continue the tactical offensive (this is from a Confederate perspective) or now do we draw back and allow the Federals to attack us? Longstreet still wanted to disengage, get around the Federal left, if possible. Lee said, "No, we're going to attack again," and he selected James Longstreet to oversee these assaults on July 3. It's somewhat ironic because fewer than half the men involved in what came to be known as Pickett's charge, the Pickett-Pettigrew assault, it should be called Longstreet's assault, fewer than half the men involved in this assault were from Longstreet's corps. George Pickett's division was from Longstreet's corps, it's the smallest division in the army, the rest of the soldiers are from A. P. Hill's Third Corps. But Lee, even with Longstreet's behavior on the 2nd, clearly believed that Longstreet was his best corps commander here. Lee didn't ask A. P. Hill to oversee this fight, he asked James Longstreet to oversee it. Longstreet suggested that maybe Hill should do it, Lee said, "No, you're going to do it." Longstreet said something to the effect that no body of troops this size can carry that position, it hasn't ever happened, it's not going to happen here. Lee said, "Let's try it anyway." So, Longstreet oversaw that assault that became the most famous assault in American military history, Pickett's charge, an assault that, in the end, was a failure and cost thousands of Confederate casualties.

But Longstreet didn't drag his feet on the 3rd. I think it's hard to criticize his performance on July 3. He didn't think that what Lee wanted to do was the best thing to do, but he did it, and he oversaw the assault, I think, quite effectively. It's July 2 where his actions at Gettysburg really can be criticized, not on July 3. Overall he behaved on the 3rd as he typically did under combat. Again, he tried to set an example. His unflappability, a word I've used several times in respect to Longstreet in combat, but that showed up again here, and I'll quote from one of the brigadier generals in George Pickett's division, the only one that wasn't killed in the Pickett-Pettigrew assault, James Kemper, who later became governor of Virginia. He described the action just before the infantry began the assault. There was an artillery duel going on, the Confederate infantry was hunkered down and just enduring this bombardment, taking many casualties on the reverse of a slope down on the southern end of the field, and Kemper described James Longstreet's behavior. He said, did Kemper:

> I made my men lie flat on the ground, a precaution which poorly protected them from the enemy's hail of shot which pelted them and plowed through them, and sometimes fragments of a dozen mangled men were thrown in and about the trench left by a single missile. While this was going on Longstreet was slowly and alone immediately in front of our entire line. He sat his large charger, with a magnificent grace and composure I never before beheld. His bearing was to me the grandest moral spectacle of the war. I expected to see him fall every instant, still he moved on, slowly and majestically, with inspiriting confidence, composure, self-possession, and repressed power in every movement and look that fascinated me.

That's Longstreet in a combat situation. That is how many, many, many men, in terms very similar to this, described him. So, he's not happy with what's going to happen, but he's trying to set an example for his soldiers just before the beginning of this assault.

Gettysburg would provide, in Longstreet's view, a very dark episode in his Confederate career; he had very bad feelings about it for the rest of his life. He didn't think the battle was fought as it should have been fought. He may have been right, but he also didn't behave the way a good subordinate should have behaved, especially on July 2.

Well, he got his wish to get away from Lee and the Army of Northern Virginia. He had talked about that, as you'll recall, before the battle of Chancellorsville when he said that it might make sense, or right after the battle of Chancellorsville, when he said it would make sense to send strength from the Virginia theater to the western theater. That debate came up again after Gettysburg, and this time Lee lost the debate. He had won the debate before, but now the decision was made to send James Longstreet and his First Corps, or two divisions of it anyway, Pickett's division was wrecked. It would take a long time to refit that division, but James Longstreet with his other two divisions, those commanded by Hood and McLaws, would go to the support of Braxton Bragg's Army of Tennessee.

So, off they went at the end of the summer of 1863 to reinforce the Army of Tennessee, and his divisions play a key role in the battle of Chickamauga, or part of them did. Longstreet got to the battlefield after the first day's fighting had already occurred on September 19, 1863. Bragg, nonetheless, put Longstreet in command of half of his infantry. He gave him command of one of the wings of the army, and the next day, the day of heaviest fighting at Chickamauga, September 20, Longstreet's part of the line broke through the Union Army of the Cumberland, drove about a third of it from the field, captured thousands of prisoners and many cannons and stands of arms, and colors, and so forth. It was a tremendous success. Part of it was do to sheer luck, but Longstreet had his troops in position to achieve the breakthrough when the opportunity arose, and here, in the only great victory the Confederate armies of the west won, these troops from Virginia, under James Longstreet's command, had played a key role. He'd gotten there just in time, was a success. Bragg's soldiers responded very favorably toward Longstreet, took an immediate liking to him, gave him an new nickname, they called him the "bull of the woods" which was another nickname—he has lots of nicknames, this is one that stuck to him for much of the rest of the war.

The rest of his time, however, with Bragg out in the west was not happy at all. He saw very soon the difference between serving under a really effective army commander, such as Lee, and serving under a man who had problems as an army commander, such as Braxton Bragg. Bragg had none of the political skills that Lee had, the high command of his army was always troubled by divisions and backbiting and arguments among officers, and Longstreet became involved in those in the wake of Chickamauga. He came in an effort to oust Bragg from army command. Jefferson Davis even became involved. Davis had to go all the way out to visit the army from Richmond to try to take care of this problem. When he got there he polled the leading subordinates in the army, they almost all said, "Get rid of Bragg," including James Longstreet. He said, "Get rid of Bragg," and then Longstreet told Davis, "Bring Joseph Johnston to command this army." Well, Davis loathed Joseph Johnston, we'll talk more about this later, and Johnston loathed Davis. The last thing that Jefferson Davis wanted to hear from someone was bring Joe Johnston out here. This is a very inept political move on Longstreet's part. It's also not a very attractive element of his personality that he jumped right into this command squabbling out in the west, but he did.

In the end, Jefferson Davis decided to keep Bragg in command and get rid of a bunch of people who were arguing against him. He didn't get rid of Longstreet, Longstreet stayed, Bragg stayed, and they had a very testy relationship when the army moved just a little bit north of Chickamauga and laid siege to the Federal army under Rosecrans that was hunkered down in Chattanooga. In the midst of that siege, Longstreet was detached, he was ordered away, in November of 1863, sent to lay siege to Knoxville, Tennessee, which had also fallen to the Federals, fallen to Ambrose Burnside, in fact, a Federal force under Ambrose Burnside, the officer who had come to grief at Fredericksburg, and whose soldiers had attacked Longstreet's well positioned Confederates on Marye's Heights and elsewhere.

This was a completely unsuccessful effort on James Longstreet's part. Here is his major independent command of the war. He's in charge in east Tennessee, and he's a long way from other armies, he is really on his own. If he had aptitude to be an army commander, this is the place to show it, and he showed absolutely none. He ordered a very unimaginative attack against the Union Fort Sanders on November 29; so much for the idea that he really understood that the defensive was more powerful than the offensive and frontal attacks were a thing of the past. This is one of the most wretchedly planned and executed frontal attacks of the entire war.

He also quarreled with a number of key subordinates after the siege. He preferred charges against Lafayette McLaws, an old friend of his, another Georgian who'd fought with Longstreet through most of the war. He leveled charges against Evander Law, another promising young officer. The charges were farcical; they had absolutely no substance, that was apparent to almost everyone. It was an instance of Longstreet's looking for scapegoats for his own failures. I talked about this tendency early at Seven Pines, he does it again here. He didn't do well at Knoxville, he wants to blame somebody else, and so, here is this parade of people for him to blame that includes Lafayette McLaws and Evander Law. Jefferson Davis was very unhappy with the charges and this whole mess in Longstreet's force. He was already upset because Longstreet had recommended Joseph Johnston. This is another mark against Longstreet in Jefferson Davis's estimation.

Longstreet also came up with a really strange notion of mounting thousands of Confederate infantry and setting them on a raid into Kentucky in this stage of the war. It made absolutely no sense at all. He is not a guy who thinks well in strategic terms. He is not someone who did well at all in this one major opportunity to operate independently. He had no aptitude, there's no question about it after this campaign. Except, perhaps, in Longstreet's mind, although even he became very discouraged at this part of the war and considered resigning and going home and taking himself out of the war. It's the least satisfactory part of the whole war for him, even a darker period of the war than Gettysburg was.

He returned to Virginia in April of 1864, he and his two divisions, and served the rest of the war under Lee. His soldiers were very happy to be back in the Army of Northern Virginia. The soldiers in the Army of Northern Virginia were very happy to have James Longstreet back, they had missed him, they considered Longstreet a key part of the army. Walter Taylor, of Lee's staff, spoke for those at headquarters when he wrote to Longstreet, "I am beside myself General with the joy of having you back. It's like the reunion of a family." And it really was. There were only 10,000 men in these two divisions by the time they got back to the Army of Northern Virginia, but the bond between them and Lee remained strong, and their happiness at seeing Lee and Longstreet together was obvious when Lee called for a review of these First Corps veterans who had come back, a review in April of 1864, just after they got back to the army. They drew up the two divisions in an open field, and Lee and Longstreet rode out to review them, and there was another one of these spontaneous demonstrations on the part of the soldiers when they saw Lee and

Longstreet together. Lee and Longstreet rode along the line, the men hadn't seen Lee in a long time, of course, hadn't seen the two men together for a long time, and one of the witnesses wrote about it this way later, said:

> I can see now the large square gatepost marking where a broad country road led out of a tall oak wood and upon an open knoll. In front of the center of our long, gray lines, and as the well-remembered figure of Lee upon Traveler, at the head of his staff, rides between the posts and comes out upon the knoll, a bugle sounds a signal, a battalion of artillery thunders out a salute, and the General reins up his horse and bears his head and looks at us, and the soldiers shout and cry and wave their battle flags and look at him again. For sudden as a wind, a wave of sentiment such as can only come to large crowds in full sympathy, something alike which came a year later at Appomattox seemed to sweep over the field. Each man seemed to feel the bond which held us all to Lee. There was no speaking, but the effect was that of a military sacrament in which we pledged anew our lives.

Others commented about how pleased they were to see Lee and Longstreet together here. Longstreet is back in his comfort zone, whether he really wants to admit it or not. Where he does best is at Lee's side at the Army of Northern Virginia. When he's not with Lee, he isn't at his best, and whatever ambitions he may have nourished for himself, at least in his own thoughts, he, I think at some level, must have been pleased to be back with Lee as well, and he immediately rendered excellent service. His corps got to the battlefield of the Wilderness, the first clash between Lee and Grant in the Overland campaign, they got to the battlefield the second day, May 6, just as disaster was about to engulf Lee's army. A. P. Hill's end of the line had crumbled. Winfield Scott Hancock, the Federal officer in charge of the assaults, had broken Hill's two divisions that were on that part of the field. Lee himself had ridden out to try to restore the line, placed himself in danger, and just as all seemed to be lost, the head of Longstreet's corps arrived on the field. Longstreet very quickly put together a counter-attack that stopped Hancock's advance, then a flank attack that drove Hancock back along the Plank Road, this is almost the same battlefield as at the battle at Chancellorsville a year earlier. It was an enormously successful performance on Longstreet's part. It showed how quickly he could take in a situation, even a very chaotic situation, in the midst of a battle he hadn't been present at the beginning of. He came in, he took control of the battle, he stabilized the situation, and then gave the Confederates the advantage with his flank attack.

But just after he launched this successful flank attack, as he was pressing forward with his staff to continue the momentum, again, the kind of behavior that Lee most prized in his lieutenants, he, like Jackson, almost exactly a year before, in almost exactly the same place, came under fire from one of his own units. One of his own units fired across the road where Longstreet and his cavalcade of staff officers and others were riding, and a bullet hit Longstreet in the throat, hit with such force that it lifted him up out of the saddle—Longstreet was a big man, he was six two, weighed more than two hundred pounds, which in a Civil War context is a very large man. The doctors said that it probably would have been a fatal wound for most people, but Longstreet's strength was such that he survived it, but it was a grievous wound. They took him off his horse, put him on the ground, he couldn't speak, at one point, however, he blew some bloody foam out of his mouth and croaked out an order and then was carried away from the field. He's gone his first day back with the army, the first combat back he is shot in this horrible way. When Lee learned of this, he was distraught. One of Longstreet's staff officers, an Englishman named Frances Dawson, remembered watching Lee's reaction of Longstreet's wounding. "We met General Lee," wrote Dawson, "and I shall not soon forget the sadness in his face and the almost despairing movement in his hands when he was told that Longstreet had fallen." Well might Lee despair. Here is his best corps commander gone at the very outset of the campaign against U. S. Grant. It had been a very auspicious return to the army for Longstreet, but it was over almost before it began.

He recuperated for a while, rejoined the army in October of 1864, he really came back too soon, he hadn't recovered from his wounds fully, his right arm was partially paralyzed the rest of his life, and he fought on through the rest of the war, through the siege at Petersburg, through the retreat to Appomattox, with Lee, always as Lee's principle lieutenant. Steadfast to the end, he told Lee not to capitulate unless Grant offered generous terms. If Grant didn't, said Longstreet, come back and let us fight it out.

The question that most comes up regarding Longstreet nowadays is: Was he a modern soldier who really understood better than Lee just how important the new weaponry was? That the tactical defensive was more important because of rifled weaponry? He's often presented that way, both by historians who point to Fredericksburg, which was a success, a very easy success, and Gettysburg where they say Longstreet was right and Lee was

128

wrong in terms of what to do. Longstreet was simply more far-seeing than Lee say many modern scholars.

Others in a more popular vein, Michael Shaara in his novel, *The Killer Angels*, and the movie *Gettysburg* based on that novel, they also present Longstreet as a modern soldier, as someone who really, really gets it better than Lee does. Lee seems sort of out of sorts, sort of out of touch in both the novel and the movie in some ways. Longstreet seems much more clear-eyed, much more able to see the power of the defensive weaponry. I don't think that interpretation holds up at all if you look at Longstreet's whole career. He was not averse to mounting assaults, as his activities outside Knoxville showed. He was also very good at it, as we've seen on a number of battlefields earlier in the war. Except Fredericksburg, his best days were always aggressive days. Every moment in which he played a key role—at Gaines's Mill, at Glendale, at Second Manassas—his powerful assault on the second day at Gettysburg, his assault at the Wilderness on May 6—all of those occasions where Longstreet is shown on a battlefield in a tactical sense, he was on the tactical offensive, and was doing very well on the tactical offensive indeed.

I think his record stands on its own merits as that of a gifted 19th-century soldier. He's one of the two best Confederate corps commanders, he along with Jackson. They occupy a stratum all by themselves, a great strength to Lee. He was a man who had reached his level of competency, although perhaps he didn't know that himself and thought that he would have done better at even higher echelons of command.

Jackson and Longstreet—the two best. Next time we'll turn to a third man who also demonstrated great capacity as a corps commander, though he is not as well known and certainly not generally treated as successful an officer as Jackson and Longstreet, and that is Jubal Anderson Early.

# Lecture Ten
# The Rise of Jubal Anderson Early

**Scope:** Ranking behind Jackson and Longstreet as Lee's third effective corps commander, Jubal A. Early followed a different path to that level of responsibility. A West Pointer who served only briefly in the U.S. Army before resigning to pursue a career in law, Early left civilian life to participate in the war with Mexico and later opposed secession as a member of the Virginia state convention in 1861. Once his home state departed from the Union, he immediately offered his sword to Virginia, then to the Confederacy, and fought in every major battle in the eastern theater, from First Manassas through Gettysburg. Progressing more slowly than either Jackson or Longstreet, he nonetheless rendered solid performances on many occasions and often found himself entrusted by Lee with difficult assignments. His ability to function in a semiautonomous manner during the Chancellorsville campaign impressed Lee and set him apart from most of his peers in the army. A profane and acerbic individual, Early admired Lee deeply and won his chief's affection in turn. Lee called the younger Early "my bad old man" and had, by the aftermath of Gettysburg, concluded that "Old Jube" possessed the skills requisite to lead an infantry corps.

## Outline

I. Early's pre-Civil War career did not center on military service.

   **A.** He graduated from West Point in the class of 1837 but soon left the army to practice law.

   **B.** He served with the First Virginia Infantry volunteers in the war with Mexico.

   **1.** He saw no battlefield action.

   **2.** He acted for a time as military governor of Monterey.

   **C.** He returned to the law after the end of the war with Mexico.

   **D.** He won election to the Virginia secession convention in 1861.

   **1.** An old Whig, he opposed secession.

   **2.** He cast his lot with his native state as soon as it left the Union.

     **3.** He accepted a commission as colonel in the Confederate army.

**II.** Early rose from colonel to major general between the summer of 1861 and the spring of 1863.

    **A.** He commanded a brigade that contributed significantly to the Confederate victory at First Manassas in July 1861.

    **B.** He suffered a wound at the battle of Williamsburg in May 1862 but returned to the army in time to fight at Malvern Hill on July 1.

    **C.** His performances during the campaigns of Second Manassas, Antietam, and Fredericksburg enhanced his reputation.

        **1.** Though a brigadier general, he more than once held temporary division command during this period.

        **2.** His command helped seal the break in Stonewall Jackson's line at the battle of Fredericksburg.

**III.** He headed a division at Chancellorsville and Gettysburg.

    **A.** Lee gave Early an important semi-independent command at Chancellorsville.

        **1.** Early held the Fredericksburg front while Lee and Jackson marched west to deal with Joseph Hooker's flanking movement.

        **2.** Early impressed Lee with his aggressiveness at the battle of Salem Church on May 4.

    **B.** Early's actions at Gettysburg triggered later debate.

        **1.** Critics argued that he should have been more aggressive on the afternoon of July 1.

        **2.** A close reading of the evidence suggests the Early acted reasonably on the first day of battle.

        **3.** His division attacked impressively on July 2.

**IV.** Early and Lee respected each other despite vast differences in personality.

    **A.** Lee affectionately called the younger Early "my bad old man."

    **B.** Early idolized Lee from the beginning days of the war.

    **C.** Early little resembled Lee as a man.

        **1.** He was exceedingly profane.

        **2.** He evidenced scant interest in religion.

        **3.** He flouted Southern marital conventions.

**D.** Early's self-reliance and aggressiveness on the battlefield suited Lee well.

## Essential Reading:

Freeman, *Lee's Lieutenants*, vol. 2, chapters 2, 35.

Gallagher, *Lee and His Army in Confederate History*, chapter 7.

## Supplementary Reading:

Early, *Autobiographical Sketch and Narrative of the War between the States*, chapters 1–26.

Osborne, *Jubal: The Life and Times of Gen. Jubal A. Early, C.S.A., Defender of the Lost Cause*, chapters 1–13.

## Questions to Consider:

1.  What does Lee's relationship with Early reveal about the commanding general's willingness to embrace subordinates of vastly different temperament?

2.  What does Early's case indicate about possible connections between prewar politics and allegiance to the Confederacy?

# Lecture Ten—Transcript
# The Rise of Jubal Anderson Early

With this lecture we begin our consideration of Jubal A. Early, who ranked behind Stonewall Jackson and James Longstreet as the third man who proved that he could lead a corps under Robert E. Lee's overall charge. Jubal A. Early followed a different path to that level of responsibility than either Jackson or Longstreet. A West Pointer who served only briefly in the United States Army before resigning to pursue a career in law, Early left civilian life to participate in the war with Mexico and later opposed secession as a member of the Virginia state convention in 1861. Once his home state departed from the Union, he immediately offered his sword to Virginia and then to the Confederacy, and he fought in every major battle in the eastern theater, from First Manassas through Gettysburg. Progressing more slowly than either Jackson or Longstreet, he nonetheless rendered solid performances on many occasions and often found himself entrusted by Lee with difficult assignments. His ability to function in a semiautonomous manner during the Chancellorsville campaign impressed Lee and set him apart from most of his peers in the army. A profane and very acerbic individual, Early admired Lee deeply and won his chief's affection in turn. Lee called the younger Early "my bad old man" and had, by the aftermath of Gettysburg, concluded that "Old Jube," as Early was called by his soldiers, possessed the skills requisite to lead an infantry corps.

Early's pre-Civil War career didn't center on military service. He's unlike many of the other individuals we'll talk about in this course in that regard. He was born in 1816 near Rocky Mount, Virginia, down near Lynchburg, in that part of the state, to a fairly prominent slave-holding family. His father held a considerable amount of slaves, his mother was one of the Hairston family, who kind of straddled the Virginia/North Carolina border and who were probably the largest slave-holding family in the entire South. So, through his mother, he is tied to the very top echelon of the slave-holding aristocracy in the South.

He graduated from West Point in the class of 1837, but didn't stay in the army very long. He left the service to practice law in 1838. He was eighteenth in his class, a respectable showing, not a great showing but a respectable one. Some of his classmates were Braxton Bragg, Joseph Hooker, John Pemberton, who would all be army commanders during the Civil War. Louis A. Armstead, who would be killed in Pickett's charge at

Gettysburg on July 3, got involved in an incident that showed that even at West Point Early had the ability to rile people up, that was an aspect of his character that would be very clear during the Civil War. He had this very sharp tongue, very much opinionated, very quick to let his opinions be known. He must have said something to Louis Armstead that absolutely provoked Armstead, because they were engaged in an incident in the mess hall at West Point where Armstead, in the end, threw a plate at Jubal Early's head, and Armstead was thrown out of West Point as a result. He ended up with an army career, but without a West Point diploma because he and Early had this altercation in the mess hall.

Early served for a while in Florida against the Seminoles in his short career, but then he got out of the army, having been promoted to first lieutenant, in 1838. He went back to Rocky Mount, studied law. That is, he decided after studying law that it was something that would suit him, and that is what he made the rest of his antebellum career doing, practicing law in this sort of backwater area of Virginia. He did stand for election to the Virginia House of Delegates, and was successful as a Whig candidate for one term in the early 1840s. He took a break from his law practice during the war with Mexico to serve with the First Virginia Infantry Volunteers; he was the major of the First Virginia Infantry during the war with Mexico. He went in in January of 1847, and remained in the service until the summer of 1848, and although he spent time in northern Mexico, he didn't see any action. He was sick for a good part of the time. He served for a while as the military governor of the Mexican city of Monterey during that service, but no combat experience for Jubal Early during the war with Mexico.

He was called Major Early, however, for the rest of the antebellum years by those who knew him in Virginia because that had been his rank in this prominent Virginia unit during that action in Mexico. He returned to practice law again after the end of the war. He was Commonwealth's Attorney for ten years, so he prosecuted a number of cases. He was very able as a lawyer, both as Commonwealth's Attorney, and he was a good defense lawyer He achieved a reputation as someone who is very quick on his feet, perhaps quicker on his feet than careful in preparation, but nonetheless successful. And again, his ability with words, his ability with arguments, shown as a lawyer just as it would when he got into altercations with either peers during the Civil War, or with James Longstreet, arguing about Gettysburg after the war. He and Longstreet locked horns after the war, and Longstreet was absolutely no match for Jubal Early as a controversialist. Early had his way with Longstreet as we will see later in the course.

He won election to the Virginia secession convention in 1861 as a Whig. He never quit calling himself a Whig. He was very conservative politically; never quit calling himself a Whig, even though the Whig party essentially disappeared in the early 1850s. Early continued to call himself a Whig, and he went to the secession convention as a conservative Whig and he opposed secession. It's not that he thought that slavery was a bad thing by any means, and the secessionists who thought that by leaving the Union to protect slavery was a good thing itself, but he didn't agree with him. He was very much pro-slavery, he just thought that slavery had been protected by the Constitution all those years in United States history, and thought that was the safest route to take. Why change something that has worked argued Early. "The Constitution will protect the institution, we don't need to secede to protect. In fact, if we do secede all bets will be off, we don't know what the result of secession will be, it might end up harming the institution of slavery and the other things that we're concerned about."

In fact, that's exactly what happened. That is what Early argued in the convention, he voted against secession right down to the very end, but when the state seceded in mid-April 1861, he quickly offered his services to the state, his military services to the state, and then accepted a commission as a colonel in the Confederate army once Virginia forces went into Confederate service. He was colonel of the 24$^{th}$ Regiment of Virginia Infantry. So it didn't take him long to transition from being an opponent to secession to being firmly on board with the Confederate war effort. He became an inveterate Confederate from then on, and remained for the rest of his life a very staunch defender of what the South had done, what the South had fought for, and the effort the Confederates had mounted to make their break with the Union permanent.

He rose from colonel to major general between the summer of 1861 and the spring of 1863. Although still a colonel he commanded a brigade at the battle of First Manassas, and it was a brigade that contributed significantly to that victory. He and his brigade were not involved early in the battle at First Manassas, they were in a position in reserve, but as the battle unfolded they were brought to the front at a critical moment in the afternoon and added their weight to the Confederate effort and turned the tide and brought the rout of the army of United States soldiers commanded by Irvin McDowell. So Early and his little command helped seal the victory, and as so many were, he was mentioned favorably in Beauregard's battle reports, and he was promoted to brigadier general, to rank from the day of the battle, in recognition of his contribution to the battle. He became a brigadier general to rank from July 21, 1861.

He was in Joseph Johnston's army on the peninsula in 1862, and as the army was falling back towards Richmond he fought in the rear guard action at Williamsburg on May the 5<sup>th</sup>, and he was wounded there. His command fought quite aggressively there, his brigade did. He launched an attack that was probably an ill-considered precipitated attack, an attack that was praised for the gallantry of the soldiers, although a number of observes questioned whether Early really needed to launch the attack. He wasn't criticized heavily for it because it was an aggressive move and many people thought it was good to be aggressive on the battlefield. Early had fit that mold. It was easy to question whether the attack should have been launched, but he attacked with great élan said many of the observers, and he got points for that. His men lost 600 casualties during the battle of Williamsburg, and Early was wounded in the shoulder. It required a furlough home to recover. He came back in time, however, to participate in the very last stage of the Seven Days' campaign; he fought at Malvern Hill with Lee's army. This was under Lee's command now, of course, although he didn't take an especially important role at Malvern Hill, but he'd done well to this point in the war.

He really started to blossom under Lee and Jackson when you move beyond the Seven Days. His performances during the campaigns of Second Manassas, Antietam, and Fredericksburg all enhanced his reputation as an up and coming officer in the Army of Northern Virginia. His first real action came at the battle of Cedar Mountain, which as we have seen earlier was a preliminary to the main battle of Second Manassas. This is when Jackson had taken his command away from Richmond, under Lee's direction, to confront John Pope's advance in central Virginia.

The battle of Cedar Mountain, fought just outside Culpepper, on August 9, 1862 featured Jubal Early's brigade in a defensive posture. Early was really the most prominent officer fighting under Jackson that day. He absolutely held his ground under very difficult circumstances, and he was praised in Jackson's report. Jackson usually didn't praise anybody, he gave all thanks to God, all credit to God, occasionally he would single out an officer, and in his report on Cedar Mountain, Jackson said that Jubal Early held his position "with great firmness." That's extravagant praise from Stonewall Jackson. Richard Ewell, who was Early's superior, Ewell was the division commander at that point, Early a brigade commander, Ewell also spoke very highly of how Early had done at Cedar Mountain.

So, it's a good start there, and at the battle of Second Manassas itself, Jubal Early, again, was probably the most prominent of all the brigadiers in Jackson's part of the army, Jackson's Left Wing of the army. Again in a defensive posture, especially on August 29, when Jackson was holding his position, Longstreet was coming into position, and the Federals under John Pope were launching very heavy attacks against Jackson. Jackson's line, more than once, nearly gave way, and Jubal Early handled his brigade very effectively on August 29, and again was prominently mentioned in the Confederate reports because of how well he had done there.

During the movement into Maryland, Early would have yet another opportunity to distinguish himself. The long day at Antietam, the day when Jackson's command more than once almost broke on the Confederate left, featured Jubal Early leading fragments of other commands. He ended up temporarily in command of a division at Antietam. He's off the Confederate left, and he shifts his command again and again to meet different threats. Their position was at one point facing north, another point facing east, and a third time part of them facing north and part of them facing east, and even a little piece of them facing south. It's a very adept performance on Early's part with strong support from some Confederate artillery that belonged to Jeb Stuart's cavalry command. But in the situation at Antietam, this long and difficult day, where more than once Jubal Early showed initiative and showed his ability to handle a brigade, and then a division, under the stress of combat. Very successful, very successful, and he came under the eye of a number of officers there. He, himself, never underestimated what he had done, he's an intensely ambitions man, intensely ambitious. He wants higher rank, believes he deserves higher rank, never slights his own performances. He wrote of his brigade between the Seven Days and Antietam, that it "has never been broken or compelled to fall back or left one of its dead to be buried by the enemy." The last is a great point of pride among soldiers, of course. You take care of your own dead, you don't leave your dead in the hands of the enemy, and Jubal Early claimed, I don't know if it's really true but it may have been, that not a single one of his soldiers killed in action or mortally wounded in action during this stretch from the Seven Days to the Maryland campaign had fallen into enemy hands.

As for his performance at Antietam in a broader sense, Early had shown "great resolution in the face of the large force opposite to him at Antietam." Lee also was very guarded in his praise of officers, and this is, if not effusive, at least a very unusual praise from Lee. So, Jackson has praised Early, Lee has praised Early, Ewell has praised Early—this stretch from Second Manassas to the Maryland campaign, Cedar Mountain, Second Manassas and Maryland/Antietam showed Early and his ability in situations that allowed crucial people to observe him and react positively.

During the battle of Fredericksburg, Early, incidentally by the time of the battle of Fredericksburg, thought he should be a major general instead of a brigadier general, thought he should have been promoted by then, should have been promoted on the basis of what he did at Antietam, said, "I temporarily led a division at Antietam, I should have a division, should have a division, should have permanent command of a division," and he probably had in mind Richard Ewell's division because Ewell had been grievously wounded in the battle of Groveton that took place on August 28, just before the main fighting at Second Manassas. That division's top slot was open, and I think there is no doubt that Early thought he deserved it. But he didn't have it, nor formally, not officially. He fought at Fredericksburg very well. I've talked about how Jackson's end of the line was not drawn particularly well at Fredericksburg, how there was a gap in part of his line and how George Meade's Pennsylvania reserves broke through that gap in the fighting at Fredericksburg. Well, one of the key units in sealing that break was Jubal Early's. Jubal Early came up from a position of support and helped seal the break on Jackson's end of the line at the battle of Fredericksburg, another very positive performance on the part of Jubal Early.

He was promoted to major general in January of 1863. How did he react? Did he say, "Gosh, it's so good of them to think so well of me and I'm happy?" No. He said, "I should have had this a long time ago." He was very grouchy about it, he was always grouchy, always in a very touchy mood it seemed, always ready to criticize, always ready to throw out a snide remark if the situation seemed to warrant it, or even if it didn't. And here he said, "Great, I've got it, I should have had it before." But anyway, he did have it, major general in January of 1863, and given command of his friend Richard Ewell's old division. Ewell, his health was simply too problematic, we'll talk more about that later. Ewell had lost a leg as a result of his wound at Groveton, and so now Jubal Early is a division commander. His first real test as a division commander would be an absolutely critical one in terms of Lee's estimate of Jubal Early, and that came at the battle of Chancellorsville in early May 1863.

Now, Lee already had decided that Jubal Early was his kind of guy. He's aggressive. He can be independent in a critical situation, as he was at Antietam. He can think on his feet. He can respond to crisis on a battlefield. All of those are plusses from Lee's point of view, the kind of person Lee wants in his army. We've talked about this again and again, and we're going to continue to talk about it because it is so important to understand the culture of command in the Army of Northern Virginia, and how that culture played out on battlefields, how different it was, as I've said before, from the culture of command of the Army of the Potomac put in place by George McClellan, the cautious culture of the Army of the Potomac, the don't-make-a-mistake culture in the Army of the Potomac. That's not what Lee wants. Jubal Early is the kind of man, believes Lee, who will fit in with his preferred, Lee's preferred style of leadership.

Lee gave Early a semi-independent role in the campaign at Chancellorsville. Here he is, a brand new major general. This is his first command as a major general at that rank, and Lee gives him, really, the most important task of all of the major generals in the Chancellorsville campaign, and that is a semi-independent one. After Hooker worked his way round Lee's left flank with that grand turning movement, a really brilliant move on Hooker's part, crossed the Rappahannock and Rapidan Rivers and came in behind Lee on April 30 and May 1, Lee and Jackson took almost all of the Army of Northern Virginia west to deal with Hooker near the Chancellorsville crossroads, Lee left Jubal Early behind at Fredericksburg to face a powerful Union force there. Hooker had left nearly 40,000 Federals at Fredericksburg under John Sedgwick to hold Lee's attention while he took the rest of the Army of the Potomac up the Rappahannock to get around Lee's left flank.

Well, Lee left Jubal Early and just 10,000 Confederates to keep an eye on all those thousands of Federals at Fredericksburg. Lee is saying, "Okay, you hold this position while we go take care of this large threat coming in from the west." You would only ask that of a commander you considered to be capable of making decisions on his own, without direct supervision, someone who could be resilient in the face of difficult circumstances, and that is what Lee believed of and expected from Jubal Early. It's a very important gesture of respect from Lee to Early, and Early impressed Lee with his performance during the Chancellorsville campaign. He was driven away from the lines at Fredericksburg in the end, no real black mark against him because the odds where such. But he especially did well at the battle of Salem Church on May 4, which is the very last act in this grand Chancellorsville drama that took place over such a broad stretch of territory in that part of Virginia. The battle of Salem Church, on the 4th, Lee deployed three of his divisions to meet the threat of Sedgwick who had been at Fredericksburg and was moving toward the rest of the Federals at Chancellorsville, two divisions that Longstreet had left behind under Lafayette McLaws and Richard Anderson, but also Jubal Early's. Of those three commanders who fought at Salem Church, only Early showed any aggressiveness. Lee was very put out with the way that McLaws and Anderson performed. They were both senior to Jubal Early, had been major generals much longer than Early. Lee himself rode to this battlefield, didn't like what he was seeing on the part of Anderson and McLaws, but did like what he saw on the part of Early. Early was the only one who launched assaults at Salem Church; he's the only one who behaved the way that Lee wanted these division commanders to behave.

So, coming out of Chancellorsville Lee put alongside Early's name not only a good performance in dealing with Sedgwick at Fredericksburg in the early stage of the campaign, but also a strong positive evaluation of Early in how he behaved at Salem Church, and Lee praised Early very strongly in the official reports. Early, overall, did extremely well during the Chancellorsville campaign, and this, I think, would be pivotal in the kinds of things that Lee would ask him to do later and in Lee's belief by May of 1864 that Jubal Early was competent to command a corps.

Early participated in the Gettysburg campaign, and his actions at Gettysburg became controversial, partly because those who defended Longstreet and were upset that Early attacked Longstreet so much for his behavior at Gettysburg after the war, those who were in Longstreet's camp, in turn, attacked Jubal Early. They say that he was not very aggressive at Gettysburg. Critics said he should have been much more offensive minded at the end of the first day's battle especially. That's the critical moment said some people later, retrospectively, when the Confederates had lost the battle. They had routed these first two Union corps on the first day, we talked about this earlier, and it is a great tactical victory for the Army of Northern Virginia on July 1 at Gettysburg. If only there had been one more round of assaults on Richard Ewell's end of the line against Cemetery Hill and against Cult's Hill. Ewell, over there with Jubal Early as his key division commander on the scene, if only they had been more aggressive Lee would have swept the Federals off that high ground and Gettysburg would have been a complete victory. That is the critique of Jubal Early at Gettysburg. He didn't do enough late in the day, he should have done more, he became timid, he became irresolute at the end of the battle.

Well, I think the evidence suggests otherwise. Early's division had fought hard earlier in the day, had played a key role in routing the Union army's 11$^{th}$ Corps, the poor corps that had been routed by Jackson's flank attack at Chancellorsville; it gets routed again on the first day at Gettysburg. Early's brigades play a crucial role in that, pushing the Federals through the town of Gettysburg, right through the town of Gettysburg, and pushed them up to the high ground south of town. Early recommended continuing the assault later, but he said continue it only if we are supported on our right flank. That meant cooperation from A. P. Hill's corps, which was off to the right. Ewell said the same thing, yes we will continue the attack. Lee had told Ewell to continue the attack if practical, take the high ground if practical late in the day. Ewell said I think we can take it, we need support on the right. Early said the same thing. Attack but only with support on the right. When it became clear that there was not going to be any support on the right, both Early and Ewell decided that it was not practical to take that high ground, and so they didn't. That became controversial later.

On the second day at Gettysburg, Early's division, two of his brigades launched a quite spectacular assault that actually got all the way to the top of the East Cemetery Hill, captured Union guns there briefly, but couldn't hold their position. Overall I think Early did fine at Gettysburg. But although he, as so many Confederates, became embroiled in the controversies that arose from Monday morning quarterbacking, post-war Monday morning quarterbacking, maybe it's Friday morning quarterbacking when it's that late in the game, looking back and trying to figure out who was really to blame at Gettysburg.

Early and Lee respected one another, and it's an interesting respect. I think they really liked each other too, and that is really interesting as well, because they were vastly different kinds of men. There personalities offer an enormous range of contrasts and very little similarity. They are similar in key military ways, and that is why they were both capable of great aggressive behavior on battlefields, which Lee prized, which we all know by now. That was certainly a mark in Early's favor, but in many ways Early did not fit the model of a Confederate officer who would be adored by his men and by the public, things that would never happen with Early, incidentally. He was never adored by his men; he was never adored by the public. His personality didn't allow those things to happen.

Early was an interesting man to look at. He was probably a little more than six feet tall, but suffered such severe arthritis, or rheumatism as it was usually described then. We don't know exactly what was wrong with him, but he was literally bent over, literally bent over. It made him look shorter and older than he really was. He had dark hair, what was left of it by the time of the Civil War, a dark beard, and his eyes were often described as black. He had a very distinctive voice, kind of squeaky and high with a pronounced southwestern Virginia twang, apparently. His voice made an impression on a number of people. He was a misogynist; he didn't like women especially, I think. He made the most fun of, saved his sharpest barbs, for men he believed either to be happily married or foolishly in love. He was relentless in his snide comments about those kinds of men. He didn't shy away from cursing; he was known as one of the most imaginative cursers in the army. Lee never cursed. Jubal Early filled his speech with "goddamns" and "Jesus Christ" and all kinds of blasphemous phrases, which certainly would not have pleased Stonewall Jackson or Lee or the other quite religious men in the army, and, of course as I've said, he was very sarcastic both in what he wrote and what he stated. Gilbert Moxley Sorrell has left a wonderful portrait and I think a quite perceptive one of Early. He said, "His irritable disposition and biting tongue made him anything but popular, but he was a very brave and able commander. His appearance was quite striking, having a dark handsome face, regular features, and deep piercing eyes. He was the victim of rheumatism, and although not old, bent almost double like an aged man. Of high scholarly and political attainments, he never married, but lived the life of a recluse in Virginia entirely apart from social and public affairs." It wasn't entirely apart from social affairs; he fathered a number of illegitimate children, at least four, and maybe as many as eight. He didn't ever marry anyone, but we do know that he had at least four illegitimate children there on the census rolls attributed to him basically, down in his part of Virginia, and there may have been four others, the evidence isn't quite so clear on that. But he didn't ever marry, that's true. He did seek out female companionship, obviously.

He was not someone who would engender a warm response in most people around him. He simply was too prickly. He labored under no illusion in that regard. He was very frank. He says at one point in his memoirs, "I was never what is called a popular man," and he wasn't, and he knew he wasn't, he said he wasn't. He idolized Lee from the beginning days of the war. Even before Lee became a great figure, Jubal Early thought he was a great soldier and said so again and again, even before the Seven Days, and Lee affectionately called Early "my bad old man." It's really the most affectionate nickname that he fastened on anyone. That's more affectionate than "my old war horse" for Longstreet. "My bad old man," it's interesting, maybe he was in Jubal Early his other side and sort of took some delight in watching Early do all the things that he himself never did, include drink plenty. Jubal Early loved to drink whiskey. Old Crow was his type; if he could get Old Crow; that's what he drank, cursing, smoking cigars, and generally behaving in a way that Robert E. Lee did not behave. The profanity set him apart from Lee, of course, very profane. No real interest in religion. There was a famous incident after the battle of Fredericksburg or late in the battle of Fredericksburg, where Early saw a chaplain clearly moving to safety in the rear and he hollered out at him, "Chaplain, where are you going?" The guy honestly answered, "General, I'm going to a place of safety in the rear." Early hollered again as the guy was getting farther away, "Chaplain, I've known you for thirty years and you've always been trying to get to heaven, and now that you get your chance you seem to be turning your back on it." There were many instances during the war when he took the opportunity to sort of put the stiletto in religious figures like that. So, he's very unlikely in that regard as well.

Flouting marital conventions, not interested in religion, very profane, very self-assured—another famous incident, Jackson saw that there was straggling in Early's command one time and he sent one of his little curt notes "Compliments to General Early: I saw straggling in your command today. Could you tell me why?" And Early wrote back, "Compliments to General Jackson: You saw stragglers in the back of my command probably because you were in the rear of my command today." The kind of response no one else would have gotten away with with Jackson, I think. It showed that Early was self-assured, and that Jackson let him get away with it, I think, shows that Jackson really valued Early as a soldier as well.

Self reliant, aggressive on the battlefield, Jubal Early promised, or seemed to promise, success at a greater level of responsibility. And as we will see next time, moving into the campaign in 1864, Lee was going to give him that greater responsibility and we'll see how Early responded to that test.

# Lecture Eleven
## Early's Path to Defeat

**Scope:** The second of our lectures on Jubal Early traces his trajectory in the operations in 1864–1865, a period during which he justified Lee's confidence in his abilities yet suffered a series of defeats that eventually brought his removal from command. He stood in for both A. P. Hill and Richard S. Ewell at different times during the Overland campaign before receiving permanent charge of Ewell's Second Corps in late May. Soon deployed to the Shenandoah Valley, he crafted a series of successes in June and July that opened a second front in the Virginia theater, brought him to the gates of Washington, and compared favorably to Stonewall Jackson's accomplishments in the Valley during the spring of 1862. The second phase of the 1864 Valley campaign, during which Early faced a far more powerful U.S. Army led by the talented and confident Philip H. Sheridan, closed with three disasters in the battles of Third Winchester, Fisher's Hill, and Cedar Creek in September and October. Left with a skeleton force in the Valley after Cedar Creek, Early lingered in command until early March 1865, when Lee, with gentle reassurances of his continued admiration, removed him. Although he ended the war on a distinctly sour note, Early had demonstrated a capacity for independent command superior to that of Longstreet and in some ways equal to that of Jackson. No former Confederate would be more active as a postwar controversialist than Early, who did much to shape the Lost Cause interpretation of the conflict.

## Outline

I. Lee judged Early's capacity for higher responsibility between the autumn of 1863 and the summer of 1864.

    A. Early stood in for Richard S. Ewell at the head of Jackson's old Second Corps during the Mine Run campaign of late 1863.

    B. Early led the Third Corps at Spotsylvania when A. P. Hill fell ill.

    C. Early permanently replaced Ewell in charge of the Second Corps in late May 1864.

       **1.** Ewell bitterly resented losing his command and held a grudge against Early.

       **2.** Early denied any role in ousting Ewell but clearly believed himself competent to lead a corps.

  **D.** Early commanded the Second Corps at Cold Harbor.

**II.** Early's most important Civil War service began with the first phase of the 1864 Shenandoah Valley campaign in June–July.

  **A.** Lee detached Early from the Army of Northern Virginia and gave him a range of goals.

       **1.** He was to defeat a Union army closing in on Lynchburg.

       **2.** He was to clear the Shenandoah Valley of U.S. forces.

       **3.** He was to cross the Potomac River and threaten Washington if possible.

  **B.** Early accomplished all Lee asked.

       **1.** He bested a group of minimally talented Federal opponents.

       **2.** He won the battle of the Monocacy on July 9, 1864, and marched to within cannon range of the U.S. capital.

       **3.** His successes depressed morale in the United States.

       **4.** Ulysses S. Grant had weakened his army to reinforce Washington's defenders at Lincoln's request.

       **5.** Early had done about as well as had Jackson in 1862.

**III.** A second phase of the 1864 Valley campaign ended with Early's shattering defeat.

  **A.** Grant placed Philip Sheridan in command of an army of more than 40,000 with which to defeat Early's 15,000-man Army of the Valley and destroy the logistical bounty of the Shenandoah.

  **B.** Early maneuvered successfully in the lower Valley from mid-July to mid-September.

  **C.** The climactic phase of the fighting in the Valley unfolded between September 19 and October 19.

       **1.** Early lost the battle of Third Winchester on September 19.

       **2.** Early lost the battle of Fisher's Hill on September 22.

       **3.** Sheridan systematically wrecked much of the Valley's economy after Fisher's Hill.

       **4.** Early's dazzling surprise attack gained initial success at the battle of Cedar Creek on October 19, but Sheridan mounted a smashing counterattack.

    **5.** In 1864, Sheridan took more than 15,000 casualties; there were approximately 12,000 in Early's army.

  **D.** Lee recalled most of Early's small army to the Richmond front before the end of 1864.

  **E.** A final defeat at Waynesboro during the first week in March 1865 prompted Lee to remove Early from command.

**IV.** Early's record as a corps commander in Lee's army was exceeded only by Jackson's and Longstreet's, and only Stonewall outshone Early in independent operations.

**Essential Reading:**

Freeman, *Lee's Lieutenants*, vol. 3, chapters 6, 15, 22, 26, 29–30.

Gallagher, *Lee and His Army in Confederate History*, chapter 8.

————, *Lee and His Generals in War and Memory*, chapters 9–10.

**Supplementary Reading:**

Early, *Autobiographical Sketch and Narrative of the War between the States*, chapters 27–50.

Osborne, *Jubal: The Life and Times of Gen. Jubal A. Early, C.S.A., Defender of the Lost Cause*, chapters 14–24.

**Questions to Consider:**

1. Where should Early's Valley campaign rank among accomplishments by Lee's subordinates?

2. Should Lee have removed Early from command sooner?

# Lecture Eleven—Transcript
## Early's Path to Defeat

The second of our lectures on Jubal Early traces his trajectory in the operations in 1864-65, a period during which he justified Lee's confidence in his abilities yet suffered a series a defeats that eventually brought his removal from command. He stood in for both A. P. Hill and Richard S. Ewell at different times during the Overland campaign before receiving permanent charge of Ewell's Second Corps in late May. Soon deployed to the Shenandoah Valley, he crafted a series of successes in June and July that opened a second front in the Virginia theater, brought his small army to the gates of Washington, and compared very favorably to Stonewall Jackson's accomplishments in the Valley during the spring of 1862. The second phase of the 1864 Valley campaign, during which Early faced a far more powerful United States army led by the talented and confident Philip H. Sheridan, closed with three disasters for Early in the battles of Third Winchester, Fisher's Hill, and Cedar Creek in September and October. Left with a skeleton force in the Valley after Cedar Creek, Early lingered in command until early March 1865, when Lee, with gentle reassurances of his continued admiration, removed him. Although he ended the war on a distinctly sour note, Early had demonstrated a capacity for independent command superior to that of Longstreet and in some ways equal to that of Jackson. No former Confederate would be more active as a postwar controversialist than Early, who did much to shape the Lost Cause interpretation of the conflict. We'll talk more about that later in the course.

Robert E. Lee judged Early's capacity for higher responsibility between the autumn of 1863 and the summer of 1864. Early replaced Richard S. Ewell at the head of Jackson's old Second Corps during the Mine Run campaign in late 1863. Ewell's health was very uncertain. He had problems with the stump of the leg that had been amputated when he was wounded during the campaign of Second Manassas, and he had to step down from command more than once. Early took his place. Lee also during this period, I think, had doubts about Richard Ewell as a corps commander arising from Ewell's performance at Gettysburg. We'll talk more about that later as well.

Early led the Third Corps at Spotsylvania, A. P. Hill's corps at Spotsylvania because Hill was incapacitated by sickness at critical moments in May of 1864. It seemed as the campaign heated up, A. P. Hill's health became more and more fragile, and Lee would put Jubal Early in temporary command of the Third Corps at more than one point in May. The campaign between Grant and Lee began at the Wilderness, as we've seen, and Jubal Early didn't distinguish himself in the Wilderness. In fact, he was involved in a slight controversy there. There was an opportunity at the end of the first day's fighting in the Wilderness, on May the 6, to launch a flanking attack against Grant's right. John Gordon, a young officer, someone we're going to spend a good deal of time on a little later in the course, Gordon said that he'd found an opening to strike the Federals and he urged Ewell, who commanded the Second Corps, to order it. Jubal Early, who was a division commander in that corps and Gordon's superior, said he didn't think it was a good idea to make this flank attack, and there was some back and forth between Early and Gordon. In the end, the flank attack was launched, and it was successful, but it would have been much more successful if it had been launched earlier. Now, Lee held Ewell primarily responsible for the failure to accomplish more there even though Early had been the one who had argued most strenuously against it. Lee reasoned that Early was the division commander, Ewell the corps commander, the final choice as to whether to do this or not lay with Ewell. So it isn't a major negative that's placed beside Early's name over this episode, although he's right at the center of it. I think it's really a larger negative placed beside Ewell's name on the part of Robert E. Lee. But, the main point here is that when anything was going wrong with a corps commander between autumn of 1863 and the first part of the Overland campaign, Lee was turning to Jubal Early as someone capable of standing in for the men, Ewell and Hill, who commanded the Second and Third Corps. Ewell stepped down, didn't really step down, was eased out of the army at the end of May 1864, and Jubal Early replaced him permanently as the head of Stonewall Jackson's old command. Early was promoted to lieutenant general on May 31.

Ewell bitterly resented losing his command and he held a grudge against Early. He believed that Early had maneuvered and schemed to take this command away from him. The two had been very close for the early part of the war. Ewell had been very supportive of Jubal Early at almost every stage of the conflict down to May of 1864. He'd tried to get Early promoted on more than one occasion. He in every way had been a very good friend and superior to Jubal Early. Early outwardly had been a very good friend of Ewell's as well, and had spoken well of Ewell, but now Ewell thought that Early had wanted his command, had coveted his command. Ewell must have known, as almost everyone did, that Early was a very ambitious man and a man who believed that he was very talented, there was no question about that, and Ewell blamed Early for this. A member of Ewell's staff, a man named

Campbell Brown who was actually Ewell's stepson, kept a famous journal, and in that journal he just pours out his enormous anger against Jubal Early. At one point he wrote that, Campbell Brown stayed at headquarters even when Ewell left and he was watching Early at one point, and he said that Early looked like a "sheep-stealing dog" as he moved around headquarters, someone who had stolen this command from Richard Ewell.

Early tried to persuade Ewell that he hadn't stolen the command. He wrote him a letter, he said, "I wish to say to you General that in the arrangement that has been made by which I'm given the corps, I've had no agency directly or indirectly, either by procurement or suggestion. I assure you General that I should regret excessively if any misunderstanding between ourselves should result." Well, this letter had no effect whatsoever. Ewell remained bitter. He and Jubal Early never spoke to each other again after June of 1864. But, Early is in command, Ewell is out, and the main reason is that Robert E. Lee believed that Jubal Early was more competent to lead the Second Corps than was Richard Ewell.

Early certainly believed he was competent to lead a corps. There is absolutely no question about that, and here he is in the command where he'd made his reputation as a brigade commander and then a division commander, under Stonewall Jackson, and then under Richard Ewell. In that famous old command he'd made his name, and now he was going to see whether he would add to his laurels at the head of that command.

His most important Civil War service, by far, would come in the Shenandoah Valley, in a campaign that would stretch from mid-June 1864 to late October 1864, and would really break down into two distinct phases. The first phase of the Shenandoah Valley campaign was played out in June and July. It began just as Ulysses S. Grant was moving across the James River in the grand strategic move that would bring him to Petersburg and would lead to the siege of Petersburg. So, while Grant is doing that, while you're heading toward a period in the eastern theater, on the Richmond Petersburg front, where the armies are going to be immobile in their trenches, you're moving toward a period at the same time in the Shenandoah Valley where there's going to be great movement. There's going to be an enormous contrast between the nature of the war on the Richmond and Petersburg front and the nature of the war carried out by Jubal Early and his opponents in the Shenandoah Valley.

Lee detached Early from the Army of Northern Virginia, gave him his orders on June 12. Early and the Second Corps left the army the next day, on the

13$^{th}$, and Lee had a range of goals for Jubal Early. He expects a lot from Early, and it's a measure of his confidence in Early that he thinks he can accomplish all of these things, or hopes that he can. It's also a clear indication that at this point of the war, with James Longstreet wounded in the Wilderness, and therefore out of the army, at least for the time being, at this point Lee believed that Jubal Early was his best corps commander, the only corps commander he had who might be able to operate in this semi-independent, or really independent, fashion that this campaign would require.

This is what Lee wanted Early to do first, the most important thing, he was to march toward Lynchburg, Virginia, an important center for communications and transportation, a canal went there, railroads came there, there were large hospital complexes situated there, supply depots, and so forth. There was a United States army bearing down on Lynchburg, and Lee believed it crucial that Lynchburg be protected. That's the first thing that Early's supposed to do. Make sure that a Federal army, this army under David Hunter, did not get to Lynchburg. Grant had been casting his eye toward the Shenandoah Valley throughout his planning in early 1864, and an initial Federal effort in the Valley commanded by an officer named Franz Sigel had ended in a little battle at New Market with a Confederate victory. The United States army had retreated. After Sigel's failure, Grant had tried again with a general named David Hunter, and Hunter had moved up the Valley, he'd gotten all the way to Lexington, he'd burned the Virginia Military Institute and some other buildings, and was now closing in on Lynchburg. So, the first thing that Early is to do is to make sure that Hunter doesn't get into Lynchburg.

If he is successful at that, Lee said, then he wanted him to march northward down the Shenandoah Valley and clear the whole valley of Federals. Make sure that that great granary of the Confederacy of Virginia would be free of a major United States presence. So that's a second goal, Lynchburg, clear the Valley. If he managed to clear the Valley, Lee wanted him to cross the Potomac River and in some way threaten Washington, try to convince Grant and the United States leaders in Washington that the threat was so important that Grant would have to deploy forces then at Petersburg and Richmond to defend the United States capital.

It's an amazing array of goals that Lee gives Early when you really think about it. Early's force is going to number fewer than 15,000 men, and Lee expects a great deal of his cranky lieutenant here. He wants him to accomplish all of this.

Jubal Early christened his little force the "Army of the Valley" and he set about absolutely fulfilling every part of this blueprint that Lee had placed in front of him. The first thing that he did was march off, to put his men—they moved partly by train and partly by foot—toward Lynchburg. They reached Lynchburg on June 17, and there was a little clash with the vanguard of Hunter's army as it approached Lynchburg, and the Confederates prevailed. There was a great scene where Jubal Early rode right out to the front, place his horse in between a couple of Confederate cannons as the Federals were approaching Lynchburg, and his profanity came out here, raised himself up in the stirrups—he didn't think much of Confederate cavalry, Early didn't, he was always at war with the cavalry, he thought they didn't fight, that all they did was steal things from Confederate civilians. He thought that's what they were best at, they would sort of maraud around the countryside and take things from civilians. He called them "buttermilk rangers," that's what he called his cavalry. There had been some cavalry and a motley array of horses in Lynchburg before these veterans under Early arrived. Anyway, Early rode out to the edge of town, right to the front lines, raised himself up in the stirrups on his horse, and shook his fist at the Federals who were coming, and said, "These are no buttermilk rangers in front of you now, you goddamned blue bucks." Many of the men around him found that sort of humorous. It gives us a key as to what kinds of oaths he might have used in different situations. Here things are going very well and he said that, I'd love to hear what he said when things weren't going well. It might have been quite spectacular cursing.

At any rate, Hunter withdrew from Lynchburg, didn't even really get into a major fight, withdrew all the way into the wilds of western Virginia and was out of the war, basically, for several weeks. So, Early had accomplished the first thing that Lee wanted him to accomplish. Lynchburg was safe. He then proceeded to the second step, and that is to march through the Valley toward the Potomac River, and he did that very expeditiously. All the way to the Potomac, cleared Federals out of the Valley, and crossed the Potomac River, swung up across South Mountain and across the Coshoctons, and came southward, then, through Frederick, Maryland. And on July 9, 1864, fought a battle just outside Frederick right along the Monocacy River. The battle of the Monocacy, in which he defeated a small Union army under a general named Lou Wallace who was not a good general. Wallace wasn't a good novelist either. He wrote *Ben Hur* later, that's probably what he's most famous for. Not a good novelist, but a worse general than he was a novelist even. Early triumphed over him on the 9th and the way to Washington was open.

It was really hot that July in that part of Maryland. It was a very exhausting march, but by or within two days after the battle of the Monocacy, Jubal Early's little Army of the Valley was right opposite the northern ring of defenses of Washington D.C. Through their field glasses the Confederate officers could see the United States Capitol. It was the closest any major confederate force came to the United States Capitol during the entire war. Abraham Lincoln rode out into the defenses at Fort Stevens to observe the skirmishing. In the famous incident there when Oliver Wendell Holmes, who was a junior officer in the United States army at that point, looked, saw the president, there were minié balls clipping around the works there, and he told him to "get down, you damned fool," Holmes did. Lincoln was amused by that.

The point is that Jubal Early had done everything that he had been asked to do by Robert E. Lee. Grant had deployed part of the Union's 6$^{th}$ Corps to help defend Washington. Early knew that he couldn't get into the Federal capital, the defenses were far too strong to do that. He skirmished for a little while outside the city and then withdrew to the lower Shenandoah Valley. As he was gong back, as the Confederate army was disengaging, his little Army of the Valley was disengaging outside Washington, Early turned to one of his staff officers and said, "Major, we haven't taken Washington, but we've scared Abe Lincoln like hell." There was some truth to that. Early's movement caught the Northern public by surprise. They had been very confident as Grant began his Overland campaign that the war was going to be over quickly. They finally had their champion in the east to vanquish this Confederate Lee that no one had been able to beat. Then the Overland campaign unfolded, far bloodier, far less decisive than the United States citizenry had expected, and now this—a Rebel army right outside the United States capital, shelling the works of the United States capital in July of 1864. No one had expected it. It had a very depressive effect on morale in the United States.

This really did panic Lincoln a little bit. Lincoln hadn't been panicked by Jackson's Valley campaign, but as Early approached Washington, Lincoln actually asked Ulysses S. Grant to bring the bulk of the Army of the Potomac back to the United States capital to protect it. Grant, to his credit, said, "Mr. President, I don't think that would be a good idea. It would send the wrong signal to the Rebels, that we've disengaged from this major campaign that we've been slugging our way through in order to get to the Confederate capital. I'll send some strength to Washington, but I'm going to keep my focus here at Richmond and Petersburg."

Early had done a great deal, he had done a great deal. I think in almost every way this campaign of Early's between June and mid-July compares very favorably to what Stonewall Jackson had accomplished in the Valley. Early had moved as rapidly, he had defeated minimally talented Union opponents such as Hunter and Lou Wallace, just as Jackson had defeated people such as Banks and Frémont and so forth. If this had been the end of the 1864 Valley campaign, if there had been no second phase, I think Jubal Early's reputation would have been much larger after the war than what it was. But there was a second phase to the campaign, and that second phase ended with Jubal Early's shattering defeat.

While Early was back in the lower Valley, that is the northern extent of the Valley near the Potomac River, after he withdrew from Washington, he continued to move around, to maneuver. He would go up to the river and then drop back. He threatened the Baltimore and Ohio railroad which dipped down toward the Potomac there, and was a major lifeline in the United States, a great deal of concern about its being safe on the part of the Federal planners. He won the Second Battle of Kernstown in July. Part of his cavalry burned Chambersburg, Pennsylvania late in July. Early took great delight in that. He said it was retribution for what the Federals under Hunter had done in the Shenandoah Valley.

Ulysses S. Grant watched all of that, he watched Sigel fail in the Valley, he watched Hunter fail in the Valley, and now he watched Jubal Early threaten the United States Capitol, threaten the Baltimore and Ohio Railroad, burn a Pennsylvania city, and he had had enough. He decided that he was going to allocate the resources necessary to end this Rebel venture in the Shenandoah Valley. He selected one of his ablest lieutenants, Philip Henry Sheridan, who had come east with Grant from the western theater when Grant came east, put him in command of an army that eventually would grow to more than 40,000 men, and told him, "I want you to do two things. I want you to wreck Jubal Early's Army in the Valley, and then I want you to lay waste to the Shenandoah Valley as an area that produces logistical support for the Confederate army. Those are the two things I want you to do." Grant was very specific about it, and in Philip Henry Sheridan he had a man who was capable of carrying out those orders.

But Sheridan didn't get to it right away. The whole month of August went by with Sheridan being very quiet really, and Jubal Early badly misinterpreted what was going on. He thought Sheridan was afraid to confront him. Early would try to goad Sheridan into fighting, and Sheridan didn't engage in a major battle in August because he had very specific orders from his superiors in Washington, his civilian superiors in Washington, not to risk a battle with Jubal Early that might not be a success. "We cannot countenance another failure in this front," said Secretary of War Edward Stanton, "so don't risk anything, don't get this going," Sheridan's superior said, "until you're sure that you will be successful." So, all of August went by, the first half of September went by, and Jubal Early's disdain for Philip Sheridan grew and grew and grew. He believed he was up against an opponent who was afraid to fight him. He believed he was up against an opponent who would be malleable and who would not pose a serious threat to Confederate operations in this part of Virginia. He could not have been more mistaken. He was absolutely wrong, because Philip Sheridan was the antithesis of that kind of careful officer; he was the antithesis of the kind of officer that the old McClellan culture in the Army of the Potomac produced. Sheridan was as aggressive as anybody in either army in the entire war, and here he had the enormous advantage, the advantage that none of Stonewall Jackson's opponents had had in 1862, of being in complete control. Sheridan is in control, he is in control in this theater, and he has one very large army, which none of Jackson's opponents had had either. He's in control, he has a large army, he has the complete support of the general-in-chief, Ulysses S. Grant, and he got his campaign going the third week of September. On September 19, Sheridan launched what proved to be a month-long offensive that absolutely shattered Jubal Early's command and, in essence, ended the Civil War in the Shenandoah Valley.

The first clash came on September 19 in a battle that came to be called the battle of Third Winchester. Early had divided his little army, he had parts of it scattered over different sections of the Lower Valley. It was a measure of his contempt for Sheridan that he would do that. Sheridan crossed Opequon Creek, attacked the part of Early's little army that he found first, Stephen Dodson Ramseur's division, and almost wrecked it. Ramseur managed to hang on long enough for the other parts of Early's army to come up, and there was a very hard fight on the 19th. In the end, Northern numbers and especially more powerful cavalry told, and Early's army retreated on the evening of September 19, having lost the battle of Third Winchester. They retreated only to Fisher's Hill, it was the only place that Early thought he could defend. The Shenandoah Valley is quite narrow there between Massanutten Mountain on the east and the Alleghenies on the west. Sheridan attacked him again on the 22nd of September in the battle of Fisher's Hill. Again, Sheridan broke the Confederate lines and Jubal Early's army streamed away from the battlefield in disarray and retreated all the way to Rockfish Gap, far up the valley.

As Jubal Early retreated up the Valley, Philip Sheridan then began to carry out the second part of Grant's instructions. He began systematically to burn anything of value to the Confederate war effort in the Shenandoah Valley. He burned both along the Valley proper, the main Valley, Massanutten Mountain, which we've talked about before, divides the Shenandoah Valley for fifty miles between Harrisonburg and Front Royal. There's the Valley proper to the west of Massanutten and the Luray Valley, or Page Valley, the narrower one, to the east. Sheridan's troopers burned on both sides of Massanutten Mountain all the way up to Harrisonburg. This was carrying out what some historians have called Grant's strategy of exhaustion. It's happening here before it happened with Sherman in Georgia. The strategy of exhaustion says you don't have to kill your opponent's soldiers to win the war, you have to just strike at the logistical underpinnings of their war effort to defeat them. If they can't get the food they need, if they can't get the supplies they need, they can't mount an effective defense. So, striking at resources, burning barns, killing livestock, burning stores of grain and fodder, that is an effective way to get at your enemy, and that is what Philip Sheridan did. This period of the Valley campaign was called the burning by the Confederate civilians who lived in the area, and when it was over Sheridan said that even a crow crossing the Shenandoah Valley would have to carry it's own rations because there was no food to be had.

Sheridan thought the campaign was over. He thought Early had been completely whipped. He was getting ready to withdraw his army from the Valley, but Early turned and struck one more blow. He marched northward, and on October 19, 1864, delivered the most astonishing surprise attack of the entire conflict. It was a complicated affair. Sheridan's army was encamped along Cedar Creek, which is a tributary along the north fork of the Shenandoah River. Not expecting an attack, Sheridan was away from the army and Early's soldiers crossed the north fork of the Shenandoah at night, worked their way around the nose of Massanutten Mountain, crossed the river again, and got into position before dawn, just right at dawn really, to launch a surprise attack, and it was enormously successful. It was a very complicated flank attack, they were up all night making the march, far more complicated, far more daring, far more risky than Jackson's flank attack at Chancellorsville, for example. This shows Early at his audacious risk-taking best.

The Confederates got into position; there were about 15,000 of them. They were attacking a Federal army of 40,000—three corps in the Federal army—and the Confederates rout two of those three Federal corps and push the third back. It's an incredible fight in the morning, very successful. Early's soldiers ran out of energy, however, before the end of the day. Sheridan came back to the army, did a very good job of putting together a counter-attack, and by the end of the day, on October 19, the end of the battle of Cedar Creek, Early had been defeated again, defeated decisively again. The Confederates retreated southward in disarray, and that was it. This was the end of major fighting in the Valley. Third Winchester, Fisher's Hill, and Cedar Creek—three unequivocal defeats for Jubal Early in the Valley. Three hard fights, three defeats.

It had been a campaign fought on a scale much larger than that of Jackson's in 1862. It's worth just a quick comparative look. Early's soldiers, according to Jed Hotchkiss, a very careful engineering officer, topographical engineer on the staff of Early who also had been on Ewell's staff, also been on Jackson's staff, one of the brilliant staff officers in all of the Army of Northern Virginia. By his careful reckoning, Jubal Early's soldiers had marched more than sixteen hundred miles during their campaign in the Valley. They had fought far more battles and skirmishes than Jackson's troops had in '62. They'd marched about three times as far as Jackson's had, and the scale of the fighting in '64 dwarfed that of 1862. We've talked before about casualties in '62, there were about 5,500 U.S. casualties and about 2,750 Confederate casualties in all of Jackson's Valley campaign battles and skirmished put together. In 1864 Sheridan suffered more than 15,000 casualties and Jubal Early's army more than 10,000. The battle of Third Winchester, and again at the battle of Cedar Creek, Sheridan's losses in each of those battles, not in the two put together, in each of those battles he lost more men than the Federals lost in the entire '62 Valley campaign put together. The scale is greater.

The impact was very important as well. Sheridan's victories in the Valley, together with Sherman's capture of Atlanta, which had come the first week in September, reelected Abraham Lincoln. These two military campaigns, that turned around that very dark, depressing, pessimistic period for the United States, did come in July and August of 1864. When Lincoln thought he would not be reelected, when it looked like the Democrats were going to win, first Sherman in Atlanta, then Sheridan in the Shenandoah Valley, turned that around and reelected Lincoln.

Lee withdrew most of the troops from the Valley after Cedar Creek. John Gordon would end up commanding the bulk of the Second Corps later. Early remained in the Valley, but at the head of very few soldiers. He suffered a final defeat at Waynesboro the first week of March 1865. It really wasn't much of a battle. It was on March 2. Jubal Early and a handful of men were overwhelmed by a more powerful Federal force. At the end of that fight, Early and literally a handful of officers and soldiers made their way eastward, across the Blue Ridge, and Early reported to Robert E. Lee's headquarters. He didn't have a command anymore. He reached there in mid-March. Lee expressed continuing confidence in Early, in his "ability, zeal and devotion to the cause." Lee wrote a very, very comforting—letter is the only thing to call it, to Early, but he also removed Early from command and sent him home to await further orders. This is a perfect example of civilian expectations effecting decisions regarding command. Lee said, in effect, the people in the Valley have no confidence in you anymore, the people in the Confederacy have no confidence in you anymore, and although I do, I believe you're still a good soldier, you're just not going to work out and I'm going to have to send you home.

Early went home, he never go another command. This is late March; Lee surrendered the second week of April, so Early doesn't participate in the surrender at Appomattox. He's back home. He doesn't have a command. He had ended the war on a very negative note.

That shouldn't obscure the fact that his record as a corps commander was exceeded only by Jackson's and Longstreet's, and in terms of his ability to operate independently, only Jackson exceeded Jubal Early in terms of his ability. Early is much better, much better, than James Longstreet, but this last phase of his career deeply tainted Early's overall record. He was a very unpopular figure at the end of the war. What people overlooked was that he had faced extremely long odds in the Valley. Even Lee admitted he had grossly underestimated Sheridan's power versus Early. He had done well, Early had, under very difficult circumstances, and then had suffered complete defeat.

We'll talk more about him as a Lost Cause writer later. But next time we will turn our attention to the only cavalryman who will be at the center of one of our lectures, and that is the colorful Jeb Stuart.

# Lecture Twelve
# "Jeb" Stuart as Soldier and Showman

**Scope:** James Ewell Brown "Jeb" Stuart earned fame as a general in Lee's army exceeded only by that of Jackson and Longstreet. Just 28 years old when the war began, Stuart was a West Point graduate who had been wounded in action on the western frontier in 1857 and had participated in the action at Harpers Ferry in October 1859 that resulted in the capture of John Brown. A cavalryman throughout his Confederate career, Stuart affected a flashy uniform that included a scarlet-lined cape, a bright yellow sash, and an ostrich plume in his hat. Those gaudy trappings should not obscure his superior record as a cavalryman whose skills at reconnaissance and screening, the crucial tasks of Civil War cavalry forces, were unexcelled on either side. He also carried out headline-catching raids in 1862 that helped boost Confederate morale at crucial times, and he led the Second Corps effectively at Chancellorsville in the wake of Stonewall Jackson's wounding. A near reverse in June 1863 at Brandy Station, the largest cavalry battle of the war, and a sub-par performance during the ensuing Gettysburg campaign stand as the only major blemishes on an otherwise fine career. When informed that Stuart had been mortally wounded at the battle of Yellow Tavern in May 1864, Lee remarked that his young lieutenant had "never brought me a piece of false information"—a high tribute for any cavalryman.

## Outline

I. Stuart spent his entire pre-Civil War career in the U.S. Army.

    **A.** He graduated from West Point in 1854, 13th in his class.

    **B.** He served in the cavalry on the western frontier in 1855–1861 and was wounded in Kansas in 1857.

    **C.** He participated in the suppression of John Brown's raid on Harpers Ferry in October 1859.

II. Stuart joined the Confederacy in May 1861 and made his mark in the first 15 months of the war.

**A.** His First Virginia Cavalry regiment launched a flashy charge at the battle of First Manassas.

**B.** He impressed Joseph E. Johnston with his skill at reconnaissance and screening during the period after First Manassas.

**C.** He achieved national prominence in mid-June 1862 with his first "ride around McClellan" during the Peninsula campaign.

    **1.** Stuart gained valuable intelligence and told Lee that McClellan's right flank wasn't well anchored.

    **2.** His accomplishment came at a time when Confederate morale needed a boost, with Richmond under attack and the western theater a disaster.

**D.** He served capably throughout the Seven Days' campaign.

    **1.** He was promoted to major general on July 25, 1862.

    **2.** Lee organized all the army's cavalry into a division under Stuart.

**III.** Stuart achieved a number of successes between July 1862 and May 1863.

**A.** He honed his skills at reconnaissance and screening during the campaigns of Second Manassas and Antietam.

**B.** His horse artillery under John Pelham played conspicuous roles in the battles of Antietam and Fredericksburg.

**C.** He rode around McClellan's army a second time in October 1862, this time in Pennsylvania.

**D.** He led the Second Corps on May 3–4 at Chancellorsville after Jackson's wounding.

    **1.** He proved to be an aggressive, effective infantry commander.

    **2.** Some officers in the army believed he should replace Jackson.

    **3.** Lee believed that Stuart was too valuable as head of the cavalry to be given command of Jackson's corps.

**IV.** Stuart's last year in the army combined successes and failures.

**A.** His darkest period came in June and July 1863.

    **1.** He almost lost the battle of Brandy Station on June 9, 1863, when he was surprised by Federal cavalry, though in the end, his men held the field.

    **2.** The battle followed a round of celebrations and grand reviews.

      **3.** Stuart suffered at the hands of some editors in Richmond.

  **B.** During yet another attempted ride around the Union army, he lost contact with Lee's army as it marched toward Pennsylvania during the Gettysburg campaign.

      **1.** His Confederate comrades and later historians have disagreed about Stuart's conduct during the campaign.

      **2.** There is no doubt Lee was disappointed in Stuart, the only time Stuart failed him during the war.

  **C.** Stuart fought well in the initial stage of the Overland campaign.

      **1.** Confederate cavalry did especially well at Spotsylvania.

      **2.** It was clear that Stuart had built a talented subordinate command.

  **D.** Stuart died of wounds received at the battle of Yellow Tavern, about five miles north of Richmond, during the second week of May 1864.

      **1.** Lee deeply lamented his death.

      **2.** Confederates across the South mourned the greatest loss of a commander in Lee's army since Jackson's death one year earlier.

**V.** Stuart combined personal dash and magnetism and solid military skills.

  **A.** He was visually the most colorful general in Lee's army.

  **B.** No cavalry commander on either side outstripped Stuart in the crucial tasks of gathering information and screening his army.

## Essential Reading:

Freeman, *Lee's Lieutenants*, vol. 1, chapters 20, 40; vol. 2, chapters 3, 18, 25, 34; vol. 3, chapters 1, 4, 11, 14, 19, 21.

## Supplementary Reading:

Thomas, *Bold Dragoon: The Life of J. E. B. Stuart.*

Thomason, *Jeb Stuart.*

## Questions to Consider:

**1.** Should Lee have given command of the Second Corps to Stuart after Chancellorsville?

**2.** Is it possible Lee's army would have achieved its great successes in 1862–1863 without Stuart's participation?

# Lecture Twelve—Transcript
## "Jeb" Stuart as Soldier and Showman

We shift from the infantry to the cavalry with this lecture as we examine James Ewell Brown Stuart, "Jeb" Stuart, the nickname formed by the initials of his first three names. Jeb Stuart earned fame as a general in Lee's army exceeded only by that of Stonewall Jackson and James Longstreet. He's one of the great figures in the Confederate pantheon. Just twenty-eight years old when the war began, Stuart was a West Point graduate who'd been wounded on the western frontier in 1857 and had participated in the action at Harpers Ferry in October 1859 that resulted in the capture, eventually the hanging, of John Brown. A cavalryman throughout his Confederate career, Stuart affected a flashy uniform that included a scarlet-lined cape, a bright yellow sash, and an ostrich plume in his hat. These gaudy trappings should not obscure his superior record as a cavalryman whose skills at reconnaissance and screening, the crucial tasks of Civil War cavalry, were unexcelled on either side. He also carried out headline-catching raids in 1862 that helped boost Confederate morale at crucial times, and he led the Second Corps, Stonewall Jackson's Second Corps, effectively at Chancellorsville in the wake of Jackson's wounding. A near reverse in June 1863 at Brandy Station, the outset of the Gettysburg campaign, and his behavior during the ensuing operations in Pennsylvania form the most problematical part of his career, of his otherwise fine career. When informed that Stuart had been mortally wounded at the battle of Yellow Tavern in May of 1864, Robert E. Lee remarked that his young lieutenant "never brought me a piece of false information"—a high tribute indeed for any cavalryman.

Jeb Stuart was born in southern Virginia down near the North Carolina border, born into a slave-holding family of significant but not really high social rank, although he was tied into the Hairston clan, that huge slave-holding family that Jubal Early was also tied into. Stuart and Early are kin in some way in that regard. He graduated from West Point in 1854; he was 13th in his class at West Point. Studying hard was never really the main object for Jeb Stuart. Jeb Stuart enjoyed life, he enjoyed life as a cadet. He was there while Robert E. Lee was superintendent, and while he was good in many of his classes he did not really excel. He won the nickname "Beauty", Beauty Stuart was his nickname in the old army, among the men with whom he went through West Point.

He became quite well known to Robert E. Lee. Lee formed a quite affectionate attachment to this young cadet from Virginia while he was superintendent of West Point. He saw a lot of Stuart, he liked Stuart while Stuart was a cadet.

Stuart went into the cavalry and served on the western frontier between 1855 and 1861. He was a second lieutenant of the mounted rifles. He was wounded in Kansas in July 1857, shot in the chest in a skirmish with some Native Americans. He happened to be in the east when John Brown and his small group of raiders took possession of the Federal installation at Harpers Ferry. Stuart went with R. E. Lee, who also happened to be in the east, out to Harpers Ferry with a small group of marines who were sent to suppress this rebellion. Stuart had known John Brown from his time in Kansas. Brown had operated in Kansas with the anti-slavery forces there. Stuart had become aware of him there, and it was Stuart who positively identified Brown as being the person holed up in the engine house at Harpers Ferry. Stuart said, "Yes it's Brown"; Stuart participated in the short action that resulted in the capture of John Brown at Harpers Ferry.

Stuart was an ardent Southern rights man. He believed in slavery, he believed in the South, and he very quickly left the United States Army as the secession crisis heated up. He joined the Confederacy in May 1861, just after his home state, Virginia, left. He'd been promoted to captain of the First Cavalry back in April, in late April, but he resigned his commission on May 14 and cast his lot with the Confederacy and went into the cavalry. He was in the cavalry first to last in his Confederate service. He was made colonel of the First Virginia Cavalry Regiment and he was present in the battle of First Manassas. He didn't play a critical role, cavalry almost never played a critical role on any real battlefield. Their hard work came before and after the battles, for the most part, not during battles. During the Civil War the presence of rifled shoulder weapons made it very hard for cavalry to be decisive on a battlefield. The infantry could shoot so far now that the infantry fire had such range that cavalry charges were a thing of the past. The horses could be shot down long before an attacking cavalry column could get at defending infantry. So, the kind of mass cavalry charges that you would have on a Napoleonic battlefield were no longer going to be workable during the Civil War. You're not expecting, if you're a Civil War army commander, you're not expecting your cavalry to play a decisive role on the battlefield.

Despite that, in this first great clash of the war at First Manassas or Bull Run, Jeb Stuart and his regiment managed to launch a little attack, a little cavalry attack, against infantry that garnered some headlines, didn't really contribute much to the outcome of the battle, but showed that he was aggressive. He also was active, somewhat active, in the pursuit of the fleeing Federals. He had a good day, in other words, as a colonel at First Manassas, and he impressed Joseph E. Johnston, the army commander along with Beauregard at First Manassas. He impressed Johnston in the wake of First Manassas with his skills at reconnaissance, carrying out the kinds of activities that cavalry were supposed to carry out. Going out and gathering intelligence, letting your army commander know where the enemy is and what the enemy might be up to. Johnston wrote in August of 1861 that Stuart "is a rare man, wonderfully endowed by nature with the qualities necessary for an officer of light cavalry. He's calm, firm, active, and enterprising."

Stuart was promoted to brigadier general in September of 1861. It helped that he had the high opinion of Joseph E. Johnston. So he's a brigadier general in the summer of 1861, even though he's a man in his late twenties. He achieved national prominence, prominence within the Confederacy and prominence, or at least an awareness, north of the Potomac among people in the United States as well during the operations outside Richmond in June of 1862, just after Robert E. Lee had taken command of the Army of Northern Virginia. He achieved that prominence with what was called his "first ride around McClellan." The situation was that McClellan's army had come within a few miles of Richmond, as we know and as we've seen. Johnston wounded at the battle of Seven Pines, Lee took command, and Lee, during the first three weeks of June was trying both to get his army together and decide how best to get at McClellan's Army of the Potomac. Lee wanted to know exactly where the flanks of the Army of the Potomac where, and that was the origin of this "ride around McClellan" by Jeb Stuart. Stuart took more than a thousand troopers. He went out to find the right flank of the United States army. He found it. He could have stopped right then and gone back and told Lee, but instead he decided to ride all the way around the Army of the Potomac and come back and tell Lee of what he had seen at the end of that. He had a real flair for the dramatic, Stuart did. Probably had some sense that this would have an impact on Confederate moral, we can't be absolutely certain about that, but, at any rate, that's what he did, took his more than a thousand troopers all the way around McClellan's army, then came back and told Lee that McClellan's right flank was in the air, it wasn't really anchored on anything. So he had carried out his intelligence gathering operation here.

Some people, at the time and later, said that he would have been better off just going out and finding where McClellan's right flank was and going right back to Lee and sharing that intelligence with Lee. As it was, say these critics, Stuart alerted McClellan that something might be up. The fact that a Confederate cavalry force had ridden all the way around his army put him on alert in a way that he would not have been put on alert if Stuart had not done that. But the benefits in terms of impact behind the lines of the Confederacy far outweighed any negative that might come in that direction of putting McClellan on alert. This was, we've talked about this before several times, it's always important to remember when things happen, what's going on behind the lines when something happens, and here we are again in June, mid-June, this operation carried out June 12–15, 1862, in mid-June. Remember, things are going very badly for the Confederacy everywhere but in the Shenandoah Valley. Jackson had just had his successes in the Shenandoah Valley, but that's the only good news. The United States is just outside Richmond, and things are horrible out in the western theater, as we've seen on more than one occasion, and news of Stuart's operation, his escapade here, whatever you want to call it, resonated with the Confederate people. Here's a great piece of news from the most sensitive theater, from the theater just outside Richmond. The armies weren't fighting here, Lee was in command, as we've seen many people didn't have high hopes for what Lee was going to do, but here was this young cavalryman. This very colorful young cavalryman has taken this body of troopers and gone all the way around the largest army of the United States. The reactions were quite dramatic behind the lines. Let me just give you a couple of those reactions.

One was from a woman named Sallie Brock Putnam who kept a very famous diary in Richmond. She said, "The *Richmond Press* teems with praises of General Stuart and his followers. Even the journals of New York do not fail to render homage to the conception and execution of this bold enterprise. It gives a fresh impetus to the cavalry service and the brilliant, dashing exploits of General Jeb Stuart and his gallant horsemen have become famous in the annals of the war."

Cate Edmondston, whom we'll quote throughout the course, the woman in eastern North Carolina, wrote on June 16, 1862, "A brilliant exploit has enlivened our army before Richmond. General Stuart with a strong force of cavalry left Richmond on a reconnaissance and made a circuit of the entire lines of the enemy. They entered in Richmond in triumph, truly a brilliant episode."

This really put Jeb Stuart on the map. He had a flair for the dramatic throughout his Civil War career. He probably did before the Civil War as well, but he did during the Civil War and this is the first real evidence of that.

He served capably during the Seven Days' campaign. He was promoted to major general on July 25, 1862, and Lee pulled together all the cavalry in his large army, placed it in one division, a cavalry division, and gave command of that cavalry division to Jeb Stuart. So here, by the end of July 1862, just a year into the war, a bit more than a year into the war, Jeb Stuart is in command of all of the cavalry in the largest army of the Confederate States. It's been quite a rapid rise for him. Lee had great confidence in Stuart and he had confidence in the cavalry Stuart led. The Confederate cavalry at this stage of the war was quite superior to the United States cavalry. This is something that has been written about by many Civil War historians. The Federal cavalry would later be as good, and by the end of the war would be better than the Confederate cavalry because they had better horses and they were better armed as the war went on. But for about the first two years of the war, Jeb Stuart's cavalry really was better than the United States cavalry. He had better horsemen, he had better junior officers—it was just more effective and he was a better officer than any of the officers that led the cavalry of the Army of the Potomac.

Lee already sensed this by the end of the Seven Days. He sensed in Stuart a lieutenant who could show great enterprise, who could get out of difficult situations by making decisions on the spot, and who could also inspirit his men. Stuart's men loved to fight and ride under him. Lee realized all of this. He also saw the characteristics in Stuart that made Stuart a great reconnaissance outpost cavalry officer. He was tireless, seemingly tireless. He could go for very long stretches without sleep. He inspired his men. As I said before, he was very aggressive, he was a brilliant horseman. He had the qualities you wanted in a cavalryman, and Lee didn't have to worry about that part of his army after the Seven Days. He was always searching for able infantry officers. As attrition took its toll there was always a question of who will take this slot or who will take that slot, but for the cavalry he found Stuart early and he knew that the cavalry was not something he would have to worry about. He had a top man in place there.

Stuart was one of the most memorable figures of the war in terms of what he looked like. He was about 5'9", that's a little more than average height during the Civil War. The average man was between 5'6" and 5'7" during the Civil War, weighed about 135 or 140 pounds. Stuart was about 5'9", weighed less than 170 pounds. He had long legs and a short torso. He looked great on horseback, everybody talked about what a great horseman he was. But the thing that was really memorable about him was his uniform, as I alluded to earlier. He had a big ostrich feather in his hat, he wore very high boots, white gauntlets, he had a sash that he always had around his waist, this scarlet lined cape, a huge very luxuriant auburn beard, and he had auburn colored hair. He was simply a very arresting figure, and he had, perhaps, the most colorful entourage of any Confederate general in Lee's army. He had a banjo player named Sweeny who went everywhere with him; he had a guy who played the bones at headquarters; and he had a group of colorful officers around him, a huge Prussian officer named Heros von Borcke who was 6'4" and added a sort of foreign touch to the headquarters. He simply was a man, Stuart, who would ride into a situation with all of this group trailing him and with his own personality and would sort of take center stage.

He's a hard-eyed soldier on the one hand, very good at what he did, and he's sort of a perpetual adolescent in some ways, craving the spotlight, craving attention, craving the approbation of Lee and his other superiors, enjoying adulation he received from civilians, especially from women. He comes as close to being a sort of movie star, or pop star, within a Civil War context as anybody who fought in the Confederacy. People would crowd around him, women would throw flowers at him, they would put garlands on his horse, and so forth, and he thrived on that, he needed that. Lee also knew about that dimension of Stuart's personality. He might have been bemused by it, but he certainly understood it, and he just accepted that as part of Stuart's persona. Stuart is a young guy, he's very good at what he does, but he also behaves in this way, and that's just the full package.

Stuart honed his skills at reconnaissance and screening during the campaigns at Second Manassas and Antietam. Lee wrote of him at Second Manassas, "During all these operations, the cavalry under General Stuart rendered most important in valuable service. It guarded the flanks of the army, protected its trains, and gave information of the enemy's movements." That passage from Lee's report defines what cavalry should do during the Civil War, and that's what Stuart did so well. Find out what the enemy is doing; prevent the enemy from finding out what your army is doing. He's brilliant at those things.

His horse artillery, under John Pelham, horse artillery differs from regular artillery in Civil War armies in that all the men in the horse artillery are mounted. The gunners are mounted; in the regular artillery the gunners walk along with the guns being pulled by horses and so forth. The horse artillery played conspicuous roles at both Antietam and Fredericksburg, helped anchor the Confederate left flank at Antietam. John Pelham was the commander of the Confederate horse artillery at this stage of the war, a very arresting young officer, very young—in his early twenties, from Alabama. Then at the battle of Fredericksburg with this huge amphitheatrical plain or setting, across which the armies were maneuvering and thousands of people could see what was happening, the Stuart horse artillery came out on the far Confederate right flank and, in effect, held up the entire Federal effort for an hour, with Pelham moving his guns first two and then one, back and forth, very dramatic, very dramatic indeed, the cavalry's horse artillery at both Antietam and at Fredericksburg.

There was a second ride around McClellan in the wake of the Antietam campaign, this time in Pennsylvania. Stuart took a larger group of horsemen, nearly two thousand of them in this instance, and headed into Pennsylvania, swept all the way around the Army of the Potomac, gathered in a number of horses, destroyed a number of things while he was in Pennsylvania, and once again garnered a number of headlines. The newspapers in the North made a great deal about this. There were woodcuts that appeared in *Harper's Weekly* and Frank Leslie's illustrated newspaper showing these Confederate troopers in Pennsylvania. There was unhappiness with McClellan at this stage of the war for not following up his victory at Antietam back in September. And here he is not only following up his victory, but the Rebel cavalry is riding all the way around his army once again. It seemed to show that the army was stationary, the Army of the Potomac is doing so little, it's so stationary, it's so lacking in aggressiveness—that a Rebel cavalry force can go all the way around it and emerge unscathed.

Once again the people behind the lines reacted very positively to this. One writer compared this exploit to Stuart's first ride around McClellan during the Richmond campaign in '62 and said, "It was not less brilliant than the grand round in June, and this was in the enemy's country." Another diarist in Richmond said, "The raid was a most brilliant affair that yielded much public property, captured or destroyed. The abolitionists are much mortified and greatly frightened," wrote this man. This was John Beauchamp Jones, the famous Rebel war clerk in Richmond who kept one of the great diaries of the war, one of the great published diaries of the war. So Stuart, again, has carried out an operation that had an impact on people behind the lines, both North and South, more important in that sense than in a strictly military sense.

He departed from his cavalry service, really, just one time in the war, and that was at the battle of Chancellorsville. After Stonewall Jackson was wounded on May the 2nd, Lee put Stuart in charge of the Second Corps. Stuart presided over the very heavy assaults on the morning of May 3, extremely hard and heavy fighting on May 3, resulted in thousands of Confederate casualties, as the two separated pieces of Lee's army tried to fight their way together at Chancellorsville. He rode up and down the line; he exposed himself to enemy fire. It was very much a hands-on leadership style that he exhibited while commanding Jackson's Second Corps at Chancellorsville, and in the end he was very successful, and Lee realized that he was successful. He proved to be quite an effective infantry commander.

Had he been named to replace Jackson, of course, he would have been promoted to lieutenant general, he was still a major general. He ended the war, or ended his life, as a major general, never was promoted to lieutenant general. He was ambitious; he probably would have liked to get that command of the Second Corps. A number of people thought he was the best man for it, including Porter Alexander. Again, this very astute critic and analyst of Confederate operations, he said that he thought that Stuart's behavior on May 3 justified Lee's giving the command to him, but Lee did not, in the end. I think the reason he didn't is because he knew how good Stuart was as the head of the cavalry, he needed someone very good at the head of the cavalry, and he believed, Lee did at this stage, that either Richard Ewell or A. P. Hill probably could be a good stand-in for Jackson. So, maybe there's somebody else who'll be good at the head of the Second Corps, I know how good Stuart is at the head of the cavalry. I believe that's Lee's thinking. So, Stuart did not get the infantry command.

His last year in the army combined successes and failures. His darkest period, Stuart's, came in June and July 1863, during the Gettysburg campaign, the preliminaries and the actual campaign itself. He almost lost the battle of Brandy Station on June 9, 1863. This was the biggest cavalry battle of the war. Nearly 20,000 cavalrymen on both sides participated in this, fought near Culpepper, Virginia. Stuart's cavalry division numbered 10,000. It's the largest command he had during the whole war, and he had held a series of reviews to show off his command. Trains full of civilians had come out and had gotten off the trains to watch mock combat carried out by Stuart's troopers. This was a sort of throwback to a sort of tournament from medieval times, and Stuart reveled in it. He held a series of balls in connection with this review or this series of reviews, and so forth. He was in all his glory in early June commanding this massive cavalry, and then, on June 9, the Federal cavalry surprised him. The one thing that should never happen to a cavalry officer is to be surprised. His job is to make sure that doesn't happen to the army. Well, it happened to Stuart in the battle of Brandy Station. The Federal cavalry pressed his troopers to the absolute limit. In the end, Stuart held the field, but just barely, and the Richmond newspapers, some of them, really went after him, said that he was puffed up with concern for his image, he'd had these balls, these mock fights, and so forth, but when the real fighting started he almost lost the battle.

It was a bad period for Stuart, and I think helped fuel his reaction, which was to try to pull off something spectacular during the Gettysburg campaign. There's been a great deal of disagreement among historians as to whether Stuart was following orders or exceeded his orders during the Gettysburg campaign. He tried to ride around the Union army again, and this time it didn't work because what happened was he moved from the western side of the Army of the Potomac, got around to the eastern side, and then the Army of the Potomac began to march northward and Stuart got caught with the Army of the Potomac between him and the Army of Northern Virginia. The result was that he was out of touch with General Lee for a good part of the early stage of the campaign. Lee didn't know what was going on. Some writers have said that Lee's orders were discretionary and Stuart was acting well within those orders. Others said that wasn't the case. I don't think any of that matters. What matters is that Stuart wasn't giving Lee the kind of information Lee needed, and Lee was disappointed in Stuart. There's no question about that. It really doesn't matter what we think about Stuart's behavior, the point is Lee thought Stuart let him down during the Gettysburg campaign. One reason the battle took place where it was was because the cavalry hadn't told Lee exactly where all of the Army of the Potomac was. The infantry sort of stumbled into a fight at Gettysburg. That wouldn't have happened had Jeb Stuart been present. Lee said after the war that "Stuart's failure to carry out his instructions forced the battle of Gettysburg," I'm quoting Lee there. "Stuart's failure to carry out his instructions forced the battle of Gettysburg." He said that in 1868. So, we can argue about it all we want, defend him, attack him, the point is Lee thought he hadn't done his job, and that really is the only time in the war when Stuart didn't carry out his functions of gathering intelligence and screening the army in the way that Lee wanted him to.

He did well in the last phase of the war. He was present during the Overland campaign and the Confederate cavalry outperformed the Federal cavalry, which was under Philip Sheridan at that stage. When Sheridan came with Grant to the Army of the Potomac, Grant made him chief of the Federal cavalry. That was his first position. He wasn't really a cavalryman, and Stuart did a better job than did Sheridan during the battle of the Wilderness and the first phase of the Spotsylvania campaign. During the battle of the Wilderness the Confederate cavalry gave Lee very good intelligence. The Federal cavalry didn't do as good a job. Grant and Meade, who was the head of the Army of the Potomac, with Grant commanding over him, they didn't have nearly as good a sense of what was going on, as did Lee. But the cavalry did its best service at the very outset of the battle of Spotsylvania. There was, in effect, a race towards Spotsylvania after the battle of the Wilderness. Spotsylvania was the next key crossroads between the Wilderness and Richmond, and whichever army got there first would be in a strong position. The Federals had the shorter route, but Confederate cavalry got in front of the Federals, part of Stuart's cavalry got in front, and slowed down the Federals enough so that the Confederate infantry was able to come up and hang on. In the course of the Spotsylvania campaign, Sheridan mounted a major raid against Richmond, 10,000 troopers or more. Stuart took part of his cavalry, interposed those troopers, about 4,500 of them, in between Sheridan and Richmond, and fought a battle at Yellow Tavern, about five miles north of Richmond, on May 11, 1864. Stuart was wounded in the stomach in that fight. He died the next day in Richmond.

Lee was very upset when he learned about this. When the note was handed to him he had other people around him, he looked up and said, "Gentlemen, we have very bad news. General Stuart has been mortally wounded." Lee paused, sort of looked away, and then looked back up and said, "He never brought me a piece of false information." Again, that's absolutely the highest tribute that an army commander could pay to a cavalry officer. That's what a cavalry officer is supposed to do, bring information. The cavalry is an intelligence-gathering arm of Civil War military forces, and Stuart excelled at that.

Later Lee said, "Among the gallant soldiers that have fallen in this war, General Stuart was second to none in valor, zeal and devotion to the cause. His achievements form a conspicuous part of the history of this army with which his name and services will forever be associated." That was a very accurate predication. That is what happened to Stuart. He is one of the great figures of the Army of Northern Virginia, along with Jackson and Longstreet.

He was mourned across the South. He's the greatest loss to the Confederate army, many people said, since the death of Stonewall Jackson almost exactly one year earlier. Stuart and Jackson had been very close. It's an odd couple if ever there was one. The dour Jackson on the one hand, essentially without humor, and the very loud and colorful and boisterous Jeb Stuart on the other hand. They did share a very profound Presbyterian faith. Stuart, for all of his showiness, was very religious. He didn't drink as Jackson didn't drink for different reasons. Jackson didn't drink because he took a drink once and liked it so much that he decided he'd better not drink anymore. That says a lot about Jackson. Stuart didn't drink because he promised his mother that he wouldn't. Stuart had a crisis at the very end when he was dying. They offered him liquor and he said that he'd promised his mother he wouldn't drink. They said, "No, really, you're going to be dead in a few minutes or a little while, and perhaps it wouldn't hurt at this stage of your life."

Stuart combined personal dash and magnetism on the one hand, and solid military skills on the other, in about equal measure. As I've said, he's visually the most colorful general in Lee's army. No cavalry commander on either side outstripped him at the crucial task of gathering information and screening the army. He's this fascinating blend of style and substance, the greatest romantic figure in the Army of Northern Virginia. Lee, as we've seen, was often presented as a romantic figure; Stuart is presented the same way only much more so. And with more reason, I would think, because he sort of cultivated that chivalric image much more than Lee would have. But he's still an excellent soldier underneath, and his loss was a great loss to the army. Lee would eventually find capable replacements in Wade Hampton and Fitzhugh Lee, but losing Stuart was still a major blow.

Well, that's our foray to the cavalry side of the Army of Northern Virginia. We'll get back to the infantry with our next lecture. We will look at Ambrose Powell Hill.

# Lecture Thirteen
# One Promotion Too Many—A. P. Hill

**Scope:** The focus in this lecture shifts to the first of two famous corps commanders who never fulfilled their early promise and stand as examples of soldiers promoted beyond their levels of competency. West Pointer Ambrose Powell Hill figured prominently in all the campaigns directed by Robert E. Lee. As the leader of the "Light Division" in the Seven Days, he showed an aggressive demeanor that sometimes bordered on the rash but often yielded rich dividends. His division mounted a memorable defense at Second Manassas and made a forced march from Harpers Ferry to the battlefield at Antietam that literally saved the day for Lee's army. Two more solid performances at the battles of Fredericksburg and Chancellorsville made Hill an obvious candidate for promotion to corps command following Jackson's death in May 1863. Lee pronounced Hill the best major general in the army and rewarded him with the new Third Corps. Hill's record at that level contained more disappointment than distinction. Often ill at critical times, he played a minor role at Gettysburg, attacked without proper preparation at Bristoe Station, and failed at the battle of the Wilderness. Lee soon discerned that he could not rely on Hill, as he had on Jackson or Longstreet, though he retained the often-fiery Virginian in command. Hill was killed in action on April 2, 1865, just a week before the surrender at Appomattox, with his glory days as a division commander in the distant past.

# Outline

**I.** Hill's antebellum career followed a typical trajectory for junior officers.

**A.** He graduated in the top third of his class at West Point in 1847.
**1.** He had been held back a year because of illness.
**2.** The delay in graduation prevented his seeing significant action in the war with Mexico.

**B.** He received various postings as a lieutenant of artillery.

**C.** He transferred to the U.S. Coastal Survey Service.

II. Hill resigned from the U.S. Army before the secession of his native Virginia and rose rapidly in the Confederate army.

   A. He entered Confederate service as colonel of the 13$^{th}$ Virginia Infantry.

   B. His highly professional demeanor and skill at drill and organization brought promotion to brigadier general before he fought in a battle.

   C. He achieved conspicuous success at the battle of Williamsburg on May 5, 1862.

      1. He was promoted to major general the same month.

      2. He was given command of the "Light Division," the largest division in the army defending Richmond.

III. Hill's actions between the Seven Days' battles and Chancellorsville won him renown as the best division commander in Lee's army.

   A. His actions at the Seven Days combined aggressiveness and impetuosity.

      1. He attacked precipitately at Mechanicsville on June 26.

      2. His soldiers suffered heavy casualties at Gaines's Mill and Frayser's Farm.

   B. His division fought a notable defensive battle at Second Manassas.

   C. A brilliant march from Harpers Ferry to Antietam on September 17, 1862, probably saved Lee's army.

   D. His division suffered a temporary reverse at Fredericksburg.

      1. Hill's defensive line was poorly drawn.

      2. The episode had no effect on Hill's reputation.

   E. His division took part in Stonewall Jackson's flank attack at Chancellorsville, but a minor wound prevented his replacing Jackson on that battlefield.

IV. Hill experienced problems with fellow generals during his time as a division commander.

   A. He quarreled with James Longstreet in the aftermath of the Seven Days.

   B. He quarreled with Jackson during the Maryland campaign.

      1. Jackson arrested Hill at one point.

      2. Lee intervened to try to diffuse the situation; only Jackson's death avoided the trial that Hill wanted.

**V.** Hill advanced to corps command when Lee reorganized the army following Jackson's death.

    **A.** Lee considered him the most talented major general in the army.

    **B.** Hill led a new Third Corps made up of elements from the First and Second Corps and units previously not with Lee's army.

**VI.** Hill compiled a disappointing record as a corps commander.

    **A.** He fumbled at Gettysburg.

        **1.** His decisions helped precipitate the battle on July 1.

        **2.** Illness caused him to disappear from action on July 2–3.

    **B.** He presided over a ghastly failure at Bristoe Station in October 1863.

        **1.** He again attacked precipitately.

        **2.** Lee expressed great disappointment with Hill's actions.

    **C.** He contributed little to the Overland campaign.

        **1.** His command gave way on May 6 at the Wilderness.

        **2.** Lee was forced to do Hill's job, as well as his own.

        **3.** Hill fell ill on several occasions.

    **D.** He suffered another rebuke from Lee at the North Anna in late May 1864.

    **E.** He rendered his best service as a corps commander during the siege of Petersburg and was killed just as the army began its retreat toward Appomattox.

## Essential Reading:

Gallagher, *Lee and His Army in Confederate History*, chapter 6.

———, *Lee and His Generals in War and Memory*, chapters 4, 8.

## Supplementary Reading:

Hassler, *A. P. Hill: Lee's Forgotten General*.

Robertson, *General A. P. Hill: The Story of a Confederate Soldier*.

## Questions to Consider:

**1.** What does Hill's career reveal about Lee's pool of possible corps commanders?

**2.** Should Hill be remembered most for his corps or division leadership?

# Lecture Thirteen—Transcript
## One Promotion Too Many—A. P. Hill

The focus in this lecture shifts to the first of two famous corps commanders who never fulfilled their early promise and who stand as examples of soldiers promoted beyond their level of competency. West Pointer Ambrose Powell Hill figured prominently in all the campaigns directed by Robert E. Lee. As the leader of the "Light Division" in the Seven Days, he showed an aggressive demeanor that sometimes bordered on the rash but often yielded rich dividends. His division mounted a memorable defense at Second Manassas and made a forced march from Harpers Ferry to the battlefield at Antietam that literally saved the day for Lee and the Army of Northern Virginia. Two more solid performances at the battles of Fredericksburg and Chancellorsville made Hill an obvious candidate for promotion to corps command following Stonewall Jackson's death in May 1863. Lee pronounced Hill the best major general in the army and rewarded him with the new Third Corps. Hill's record at that level contained more disappointment than distinction. Often ill at critical times, he played a minor role at Gettysburg, attacked without proper preparation at Bristoe Station, and failed in the battle of the Wilderness. Lee soon discerned that he could not rely on Hill as he had on either Jackson or Longstreet, though he retained the often fiery Virginian in command. Hill was killed in action on April 2, 1865, just a week before the surrender at Appomattox, with his glory days as a division commander in the distant past.

Hill is another Virginian. That has been one of the themes in this course as well. Most of the men we've looked at were Virginians. There were complaints within Lee's army among the non-Virginians that it seemed that all the great positions went to officers from Virginia. Longstreet is an exception to that, but Jackson was a Virginian, and Early a Virginian, and Jeb Stuart a Virginian, and here we have another Virginian, Ambrose Powell Hill, born in Culpepper, Virginia, in 1825. As the others we've mentioned, he came from a small slave-holding family, a quite comfortable slave-holding family financially, and, as all the others we've talked about so far, went to West Point where he graduated in the top third of his class in 1847; he was 15th. He actually should have been in the class of 1846, but he was held back a year because of illness. The delay in graduation meant that he missed out on the key action between the war with Mexico. He did go to Mexico; he was a second lieutenant of artillery. He got to Mexico, but he got there after Scott's famous campaign had been completed. He spent some time in Mexico but didn't see any significant service. He didn't win any brevets; he didn't punch the tickets the other men we've looked at were able to punch in Mexico, and it was because he came out of West Point a year late.

In fact, his entire antebellum career in the United States Army doesn't have a great deal of substance to it. He was an officer the whole time. He received various postings as a lieutenant of artillery. He later transferred to the United States Coastal Survey Service, but he didn't really do anything that stood out. He didn't fight against the Native Americans on the frontier or against Seminoles in Florida in a significant way. He didn't have any of the things on his resume that some of the officers we've looked at did have—a really quite unremarkable antebellum career.

He resigned from the United States Army before the secession of his native Virginia, and he rose very rapidly. He resigned on March 1, 1861, a full six weeks before Virginia voted to leave the Union. He entered Confederate service as a colonel of the 13th Virginia Infantry and he was posted to the lower Shenandoah Valley where his commander was Joseph E. Johnston very early in the war. His highly professional demeanor and his skill at drill and organization, rather than anything he did on any battlefield, brought his promotion to brigadier general in February 1862. He's made a brigadier general before anyone sees what he can do on a battlefield. It's an interesting illustration of the different ways that officers reached the level of general in the army in Virginia.

He first fought at the battle of Williamsburg—the first notable service that he rendered—on May 5, 1862 as part of Longstreet's division. He was praised in the reports for keeping his brigade very well in hand in that battle, a battle that was really a covering action as Johnston's army retreated up the peninsula towards Richmond. His service at Williamsburg resulted in a promotion to major general, which came on May 27, 1862. So, he's a major general with service really only in this one fairly modest battle. He was given command not just of any division, but of a division he termed a "Light Division." It's the largest in Lee's army, six full brigades. It's more than 12,000 strong during the fighting outside Richmond. In the later stages of the war that's the same size as a corps would be and it's larger, or about as large, as the Federal infantry corps at Gettysburg, for example. It's a very big division.

His actions between the Seven Days' battles in June and July 1862 and the battle of Chancellorsville won him renown as the best division commander in Lee's army. His actions at the Seven Days combine aggressiveness and impetuosity. Lee was trying to strike at McClellan, as we've seen before. McClellan had gotten his army into a position where a third of it was north of the Chickahominy River and two-thirds of it south of the Chickahominy River. Lee decided the best way to get at the Federals was to build most of his strength opposite the one third of the Federal army that was north of the river. He would smash that part of the Army of the Potomac and then turn his attention to the rest. The idea was to bring as much power to bear on FitzJohn Porter, the Federal officer commanding north of the Chickahominy. This plan resulted in the battle of Mechanicsville on the 26th of June. This was one of the instances where Stonewall Jackson didn't do his job. Jackson was supposed to come onto the field, he was a key part of Lee's plan, and as we've seen, he didn't get there. A. P. Hill was on the scene, and A. P. Hill was chafing to get into action on the 26th of June. He waited and he waited—no sign of Jackson, no sign of action. Noon came, early afternoon came and went, and finally about three o'clock, A. P. Hill couldn't stand it any longer and he attacked on his own. He didn't tell Lee what he was doing; he just went and precipitated the battle of Mechanicsville. There was heavy fighting there that day. Other Confederate units became involved, and in the end FitzJohn Porter retreated a little ways—didn't retreat to the other side of the Chickahominy, but he retreated to the area of Gaines's Mill. And there, the next day, there was another major battle. Jackson, again, late, as we've seen. A. P. Hill, again, fought, his division did, at Gaines's Mill and fought again at Frayser's Farm—very heavy action in all of these battles at Mechanicsville, Gaines's Mill, Frayser's Farm. Three of the Seven Days' battles A. P. Hill's division is heavily engaged, the first unit engaged at Mechanicsville.

Casualties during the Seven Days were very heavy for his division. Losses among his officers were very heavy. He had two colonels killed, two brigadier generals, eleven colonels and six lieutenant colonels were wounded. Hill's performance at the Seven Days, if we were going to give him a report card, would be mixed. On the positive side, from someone such as Lee who would be judging this, was the aggressiveness—that's good. Hill wants to get is men in action. Hill wants to strike a heavy blow against the enemy. But, against that aggressiveness you have to array the behavior that seems too aggressive. It was rash; it was precipitant. He'd moved in Mechanicsville in ways that he shouldn't have. You need to tell your commanding general what you're doing. You need to wait until you get orders to go into action in that situation, and A. P. Hill didn't do that. He did not do that. But Lee, on the whole, came away from the Seven Days with a positive estimate of A. P. Hill. A. P. Hill went by his middle name, he went by Powell Hill or A. P. Hill. No one called him Ambrose Hill. It was very common in the mid-19th century for men to go by their middle names, often their mother's maiden name. At any rate, Hill went by Powell. His soldiers called him "Little Powell." No one called him Ambrose as far as I know.

Hill's division mounted a notable defense at the battle of Second Manassas at the end of August. He was part of the great flanking march that Jackson made that went up and around John Pope's right flank and came in from the rear to the depot at Manassas Junction. A. P. Hill's soldiers were some of those who helped either consume or destroy or haul away that vast store of materials that the Federals had gathered there. On the 29th of August, as Pope was pressing and pressing against Jackson's line, unaware was Pope that James Longstreet was on the field. In a quite remarkable bit of obtuseness, Pope never did concede that Longstreet was on the field. He thought he was just facing Jackson. All of his attention was against Jackson, and it was very heavy attention indeed. Whatever his failings, John Pope was willing to launch heavy assaults, and he did that, and A. P. Hill's division did a very good job on the 29th of August maintaining its position on the battlefield. In one very famous episode, one of his units, having fired all of its ammunition, was reduced to throwing rocks at the attacking Federals. That's been overdone, but the point is, it's a defense in quite serious circumstances at Second Manassas—holding the line while Longstreet got in place to launch his famous and powerful attack on August 30.

A. P. Hill rendered even greater service during the Maryland campaign. In fact, he was involved in one of the most dramatic moments in the entire history of the Army of Northern Virginia. He was left behind at Harpers Ferry to see after the prisoners and all the loot that had fallen to Jackson when he captured Harpers Ferry; 12,500 United States soldiers surrendered at Harpers Ferry to Stonewall Jackson on the 15th of September. It's the largest surrender of United States soldiers until the fall of the Philippines during World War II.

A. P. Hill was left behind, and his Light Division, to oversee that while Jackson took the rest of his corps and soldiers to join Lee for the battle that would take place near Sharpsburg at Antietam. In the course of the day of the battle of Antietam, while the fighting raged between McClellan and Lee at Antietam, A. P. Hill made a heroic march to reinforce Lee from Harpers Ferry to the battlefield at Antietam. It was about seventeen miles. He left some of his division behind at Harpers Ferry, but took the bulk of it to the battlefield, and by pressing them to the absolute limit he got them there about four o'clock in the afternoon, a bit before four o'clock, and they came onto the battlefield at precisely the point where they would have the most impact.

The Federals had almost carried the day when A. P. Hill and his troops appeared. They were, literally, within about three hundred yards of taking control of the road that tied Lee to the forge over the Potomac River. If the Federals had taken control of that road, Lee's army would have been in extreme circumstances at Antietam. As it was, the whole day had unfolded as a series of near disasters for the Army of Northern Virginia. Rushing troops from his right to his left, time and again did Lee, from Longstreet's wing to Jackson's wing, to hold the line, but all of that had not been enough by the end of the day. The Federals under Ambrose Burnside were making their way inexorably toward the road that led to the Potomac forge and the Army of Northern Virginia had just about played out it's string.

Just at that moment, as if scripted by someone in Hollywood, the leading elements of A. P. Hill's division appeared on the battlefield, and they came in right on the flank of the Federals that were attacking, right at the key moment, right at the key place, and they allowed Lee's army to hang on, barely hang on, and achieve a tactical stalemate at Antietam, although it would be a strategic defeat, of course, because Lee would retreat the next day. But here Hill rendered probably the best service of his entire Confederate career.

Now, he had violated all of Stonewall Jackson's marching principles. Jackson sometimes pushed his men mercilessly, but he had an idea of how men were to march. You were to march two miles an hour, rest for ten minutes every hour, march fifty minutes, rest ten minutes, stop for lunch, and so forth. Hill did none of that as he pushed his men on this seventeen-mile march. Almost half of his men fell out of the ranks in getting from Harpers Ferry to Antietam, so hard was the pace. But in the end it paid off, and A. P. Hill did a splendid job.

His division suffered a temporary reverse at Gettysburg. His was the division that included the gap in Jackson's line. I've alluded to this a couple of times, there was a gap between a couple of A. P. Hill's brigades. The Federals made a temporary lodgment, but quite soon the line was restored. This episode didn't really have a negative effect on Hill's reputation. His division took part in Stonewall Jackson's flank attack at Chancellorsville, and Hill should have succeeded Jackson in command of the corps when Jackson was wounded on the night of May 2, but very quickly after Jackson was wounded Hill received a minor wound that prevented his taking command of the Second Corps, and, of course, in the end Jeb Stuart took that command. It should have been Hill, it wasn't because of this minor wound.

This is the end of his career as a division commander. It is on the whole a very good career, and in some ways a brilliant career, some parts of it among the best performances that any division commander had put in in the course of the war. But there were also some troubling parts of his record as a division commander, and one of the key ones was that he quarreled a lot with superiors. He had a hard time with superiors in some ways. He was a very touchy man about his personal honor and prerogatives—very, very touchy. If he perceived a slight from someone, he reacted, sometimes overreacted, very quickly. He quarreled with James Longstreet in the aftermath of the Seven Days. This drew out newspaper accounts of what their two divisions had done during the Seven Days. Longstreet was the senior major general, A. P. Hill the junior major general in this instance. Each of them thought the newspapers had not been giving full credit to their divisions, and it became quite a heated debate. At one point Longstreet ordered that Hill be arrested. R. E. Lee intervened and in his usual smooth way took care of the problem by easing A. P. Hill out from under Longstreet's authority and put him under Jackson's authority. We'll see that that didn't help in a minute, but that was the short-term resolution. One of Longstreet's staff officers described it this way, he said that:

> In the course of this discussion after the Seven Days, angry letters passed and intimate friends were called in and a hostile meeting between the two generals was almost certain. General Lee, however, heard of it and acted quickly and effectively, using his unvarying tact and great influence. He brought matters through other friends to an adjustment honorable to both Longstreet and Hill. A few days later, General Hill's division was shifted out of reach of Longstreet's command and nothing more was known of the affair.

This officer added that later on Longstreet and Hill became fairly good friends. But Hill is out from under Longstreet now; he's under Jackson. And he and Jackson got into an even worse quarrel than he and Longstreet had gotten into.

He quarreled with Jackson during the Maryland campaign. This dispute arose out of marching orders. It was really a minor point. Jackson, very rigid; Hill, very touchy, and Jackson arrested Hill at one point. Lee intervened again. Lee was very—Lee just—he basically said, "Listen, this isn't worth fighting about, General Jackson or General Hill, let's just talk about this, let's make it go away." Neither of them was willing to make it go away. Jackson rigid, Hill rigid in his own way; Hill insisted on a trial to vindicate himself. He wanted to make a point. "I will have a trial," he said. Lee, although exasperated, couldn't deny him a trial, and this whole matter was still hanging there at the time of Chancellorsville when Jackson was killed, and that was the end of it. So, there's this side of A. P. Hill, this very touchy side, that sometimes gets in the way, but, on balance, a very good division commander. Good in battle, good at taking care of his men outside of battle.

He had been advanced to corps command when Lee reorganized the army following Jackson's death. Lee considered him the most talented major general in the army. There was no question about that. As early as October 1862, Lee had written to Jefferson Davis that "next to Jackson and Longstreet," as Lee put it, "I consider A. P. Hill the best commander with me. He fights his troops well and takes good care of them." This is right after Antietam, just about six weeks after Antietam, when he wrote that. During the next spring, during the next May, when he was really forced to find a replacement for Stonewall Jackson, Lee, again, commented on A. P. Hill. He wrote to the president again. He said, "I, for the past year, felt that the corps of this army were too large for one commander." He thought that in the wooded terrain where the army maneuvered it would make sense to have smaller corps, that 30,000 men was too many men for one person to oversee in this kind of fighting. That's how many Jackson and Longstreet often commanded. Lee added, "Nothing prevented my proposing to you that we reduce their size and increase their number but my inability to recommend commanders." Now Lee had to recommend someone because Jackson was dead, and one of those he recommended was Hill. He reaffirmed his belief that Hill "was the best soldier of his grade with the army." So, again, in the fall of '62 and then again in spring of '63, Lee says the best major general I have, the best division commander I have is A. P. Hill.

Hill led a new Third Corps. Richard Ewell, as we'll see in our next lecture, was made the actual replacement for Stonewall Jackson in the Second Corps, but the commands were reshuffled and a new Third Corps created, and that corps went to A. P. Hill. It was made up of elements from the First and Second Corps, together with a few new troops that were brought to the army. So, here he is in command of the Third Corps. This is a new corps structure. The old corps structure had been in place for nearly a year with Jackson and Longstreet's commanding about half the army. Now you have a new three corps structure and it will receive its first test in the Gettysburg campaign. And A. P. Hill, from the beginning, compiled a disappointing record as a corps commander in the Army of Northern Virginia.

He fumbled at Gettysburg. His decisions helped precipitate the battle on July the 1st. We know the situation—Stuart's cavalry hadn't really been doing what it was supposed to do. Lee didn't know exactly what the situation was in front of the Army of Northern Virginia. He had ordered the concentration of the army along the eastern face of South Mountain, in the vicinity of Gettysburg, Gettysburg the cash town, and the army was coming together. Lee had issued orders not to bring on a general engagement until all of his commands were up and the army was back in one piece. A. P. Hill, on the morning of July 1, authorized one of his division commanders, Harry Heath, to take his division toward Gettysburg, to go on in and see what he could find there. That isn't what infantry divisions do; infantry divisions don't just march off to see what's ahead of them. That's what cavalry does, not infantry divisions. Now, Hill did tell Lee what he was doing—this isn't as he was in Mechanicsville. He told Lee what he was doing, and off went Harry Heath. And Heath collided with John Buford's cavalry at Gettysburg, and the battle began, as we know, July 1.

Hill oversees the action of his division, action that in the end was very successful. Although at the end of the day, when Richard Ewell said that he wanted—that he would continue the fight but needed support on his right flank, that is on Hill's end of the line, Hill said that his divisions were too fought out to fight anymore, that they had had a long day and couldn't fight anymore, and Lee, who was present with Hill, took his word for it and put the whole burden on Ewell. Part of the problem may have been that Hill was sick on the 1st of July. This would be a common occurrence for his entire tenure as a corps commander. This is the first time we see it. Arthur James Lyon Freemantle, who was a British officer, I've mentioned him before, who traveled across the Confederacy in the spring and summer, 1863, and found himself with Lee's army at Gettysburg, and left some of our most famous anecdotal accounts of the battle, saw Hill on July the 1st and wrote in his diary, "General Hill came up and told me that he had been very unwell all day, and, in fact, he looks very delicate," wrote Freemantle. He was so delicate that he essentially disappears for the rest of the battle of

Gettysburg. One of the hardest things to figure out regarding the battle of Gettysburg is what A. P. Hill is doing. It's hard even to know where he was.

On the third day, with the Pickett-Pettigrew assault, over half of the soldiers involved belonged to A. P. Hill's Third Corps, and yet Lee put James Longstreet in command of that assault. I think that says two things. It says first that Lee trusted Longstreet more than he did Hill. But it also says that Hill may have been so incapacitated physically that Lee didn't think that he was up to orchestrating this assault. So, Gettysburg is not a high point for Hill, not a good start.

He then presided over a ghastly failure at Bristoe Station in October 1863, October the 14th. Here he is back to his Mechanicsville model. He attacked without any preparation, attacked very rashly, and suffered 1,500 casualties to absolutely no purpose at Bristoe Station. Lee was very upset. Lee rode over the battleground with Hill afterward and said, "Well, well, General, bury these poor men and let us say no more about it." That is a rebuke from Robert E. Lee. Lee is not going to say, "Goddamn it Hill, you really did poorly here." To say what he said, in effect, conveys that message, however. Bury these poor men and let's don't even talk about it anymore. Jefferson Davis, in commenting about Bristoe Station, said, "There was a want of vigilance on A. P. Hill's part." So, this is twice in a row Hill hasn't done well.

The Wilderness brought more bad news for anyone who was hoping that A. P. Hill would do well. On the night of May 5, after very hard fighting, Hill decided to leave his lines, his divisions, as they were, and they were not in tremendous position. He didn't try to put together a stronger defensive line that night, and very early the next morning Winfield Scott Hancock, of course, smashed through A. P. Hill's division. Hill, and others, would say that he expected James Longstreet to relieve him that night, and he probably did, but the point is he wasn't sure Longstreet would be there and he should have taken precautions. He didn't, and his two divisions in place were routed the next morning. Lee rode into the maelstrom of the fighting at the Widow Tapp Farm and tried himself to rally these troops. Hill wasn't doing it. Lee—this was one of the instances where Lee starts behaving as an army commander and a corps commander at the same time, not a good May the 6th at the Wilderness for A. P. Hill.

During the Spotsylvania campaign Hill fell ill again. Early replaced him, we've talked about that before. This pattern—historians have speculated a great deal about exactly what was wrong with Hill. It seems that as he went up in responsibility he more often fell ill, and of course stress could be part of it, stress is critical in all kinds of illnesses. Some thought these were purely psychosomatic, some historians have. Others thought that they were residual effects from malaria that he had contracted earlier in his life. The most recent theory is it was chronic prostatitis arising from a bout of gonorrhea that Hill had had while he was a cadet at West Point. He'd gone to New York City and visited some of the prostitutes there, apparently, and had come back with gonorrhea. It's all in the medical records at West Point. No one got away with gonorrhea undetected at West Point because they were meticulous. Custer also has gonorrhea on his records at West Point. The point is, something was incapacitating Hill, and it was doing it more often than it had when he was a division commander. Lee simply couldn't rely on him.

The North Anna is another problem, this is at the end of May, and I alluded to this before. This is when Hill repulsed a Federal assault, but then didn't follow it up. This is sort of the opposite problem of what happened when he was too rash. Here he beat back a Union assault, but he didn't follow it up, and Lee was even harsher with him here than he had been at Bristoe Station. He said, "Why'd you not do as Jackson would have done, thrown your whole force upon those people and driven them back?" Lee didn't ever talk to any other corps commander during the entire war in this way, not in this way. We'll see that he had to speak very bluntly with Richard Ewell at about this same time, but it didn't have the edge that this comment to A. P. Hill had.

Hill probably rendered his best service as a corps commander during the siege at Petersburg. He seemed to rebound a bit within that framework and fight well defensively as Grant probed and extended the lines in the course of that long siege. A. P. Hill seemed to show some of his old ability within this framework of the siege of Petersburg. The army isn't out and maneuvering anymore. It maybe was a little bit better for his health that he didn't have to be quite as active, didn't have to be on the move like he did during the Gettysburg campaign or during the early stage of the Overland campaign. It is very difficult to untangle precisely how much of Hill's problems stemmed from simple inability to operate at this level, or stem from the fact that physically he really was in such poor shape that it was affecting his ability to operate as a corps commander in Lee's army. He fought right down almost to the very end of the war. As the Confederates were getting ready to abandon the lines on the Richmond-Petersburg fronts at the very beginning of April, A. P. Hill rode out toward the front, this is on April 2. There were a few Federals out in a skirt of woods near him. Hill had a single staff officer with him, and Hill was out in front of this staff officer. The Federals saw him, they shot at him, and they killed him—killed right at the very, very end of the war. Lee was very upset. It seemed such a tragic waste that this officer would die so late in the war when it was clear that the Confederacy was not going to win, but here's another corps commander killed in action.

Overall I think we must reckon A. P. Hill a failure as a corps commander, just as we have to reckon him a success as a division commander. I think that is what Lee would have said, and Lee never replaced him at the head of the Third Corps, not permanently, because there wasn't anyone available that was better. This is what we always have to keep in mind. There isn't a large group of men able to command corps just waiting over here to step in and do a good job. It's a very hard task to find someone who can look after in camp and on a battlefield this many men, and Lee simply didn't have anyone he thought made sense to step in and take A. P. Hill's place. There's no obvious replacement, and so there he is. He stays in place, he's with the army until right at the very end.

His case underscores how few men really possess the talents to command a corps. There is another man just like this, who fought through much of the war with Hill, and that was Richard S. Ewell, and we will turn our attention to Dick Ewell in our next lecture.

# Lecture Fourteen
## Forced from Center Stage—Richard S. Ewell

**Scope:** Richard Stoddert Ewell's record, like that of A. P. Hill, marked him as one who could not make the transition from division to corps command. Ewell came to the Confederate army as a West Pointer who had led dragoons on the prewar western frontier. He commanded a division with some success under Stonewall Jackson in the 1862 Shenandoah Valley campaign and in the Seven Days' battles. A severe wound in late-August 1862 at Groveton, a preliminary to the battle of Second Manassas, cost him a leg and kept him away from the army until the reorganization following Jackson's death. Although Lee had not directed Ewell except for a short period, he selected him to replace Jackson as head of the Second Corps. This decision seemed sound when Ewell performed well in the preliminary phase of the 1863 Pennsylvania campaign, but Lee rapidly lost faith in Ewell because of what he perceived, whether fairly or not, to be indecisiveness on the first day at Gettysburg. Further problems at the Wilderness and Spotsylvania convinced Lee that Ewell had to go, a difficult decision made all the harder by Ewell's insistence that he be retained in command. Exiled to command troops guarding Richmond's defenses, Ewell joined the general retreat toward Appomattox in April 1865 and was captured at the battle of Sailor's Creek.

## Outline

I.  Ewell can be accurately described as a soldier's soldier.

    **A.** He graduated in the top third of his class of 1840 at West Point.

    **B.** He won a brevet for gallantry in the war with Mexico.

    **C.** He spent the bulk of his antebellum military career on the western frontier.

        **1.** He won a reputation as an effective frontier officer and was wounded in 1859 in a skirmish with Apaches.

        **2.** The Arizona constitutional convention acknowledged Ewell's contributions by naming a territorial county for him (the name was changed when Ewell joined the Confederate cause).

**II.** Ewell achieved early success in Confederate service.

    **A.** He commanded a brigade that saw limited action at First Manassas.

    **B.** He was promoted to major general in early 1862 and assigned to Stonewall Jackson's command in the Shenandoah Valley.

    **C.** Ewell and his division played a prominent role in the Valley campaign.

        **1.** They fought at Front Royal, First Winchester, Cross Keys, and Port Republic.

        **2.** Ewell experienced decidedly mixed feelings about Jackson.

    **D.** Ewell's division remained under Jackson during the Seven Days and the campaign of Second Manassas.

        **1.** It fought at Gaines's Mill but otherwise was lightly engaged during the Seven Days.

        **2.** It fought at Cedar Mountain on August 9.

    **E.** Ewell received a serious wound at the battle of Groveton on August 28.

        **1.** His left leg was amputated.

        **2.** His career as a division commander was over.

**III.** Corps command and eventual frustration marked the remainder of Ewell's Confederate career.

    **A.** He was assigned a revamped Second Corps in the reorganization following Jackson's death.

        **1.** Lee did not know Ewell well and had some doubts about him.

        **2.** Knowledge of Jackson's high opinion of Ewell probably played a role in Lee's decision to advance Ewell.

    **B.** Ewell disappointed Lee in the Gettysburg campaign.

        **1.** He began well on the march northward and won the battle of Second Winchester in mid-June 1863.

        **2.** His decision not to attack Cemetery Hill and Culp's Hill on the evening of July 1 at Gettysburg proved to be controversial.

            **a.** Many comrades and later writers criticized him.

            **b.** Ewell had good reasons for not attacking, knowing that he lacked support on his right.

            **c.** Lee saw the failure as evidence of Ewell's tendency to vacillate at moments of crisis.

            **d.** Ewell suffered from invidious comparisons to Jackson.

**C.** Ewell fell ill during the winter of 1863–1864.

**D.** Lee removed Ewell from the army during the Overland campaign.

  **1.** He believed Ewell lost his composure twice at Spotsylvania, on May 12 and May 19.

  **2.** He tried to ease Ewell out of the army because of his fragile health.

  **3.** Ewell forced Lee to be more blunt and tell him that he was no longer capable of field command.

  **4.** Ewell did not fit Lee's model of an aggressive, self-reliant corps commander.

**IV.** Ewell remained in service to the end of the war.

  **A.** He commanded the Richmond defenses by leading the local home guard.

  **B.** He was captured at the battle of Sailor's Creek during the retreat to Appomattox.

### Essential Reading:

Freeman, *Lee's Lieutenants*, vol. 1, chapter 23; vol. 2, chapter 6; vol. 3, chapters 2, 6, 9, 20, 22, 35.

Gallagher, *Lee and His Army in Confederate History*, chapter 6.

————, *Lee and His Generals in War and Memory*, chapters 4, 8.

### Supplementary Reading:

Hamlin, ed., *The Making of a Soldier: Letters of General R. S. Ewell.*

Pfanz, *Richard S. Ewell: A Soldier's Life.*

### Questions to Consider:

**1.** Did Ewell make a substantial contribution to the success of Lee's army?

**2.** Did Ewell make reasonable decisions on the first day at Gettysburg?

# Lecture Fourteen—Transcript
## Forced from Center Stage—Richard S. Ewell

Our next lecture will consider Richard Stoddert Ewell, whose record, like that of A. P. Hill, marked him as one who could not make the transition from division to corps command. Ewell came to the Confederate army as a West Pointer who had led dragoons on the prewar western frontier. He commanded a division with some success under Stonewall Jackson in the 1862 Shenandoah Valley campaign, as well as in the Seven Days' battles. A severe wound in late-August 1862 at Groveton, a preliminary to the battle of Second Manassas, cost him a leg and kept him away from the army until the reorganization following Jackson's death. Although Lee had not directed Ewell except for a short period, he selected him to replace Jackson as head of the Second Corps. This decision seemed sound when Ewell performed well in the preliminary phase of the 1863 Pennsylvania campaign, but Lee rapidly lost faith in Ewell because of what he perceived, whether fairly or not, to be indecisiveness on the first day at Gettysburg. Further problems at the Wilderness and Spotsylvania convinced Lee that Ewell had to go, a difficult decision made all the harder by Ewell's insistence that he be retained in command. Exiled to lead troops guarding Richmond's defenses, Ewell joined the general retreat toward Appomattox in April 1865 and was captured at the battle of Sailor's Creek.

Ewell can be described, I think, quite accurately as a soldier's soldier. He was born in Georgetown, District of Columbia, in 1817. He went off to West Point where he graduated in the top third of his class in 1840. He went into the dragoons, was promoted to first lieutenant in 1845, and participated in the war with Mexico. He won a brevet for gallantry to the rank of captain at Churubusco and Contreras with Winfield Scott's army, as so many of the officers we're looking at were. He spent the bulk of his antebellum career out on the western frontier, and especially on the southwestern frontier. He was often ill while he was there; he perhaps had malaria, we're not sure, but he took to a habit of eating a very bland diet. He suffered from a very nervous stomach, loose bowels, and other ailments, physical ailments, that began when he was a fairly young man and continued on through his entire life. It's a problem very much during the war, but it was there before the war.

He was a captain of dragoons by 1849 and he won a reputation as a very effective frontier officer. He really was in his milieu many times out in the southwest. Many times later in life he would recall very fondly his service in the southwestern area of the United States, the Arizona territory, which is where he spent a good deal of time, and a number of his contemporaries who served with him during the Civil War commented on this. Richard Taylor, for example, the son of Zachary Taylor, who wrote perhaps the most literate of the Confederate memoirs. It's almost too self-consciously literate, straining with illusions to various works of literature from the past. But Dick Taylor had a good eye for people, and he said that Ewell's whole military life had been passed on the plains where, as he often asserted, he had "learned all about commanding fifty United States dragoons, and forgotten everything else." In this he did himself injustice, said Taylor, as his career proves, but he was of a singular modesty.

He also had a great sense of humor, Ewell did. If you read Ewell's letters from the prewar and wartime years you often get a Mark Twain-like quality as you go through, a very nice eye for the ridiculous and a nice turn of phrase. Another soldier who knew him during the war said that Ewell "served with distinction in Mexico and all his life against Indians. He was without a superior as a cavalry captain and a most extraordinary person in some ways."

He did such a good job in Arizona that the Arizona constitutional convention named a territorial county after Ewell before the war. They changed the name when Ewell joined the Confederacy, but for a brief time Dick Ewell had a county named after him. He was wounded in 1859 in a skirmish with the Apaches. He found army life satisfying. He liked frontier life; he did a good job before the war as a frontier officer.

He resigned from the United States Army in early May 1861. He was a brigadier general in the Confederacy in mid-June 1981. He commanded a brigade at First Manassas, but didn't see much action there. Nonetheless, promoted to major general in 1862 and assigned to Stonewall Jackson's command in the Shenandoah Valley, and here began a very important association between Ewell and Stonewall Jackson. Ewell would make his reputation under Stonewall Jackson. He would have a sort of love/hate relationship with General Jackson, especially early on, in many ways. His division, Ewell's division, played a prominent role in the Valley campaign in 1862. This is his real entrance onto the Civil War stage, this is where he steps out from the shadows, so to speak, and begins to carve a record that brings him to the attention of people who are ranking officers throughout the Confederacy, both fellow soldiers and politicians in Richmond.

He is a very odd-looking man, there's no question about it, odd-looking not only in his physical features, but also in his personal habits. A number of people commented on that. Dick Taylor provided an absolutely devastating portrait of him that I think has had a significant effect on how subsequent generations of historians and other writers dealt with Ewell. They haven't dealt with him as seriously as they might because of the sort of comical portrait that Dick Taylor offered of Dick Ewell. Let me read what Dick Taylor wrote about him. They fought together under Jackson in the Valley campaign. Taylor wrote that Ewell:

> had bright, prominent eyes, a bomb-shaped, bald head, and a nose like that of Francis of Valois, which gave him a striking resemblance to a woodcock. This was increased by a bird-like habit of putting his head on one side to utter his quaint speeches. He fancied that he had some mysterious internal malady, and would eat nothing but a preparation of wheat, and his plaintive way of talking of his disease, as if he were someone else, was droll in the extreme. His nervousness prevented him from taking regular sleep, and he passed nights curled around a campstool in positions to dislocate an ordinary person's joints. On such occasions, after a long silence, he would suddenly direct his eyes and nose at me with, "General Taylor! What do you suppose President Davis made me a major general for?"–beginning with a sharp accent and ending with a gentle lisp.

Well, that's the character, according to Dick Taylor, and others have presented a quite similar portrait of Richard Ewell. I'll quote one more, Moxley Sorrell, the staff officer on James Longstreet's headquarters, he said, "Ewell was bald as an eagle and he looked like one, had a piercing eye and a lisping speech. A perfect horseman and lover of horses, especially race horses, he never tired of talking of his horse, Tangent, in Texas, who appears never to have one a race, and always to have lost his owner's money, but the latter's confidence never weakened, and he always believed in Tangent." That is Dick Ewell. Sometimes it's hard to get beyond these descriptions of Dick Ewell as a quasi-comical figure to get at the soldier.

As a soldier under Jackson, he fought at Front Royal, at First Winchester, and at Cross Keys at Port Republic during the Valley campaign. As we've seen, these are all small battles, not a large battle at all, but Ewell is in the thick of things and on the whole doing a very good job and gaining the approbation of the stern Stonewall Jackson. Not heavy casualties, but good work on the whole. In the course of this campaign, Ewell was often frustrated by Jackson; Jackson wouldn't tell him what was going on. We've talked about this. This was an element of Jackson's military personality. Ewell would be told to do things that didn't make sense to him. If Jackson had told him why he wanted him to do them, I think Ewell would have been in a better frame of mind, but he often was in the dark and he would rail against Jackson to Dick Taylor and to others who might be close by to hear. Taylor wrote, "He always spoke of Jackson, several years his junior, as old, and told me in confidence that he admired his genius but was certain of his lunacy, and that he never saw one of Jackson's couriers approach without expecting an order to assault the North Pole." That is Ewell serving under Jackson, sort of kept off balance by Jackson—admired him, exasperated by him, but emerging from the Valley campaign, like Jackson, with a much-enhanced reputation.

His division remained under Jackson during the Seven Days and Second Manassas campaigns. Ewell fought at Gaines's Mill, but otherwise was lightly engaged in the Seven Days, partly because he's under Jackson. Jackson is never doing what he's supposed to be doing during the Seven Days. His division also fought at Cedar Mountain during the early stage of the Second Manassas campaign. He was very praise worthy of Jubal Early at Cedar Mountain. I mentioned before that he looked after Jubal Early, tried to see that Jubal Early was advanced, sort of took Jubal Early under his wing. He's senior to Early at this stage of the war, very generous to him. He is a generous man. Almost no one dislikes Richard Stoddert Ewell, Dick Ewell as his men called him. Almost no one disliked him. He is a very attractive personality in terms of his generosity, his willingness to share credit, his self-deprecating qualities—very, very attractive in those ways, and very willing to share the limelight with others and to put others forward, to make sure that they get their full measure of credit, even if it meant a somewhat diminished measure of credit for himself. He's a real contrast to Jubal Early, for example, in that regard; a contrast to James Longstreet in that regard. Stonewall Jackson just floated above that whole notion. He couldn't care less what anybody was saying about anything. In the end God would decide whether you burned forever or went to heaven, and that's what mattered to Jackson. Let the others worry about reputations on the battlefield. Ewell much less concerned about that than any of those he fought with.

He did a good job at Cedar Mountain, but in the next phase of the Second Manassas campaign he was grievously wounded. After Jackson had moved up around Pope's flank and destroyed the depot at Manassas Junction, he took up an offensive position near the old Manassas battlefield, inviting the Federals to attack him so that they would be set in place for Lee to come up with the rest of the army. That is what the battle of Groveton on the 29<sup>th</sup> of August consisted of. Show yourself to the enemy, from a Confederate perspective, suck them into a battle, and fix them there until the whole army can be up. Richard Ewell was in the middle of that battle, when in the course of it received a horrible wound in his left leg, and his left leg had to be amputated as a result of that. His career as a division commander was over. It was a long and painful recuperation for Richard Ewell. He missed the rest of the Second Manassas campaign, obviously, he didn't take part in the Maryland campaign, he didn't take part in the Fredericksburg campaign, he wasn't even back in time for Chancellorsville. It is a long and difficult recuperation. He comes back into the scene, he comes back onto our radar screen, in the wake of Jackson's wounding, when he comes in promoted to lieutenant general and takes command of the Second Corps. That corps command and a great deal of frustration would mark the rest of Richard Ewell's career as a Confederate soldier.

He was assigned a revamped Second Corps in the reorganization following Jackson's death. In recommending him for promotion, Lee called him an "honest, brave soldier who has always done his duty well." Very tepid praise indeed compared to what Lee said about A. P. Hill at the same time. He said that A. P. Hill was the best general in his grade, in this army. He'd said it before about Hill. Here he says essentially that Richard Ewell's a guy who's done his job. Part of what's going on is he didn't know Ewell very well. Ewell had not served under Lee, directly under Lee's eye, except for a very brief time just outside Richmond. He'd been serving under Jackson, off in the Valley, been detached from Lee's command during the Second Manassas campaign. Lee simply didn't know Ewell very well.

He did, however, have some doubts about him. At least, that is what Lee said after the war. He told, in conversation, he told a former staff officer from the Second Corps after the war, Lee said he made Ewell a lieutenant general with full knowledge "of his faults as a military leader. His quick alternations from elation to despondency, his wont of decision, and the like." In other words, Lee said retrospectively, he thought that Ewell might be a man who would vacillate in a crisis, someone who might not be able to make up his mind. Now, he'd never had to worry about that before because anyone serving under Stonewall Jackson was told exactly what to do, might not be told why he was supposed to do it, but was told exactly what to do— do this, this, and this. Under Lee's style of leadership you didn't get that specific direction if you were a corps commander, as we've seen. Lee gave a great deal latitude to officers such as James Longstreet and Stonewall Jackson. They could sort of find their own way within a broad charge, not Dick Ewell under Jackson.

Now, here is Lee putting a man he doesn't know that well in charge of the corps led by his late, great lieutenant Stonewall Jackson. Probably a key factor in selecting Ewell was that there was a sense that Jackson had a very high opinion of Richard Ewell, and that had Jackson been selecting a successor he might have chosen Richard Ewell rather than A. P. Hill. Both served under Jackson, but it seemed, the scuttlebutt in the army was, that Ewell would have been Jackson's choice. That may have influenced Lee's decision, we can't be absolutely sure about that. What we can be sure about was that it didn't take long for Ewell to disappoint Lee as a corps commander.

Now, he didn't do it immediately. On the march northward towards Gettysburg, Richard Ewell seemed to be doing a splendid job. He marched quickly through the Shenandoah Valley. He won a little victory at Winchester, the Second battle of Winchester; there are three of them during the course of the war. Jackson won the first one against Banks; Jubal Early lost the third one against Sheridan, here's the second one. The Second battle of Winchester won by his corps as they were marching toward Pennsylvania. It was a tidy little victory, captured several thousand Federals, and people around him were thinking maybe this man really is going to be a good successor to Stonewall Jackson.

Things seemed to be going very well with Dick Ewell, but that idea stopped as soon as the fighting began at Gettysburg on July 1. Ewell's corps came onto the field after A. P. Hill was already engaged. Two of Ewell's divisions did very well—Jubal Early's division coming in and helping to smash the Federals north of town; Robert Rodes's division also playing a key role. But the moment of crisis, the moment of decision, that changed many people's minds about Ewell, most importantly Lee's mind about Ewell, was late in the day when the Federals had withdrawn to the high ground south of Gettysburg, and Lee sent an order to Ewell to take the high ground if practicable. That's the kind of order that Lee would have given Jackson, that's the kind of order Lee would have given Longstreet, and they would have read in that, "I want you to take the high ground." That's what Lee is really saying there. He's saying it in a way that gave latitude to the lieutenant, but with the implicit understanding, I think, that Lee wanted that done.

Well, there's a problem here. If Lee really believed, as he said after the war, that Ewell was prone to vacillate and needed closer direction, maybe he should have told Ewell, "Take the high ground south of town," don't tell him "Take it if practicable" and give him some wiggle room. But at any rate, Lee sent this discretionary order and Ewell on the ground, Lee is a long way from the sight, Ewell is off on the Confederate left, he's standing on low ground looking up at Cemetery Hill and east Cemetery Hill. He doesn't know how many Federal troops are up there, but he knows there are thousands. There's a report of a Federal column coming in against his left. One of his three divisions hasn't reached the battlefield yet, that of Allegheny Johnson; Rodes's divisions and Early's divisions had already been fighting hard all day. Ewell took into account all of these factors, and responded to Lee by saying, "I will try to take that ground, but I need support on my right flank." In other words, I'll attack but I need A. P. Hill to assist me on my right. As we saw in our last lecture, Hill is over on the other part of the battlefield with Lee and he tells Lee, "My men are fought out. They can't fight anymore today." So, Lee throws the burden back on Ewell. He agrees with Hill, or at least defers to Hill, in that respect, and so it comes back to Ewell and in the end Ewell decides not to attack the high ground on the afternoon of July 1, and it becomes very, very controversial.

Now, his staff officer and stepson, Campbell Brown, whom I quoted about Early looking like a sheep-stealing dog earlier, this is what Campbell Brown wrote. He wrote, "It was, as I have always understood, with the expressed concurrence with both Rodes and Early, and largely in consequence of the inactivity of the troops under General Lee's own eye," that is Hill's troops, "that General Ewell finally decided to make no direct attack," and that is absolutely right. Early said, "Yes, attack but we need support on our right." Rodes said, "Yes, attack but we need support on our right." When the support wasn't forthcoming from the right, I think all of the men on the scene, on Ewell's end of the line, both corps commander and the two division commanders present, Early and Rodes, decided it wasn't a good idea to attack. Too many factors militated against it, and Ewell decided to wait until his third division came up, Allegheny Johnson, Edward Allegheny Johnson's division, and to employ them. Well, they got up too late to do anything.

The bottom line was, this opportunity, if there was one, to attack on the afternoon of July 1 was passed by, and there was no final blow during this day that had seen so much success for the Army of Northern Virginia, and much of that success on Ewell's end of the line. Ewell had been very aggressive when he first arrived on the battlefield. He committed Rodes's division, he'd committed Early's division, and they had achieved a great deal. But now they decided it was prudent, taking everything into consideration, not to attack late in the day, and the second guessing was enormous about this, especially the postwar retrospective second guessing. "Oh, if only Jackson had been there," that was the leitmotif through most of this criticism. "If Jackson had been there he'd have just gone up the hill, routed the Federals, and it would have been a tremendous victory and then we'd have marched to Washington," said these former Confederates, "and then the war would have been over, and independence," and they just played out this whole scenario that if only Jackson had been there instead of Dick Ewell. There's Dick Ewell, they say, wringing his hands on the low ground, looking up and deciding that he can't risk anything, whereas the mighty Stonewall would have just pulled his troops into order and gone up the hill and won the day. Poor Ewell was in the situation, and this would have been inevitable with any successor to Jackson, of being compared to Jackson, the sainted Jackson, the just-lost Jackson, the Jackson of Chancellorsville, Lee's right arm. He's gone, and now we have Dick Ewell, the chirping woodcock, who only eats wheat, who can't decide to attack the high ground. How can you win in that kind of comparison?

Well, of course, you can't, and Dick Ewell didn't, and especially didn't after the war. Not many comments during he war, although some people may have believed that he should have been more aggressive at Gettysburg even at the time. The one that mattered, there's really only one person who matters here in terms of Ewell's functioning in the Army of Northern Virginia, what did Lee think about Ewell's performance? Lee clearly was disappointed. Lee clearly believed that when he said attack that high ground if practicable that Ewell was going to attack it, and he put a very large negative mark beside Ewell's name because Ewell didn't attack on the afternoon of July the 1<sup>st</sup>. Later Lee said that Gettysburg had been a failure because, as he put it, the "imperfect halting way in which my corps commanders, especially Ewell, fought the battle and gave victory finally to the foe." For all those who attacked James Longstreet after the war, they should know that it's not Longstreet that Lee singled out, he said all of his corps commanders fought imperfectly and in a halting way, but he singled out Ewell as having done the worst job.

Now, it can't be Ewell early on the day of July 1 because he did a great job. It all comes down to this one key moment when in Lee's mind there should have been another push. This is Lee's killer instinct, the killer instinct that

Jackson surely did share. I have no doubt that if Jackson had been in Ewell's place he would have tried to capture the high ground. Whether he would have captured it or not is another question entirely, and the notion that taking that high ground would have given the Confederacy independence is, I think, very silly. The Army of the Potomac would simply have taken up another defensive position closer to Washington and the campaign would have unfolded some way, but it wouldn't have unfolded with Washington falling to Lee's army and the Confederacy being independent on the spot. I don't think that would happen. But, here's poor Dick Ewell at the vortex of this argument. I think there were good reasons for not attacking. Lee didn't agree, and this cast a shadow over Richard Ewell as far as Lee was concerned.

Well, the next fall and winter, the autumn of 1863 and winter of 1863-64, Ewell suffered a good deal of discomfort associated with his stump of his amputated limb. He had to step aside in various moments and Jubal Early replaced him, as we've already seen, in temporary command of the Second Corps. He was back in time for the opening of the Overland campaign, and once again he let Lee down, at least from Lee's perspective. Ewell did not do a very good job. There were grumblings by then among officers in his army, in his corps, as well. Robert Rodes didn't have a high opinion of Richard Ewell. He liked Ewell as a man but did not have a high opinion of Richard Ewell as a corps commander. Some of the staff officers also made deprecating remarks about Ewell.

Ewell got married in that period between Gettysburg and the period after his terrible wound and he lost his leg. He got married to a very wealthy widow named Lucinda Brown who had very large holdings in Tennessee. Ewell, in his iniminitable way, always referred to her as the "Widow Brown" rather than as his wife or as Mrs. Ewell. He'd say well, the Widow Brown is doing this or doing that, and many of the staff officers, and of course, notions about gender and proper roles for men and women certainly entered the picture here, they thought that Mrs. Ewell, Mrs. Brown, the Widow Brown, exercised entirely too much influence over Richard Ewell, and thought that maybe she, rather than Dick Ewell, was really in command of the corps. That's what some of them said in a really nasty way as you more toward the Wilderness and beyond. But, once the Overland campaign opened, Ewell is very quickly put in the hot seat, and he fails three times as far as Robert E. Lee is concerned, and that was it for Lee. He'd had doubts about him as it was, doubts about his health, doubts about his competency. I talked in the lecture about Jubal Early, about the debate flank attack on May the 6th—

should there have been an early, stronger flank attack? Lee thought yes, he blamed Ewell for not launching that. That's a mark against Ewell. But the real problems came during the battle of Spotsylvania, and they came on two occasions at Spotsylvania.

On May 12, when Winfield Scott Hancock's massive Union assault overran the salient, the line, the portion of Lee's line that jutted out in a great inverted "U" in the middle of the line, overran it, smashed a good part of Ewell's Second Corps. Ewell went to the scene of the crisis but was not under control. Lee could not tolerate officers who couldn't exercise self-control; you needed to remain in control of yourself to give a good example to the men believed Lee, and he saw Ewell thrashing around amidst this chaotic situation, cursing, riding back and forth, and he was very disappointed in Ewell at that stage. We'll talk more about that a little bit later in the course.

So, here is Ewell in a crisis, not maintaining his composure, not keeping his head, not doing the things that an officer in full control of his military faculties would do. A week later, on May 19, late in the two weeks of fighting at Spotsylvania, Ewell took part of his corps on a sort of feeling operation to find where the Federal right flank was and fought a battle at a place called the Harris Farm. This is part of the overall Spotsylvania campaign, and once again Lee believed Ewell lost control of himself and his corps. His corps—the fighting had been so savage through the Overland campaign that Ewell's Second Corps, the once mighty Second Corps, was down to 6,000 men by the time of the fight at the Harris Farm. But Ewell got out, he got embroiled in this fight, and in essence said, "I can't seem to disengage," and Lee was very disappointed in him again. I think Lee had, by that point, made the decision to get rid of Richard Ewell.

His pretext came a little bit later in May when Ewell, for health reasons, stepped aside very briefly, very briefly, and Jubal Early was put in as his replacement. Then Ewell came back and said, "I'm back up to speed, I'm ready to resume command," and Lee said, "No, I don't think so." Lee tried at first to be very gentle about it and said, "Your health is so fragile, I'm not sure you are really up to this kind of campaigning, I'm worried about you." So, poor Ewell went and got affidavits from surgeons who said, "Yes, he's up to field command." Lee, in the end, was forced to say, "No, you're not up to field command, and it isn't because you're sick, it's because you aren't up to field command." You can't do your job is in essence what Lee told him. Ewell did not fit Lee's model of a self-reliant, aggressive officer in command of a corps, and he simply had seen enough by the end of May.

More important, he had somebody in mind to replace Ewell, and that was Jubal Early. He didn't have that with A. P. Hill. There was no logical successor for A. P. Hill. There was a logical successor for Ewell, and Lee made the move.

Ewell was relegated to commanding the troops, the kind of second and third-rate troops, in the local home guard defending Richmond. That's where he went for the rest of the war. He doesn't have a command with the Army of Northern Virginia; he commands in the Richmond defenses. He took that command as part of the retreat after Richmond and Petersburg fell, and participated in the battle at Sailor's Creek on the 6th of April. Ewell was captured there along with 6,000 other Confederates, including, as we've seen, Lee's son, George Washington Custis Lee.

Ewell is, in many ways, a sad story of a soldier, ravaged by wound, and promoted beyond his level of competency. He's a man, because of certain personal characteristics, who has come down to us as a caricature. That's unfortunate as well. I think there is a lot of solid accomplishment with Richard Ewell, but most of that came before, almost all of it, came b efore he was promoted to lieutenant general. He and A. P. Hill share that characteristic.

Our next lecture is going to examine John Bell Hood. He shares a great deal with Ewell, another man who suffered horrible wounds, terrible physical ailments, in the course of his service as a Confederate general, and who also was promoted beyond his competency, not one level beyond, but two levels beyond. We'll look at the interesting case of John Bell Hood in our next lecture.

# Lecture Fifteen
# A Straight-Ahead Fighter—John Bell Hood

**Scope:** John Bell Hood personified the type of offensive spirit Lee sought to inculcate in the Army of Northern Virginia's officer corps, leading first a brigade, then a division with dash and considerable success between the Seven Days and Gettysburg. More than six feet tall, blond, and a West Pointer whose undistinguished record in the classroom prompted friendly gibes from his peers, Hood made his name with a powerful assault at Gaines's Mill and superior leadership at Second Manassas and Antietam. Promoted to major general in the autumn of 1862, he played a minor role at Fredericksburg, missed Chancellorsville when his division was deployed to southeast Virginia with James Longstreet, sustained a serious wound on the second day at Gettysburg, and was wounded even more grievously at the battle of Chickamauga in September 1863. Hood never returned to the Army of Northern Virginia. Despite his wounds, he was promoted first to corps and later to army command in the western theater, gaining no distinction in either case. Few division commanders on either side in the Civil War matched Hood's ability to lead men in combat, and his actions in 1862 formed a notable element in the success of the Army of Northern Virginia. His last two promotions, however, revealed a man sadly lacking in the requisite administrative and political skills for higher command and thrust him into situations that made failure, rather than aggressive achievement, the dominant feature of his Confederate record.

# Outline

I. Hood brought experience with Robert E. Lee to his service in the Army of Northern Virginia.

   A. He attended West Point while Lee was superintendent.
      1. He graduated in the bottom quarter of the class of 1853.
      2. Though he would have preferred the cavalry, he entered the infantry because his class rank was low.
   B. He served in the infantry and cavalry in the 1850s.

> > 1. He suffered a wound fighting Native Americans in Texas in 1857.
> > 2. He served with Lee in the Second Cavalry in Texas, which deepened his admiration for the older man.

> II. Hood commanded what became the most famous brigade in the Army of Northern Virginia.
> > A. He led the 4$^{th}$ Texas Infantry as a colonel in the first part of the war.
> > B. He subsequently commanded a brigade that included all of the Texas soldiers in the Virginia army.
> > > 1. This unit became known as Hood's Texas brigade.
> > > 2. The brigade distinguished itself at the battle of Eltham's Landing and, especially, at Gaines's Mill during the Seven Days' campaign.
> > > 3. Hood won a reputation for fearless and aggressive leadership in combat.

> III. Hood's record between July 1862 and September 1863 boasted some of the finest accomplishments in Lee's army.
> > A. His division helped break the Union lines at Second Manassas.
> > B. His division fought steadfastly at Antietam.
> > C. His division held the Confederate center at Fredericksburg.
> > D. His division missed Chancellorsville while with Longstreet at Suffolk.
> > E. His division gained distinction during fighting on the second day at Gettysburg.
> > > 1. Hood opposed making the assault as Longstreet ordered.
> > > 2. Hood was grievously wounded, suffering permanent loss of the use of his left arm.
> > F. His division helped break the Union lines at Chickamauga.
> > > 1. Hood exercised his typical style of leadership at the place of danger.
> > > 2. He suffered a wound that cost him his right leg.

> IV. Hood's style of generalship at the brigade and division levels perfectly suited the military culture Lee created in the Army of Northern Virginia.

**A.** Hood was aggressive in tactical offensive fighting.

**B.** He produced positive results but often at the price of enormous casualties.

**C.** His Texas brigade was widely considered the best shock troops in the army.

**V.** Hood achieved no further distinction after he left Lee's army.

  **A.** He compiled a mixed record as a corps commander in the western theater under Joseph E. Johnston.

  **B.** He engaged in political maneuvering regarding command of the Army of Tennessee during the Atlanta campaign.

  **C.** He failed as an army commander during the later stage of the Atlanta campaign and in Tennessee in 1864.

  **1.** He has been unfairly criticized for his activities at Atlanta.

  **2.** He lacked crucial skills necessary to lead an army.

  **D.** Hood's example underscored the danger of promoting officers beyond their level of competence.

### Essential Reading:

McMurry, *John Bell Hood and the Southern War for Independence.*

### Supplementary Reading:

Hood, *Advance and Retreat: Personal Experiences in the United States and Confederate States Armies.*

### Questions to Consider:

**1.** Was promotion beyond the level of competency inevitable in such cases as Hood's?

**2.** How could the Confederacy have made the best of Hood's talents?

# Lecture Fifteen—Transcript
# A Straight-Ahead Fighter—John Bell Hood

John Bell Hood personified the type of offensive spirit Lee sought to inculcate in the Army of Northern Virginia's officer corps, leading first a brigade and then a division with dash and considerable success between the Seven Days and the campaigns that unfolded thereafter down through Gettysburg. More than six feet tall, blond, and a West Pointer whose undistinguished record in the classroom prompted friendly gibes from his peers, Hood made his name with a powerful assault at Gaines's Mill and superior leadership at Second Manassas and Antietam. Promoted to major general in the autumn of 1862, he played a minor role at Fredericksburg, missed Chancellorsville when his division was deployed to southeast Virginia with James Longstreet, sustained a serious wound on the second day at Gettysburg, and was wounded even more grievously at the battle of Chickamauga in September 1863. Hood never returned to the Army of Northern Virginia. Despite his wounds, he was promoted first to corps and then to army command in the western theater, gaining no distinction in either case. Few division commanders on either side in the Civil War matched Hood's ability to lead men in combat, and his actions in 1862 formed a notable element in the success of the Army of Northern Virginia. His last two promotions, however, revealed a man sadly lacking in the requisite administrative and political skills for necessary higher command and thrust him into situations that made failure, rather than aggressive achievement, the dominant feature of his Confederate career.

Hood brought experience with Robert E. Lee to his service in the Army of Northern Virginia. He was a Kentuckian by birth. His father was a physician and a planter. He had wanted Hood to pursue a medical career, and probably maintained the planting interest as well, but Hood from the very beginning wanted to be a soldier. That is what drew him—the life of a soldier, the sort of romantic aura of the soldier's life. He wrangled an appointment to West Point, wrangled might be too harsh a verb, he was appointed to West Point with help from a relative, from an uncle, actually, who was a member of Congress, and he didn't do very well at West Point. This is not a student that we're talking about here. He graduated near the bottom of his class of 1853. He was 44th of 52 in the class of 1853. He was at West Point while Lee was superintendent, and that began a relationship with Lee in which Hood looked to the older man and the superior officer as a model. Hood modeled himself on Lee, or thought he did in many ways, although in terms of personality and gifts he and Lee were very different, but he did admire Lee while Lee was the head of the academy.

He wanted to go into the cavalry after he graduated, did Hood, but he was so far down in the ranking of the cadets that he ended up in the infantry. He ended up in the 4th United States Infantry, and he served in the infantry out in California in an early part of his career. When he found out that the government was creating two new cavalry regiments in the mid-1850s he began to lobby very hard for a position in one of those cavalry regiments. He wrote to all kinds of people, including the secretary of war, Jefferson Davis, saying, "I want to be in the cavalry, I want to be in one of these two regiments." This began a pattern that would be consistent throughout the rest of Hood's life of being willing to go outside normal channels in order to get what he wanted, and what he usually wanted was promotion and a better position. He's ambitious as a young man, he will be ambitious throughout his career, and there's a scheming dimension to his personality that we will see again and again. It is one of his less attractive traits. It comes up in a minor way here when he wants one of these positions in the cavalry.

Well, he got one. He was assigned to the Second Cavalry. Lee was lieutenant colonel of the Second Cavalry, as we saw in one of our early lectures. So, here he finds himself back with Lee, and they both serve in Texas.

He was wounded fighting Native Americans in Texas in 1857. He had an arrow—took a wound through his hand with an arrow. It was a painful wound. He tried to pull the arrow through at one point, but the feathers got caught. So then he, in the end, ended up yanking it out the other way—a very painful wound. It didn't disable him for a long time, but it was a painful wound.

His respect for Lee deepened while they were both in the Second Cavalry, and he carried into the Civil War this admiration for Lee that would grow deeper and deeper once he found himself as a lieutenant in Lee's Army of Northern Virginia. He commanded what became the most famous brigade in the Army of Northern Virginia, and gave his name to it early in the war. He resigned from the U. S. Army at the very outset of the war, actually before the fighting started. He'd been promoted to first lieutenant in April of 1861, but got out of the army shortly after that, out of the United States Army. As he put it at the time, "I see no hope of reconciliation or adjustment, but a very strong indication of a fierce and bloody war." He predicted the war would not be short at a time when many people were predicting that it would be short. He had no idea, of course, just how bloody it was going to be for him in a personal sense.

He was given the colonelcy of the 4th Texas Infantry early on. He loved Texas. Although a native Kentuckian, he really considered himself an adopted Texan. He enjoyed his time in Texas. Many people didn't enjoy their time in Texas in the 1850s. It was a very harsh landscape, a brutal climate in many ways, but Hood liked it and said later that he planned to make his life in Texas because of his service there. He was thinking this way before the war. Now he ends up in command of this regiment of the Texas Infantry that was part of a brigade that included all the Texas troops in the eastern army. The brigade was commanded by a man named Louis T. Wigfall, who would later be a senator from Texas in the Confederate congress. Here are these Texans in the eastern army, and Hood was commanding one of the three regiments—the 1st and the 4th and the 5th Texas are out in the army in the east. The rest of the Texas troops served out in the west.

He was made a colonel in September of 1861, and his combative personality showed even before he participated in a battle. He was trying to teach his men, as he later explained and plenty of witnesses said that this was the case, trying to teach his men to think aggressively, to think that when we do get on a battlefield we're going to make things happen. As one officer wrote of Hood in this period before he'd even been in a battle, "He tried to get his troops, even though no battle was imminent, in the frame of mind where when they did find themselves in a raid against the Federals they would go after them, they would go after them and try to hurt them."

This is what Hood wrote about it, "I lost no opportunity whenever the officers or men came to my quarters, or whenever I chanced to be in conversation with them, to arouse their pride, to impress upon them that no regiment in the army should be allowed to go forth upon the battlefield and return with more trophies of war than the 4th Texas, that the number of colors and guns captured, and prisoners taken, constituted the true test of the work done by any command in any engagement." He's setting a high standard. Those are the things that count. That is how they kept score during the Civil War—did you capture someone else's colors, did you capture any cannons, did you take prisoners? Hood is doing this before he has even been in a battle. He subsequently commanded the brigade that had been Louis Wigfall's, and it became known as Hood's Texas brigade, and as I said a minute ago, it would become the most famous brigade in the Army of Northern Virginia.

The brigade distinguished itself at the battles of Eltham's Landing, and later at Gaines's Mill, during the campaign outside Richmond in 1862. Eltham's Landing was on May 7. It was a little action, a rear guard action, as Joseph Johnston's army was withdrawing toward Richmond. Williamsburg had been another one. Eltham's Landing is one in that sequence of little clashes. Hood showed an ability to handle his men in combat there. He launched an effective little attack. But at Gaines's Mill he really made his mark. That is his coming out battle, so to speak, during the Civil War. The battlefield at Gaines's Mill was a very striking one. The Federals, under General FitzJohn Porter, were arrayed on high ground up above a stream that ran through the battlefield. There were several lines of Federal troops leading up to the crest of this high ground, with a lot of artillery supporting them behind. Lee wanted to strike early in the day. Jackson was late in coming as we've seen, but in the course of June the 27$^{th}$, 50,000 Confederates launched assaults against the Federals at Gaines's Mill—very bloody assaults. They hadn't carried the day even late in the action, and that is when John Bell Hood and his command, his brigade, came into play. They participated in one of the last assaults of the day, Hood leading in person. They went across the stream. They covered an open ground before even getting to the stream, struggled across the stream, and fought their way through all the lines of Federals up to the top, and achieved a quite remarkable success through this frontal assault across difficult terrain.

Hood came to everyone's attention because of this. He'd already come to attention because of the little thing at Eltham's Landing. He'd been praised in some of the reports by some superiors, but this was a major battle. He was leading in person, and he, at the very last part of this daylong fight, managed to achieve the breakthrough that prompted the retreat of the Federals who were on the north side of the Chickahominy to the south side of the river. Lee certainly took note of Hood at the battle of Gaines's Mill. The brigade lost very heavily at Gaines's Mill. Hood's old regiment, the 4$^{th}$ Texas, lost 50% of its men. When he rode out among the men afterwards, Hood, he broke down. He had to compose himself. He saw, he learned what their losses had been, he rode off to the side, sort of choking back tears, and the men commented at the time that that made the bond between them and him even stronger. He had the ability to forge this kind of bond with his troops. Some officers had it, some didn't. We've seen that Jubal Early didn't have it, but John Bell Hood did. The Texans were intensely loyal to him, one reason they kept his name through the rest of the war, Hood's Texas brigade, long after the time he ceased to command it.

Lee was very much impressed with John Bell Hood because of the fight at Gaines's Mill, and he also was impressed with the way that Hood had been able to manage the command before he got there. He thinks that Hood is not only good in combat, but also a good administrator. That's not quite right. Lee would learn more about that later. But at this stage he has a very positive sense of what Hood was and could be as a soldier.

Hood's record between July 1862 and September 1863 offered some of the finest moments for any division commander in all of the Army of Northern Virginia. He was in Longstreet's wing; he would always fight under Longstreet when he was with Lee's army. He's in the Right Wing, and then in the First Corps, of the Army of Northern Virginia, and as a brigadier general he was put in command of a division. W. H. C. Whiting's division needed a commander because Whiting was ill, and Hood, although not promoted to major general, was given division command after the Seven Days. So, again, an expression of belief in what this young officer might become in giving him this command, although just a brigadier general.

He had a very striking appearance. He did, we've talked about these officers who looked like soldiers and those officers who didn't look like soldiers, and John Bell Hood looked like a soldier. Moxley Sorrell said, "In appearance he was very striking; in age only thirty-four years old. He had a personality that would attract attention anywhere. Very tall," (He was 6'2", very tall for his time.) "Very tall and somewhat loose jointed. A long, oval face shaded by a yellowish beard, plentiful hair of the same color, and a voice of great power encompassed." Many of his soldiers talked about how far his voice would carry on the battlefield, which was a feature soldiers would note. It's hard to be heard on a battlefield amid the din; John Bell Hood had a very piercing voice apparently that could be heard above the sounds of battle.

Sorrell went on to comment about one other element of Hood's personality, however, in this same descriptive passage, he said, "With very winning manners he is said to have used these advantages actively for his own advancement, but apart from that, his services in the field were of the best." That's a very kind way of saying that John Bell Hood would maneuver for advancement. Sorrell was a key staff officer on Longstreet's staff, and he understood this part of Hood's personality very well.

Hood's performances at Second Manassas and Antietam were of the highest order. His division was involved in the grand attack at Second Manassas on August 30 that broke the Federal lines. He was very aggressive there.

Again, hands on leadership at Second Manassas. His division at Antietam moved into the fight when Jackson was being pressed to the very edge by the heavy Union pressure early in the day toward the cornfield. Hood's men in Longstreet's wing were farther south in the line, but just as they were getting ready for breakfast, the first hot meal, as the soldiers said, that they had had in a long time, that was interrupted. They were thrown into the battle, and they moved into that horribly bloody action along the cornfield and the ground just south of the cornfield, delivered a powerful blow, and then held their own as more Confederate reinforcements came up. It was a very dramatic moment, and it was a very successful effort on John Bell Hood's part.

He'd gone into the Maryland campaign under a cloud, in fact, under arrest. He'd gotten into a dispute with a senior officer named Evans, Nathan G. Evans. It involved some captured wagons. Hood's men captured some wagons, and Hood was using them to haul some of his wounded and others around in. Evans said he wanted the wagons, Evans was his superior officer, and Hood said, "No. My men captured the wagons, we're going to use them." So, Evans arrested him, and as the army went north, as it began to fight, during the fighting at South Mountain on September 14 just before Antietam, Robert E. Lee was watching some of the soldiers go into battle, the men of Hood's old command, and as they walked by Lee, the soldiers looked to Lee and chanted, "Give us Hood, give us Hood." Lee asked Hood to apologize to Evans and in a very A. P. Hill-like response Hood said, "I'd love to, but I can't. Personal honor won't allow me to apologize to Nathan Evans." Lee temporarily suspended Hood's arrest so that Hood could be in command during the battle of Antietam.

This whole episode, as others we've looked at, let's go to Lee for just a minute, demonstrate what kinds of political skills Lee needed to deal with all these prima donnas in his army. He has all of these eagles and all of these touchy fellows, or at least many of them, that seem to be looking for personal slights, and Lee has to try to maneuver among all of these little problems and keep the army functioning. He made a good choice on the march to Antietam because Hood did such a good job in that battle. It was a very bloody job he did on the 17th. He wrote in his own memoirs of "the most deadly combat that raged 'til our last round of ammunition was extended. The 1st Texas Regiment had lost in the cornfield fully two-thirds of its number." They actually lost 80% of its number. "Whole ranks of brave men were mowed down in heaps to the right and left. Never before was I so continuously troubled by far that my horse would further injure some wounded fellow lying helpless on the ground." So, Hood's late summer and early autumn were very successful with the army.

Promoted to major general in October of 1862, and his division participated in the battle of Fredericksburg. He didn't have a big role. He's sort of in the center of the Confederate line at Fredericksburg, he didn't have much to do. Longstreet, in retrospect, was unhappy with Hood's performance at Fredericksburg. He believed that he should have moved out and attacked the Federals in flank who were confronting Stonewall Jackson a little bit farther to the south. Hood didn't do that. He didn't have orders to do it, not direct orders to do it, but Longstreet thought he'd been given orders that were at least suggestive that he should do that. Hood didn't do it. Longstreet later was unhappy. But, Fredericksburg had no negative effect on John Bell Hood's reputation within the army.

His division missed Chancellorsville. His was one of the two divisions that went to southside Virginia along with George Pickett's when Longstreet went down for the Suffolk campaign, which we talked about when we discussed Longstreet's career. So, he's not present at Chancellorsville. He didn't do much at Fredericksburg. He was critical of Longstreet after the Suffolk campaign. That was another one of his characteristics as a soldier, willingness to criticize superiors. He did it behind the scenes, he did it in Richmond, he did it elsewhere, but this, again, is Hood kind of maneuvering off stage to make himself look better or make his superiors look not quite as good as they might have. Not a pretty part of his overall package as a general.

By the end of the spring and early summer of 1863, Hood was clearly a very able division commander who had performed very well in difficult circumstances in the army, but he was also a very ambitious man. He wanted a corps. He wanted to be a corps commander. He wanted to be a lieutenant general. He believed that his record as a division commander justified it, and in one way or another he made various people know that he felt this way. He even let Lee know it in an indirect way. And when Jackson died, this ambition, I think, came even more to the fore. Okay, now Jackson's dead, now the army needs another corps commander, what about me thought Hood in effect. Well, Hill had a longer record as a division commander, and a better one in Lee's judgment, although Lee thought that Hood had done a very good job. He told Jefferson Davis that Hood was a "capital officer." He said that he was improving, said Lee, and he should be seriously considered for corps command at some point. So, Lee has a very positive view of him. Not as positive as Hood's view of himself.

He didn't get the corps, of course, after Jackson died. Hill got one, Ewell got the other. So, Hood is still a division commander during the Gettysburg campaign. As with the rest of Longstreet's corps, he wasn't involved on the first day, but he did play a role on the second day. He's involved in those heavy assaults that Longstreet launched against the Union left, that very heavy fighting that went off, in Hood's instance, toward Devil's Den and up toward Little Roundtop. After the long march to get around to get into position to attack, Hood got on the ground. We discussed this a bit in our talk about James Longstreet. He looked at the field ahead of him and said, "Wait a minute, we're not far enough around the flank. If we go a little bit farther to our right, we'll get all the way around the Army of the Potomac's left flank, and we can come in either right on the flank or even on the left rear," and he told Longstreet that, and Longstreet said no. He made the plea again, he made it three times, to please be allowed to go around, to get all the way around the Federal flank before he launched his assault. In the end, Longstreet said, "No, you're going to go in the way that General Lee wants us to go in," and Hood did, but he made the attack under protest. He made it, he made it under protest. Just after the attack got going, right by the edge of a farm called Bushman farm at Gettysburg, Hood was wounded, very badly wounded, at the outset of his attack. He had permanent loss of the use of his left arm. Initially they weren't sure they would be able to save his arm. In the end he was able to save it, the physicians were able to save it, but not save it in a way that it would be useful for the rest of his life.

While recuperating in Richmond, he criticized operations in Pennsylvania, including James Longstreet's part in those operations, and he angled for promotion. This was typical of him. He became a sort of lion of the parlor set in Richmond, a guest at many of the evening parties and dinners where the generals were celebrities. Hood was one of the real celebrities, this tall, striking looking blond guy, his arm in a sling from his wound at Gettysburg. He was much prized as a dinner companion, and he made it known that he thought he had done well, others hadn't done so well, and that maybe he should be promoted. He was also unhappy about the fact that his division had lost so heavily during the fight on the afternoon of July 2. Not so much just the losses, but that he wasn't able to fight the way he wanted to. His commands always suffered a lot of casualties, but it was critical of Longstreet, even alluded to this in his memoirs, his unhappiness at Longstreet at Gettysburg. He said, "The losses were very heavy, as shown by the reports, and have often caused me to more bitterly regret that I was not permitted to turn Roundtop Mountain." Even in 1879 and '80, when he was taking care of these memoirs, he was still upset with Longstreet.

He recovered in time to go with Longstreet off to north Georgia and the Chickamauga campaign. His division was in the thick of the fighting on September 20 at Chickamauga when the Confederates gained their great success, but he was wounded again, this time even worse than he had been at Gettysburg. This time he was shot in the right leg, a hideous wound. They amputated the leg at the hip. Almost no one survived that type of amputation during the Civil War. You could survive if they took it off at the knee, or maybe even a little above the knee. Hood lost his leg at the hip. He recovered from that as well. Longstreet praised him and recommended him for corps command, and Hood would be promoted.

What about his style of generalship when he was with the Army of Northern Virginia? As a brigade and division commander he perfectly suited Lee's military culture in the army. He is aggressive; he is powerful in launching assaults. He's always looking for openings and for pressing the advantage in tactical offensive fighting. He absolutely fits Lee's model in that regard. He produced positive results often at an enormous cost. His commands, whether it's the 4th Texas, or the Texas brigade, or his division at Manassas, or his division at Antietam, or his division at Gettysburg, if you serve under John Bell Hood you have a pretty good chance of getting shot because of this whole attitude towards what constitutes a good fight. Going back to his comments to the 4th Texas early in the war, "We're going to capture flags, we're going to capture prisoners. That's how we're going to gauge what kind of battle we have." That is how he behaves on the battlefield. His men make his reputation go up and up and they make their own reputation go up, the Texans especially, but they pay a price for it. Moxley Sorrell said that as a major general in command of a division, Hood "might be considered an ideal officer of that rank in command." What he meant in that, although he didn't have to say it, was in the Army of Northern Virginia. Hood was just what Lee wanted in that regard, his Texas brigade widely considered the best shock troops in the army, even by other brigades that thought that they were very good. Lee commented that he wished he could get a lot more Texans in the army, because the Texans did such a good job. At a review one time he was with someone, the Texans marched by, their uniforms were very shabby, a lot of them had repaired the seats of their pants so often that their underclothes were showing through, and this guy commented negatively about that, and Lee turned to him and said, "Don't worry about that. Nobody ever sees the backs of my Texans." He loved these soldiers from Texas, he liked the way Hood handled them, and Hood's name attached to that unit conveyed this sense of aggressiveness and success in offensive combat that has a lot to do with how people remember Hood.

He didn't achieve any distinction after he left Lee's army, neither as a corps commander fighting under Joseph Johnston during the Atlanta campaign, a period characterized by his going behind Johnston and complaining to people in Richmond saying that Johnston wasn't doing a good job and maybe he should be replaced. Implicit in much of this, of course, was if we replace him maybe I'd be a good person to take his place. He eventually did replace Joseph Johnston, and he presided over the loss of Atlanta. He first attacked in army command of the Army of Tennessee at Atlanta. He's been very heavily criticized for that. I cut him some slack there because he understood why he had been put in command of the Army of Tennessee. Joe Johnston had retreated all the way from north Georgia to Atlanta without fighting a major battle, really. The Davis administration and many people behind the lines in the Confederacy believed that Johnston had given up too much without enough of a fight. Hood, they believed, would put up that kind of a fight. He went on the offensive when he took command, three battles in a row, the battles of Atlanta, Peachtree Creek and Ezra Church, 20,000 casualties very quickly, and then he just had to withdraw into the defenses. So, he lost Atlanta in the end anyway, and then failed dismally in what is called Hood's Tennessee campaign, which is a foray into Tennessee in November and December of 1864 characterized by a bloody repulse at the battle of Franklin in early November, and then an ineffective siege and bloody rout at the battle of Nashville in mid-December.

After those two defeats, as the army was retreating out of Tennessee in terrible weather, Hood was seen more than once, seen by more than one witness, I should say, just weeping in his tent. He was an absolutely broken man by that stage of the war, and he serves as a sort of metaphor for the Confederacy in some ways. He began the war as this vigorous, virile, six foot two inch officer, all aggressiveness and willingness to get at the enemy. Then he has an arm crippled. Then he loses the leg. Physically he's a wreck by the end of the war, and he's also had almost all of his aggressiveness pounded out of him because of the defeats that he suffers while in army command. He steps aside as an officer in the wake of his Tennessee campaign in 1864.

Lee understood Hood as he understood so many officers. He was a great man in terms of reading the talents of subordinates, was Lee. When asked one time about Hood's fitness for higher command, Lee chose his words carefully, as he always did, and said that in his opinion he would have been a very good soldier at the levels at which he operated, but he said that he thought Hood was all of the lion and none of the fox—all of the lion and none of the fox. A lion is a great thing to have commanding a division, smiting the enemy in a tactical sense on the battlefield, but you'd better have a little more of the fox in an army commander, and John Bell Hood didn't have those attributes necessary. The complexity in thinking, the ability to deal with people, the ability to deal effectively with politics as with subordinates, to command an army. Hood is an absolutely perfect example, even more so, than Richard Ewell and A. P. Hill, I think, a perfect example of promoting officers beyond their level of competency. Take a man who is very good as a brigade commander, very good as a division commander, and then moving him up another notch. That is a problem in Hood's case, a very striking problem. It's also inherent in the system. In a war such as this where so many officers are being shot or so many officers are leaving service for other reasons, you have to keep moving people forward. Some are going to work out, some are not. John Bell Hood did not work out once he left Lee and the Army of Northern Virginia.

Well, we'll turn from our biographical approach that we've been following with our next lecture. We're going to have two lectures that will explore the ways in which Lee dealt with various problems of replacing people under his command, whether he could make hard decisions regarding subordinates, and we're also going to look at the terrible problem of attrition in the Army of Northern Virginia, one of the great problems throughout the war, in maintaining an effective corps of leaders.

# Lecture Sixteen
## Could Robert E. Lee Make Hard Decisions?

**Scope:** Many of Robert E. Lee's contemporaries, as well as numerous historians from the late 19th century onward, suggested that he was too much of a gentleman to make hard decisions regarding personnel. The historical record suggests otherwise. Lee possessed well-developed skills as a military politician, and he found ways to ease generals who had disappointed him out of the Army of Northern Virginia with minimal disruption. He replaced a number of division commanders during the reorganization following the Seven Days, adeptly juggled officers among commands to find combinations that would best serve the needs of the army, and when necessary, directly confronted generals who had disappointed him. The first month of the Overland campaign, when both Richard S. Ewell and A. P. Hill failed on the battlefield, affords excellent insights into Lee's method of dealing with such occurrences. It also reveals Lee's clear understanding of the special challenges posed by fighting a massive war with officers and men who were not trained as professional soldiers.

## Outline

I. Lee has been criticized as a gentleman who lacked the hard edge necessary to weed out failures among his subordinate command.

  **A.** Critics argue that he allowed senior subordinates too much authority even when they failed to exercise effective leadership.

  **B.** Critics also insist that his personality was such that he could not confront those who disappointed him.

II. In fact, Lee demonstrated superior management skills in shaping his high command in the face of changing circumstances.

  **A.** He brought fundamental change to the upper echelons of the army in the aftermath of the Seven Days' campaign.

  **1.** A number of senior division commanders left the army.

  **2.** Lee divided his infantry between Stonewall Jackson and James Longstreet.

    **B.** He implemented a second major reorganization after Chancellorsville and Jackson's death.

        **1.** He created a Third Infantry Corps.

        **2.** He kept Longstreet in charge of the First Corps and advanced successful division commanders to head the Second and Third Corps.

**III.** The first month of the Overland campaign affords numerous insights into Lee's ability as a military politician and manager.

    **A.** He coped with mounting evidence that Richard S. Ewell and A. P. Hill lacked the capacity for corps command.

        **1.** He intervened personally during crises on Ewell's and Hill's fronts at the Wilderness and Spotsylvania.

        **2.** He replaced Ewell with Jubal A. Early when Ewell's loss of control on the battlefield became evident.

        **3.** He retained Hill because no capable replacement was at hand.

    **B.** Longstreet's wounding at the Wilderness forced Lee to rely on Richard H. Anderson as a replacement.

        **1.** Lee knew Anderson did not possess first-rate skills but had no obvious alternative candidate.

        **2.** Lee kept a much closer eye on Anderson than had been necessary with Longstreet.

    **C.** After Hill publicly berated an officer, Lee explained to Hill why professional soldiers had to be somewhat tolerant of failures on the part of volunteer officers.

        **1.** They were engaged in a massive war and had to do the best with the material at hand.

        **2.** They must try to teach the nonprofessionals how to be effective officers.

        **3.** Political considerations demanded that volunteer officers not be humiliated or summarily removed.

**IV.** Lee demonstrated admirable flexibility in handling subordinates and problems of command.

    **A.** He allowed wide latitude to deserving officers.

    **B.** He kept a closer eye on those less talented, such as Ewell and Hill.

    **C.** He removed officers if a capable replacement, such as Early, was available.

**D.** He coped with a series of crises brought on by attrition among his subordinates.

## Essential Reading:

Freeman, *R. E. Lee: A Biography*, vol. 4, chapter 11.

Gallagher, *Lee and His Army in Confederate History*, chapter 6.

## Supplementary Reading:

Freeman, *Lee's Lieutenants*, vol. 1, chapters 41–43; vol. 2, chapters 15–17, 36–37; vol. 3, chapters 10–11, 22, 25, 28, 34.

## Questions to Consider:

1. Are administrative and political skills as important in a field commander as a sound grasp of strategy and tactics?
2. Can any army that contains a large proportion of volunteer officers achieve real stability of command?

# Lecture Sixteen—Transcript
# Could Robert E. Lee Make Hard Decisions?

With our next pair of lectures we're going to depart from our biographical emphasis to explore topical questions, and we'll start with an examination of whether Robert E. Lee could make hard decisions regarding personnel in the high command of the Army of Northern Virginia. Many of his contemporaries, as well as numerous historians from the 19th-century onward, suggested that he was too much of a gentleman to make difficult decisions regarding personnel. The historical record suggests otherwise. Lee possessed well-developed skills as a military politician, and he found ways to ease generals out of the army who had disappointed him, and he did it with minimal disruption in almost every case. He replaced a number of division commanders during the reorganization following the Seven Days, as we've seen. He adeptly juggled officers among commands to find combinations that would best serve the interests of the army, and, when necessary, he directly confronted generals who had disappointed him. The first month of the Overland campaign between Lee and Grant in May and early June 1864, when both Richard S. Ewell and A. P. Hill failed on the battlefield, affords excellent insights into Lee's method of dealing with such occurrences. It also reveals Lee's clear understanding of the special challenges posed by fighting a massive war with officers and men who were not trained as professional soldiers. We always need to remember that these are citizen armies that the generals on both sides are working with. There's a cadre of West Pointers present in both armies, of course, in key positions, but the vast majority of men in uniform on both sides, officers and men in the ranks, are not soldiers. They are people who have been doing various things in civilian life just before the war, and now they are in uniform and they are trying to manage the very different circumstances of being in combat or being in camp in between campaigning seasons.

Lee has been criticized as a gentleman who lacked the hard edge necessary to weed out failures among his subordinate command. I think this view is very closely related to that of him as a sort of romantic throwback to a more knightly or chivalric age, someone who wasn't really attuned to the very ugly necessities, sometimes, of fighting the kind of war that Ulysses S. Grant or William Tecumseh Sherman seemed to be quite comfortable fighting. Again, Lee is often compared to Grant and Sherman. He is simply too schooled in the arts and attitudes of a gentleman to get right in someone's face and say, "You're not doing a good job, and I'm going to get rid of you." That is the view of Lee; that is the view. This is part of a broad effort, I think, on the part of many former Confederates after the war to turn Lee into a sort of saintly figure. They really tried to airbrush out all of the negative aspects, some might say human aspects, of his personality. They didn't deal with the fact that he had a very harsh temper. He could lose his temper very quickly and snap at people. Any part of Lee that didn't fit this sort of serene model of an officer who was an ideal in any way was pushed out of the way, and I think this notion that he was a gentleman who couldn't become very harsh with his subordinates is part of that larger picture.

Critics argued that Lee allowed senior subordinates too much authority—this was part of his gentle hand. He didn't keep a close enough rein on them and that often led him and the army astray. You will see in this connection the example of Richard Ewell at Gettysburg offered again and again and again. Why did Lee give so much latitude to Richard Ewell on the first day at Gettysburg? Why didn't he tell Ewell what he wanted him to do? And, look what happened when he didn't tell Ewell what he wanted him to do. The former Confederates would often say that Jackson, as we've seen, would have done it. If Lee had only exercised a tighter rein, if only he had not been so casual, so willing to give latitude to a problematical subordinate, things would have gone better at Gettysburg.

Critics also insist that Lee's personality was such that he couldn't confront, as I suggested, those who disappointed him. This is the key part of this argument, that as a gentleman he would find ways around direct confrontations. He would do almost anything to avoid direct confrontation. Let me just give you a flavor of what some of the people who fought with Lee said in this regard, and then give you a more modern twist on it.

A. G. L. Freemantle, our British friend, our British diarist who traveled with the army, stated in his famous account that Lee's "only faults so far as I can learn arise from his excessive amiability," that wonderful Jane Austin use of "amiability" there. Walter Taylor, who spent more time with Lee than any other officer during the war probably, he's on Lee's staff, noted in his widely cited post-war memoir—remember, this is his post-war take, it's very important in assessing evidence to note whether it was written in the midst of the war or written retrospectively, because often there is another agenda in place in retrospective writings. This is in Taylor's retrospective assessment of Lee. He wrote, "If it should be the verdict of posterity that General Lee in any respect fell short of perfection as a military leader, it may be perhaps be claimed that he was too careful of the personal feelings of his subordinate commanders, too fearful of wounding their pride and too solicitous of their reputation." Taylor went on to say that this tendency prompted Lee to retain in command men "of whose fitness for their position he was not convinced," and often led him "either avowedly or tacitly, to assume responsibility for mishaps clearly attributable to the inefficiency and neglect or carelessness of others." Finally, Jefferson Davis after the war also wrote that Lee's "habitual avoidance of any harshness, which caused him sometimes instead of giving a command to make a suggestion was probably a defect," and Davis may well have been thinking of Richard Ewell in that regard.

Perhaps inevitably, in the $20^{th}$ century a psychological dimension has been added to this longstanding interpretation of Lee as being unable to exercise a firm hand. A psychiatrist and a journalist wrote an article in which they claimed to locate in Lee's boyhood the reason for his habit of never confronting anyone. They said that he saw Lighthorse Harry Lee shame his mother repeatedly as a young boy, and "Robert E. Lee would grow up not to repeat the act of shaming, but to take the only other alternative—never to shame anyone at almost any cost." These authors say that this carried over into his style of command. "Shame witnessed and shame felt were the source of his inability to control his subordinates. Lee could not confront the wayward lieutenants for fear of shaming them. He was determined never, if at all possible, to let them feel humiliated as he had painfully seen his mother humiliated."

Well, you can reach that conclusion, I think, as long as you don't look at the way Lee acted during the war, then you can conclude that he never confronted anyone, he never was willing to be harsh with anyone, he never was willing to make the difficult decisions. But if you look at the record I think a very different picture emerges. Lee, in fact, demonstrated superior management skills in shaping his high command in the face of changing circumstances.

There are three main reorganizations of the army while it was under Lee's control. We've talked about each of them already to this point in the course. The first came, as we've seen, in the wake of the Seven Days. During that period Lee brought fundamental change to the high command of the Army of Northern Virginia, and if we look at this and the other reorganizations we'll see that it's obvious he could and did make hard decisions. He got rid of a number of senior division commanders after the Seven Days. I've mentioned this a couple of times already. John Bankhead Magruder, perhaps the most prominent of them, and he had a confrontation with Magruder, which we'll discuss when we get to Magruder later in the course. But Benjamin Huger, Theophilus Holmes, Gustavus Woodson Smith,

William Henry Chase Whiting, all of those men go away from the army and don't come back. They usually go out to the trans-Mississippi or to the west somewhere, sort of a dumping ground for people who didn't quite work out in the Army of Northern Virginia. Many of them end up in that epicenter of Civil War military action, Arkansas, or parts of Texas.

Many of these men did not want to leave the army defending Richmond. It isn't a question of they were unhappy with Lee and Lee unhappy with them and there was a mutual agreement that it would be better if they went somewhere else. They went because Lee didn't want them in the army anymore, and he found one way or another to make sure that that happened. But it's an almost wholesale cleaning of house at the division level after the Seven Days, and he pulled up the two men in whom he did have confidence, as we've seen. He divided his infantry between Longstreet and between Stonewall Jackson, and he gave great latitude to Longstreet and Stonewall Jackson, great latitude to both men, and this structure put in place after the Seven Days lasted just about—well, it lasted for that first great period of Lee's command of the army, from the end of the Seven Days down through Jackson's death at Chancellorsville. That's the period of the army's most famous victories. That's the period when the army and Lee became the most important national institution in the Confederacy, and it's a period when Lee gives his principle lieutenants, Longstreet, Jackson, and Jeb Stuart, very wide latitude. Now, no one criticizes him for giving too much latitude during this period. He granted the latitude, the system worked beautifully. The army functioned well. He assigned each man, as we've seen, the kinds of duty he was best at, and Jackson could make his big flank marches and James Longstreet could deliver his powerful blows on the battlefield, and it worked very, very well. There's not a more smoothly functioning high command system in place in any army on either side during the Civil War.

He implemented his second major reorganization after Chancellorsville. Again, as we've seen, Jackson's death is what prompted that. He has the question: Should I go to two corps or go to three? As we know, he went to three corps. He created the new Third Infantry Corps. He kept Longstreet in charge of the first and he advanced two very successful division commanders in A. P. Hill and Richard S. Ewell to command of the Second and Third Corps. This structure remained in place from May of 1863 until May of 1864, and Lee, at first, granted the same wide latitude to his chief subordinates within this structure. Of course he did to Longstreet, Longstreet had long since proved that he could do very well with that kind of latitude, and he continued to do well with that latitude. Jeb Stuart's the same way. Give Jeb Stuart latitude, and he'll do well. Stuart let Lee down at Gettysburg in my view, as I have said, but Lee treated that as the aberration it was. He continued to let Stuart have a good deal of room within which to execute his orders.

So, it made sense with Longstreet and Stuart to continue the old pattern, and Lee didn't know that it wouldn't work with A. P. Hill, a brilliant division commander whom Lee had long thought capable of commanding a corps, didn't know that it wouldn't work with A. P. Hill and didn't know it wouldn't work with Richard Ewell. He found out that it wouldn't work with those two men at Gettysburg, and then later in the autumn and winter of 1863-64, and as we'll see he changed his method of command with Ewell and Hill once he figured out that he couldn't follow the old ways with them. But initially I believe it made sense to continue the same model. The model had worked before. He still had two of the three men from the old model in place during/after this second reorganization. He still had Longstreet and Stuart there, so why change the model until circumstances suggest that the model wasn't going to work anymore.

The first month of the Overland campaign affords numerous insights into Lee's ability as a military politician and manager. This is the period that saw the third major reorganization of the high command. This is going to be a reorganization again brought on by both casualties and failures among the high command. This is the third time that Lee has to do this, and this first six weeks, four to six weeks, of the confrontation between Lee and Grant offers us a wonderful case study, a case study that tests some of these criticisms of Lee as being too gentle with his top subordinates. We can look at specific circumstances here and see that that was not the case. He coped during this period with mounting evidence that both Ewell and Hill lacked the capacity to command an infantry corps. He intervened personally during crisis on Ewell and Hill's fronts at the Wilderness and Spotsylvania, intervened in a way that would have been unthinkable with Stonewall Jackson or James Longstreet. Lee didn't look over the shoulder of Stonewall Jackson, he didn't look over the shoulder of James Longstreet, and wonder if he was going have to jump in at some critical moment of the battle to do their job for them. Sometimes he would be with them on a battlefield—he was at Antietam, he was elsewhere, at Fredericksburg they were together at different times, but it wasn't because Lee worried and thought that his personal intervention was necessary to make certain that the battle went the way that he wanted it to go. He trusted Longstreet, he trusted Jackson, and that was trust built on excellent performances along the line. What he does with Ewell and Hill shows that he is changing his attitude and his style of leadership, his style of management, as the Overland campaign unfolds.

It happens in the battle of the Wilderness with A. P. Hill. When Hill, on the morning of May 6, sees his two divisions disintegrate, the situation seems almost beyond retrieving, and Lee rides right into the midst of the battle, the Widow Tapp Farm, rides out among the guns of a battalion commanded by an officer named Poague, and tries to rally troops. That's not an army commander's job. The corps commander and the division commander should be doing that, but Lee, I believe, does not have faith in A. P. Hill at that point, so there he is, out in the midst of things. As soon as Longstreet rides out on the battlefield, when the First Corps arrives in the nick of time on the morning of May 6, Longstreet arrives on the battlefield and sort of jokingly tells Lee, "I'll be happy to go off where it's safe if you want to do my job, but why don't you just let me do my job?" Lee withdraws and Longstreet does his job. There is a tremendously striking contrast between attitudes, the attitude on Lee's part toward A. P. Hill that morning and toward James Longstreet. So, he's finding out with Hill that he's going to have to have a different kind of managerial style.

He finds it out even more spectacularly with Richard Ewell. This is the period of the famous "Lee, to the rear" episodes. The first is in the Widow Tapp's field the morning of May 6. The soldiers see Lee come out. They know he's not supposed to be there. That's not where the army commander should be. They grab his horse's bridle, Traveler's bridle, and they say in effect, "We're not going to go into the battle until you go to a place of safety." The Texans of Hood's old Texas brigade tell Lee that on the morning of May 6. It happens again with Richard Ewell at the center of things on May the 12th in the Mule Shoe at Spotsylvania. During that great crisis when Hancock's troops overran part of Ewell's Second Corps, Lee again rode to the front. Ewell was out there very ineffectively trying to deal with the crisis. Lee rode out and took control of the situation. Again, the soldiers, different soldiers from a different corps, grabbed at his horse's bridle and told him to go back or they wouldn't go into the battle. They, again, understood that he shouldn't be there, but he wasn't trusting Richard Ewell.

It happened again on the 19th with Ewell, the battle of the Harris Farm. Lee didn't ride out there, but he, in effect, told Ewell, "Listen, either get control of your corps or I will get control of your corps," and Hill by that time was ill. So, he's changing his leadership style with Hill and Ewell, and eventually he decided he had to replace them. He had to replace them, and

Ewell was the one, he had to replace Ewell—we'll talk about Hill in just a minute, but Ewell is the key test here. Ewell is the test that proves that Lee, when he had decided that alternatives had been exhausted, excuse me, that the circumstances had shown that one of his lieutenants simply wasn't going to be up to the job, and in a situation where there is an alternative, he would confront the person who wasn't doing his job and get rid of him. He decided this over a period of months with Richard S. Ewell, and let's look at Ewell quite closely because he's such an important case.

Lee believed in the winter of '63–'64 that Ewell's health, together with his somewhat halting action at Gettysburg, had raised serious red flags as to whether he should continue with Richard Ewell in command, and there was an exchange between them that winter. He was quite blunt with Richard Ewell during the winter. He said that it was up to Ewell to decide whether his health was good enough to continue in the field. Lee wrote to him, "I don't know how much ought to be attributed to long absence from the field, general debility, or the result of your injury, but I was in constant fear during the last campaign that you should sink under your duties or destroy yourself. I last spring asked for your appointment provided you were able to take the field. You now know from experience what you have to undergo and can best judge of your ability to endure it. I fear we cannot anticipate less labor than formerly." Lee's putting him on notice here, are you going to be up to your job physically or not? I have real doubts about you.

Ewell assured Lee that he would be up to it, but events in the Mule Shoe suggested otherwise. I think Lee was horrified when he saw Ewell's behavior on the morning of May the 12th, in these wild circumstances in the Mule Shoe. One witness wrote that Lee "in the calmest and kindest manner sought to rally the soldiers, whereas an agitated Ewell bellowed 'Yes, goddamn you, run, run, run you men. The Yankees will catch you. That's right, go as fast as you can, goddamn it.'" Well, that's not the kind of behavior Lee wants on the part of his corps commander there. Ewell was riding around, flailing, shouting, cursing, and Lee did not think that's how a corps commander should behave. He at one point said, "General Ewell, you must restrain yourself. How can you expect to control these men if you have lost control of yourself? If you cannot repress your excitement, you had better retire." Loss of control—Lee would not tolerate loss of control on the part of a senior subordinate, and here Ewell was exhibiting the thing that Lee most did not want to see in his subordinates.

Ewell fell ill a little bit later in May, he had to step aside, and when he tried to come back this whole question came to a head. Lee had decided by then, he'd been watching Jubal Early very carefully for a long time, as we've seen in the class, and Lee had decided that Early was up to corps command, and now he decided that it was time for Ewell to go. At first, he tried, in order to save face for Ewell, to make it seem that it was simply because of Ewell's health that Lee was going to ask him or going to remove him from command. In early June, he wrote about Ewell to the adjutant inspector general of the Confederate army, a man named Samuel Cooper. Lee wrote, "Although now restored to his usual health, I think the labor and exposure in which he would be inevitably exposed would at this time again incapacitate him for field service. The general, who has all the feelings of a good soldier, differs from me in this opinion," admitted Lee, "and is not only willing but anxious to resume his command. I, however, think that in the present emergency it would jeopardize his life, and should his strength fail it would prove disadvantageous to the service."

Lee's trying to say, "Okay, Ewell's not up to it physically," but Ewell wouldn't have it. Ewell said, "Yes I am up to it physically." As I said earlier, he got affidavits from surgeons saying that he was up to it. He went to see Lee directly on the morning of June 8, and this was a very difficult session between the two of them. Lee at first tried to put Ewell off by saying he was worried about his health and Ewell wouldn't have it. Ewell said he'd been very anxious when he was out of command and he wanted to come back. Ewell then said, "Well, do you really think Jubal Early's better than I am as a general?" He asked Lee bluntly that, and Lee said, "It's due Early in the corps that he receive the appointment, the permanent appointment, to command the Second Corps." Somewhat pathetically, it was then Ewell said that he would go somewhere to be out of the way. Lee said, "You're not in the way, but you'd better take care of yourself."

After the war, Lee put it much more succinctly in discussing the case of Ewell with a former staff officer. Lee said, "I tried to put him off by sickness, but when Ewell insisted I told him plainly I could not send him in command." Well, how direct and blunt can you get with a senior subordinate who's standing right in front of you? Who says, "I want to come back into command," you say, "I'm worried about your health," he says, "I want to come back in command, my health is fine," and then you say, "I'm sorry, you're out of the army" This test case of Ewell, I think, puts the lie to the whole notion that Lee couldn't deal directly with subordinates. He liked Ewell, everybody liked Ewell, so he can even do it with someone he really likes. Ewell isn't someone he just wants to get rid of because no one likes Ewell.

Hill was a different case, as we've seen. The key difference is there was no Jubal Early waiting in the wings to replace Ambrose Powell Hill. Lee had a capable replacement for Ewell, so he could move Ewell out, send him to the defenses of Richmond. There's no comparable officer waiting to replace A. P. Hill. Lee had already used one of the able officers, not a brilliant officer, but a good officer, when Longstreet had been wounded. Remember, the whole high command is fracturing here in this month of May. Longstreet's the first to go, shot down in the Wilderness. Lee has to replace him first, and he replaces him with a man named Richard H. Anderson. Now, he knew Anderson didn't have first-rate skills. He was a solid division commander; he'd been a commander at that level for much of the war. Lee took into consideration the fact that Anderson originally had fought under Longstreet in the old First Corps. He then had been moved to the Third Corps during the reorganization after Chancellorsville. Lee new that the men in Longstreet's corps, many of them were familiar with Anderson, and thought that would be a good factor. Here's a known quantity from the men's point of view coming back to head the First Corps to replace James Longstreet. He seemed to be, on balance, the best of the choices available.

Early was also available at this juncture, but I think Lee was already thinking Jubal Early's going to replace Ewell. So, all right, if Early's going there, to whom will I look to replace James Longstreet? And he decided it would be Richard H. Anderson, but he kept a very close eye on Richard H. Anderson. He did not give Anderson great latitude as he had with the other soldiers, another clear indication that Lee could adjust his style of command to suit the strengths and weaknesses of a particular lieutenant. He sent far more specific orders to Anderson, sent more orders period to Anderson. He does sort of look over Anderson's shoulder. He knew Anderson wasn't going to be brilliant, but he thought that Anderson would do okay, and he did do okay. He didn't so a really exceptional job.

There's also a wonderful illustration of Lee's understanding of the complexities of being a professional in a non-professional army that comes out in the Overland campaign, during the Spotsylvania period of it, and it again deals with A. P. Hill. On May 18, at Spotsylvania Hill, he lost patience with one of his brigade commanders, a Georgian named Ambrose Wright. Wright did something that Hill didn't like, and Hill, in Lee's presence, was sputtering and fuming and said that he thought he was going to convene a court of inquiry to deal with Ambrose Wright he was so unhappy with Ambrose Wright, and Lee took the opportunity to lecture to

Hill, really to lay out for Hill what a commander should be doing in an army such as he and Hill functioned in. He, in effect, said, "Listen, you don't get it, and let me tell you what's going on here." He said, "These men," this is Lee to Hill, "these men are not an army. They're citizens defending their country." He said, "Wright's not a professional soldier, he's a civilian fighting for his people's independence. I have to make the best of what I have and lose much time in making dispositions," explained Lee. Then he looked to Hill and said, "Surely you understand this." Of course, Hill didn't seem to understand it. Lee said that if Hill humiliated Wright by calling for an official inquiry he might offend the people of Georgia, which would in turn hurt the Confederate cause. "Besides," asked Lee pointedly, "whom would you put in his place?" That's the key question again. All right, get rid of Ambrose Wright, humiliate Ambrose Wright, and then what are you going to do? Do you have somebody better than Ambrose Wright to put in his place? The answer was no. Lee said, "You'll have to do what I do. When a man makes a mistake, I call him to my tent, talk to him, and use the authority of my position to make him do the right thing the next time."

I've often wondered if Lee was really saying all these things to Hill not so much about Ambrose Wright, but about A. P. Hill because all of this is true about A. P. Hill. Lee was making due with the best he had, A. P. Hill. If he got rid of Hill, what would Lee do? There's not somebody better than A. P. Hill, as problematical as Hill is, Lee doesn't have someone right at hand to put in in his place. He's telling Hill, "Look at the big picture, look at the political considerations, look at the pool of available material, look at everything before you make a precipitative decision regarding someone like Ambrose Wright." The key here is there weren't always capable replacements. Lee's handling of Hill showed that.

I believe that overall Lee demonstrated admirable flexibility in handling subordinates and problems of command. I think he's much like Dwight D. Eisenhower in that regard. He has a real politician's touch in dealing with these often difficult subordinates. I've often thought that Dwight Eisenhower, when he woke up in the morning, might have had as his first thought, "My God, Montgomery and Patton are still both in my army. How am I going to deal with these two raging egos?" Well, Lee also had to deal with those kinds of things, and as Eisenhower did, he often performed very deftly in that regard.

He allowed wide latitude to the deserving officers, to the Jacksons and Longstreets and Stuarts and Jubal Earlys in the Shenandoah Valley in 1864, in Early's case. He kept a closer eye on those less talented—Ewell and Hill, by the time of the Overland campaign, Richard Anderson. He removed officers if a capable replacement were available, as in the case of Early's being available to replace Ewell. But in many cases, to use his language in talking to Hill, he had to make the best of what he had. He had to make the best of what he had. We always have to remember that the United States had never been engaged in a war on this scale. The army had been tiny at the time of Fort Sumter, fifteen thousand men total, officers and men in the ranks. Then you go to three million men in uniform. What are the odds of finding adequate commanders in an army that expands from fifteen thousand to three million, to find enough men who can deal with all of the difficulties of trying to lead men into battle and to keep them in good shape in camp? All of these men commanding corps have never commanded more than a handful of soldiers in the field in the best of circumstances. Richard Ewell, forty or fifty dragoon; A. P. Hill, not even that many; James Longstreet—he's a paymaster at the outset of the war. Lee had been a staff officer. It's a miracle of sorts that as many capable men stepped forward at as many levels as they did, but the point is there's not a huge pool from which Lee could draw. He couldn't be guaranteed of a steady supply of talented men to replace officers who failed him or officers who were killed or wounded in battle.

That was a huge headache for Lee throughout the war, attrition. Attrition in the high command, part of it arising from the expectations on the part of men of how their officers would behave in battle, and it is that question that we will turn to next time—that topic, the topic of attrition, that ravaged the high command of the Army of Northern Virginia.

# Lecture Seventeen
# The Problem of Attrition

**Scope:** One factor Lee could not control was the loss of able subordinates to wounds on the battlefield. Attrition among generals in the Army of Northern Virginia sometimes exceeded 25–30 percent in a single campaign, and the search to replace officers who fell in battle forms a leitmotif through the history of the army. This lecture focuses on three periods—the aftermath of Chancellorsville, when Lee sought to fill Stonewall Jackson's place; the aftermath of Gettysburg, a battle in which roughly one-third of the army's generals were killed, wounded, or captured; and the first six weeks of the confrontation between Lee and Ulysses S. Grant, when James Longstreet, Jeb Stuart, and a number of less famous generals were killed or severely wounded. The ghastly toll of generals in the army, which began early and continued until the very last scenes in the drama, illuminates the fragile structure of the army's high command.

## Outline

I. Generals faced enormous dangers on Civil War battlefields.
   A. Officers commanding brigades were expected to lead from the front.
      1. Soldiers demanded heroic leadership from their brigadier generals.
      2. Such leadership exacted a heavy toll among promising officers. Two dozen brigadier generals were killed in the C.S.A. alone.
   B. Division and corps commanders also often exposed themselves to danger.
      1. Four corps commanders in the Army of Northern Virginia were killed or badly wounded in battle: Jackson, Stuart, Longstreet, and Hill.
      2. One-third of the army's division commanders were wounded at Gettysburg.
   C. Some campaigns exacted a particularly high price in officers.

      **1.** Roughly one-third of the army's generals became casualties during the Gettysburg campaign.

      **2.** The Overland campaign proved equally costly.

**II.** Lee reshuffled his high command because of Jackson's death after Chancellorsville.

    **A.** Lee wrestled with the question of whether to have two or three corps.

      **1.** His decision to add a third corps required promoting two major generals.

      **2.** He had to choose from among several prominent officers:

        **a.** Jeb Stuart

        **b.** A. P. Hill

        **c.** Richard S. Ewell

        **d.** John Bell Hood

    **B.** Lee had to select generals to replace the new corps commanders at the division level.

    **C.** Additional changes rippled down through the ranks.

**III.** The aftermath of Gettysburg presented a different situation.

    **A.** Losses were higher than after Chancellorsville.

      **1.** Seventeen of the 52 generals who had begun the campaign were dead, severely wounded, or had been captured.

      **2.** George E. Pickett's division had been wrecked and would not figure prominently in the army's operations during the next year.

    **B.** Lee had to replace no corps commander.

    **C.** The absence of a major campaign for the rest of the year took some of the pressure off dealing with these losses.

**IV.** The Overland campaign brought a virtual collapse of the army's high command.

    **A.** James Longstreet was lost for months with his wound at the Wilderness.

    **B.** Jeb Stuart was mortally wounded at Yellow Tavern.

    **C.** Richard S. Ewell and A. P. Hill suffered physical problems and otherwise failed to meet Lee's expectations.

**D.** Shuffling commanders to fill vacancies gave opportunities to promising young officers.

    **1.** John B. Gordon's brilliant actions at Spotsylvania earned him promotion to major general.

    **2.** Stephen Dodson Ramseur similarly received a major general's commission based on his consistently fine work as a brigadier.

**E.** However promising were such men as Gordon and Ramseur, their promotion could not offset the loss of so many senior officers.

## Essential Reading:

Freeman, *Lee's Lieutenants*, vol. 2, chapters 16, 36–37; vol. 3, chapters 10, 18, 25, 28, 34.

Gallagher, *Lee and His Generals in War and Memory*, chapter 4.

## Supplementary Reading:

Welsh, *Medical Histories of Confederate Generals.*

## Questions to Consider:

**1.** Did Confederate attitudes toward the need for personal courage guarantee a devastating rate of attrition among general officers?

**2.** Why was attrition higher among Confederate generals than among their U.S. counterparts?

# Lecture Seventeen—Transcript
# The Problem of Attrition

We continue our topical interlude with a look at the problem of attrition among general officers in the Army of Northern Virginia. One factor Robert E. Lee could not control was the loss of able subordinates to wounds on the battlefield. Attrition among generals in the Army of Northern Virginia sometimes exceeded 25-30 percent in a single campaign, and the search to replace officers who fell in battle forms a leitmotif through the history of the army. This lecture will focus on three periods—the aftermath of Chancellorsville, when Lee sought to fill Stonewall Jackson's place; the aftermath of Gettysburg, a battle in which roughly one-third of the army's generals were killed, wounded, or captured; and the first six weeks of the confrontation between Lee and Ulysses S. Grant, when James Longstreet, Jeb Stuart, and a number of less famous generals were killed or severely wounded. The ghastly toll of generals in the army, which began early and continued until the very last scenes in the drama, illuminates the fragile structure of the army's high command.

Before we get to attrition let me just say briefly that there were a number of concerns that were on army commanders' minds pretty much every day, day in and day out, and they are not necessarily what we would consider strictly military concerns. They are not strategic, they're not tactical, they're not: Do we have enough cannons in the army or enough ammunition for the men? But things such as: Do we have enough food? Are the men clad? Do they all have shoes? Do they have enough socks? Do the animals have enough food and fodder? Logistics are probably on Lee's mind day in and day out more than anything else, just feeding the army, the men, the animals, these tens of thousands of men, and it's not only the white soldiers who have to be fed in the Army of Northern Virginia, of course, what really has been airbrushed out of the story of Confederate armies in the Civil War, and United States armies to a lesser extent, is, on the Confederate side, there are thousands of slaves, not slaves fighting for the Confederacy as some of the weird works that have come out recently would suggest, these aren't black Confederate soldiers, but slaves who've been placed into situations where they're working in support of the Confederate army. They're teamsters, they're cooks, and they're doing all kinds of non-combatant things, not because they want to but because that's what they're being made to do. They also have to be fed and clothed.

So, if Lee's army has 65,000 men in it at the time of the Overland campaign, you may have to add as many as 10,000 slaves with the army who also need to be supplied with the things they need to do their jobs, together with the thousands of animals that labor alongside the soldiers, who pull the cannons and pull the wagons, the tens of thousands of animals with the army. It's an enormous problem keeping these armies supplied, an absolutely enormous one, and it is something that would always be on Lee's mind. If you read his letters throughout the war, he probably devotes more time, his correspondence with Jefferson Davis, his correspondence with various governors across the Confederacy, and so forth, probably more attention devoted to the problem of feeding his army and equipping his army than to any other single topic. That is a theme going through the history of the army. He can, to a degree, control that by asking for more of this and wheedling things out of the government, and so forth. He has some control there, and I think Lee often exaggerated the condition his army was in in order to get supplies. Something he didn't have control over, however, is something we're going to focus on now, and that is attrition in the army.

We can start from the position that generals faced enormous dangers on Civil War battlefields. It was a much more dangerous business being a general in the Civil War, whether you were in a United States uniform or a Confederate uniform, than it is to be a general now, or it was to be a general in World War II, or than it was to be a general in World War I, or than it was to be a general in the Spanish-American War. The circumstances for generals change after the Civil War. It's a bloody business to lead men in battle in the rank of general during the Civil War. Officers commanding brigades in Lee's army were expected to lead from the front, literally to lead from the front. This was also true in the United States, but losses among Confederate officers were higher than they were among United States officers during the Civil War. No one has ever tried to explain that in a precise way. I believe part of it had to do with the ethos of honor among the slaveholding officers in the Confederacy. There was a sense that they were honor-bound to behave in a certain way on a battlefield, that honor dictated that you place yourself at enormous risk at the front of your troops.

There was also a sense on the part of soldiers in the ranks that officers better behave that way or the soldiers were not going to fight hard for them. You are going to lead me, the soldiers said, or I'm not going to do what you want me to do. Don't you tell me to go attack Cemetery Ridge, you go and I will follow you. That is the attitude among soldiers in the Army of Northern Virginia and elsewhere. One perceptive foreign observer, a professional soldier himself, who was just interested in seeing how this American war was being played out, he wrote directly on this point, and he said that every ounce of authority that officers in the Confederate army enjoyed was purchased with their blood, a very graphic way to put it. If you want me to follow you, by God, you'd better put yourself at the same risk your asking me to put myself or you're not going to get a performance out of me, and Confederate officers did that.

Northern officers did as well, don't misunderstand me here, but the casualty rates are higher among the Confederates at the rank of general officer—more dangerous being a Confederate general if you go by the numbers than if you were a United States general. This kind of leadership exacted an enormous toll among promising officers. More than two dozen brigadier generals were killed or mortally wounded in the Army of Northern Virginia during the period of Lee's tenure of command. Two dozen—generals, brigadier generals—killed or mortally wounded. Brigadier generals are out in front. It's dangerous for them. They're the lowest ranking generals, the one-star generals.

All right, we can sort of accept why that might be the case, but what about the higher ranking generals, though? Are they doing better? In fact, division and corps commanders also expose themselves to great danger on the battlefields of Lee's army, the lieutenant generals, the three-star generals, the two-star generals, the major generals. Four corps commanders in the Army of Northern Virginia were killed or badly wounded in battle. We've followed them along already in this course. Stonewall Jackson died of wounds after Chancellorsville. Jeb Stuart died of his wounds at Yellow Tavern. A. P. Hill killed just at the very end of the war in action. James Longstreet severely wounded in the throat there on the Plank Road in the Wilderness. Now those, that group of generals, include the three most famous subordinate commanders in the history of the Army of Northern Virginia—Jackson and Stuart and Longstreet, two of them killed, one of them grievously wounded. Most officers would have died from the wounds that Longstreet received. Longstreet was so strong that he managed to survive it. But, these aren't just some of the lieutenant generals and major generals of the army, these are the very top ones. One-third of the army's nine division commanders were wounded at Gettysburg. There were nine men commanding divisions there, three of them became casualties—William Dorsey Pender, and he died later of his wounds, he led a division in A. P. Hill's corps; Henry Heath, another one of Hill's division commanders, was wounded at Gettysburg; and, as we've seen, John Bell Hood had his arm mangled at Gettysburg and was out for a while after that.

Now, if you count replacements it's actually even worse than that at Gettysburg because Isaac Ridgeway Trimble replaced Dorsey Pender. Trimble was badly wounded during the Pickett-Pettigrew assault. And Pettigrew, Johnston Pettigrew, who replaced Heath, was wounded during the army's retreat to the Potomac River, and he died as well. So, you really have five major generals who become casualties at Gettysburg, not the three. Three of the nine who went into the battle as division commanders, and then two replacements wounded as well.

Some campaigns exacted a particularly high price in officers. Gettysburg, of course, was one of those. I've already mentioned roughly a third of the army's generals became casualties during the Gettysburg campaign. Lee's army marched north with 52 general officers in June of 1863. Officers from lieutenant general down to brigadier general, there were 52 of them in this army of 75,000 men. A third of them become casualties of one kind or another, and I'm including captured. James J. Archer was captured on the first day's fighting. He's the first general officer in the army under Lee's period of command who was taken prisoner during battle by United States forces. So, there's one captured, the rest are killed or wounded. That is a catastrophic proportion. It's a proportion—the army as a whole loses a third of its strength, at least, during the Gettysburg campaign, but the losses among general officers are as high as the losses among soldiers in the ranks. That's an astonishing statistic. All right, we can understand that the poor guys shouldering muskets would be shot down in profusion in the kind of fighting that took place at Gettysburg and on other Civil War battlefields, but that their general officers would fall in the same proportion is quite remarkable, and the implications for command are enormous. You cannot have that kind of loss of leadership, we're talking about generals here, the same thing is true of the field grade officers and company grade officers, going all the way down the ranks of the army. The implications for the cohesion and integrity of the army are enormous when you've removed so much of the command structure. This is in one campaign. This is in a matter of weeks.

The Overland campaign proved equally costly. We will talk more about that in a few minutes. We can use the men that we're looking at in this course as a population to gauge just what a problem attrition was in Lee's army. These are the top men in many ways in the army that we're dealing with. We're dealing with most of the most important ones, and selected junior officers who put in superb performances time and time again. So, this isn't just a random group of officers in the army, these men are essential to the army. Our fifteen key officers, Lee would be sixteen and we won't count him, the other fifteen, these fifteen officers underscore the problem of attrition. Of our fifteen, Jackson, corps commander, killed; Stuart, a corps commander, killed; Hill, a corps commander, killed; and two younger officers we'll talk about in later lectures in the course, Robert Emmett Rodes and Stephen Dodson Ramseur, also killed in action. So, there, five of our fifteen are killed or mortally wounded.

Drop down to those just wounded: James Longstreet, grievously wounded in the Wilderness; Jubal Early, wounded at the battle of Williamsburg; Richard Ewell, grievously wounded at Groveton, lost a leg as we've seen; John Brown Gordon, whom we haven't looked at yet, was wounded multiple times; Edward Porter Alexander, another young officer we'll look at in a subsequent lecture, wounded; Joseph Johnston, an army commander, wounded in the chest as we saw at Seven Pines; George Pickett, we'll talk about him later, wounded; John Bell Hood, just as severely wounded as you could be and not die, an arm crippled, a leg taken off at the hip. Eight of our officers then, eight of them are wounded severely. That is thirteen of our fifteen. The only men out of our entire group who were not wounded during the war were P. G. T. Beauregard, whom we'll look at in a later lecture, and John Bankhead Magruder, who will also come up in a later lecture. Thirteen of our fifteen become casualties, five killed or mortally wounded.

Lee reshuffled his high command after Chancellorsville because of Jackson's death. It's attrition that brings that reorganization, and attrition always had this effect. It forced Lee to try out new officers. It forced him to bring up to the next level a quantity known at the lower level but unknown at the new level, because men usually stepped up in grade to replace someone who'd been lost. Lee could have a firm handle on how they'd done before or he wouldn't have been considering their promotion, but he couldn't know how they would function at the next step up. That's always, always, always a large element of chance and some doubt as to whether officer X, who is a wonderful brigade commander, can lead a division, or whether officer Y, who is a very competent division commander, can lead a corps.

Lee's decision to add a third corps after Chancellorsville, of course, required promoting two major generals. He's not just going to promote one to replace Stonewall Jackson, he's going to have to find two, and he had, really, four men from among whom he would make these choices. He had Jeb Stuart, we've talked about this, he'd done such a wonderful job with the cavalry that Lee decided in the end he probably shouldn't make him an infantry corps commander. He had A. P. Hill, the obvious choice because he'd been such a great division commander. He, if anyone seemed a certain thing, I think A. P. Hill did to Robert E. Lee, and we know, of course, how that came out. Richard Ewell, the second most obvious choice. John Bell Hood was the fourth, who was, at least, a possibility as a corps commander. A little bit longer shot. He actually had a better combat record than Richard Ewell did, but Ewell was in his late forties, a man of more experience than John Bell Hood, who was only in his mid-thirties, and Ewell also had the blessing of Stonewall Jackson, as we've seen, or at least people believed that he did. But Lee, in making these two choices, brought on by the death of Stonewall Jackson, really only had four men to choose from.

He made the selections, and we know those didn't work out very well. But, in choosing men to move up to the corps level he also had to make new division commanders. This is the effect that all of these attempts to fill the places of men killed or mortally wounded, or wounded so badly they leave the army. It's the effect it always has. You don't just replace—it ripples down all the way through every level of command. You're bringing people up from lower levels to replace the men lost at the higher levels. Lee had to select generals to replace the new corps commanders at the division level. As I said a few minutes ago, there are nine divisions in the Army of Northern Virginia at this stage of the war, and Lee had to keep all of them filled. What he does after Chancellorsville is make Robert Rodes a permanent division commander. Rodes had commanded a division temporarily at Chancellorsville as a brigadier general. Now he's made a major general. A. P. Hill is replaced, has to be replaced at the division level, he's replaced by William Dorsey Pender, and then Henry Heath is also promoted to division command. So, you have three new permanent major generals after Chancellorsville, which means that going into Gettysburg a third of your division commanders are reasonably new to that level of command and you're not going to know exactly how they're going to do, and the changes then went on down through the ranks. You had to have colonels who had to become brigadier generals, you had to have lieutenant colonels who would become colonels, majors who would become lieutenant colonels—it goes all the way down and you have this constantly shifting cast of leaders, many of whom had not proved themselves at the level at which they were exercising command.

The aftermath of Gettysburg presented a different situation. Losses were higher than at Chancellorsville, 17 of 52 generals killed or wounded or captured. George Pickett's division had been wrecked, wouldn't figure prominently in the army's operations in the next year, but Pickett hadn't been shot. No corps commanders were killed at Gettysburg, so you didn't have to deal with the problem, as after Chancellorsville, of replacing a corps commander. However, Lee came away from Gettysburg with doubts about Ewell and Hill. So, that has to be in his mind. That's not attrition in terms of being killed or wounded on the battlefield, but it's a different kind of attrition. People demonstrating that they were not really up to their level of command.

The absence of campaigning during the rest of the year took some of the edge, some of the pressure off dealing with some of these losses. He didn't have to hurry. After Chancellorsville, the army was headed north within a few weeks for the Pennsylvania campaign. After Gettysburg, it's going to be ten months before there is major action again in Virginia, and so Lee has more time to deal with this. However, that was a period during which new questions came up about Ewell and Hill, as we've seen. Hill at Bristoe Station badly bungled his role there. Ewell becoming sick in the winter, having to be replaced by Jubal Early on a temporary basis. So, there's looming attrition in respect to two of the corps commanders, even though there is not campaigning.

The Overland campaign of 1864 brought a virtual collapse of the army's high command, and it's absolutely breathtaking the degree to which top command simply fell apart within a matter of a few weeks. I cannot overstate the calamitous nature of this fracturing of the leadership in the army. James Longstreet lost for months with his wound from May 6. He's the top officer in the army under Lee; he's the only reliable corps commander. He's gone for five months. He might have been gone for the rest of the war, his wounds were so horrible, but as it turned out he was gone for five months. The point is the best guy is gone right at the outset; two days into the new campaign James Longstreet is gone. James Longstreet is gone, and Richard Ewell and A. P. Hill suffering physical problems and otherwise failing to meet Lee's expectations. All three of the infantry corps commanders are either being wounded or letting Lee down, and that meant that Lee had a problem at the top of every corps, and Jeb Stuart's killed, or mortally wounded, at Yellow Tavern. All four of his top subordinates are gone within one month. Nothing like that had happened before.

After the reorganization after Seven Days, as we've seen, that structure remained in place all the way to Chancellorsville the following spring. After the reorganization following Chancellorsville, that structure remained in place for over a year. Here, the structure is gone within a month, gone within a month, and the result was that Lee faced a crisis of command unprecedented in the war, and it dumped so much on his shoulders, there was so much uncertainty at the top levels of his subordinate command, that he was, for the only time in the war, offered an opportunity that he couldn't even try to take advantage of. This came at the North Anna in late May. The armies had moved south after Spotsylvania. Lee was in a position just south of the North Anna, and Grant got his army into a very awkward position opposite Lee. Part of his army on one side of the river, part in the middle on the other side, and his other wing on the south side of the river as well. The river, in other words, would have had to have been crossed twice by men from Grant's right to move over to Grant's left, a very vulnerable position.

Lee knew the Union army was vulnerable, but for the only time during the war Lee's health was so uncertain that he literally couldn't get out of his cot and exercise command. He could not do it. He was confined to his cot, immensely frustrated. If this had happened in May of 1863, while Jackson was alive, he would have had Stonewall Jackson attack Grant's army. He would have had James Longstreet attack Grant's army if Longstreet hadn't been wounded in the Wilderness. He might even have had Jubal Early do it a little bit later in the war, after he knew that Early could command a corps. But at this moment, in late May, with Longstreet wounded, with Hill and Ewell letting him down, Lee would not entrust this kind of operation to anybody. He had no one he could trust at the level of corps command, and so he did nothing, he did nothing. He lay in his cot and he railed at the situation that prevented him from trying to take advantage of this opening that Grant had given him.

This is a measure of how disastrous the breakdown of the high command was in the first part of the Overland campaign. There's nothing comparable to it in the rest of the war. There's a paralysis of the high command, this utter absence of known quantities at the corps level. Attrition here had put Lee in a position where for really the only time in this entire part of his confrontation with Grant. He had Grant at a tremendous disadvantage; he could do nothing about it because he had no lieutenant near at hand who could step up and carry out the job. So the high command, the very top part of the high command, falling apart during the first part of the Overland campaign.

During this same period six brigadier generals were also killed or mortally wounded in May, six brigadier generals. That's more than at Gettysburg. There weren't that many killed at Gettysburg. I think there were five at Gettysburg. There are six in this first part of the Overland campaign.

Truly, a very, very problematical period for the command of the Army of Northern Virginia.

What Lee had to do was shuffle commanders to fill vacancies, and in doing this several very bright young officers are going to come to the fore. This is also how it works during the war. Sometimes these things work out very well. At the corps level here it is not working out very well. You're not having men, there are not men readily available, only Early is going to step forward to prove that he is up to corps command out of this malaise from the month of May in 1864, but that's not going to be the case among lower ranking officers. There are some men who are going to step forward and do very well, very well indeed. Some of the division commanders perform especially well in the Wilderness and Spotsylvania. Robert Rodes, perhaps best of all of those. We'll talk about him in a subsequent lecture. But, among brigade commanders you have men who step up to the division level here in the Wilderness and Spotsylvania, and they do so because of casualties and other changes that are brought on by changes. John B. Gordon is an example. We'll have a lecture about Gordon, a truly remarkable non-professional soldier in the Army of Northern Virginia, but his example illustrates how young men who are in a position to do well are able to make a move up because of the loss of officers above them.

Gordon did very well both at the Wilderness, when he came up with a plan—the flank attack against Grant's right on May 6, we've talked about that, where Lee was so unhappy with Richard Ewell for not following through with that. It was Gordon's idea. Lee took note of that. But also in the Mule's Shoe at Spotsylvania when Richard Ewell was behaving so badly and Lee was on the scene, Lee was aware that John Gordon was also in that critical situation and he was behaving very well. He had his troops in hand. He had his troops, he was in temporary command of a division at that point, still only a brigadier general, but doing so well that Lee made a note, I'm sure, on the spot that that, together with how well Gordon had done in the Wilderness, meant this young guy could handle the responsibilities of moving up, and so he did. He was moved up, promoted to major general, and given command of a division, permanent command of a division.

In that same Mule Shoe, on that same morning, another young officer distinguished himself, Stephen Dodson Ramseur of North Carolina. Ramseur had been one of the hardest hitting brigadiers in the army for a good long while. We'll also talk about him in a later lecture. Lee had been making notes about Ramseur, mental notes about Ramseur, as the campaigns unfolded from 1863 and into 1864. Ramseur had done well at

Chancellorsville and done well at Gettysburg, and had a minor but very successful role in the battle of the Wilderness, but here in the Mule Shoe, again, amid these very difficult circumstances, Ramseur stepped up and had his brigade so well in hand and applied it so effectively in a very difficult situation, that Robert E. Lee took note of it, and Ramseur, before the end of May, was promoted to major general and was given command of a division in the army.

So, here are two success stories in terms of young men who would step up because of problems above them, but there aren't going to be nearly as many of these. These are nice stories, these are men who will contribute to the rest of the history of the army in a positive way, but they can't offset the fact that the very top guys aren't doing that well. What this phase of the Overland campaign really demonstrates more graphically than any other period of the war, in terms of Lee's army, is that there is a very small pool of men capable of commanding at the corps level, a very small pool. Out in the western Confederate armies they really never developed any first-rate corps commanders. Of all the top commanders who lead a corps in the Confederacy, not one served in the Army of Tennessee, not one served under John Pemberton's army along the Mississippi River. They're all in the Army of Northern Virginia. When I say all who proved that they could command a corps, you can count them on the fingers of one hand. This is in a Confederate army that numbers close to a million men, nine hundred thousand or so, in the course of the war. Among all of those men, among all the officers, the West Pointers, the two hundred and fifty-some West Pointers who cast their lot with the Confederacy, you only come up with a handful of men who can command a corps. They just all happened to be in Lee's army, and if you start to lose them at the rate that you are at this phase of the war, there's not much that can be done about it.

This is a very important fact going back to our last lecture in this criticism of Lee, Lee not taking people out who were not doing a spectacular job. That overlooks this fundamental fact, the fundamental fact is there are never enough men to command a corps effectively, just as there are never enough men to command an army effectively—there's one, as we've seen, there's Lee. There are never enough men to command a corps effectively. You can't just reach into your bag of possible corps commanders and pull out a great officer when something happens to one of the men who are commanding at that level. You cannot do it. Lee was lucky to have Jubal Early in the wings, although even Early had his problems. He was a crotchety person and wasn't good at many things, but he was plenty good to lead a corps. We've just exhausted the list of potential corps commanders that Lee had as he watched this disaster unfolding. It must have seemed at sometimes like it was in slow motion, and at other times like it was happening at warp speed as the army fought in May. What am I going to do, Longstreet's gone? All right, I have to replace him. I've got doubts about Ewell and A. P. Hill is sick again, and now I have to confront Ewell, and Hill's sick again now, and what am I going to do with him?

In the end, Lee simply began to do more himself. He solved the problem of not having enough good corps commanders by, in effect, becoming a corps commander himself, as he did at the Wilderness, at the Widow Tapp Farm, as he did at Spotsylvania, in the Mule Shoe, and the problem with having all that burden on Lee is shown absolutely starkly through the situation at the North Anna. Lee's doing everything, and Lee isn't up to it for reasons of health, the army becomes paralyzed.

So, attrition is a theme through the history of the army. The one bright side of attrition is it brings bright young officers to the fore, and what we will begin with our next lecture is a series of four lectures on some of the very brightest of the young men who became generals in the Army of Northern Virginia.

# Lecture Eighteen
## Younger Officers I—Robert Emmett Rodes

**Scope:** The development of younger officers provided the best means of replacing generals lost in battle. This is the first of four lectures that will examine a group of talented commanders who began the war as junior officers, climbed rapidly on the basis of excellent performances to positions of considerable authority, and directly controlled much of the most successful fighting in the army's history. Robert Emmett Rodes, 32 years old and a graduate of the Virginia Military Institute when the war opened, earned distinction as a brigade commander during the 1862 Maryland campaign and made his debut as a division leader at Chancellorsville. After a lackluster performance at Gettysburg, he hit his stride during the Overland campaign, where his aggressiveness, alertness, and powerful counterattacks at Spotsylvania helped avert disaster on May 12. Twice wounded in 1862, he was killed in the Shenandoah Valley at the battle of Third Winchester in September 1864. A perceptive member of Jubal Early's staff remarked that the army "never suffered a greater loss save in the Great Jackson."

## Outline

I. Rodes entered Confederate service without West Point training or experience in the U.S. Army.

    **A.** He graduated from the Virginia Military Institute in 1848 at the age of 19. V.M.I. contributed hundreds of officers to the Army of Northern Virginia, which became a distinct advantage for Lee's army.

    **B.** Rodes pursued various activities before the Civil War.
        **1.** He taught at V.M.I. for two years.
        **2.** He worked as an engineer on railroad projects in several states.

II. Rodes spent the war's first year commanding a regiment or a brigade.

    **A.** He served as colonel of the 5th Alabama Infantry.
        **1.** The regiment stood on the periphery of the battle of First Manassas.

  **2.** Although lacking combat experience, Rodes was promoted to brigadier general in October 1861.

 **B.** He earned a strong reputation as a brigade commander.

  **1.** His brigade was present at the battle of Williamsburg.

  **2.** Rodes was badly wounded at the battle of Seven Pines.

  **3.** He played key roles at the battles of South Mountain and Antietam during the 1862 Maryland campaign.

   **a.** His brigade mounted a stalwart defense on September 14 at South Mountain.

   **b.** He received a second wound while defending the Sunken Road at Antietam.

  **4.** The brigade stood outside the arena of major action at the battle of Fredericksburg.

**III.** Chancellorsville and Gettysburg marked Rodes's first two battles in division command.

 **A.** He fought as a temporary replacement for Daniel Harvey Hill at Chancellorsville.

  **1.** His division spearheaded Jackson's flank attack on May 2.

  **2.** He was promoted to permanent command of the division on the basis of his actions.

 **B.** Rodes added nothing to his reputation at Gettysburg.

  **1.** Two of his brigades were wrecked in fighting on July 1.

  **2.** His division nonetheless helped Lee win a decisive tactical triumph that day.

  **3.** He played a secondary role for the rest of the battle.

**IV.** Rodes forged an enviable record as a division commander during 1864.

 **A.** He ranked among the Confederate heroes at Spotsylvania.

  **1.** His division helped restore Lee's lines in the Mule Shoe salient on May 12.

  **2.** His activities stood in stark contrast to those of his corps chief, Richard S. Ewell.

 **B.** He accompanied Jubal Early and the Second Corps to the Shenandoah Valley in June 1864.

  **1.** He participated in the successful first phase of the campaign that approached the outskirts of Washington.

  **2.** He fought well at Third Winchester on September 19.

3.   A mortal wound at Third Winchester, his fourth during the war, ended a promising career.

**V.**   Rodes typified many successful younger officers in Lee's army.

   **A.**   He led by example and was wounded three times before being mortally wounded.

   **B.**   He demonstrated initiative and manifested a strong predilection for the offensive.

   **C.**   He was killed before the close of the conflict.

## Essential Reading:

Krick, *The Smoothbore Volley That Doomed the Confederacy*, chapter 5.

## Supplementary Reading:

Freeman, *Lee's Lieutenants*, vol. 2, chapter 36; vol. 3, chapters 20, 22, 29.

## Question to Consider:

1.   How much of a corps commander's record depended on the performance of his division commanders?

2.   Does Rodes's career suggest that timing, perhaps as much as talent, played a critical role in determining how quickly officers advanced?

# Lecture Eighteen—Transcript
## Younger Officers I—Robert Emmett Rodes

With this lecture we move back to our biographical format. We're going to look at the development of younger officers, the young officers who provided the best means of dealing with the problem of attrition, which we discussed last time. This is the first of four lectures that will examine a group of talented commanders who began the war as junior officers, climbed rapidly on the basis of excellent performances to positions of considerable authority, and directly controlled much of the most successful fighting in the history of the army. Robert Emmett Rodes, 32 years old and a graduate of the Virginia Military Institute when the war opened, earned distinction as a brigade commander during the 1862 Maryland campaign, and made his debut as a division leader at Chancellorsville. After a lackluster, or at least somewhat lackluster, performance at Gettysburg, he hit his stride during the Overland campaign, where his aggressiveness, alertness, and powerful counterattack at Spotsylvania helped avert disaster on May 12. Wounded three times in 1862 and 1863, he was killed in the Shenandoah Valley at the battle of Third Winchester on September 19, 1864. A perceptive member of Jubal Early's staff remarked that the army "never suffered a greater loss save in the Great Jackson."

Rodes is another Virginian. He was born in Lynchburg in 1829. A family of considerable means, that you've heard me say again and again, most of these young officers came from the slave-holding class and the older ones as well. Rodes's family is not at the very top of the slave-holding aristocracy by any means, but certainly a family of comfortable circumstances. Rodes entered Confederate service without West Point training or experience in the United States Army, and we're going to use him as a case study of how non-West Pointers, with some military background, however, could enter Confederate service and do very well as Confederate officers.

He graduated from the Virginia Military Institute in 1848 at the age of 19. He had an excellent record at V.M.I. His older brother had attended the school as well. He did especially well in engineering and mathematics, and it's worth a few minutes here to talk about the Virginia Military Institute and Confederate military history. We often think of West Pointers as the principle cadre of officers in both the United States and the Confederate armies, and it's true that they held most of the top positions, but the Confederacy had a distinct advantage over the United States, especially in the eastern theater, especially in quality of officers in Lee's army versus those of the Army of the Potomac early in the war because V.M.I., the Virginia Military Institute, contributed hundreds of officers to military service. There's no comparable school north of the Potomac River that does this. By the end of the Civil War, I think something like 1,700 men had gone to V.M.I. Virtually all of them served in the Army of Northern Virginia.

This gave the Army of Northern Virginia a leg up in terms of having, in some cases, company-grade officers and in some cases field-grade officers—either lieutenants or captains or majors, lieutenant colonels and colonels—who had the benefit of serious military/engineering training from V.M.I. V.M.I. consciously modeled on West Point. The cadets at V.M.I. got many of the same kinds of training that cadets at West Point got, and the fact that almost all of these men, hundreds and hundreds of them, went into the Army of Northern Virginia really helped strengthen the subordinate command of the Army of Northern Virginia in ways that no other army could claim, either United States armies or Confederate armies. It's a source for very able men in many instances that simply wasn't available elsewhere.

There were also a lot of men in Lee's army who attended the military college of South Carolina, The Citadel. The also went, many of them, to the Army of Northern Virginia and that made this advantage even greater, at least until about the mid point of the war when many of the true non-professionals who held comparable rank in the Army of the Potomac and other United States armies had learned their craft and had become quite adept at being officers at whatever rank they held. Until then there is this built-in advantage for Robert E. Lee and his army. It's not just Lost Cause myth making that Lee's army was better in some ways, it actually was better in some ways early in the war. And one of the reasons it was better was because so many men, such as Robert Rodes, had received training at V.M.I., fewer of them at The Citadel and other places, and had gone into Confederate service. They had come in knowing what a drill manual was, they didn't have to sort of learn as they went along. There is an image, and it's actually an accurate image, of some of these colonels of regiments in the Civil War, both Confederate and Federal, who literally don't know which way is up in terms of drilling men. They'll have a copy of *Hardee's Tactics* or some other tactical manual, studying at night, and then trying to train their men the next day, or sometimes out on the parade ground holding the manual of drill and trying to drill the men. There is a great difference between that kind of person, who probably will learn what is going on eventually, Joshua Lawrence Chamberlain is a good example of that, somebody who had to teach himself all of these things as he went along, and someone like Robert Rodes, who had spent four years at a military school and came out knowing a lot of these things. So, V.M.I. is a great source for officers for the Army of Northern Virginia. It gives an advantage to the Army of Northern Virginia that no other army can claim.

Robert Rodes is the best of the V.M.I. graduates who fought for the Confederate states. He pursued various activities before the Civil War. He had such a great career at V.M.I. that they brought him back to the faculty immediately after his graduation. He taught there for two years. He then went out and worked as an engineer. V.M.I., like West Point, was primarily an engineering school. You learned military things there, you learned how to drill and so forth, you learned some artillery tactics, but mainly it's an engineering school, and V.M.I. engineers worked on all kinds of railroad projects and other projects across Virginia and the South. For his part, Rodes worked on railroad projects in Virginia, in Texas, in Alabama, in North Carolina, in Missouri—he moved around a lot in the 1850s.

When war came he unhesitatingly joined the Confederacy. He was in right at the outset of the war, and he began with an Alabama unit, the 5$^{th}$ Alabama Infantry. He had spent a good deal of time in Alabama during the antebellum years, and he starts out as colonel of the 5$^{th}$ Alabama. His regiment was at First Manassas, but not really involved in any significant way. They were on the periphery. He didn't have any combat experience, very early in the war in other words, and yet he was promoted to brigadier general in October 1861, even though he hadn't done well on any battlefield. He impressed a number of superiors. He impressed P. G. T. Beauregard, his army commander at that time, more important he impressed Richard S. Ewell, and in his usual, generous way, Dick Ewell went to great lengths to see Rodes promoted. He thought Rodes was a good officer and he bent every effort, did Ewell, to get Rodes advanced. He was impressed with the professional demeanor and attitude of Rodes, as were other superiors. They were impressed at how well drilled his unit was, the V.M.I. training certainly paid off there. One observer remarked on the phenomenon of Rodes's popularity despite his rigor in training. Many of these volunteer soldiers detested West Pointers who tried to treat them as they would treat professional soldiers in the United States army, which is to say to basically treat them like dogs. Being a soldier in the antebellum army was not a very popular thing to be, and it was a very rough life, huge desertion rates in the antebellum years, up to 30 percent often in one year would desert. The officers were very hard on the men, on these professional soldiers. Well, many of them tried to be hard on these volunteer soldiers, and it often didn't work. The volunteer soldiers would say, "You can't talk to me that way, you can't treat me that way."

Well, they didn't respond to Rodes in that manner. He was able to drill them very efficiently, and yet still earn their respect. One soldier wrote, "The stern and military precision of General Rodes were not such as to render him a favorite with the citizen soldier, but his troops always admired his ability, and the sight of him was sure to extort a cheer, which is rarely given to any besides General Jackson." So, he trained his men well, he also forms a strong bond with his soldiers here, although they hadn't been in combat, and he's promoted to brigadier general in October 1861.

He fights during the Richmond campaign, the extensive Richmond campaign of 1862 that extends up the peninsula and culminates in the Seven Days' battles. It begins with Joe Johnston in command and ends with Robert E. Lee in command of the army. Rodes's brigade was present during the battle of Williamsburg on May 5. We've talked about that battle before, a rear guard action. He performed largely in a reserve capacity there, but he had a much more important role at the battle of Seven Pines at the very end of May in 1862, the battle in which Joseph Johnston was wounded. He was very effective in handling his brigade in that mismanaged battle, and he was badly wounded in the arm during the fighting. He was prominent enough so that some bad poetry was even written about his role in the battle of Seven Pines. It was entitled "Rodes's Brigades Charge at Seven Pines." It's forty stanzas of absolutely mind-numbingly wretched poetry, but the fact that he came to someone's attention to the degree that this poem would be written and then published is significant. This is his debut battle, really, the battle of Seven Pines, and he's badly wounded. He would be out of action for a couple of months. He'll try to come back too soon, actually. He tries to come back during the Seven Days, but he's really not up to it.

He played key roles at the battles of South Mountain and Antietam during the 1862 Maryland campaign. His brigade mounted a stalwart defense on September 14 at South Mountain. South Mountain is the battle that comes immediately after George B. McClellan, through sheer luck, came into possession of a copy of Lee's entire strategic blueprint for the Maryland campaign, Special Orders, No. 191. An extra copy had been made, two copies sent to D. H. Hill, and one had been dropped inadvertently and Federal soldiers found it and moved it up the chain of command, and McClellan ended up with Lee's entire strategic blueprint. McClellan actually roused himself to a forward movement the next day, not the day he found it of course, it took a while to work himself into an offensive mode, but the fighting took place on the 14th at the gaps of the South Mountain range, in Crampton's Gap, in Fox's Gap, in Turner's Gap. Rodes was in Turner's Gap. These gaps had to be held long enough for Lee's army to get to at least a reasonably good position on the western side of the South Mountain range, and the brigade under Robert Rodes did a superbly job, probably saved the day for the Confederates on the Turner's Gap end of the line, did a very good job there.

Rodes was wounded again at the battle of Antietam. His brigade was stationed in the Sunken Road, which later became the "Bloody Lane." It's one of the focal points of the battle of Antietam, the middle phase of the battle of Antietam. Rodes's brigade of Alabamians, all Alabama regiments here, fought there in the middle phase of the battle. At one point Rodes was assisting a staff officer away from the fighting, a wounded staff officer, and when he turned around to return to his brigade line he was wounded by a shell fragment in the thigh. It didn't compel him to leave the battle, but it is his second wound already in 1862. He, again, came to the attention to superiors here. Although his brigade was driven out of its position, he did a good job at Antietam. So he has done well three times in 1862 and been wounded twice in the course of that.

His brigade didn't play a key role at the battle of Fredericksburg at the end of 1862, but if we were charting his actions throughout that year and trying to gauge whether he had potential to operate at a high level, we would give him overall high marks for the summer and autumn of 1862 and say, "Yes, he should be considered for advancement. He probably has what it takes to command at a higher level."

Chancellorsville and Gettysburg marked Rodes's first two battles in division command. He had a lot of people pushing him forward for promotion to major general. The Alabama delegation to the Confederate congress even got involved in it. There's some of the attitude here that Virginians were getting too many of the top positions in the army. Well, Rodes is born in Virginia, but he is associated with Alabama at this stage of the war because the troops he led were Alabamians, both initially a regiment of them, and then later a brigade of Alabamians, and the members of the Alabama delegation to the congress pushed him. Others did as well, and he was put in temporary charge of D. H. Hill's division just before Chancellorsville.

Daniel Harvey Hill is an important officer in the army who just missed the cut for this course, incidentally. He almost was included among our subjects in this course, but he didn't quite make it. He's no relation to A. P. Hill. He's a very colorful soldier. He was only with the army for about half of the war. In the end I decided not to use him, but he is someone who is very quotable. At one point one of his soldiers asked for a transfer from the infantry to a band in a regiment, and Hill scribbled down that "shooters, not tooters, were needed in his command" and he denied this man's request.

At any rate, Rodes is given temporary command, he's still a brigadier general, of Daniel Harvey Hill's division before Chancellorsville, and his division spearheaded Stonewall Jackson's famous flank attack on May the $2^{nd}$. There's a scene with Rodes and Jackson and other V.M.I. related officers just before Jackson launched his attack. Jackson, of course, taught at V.M.I. Rodes taught there and attended there. Jackson turns to Rodes, and they are thinking about V.M.I., and Jackson says, "The Institute will be heard from today," the Virginia Military Institute, and Rodes did a superlative job on May the $2^{nd}$. People who wrote about the famous flank attack almost all said that after Jackson, Robert Rodes was the most important component in that successful effort.

He, by strict army standards, should have commanded the Second Corps after Jackson was shot down. Jackson wounded, then A. P. Hill wounded, well the next one there was Robert Rodes, but he was only a brigadier general. It's very hard to say a brigadier general should command a corps, and in the end, of course, and not a long time later, but fairly quickly, Lee, of course, brought Jeb Stuart over to command. One of Rodes's aides later wrote that "Rodes distrusted his ability to take command of the corps," and then added, "I've always thought he threw away the opportunity of his life. Modesty was a mistake in that crisis." Rodes said that Stuart should have it, and I think he was right. He was just a brigadier general. He'd only commanded a division for a couple of days in action. I think it would have been asking a lot for Rodes to move up to corps command at that point. But as a division commander he did very, very well there, and he clearly—it was a punctuation mark, Chancellorsville was, to the statement that this man should be watched for promotion to major general. That settled the issue. He's also wounded again, wounded at Chancellorsville. That is now his third wound. He's been in the war, and he's getting wounded repeatedly.

So, now he's a major general. He's a major general in permanent command of a division in Richard Ewell's corps, when the army marches northward to Gettysburg in June and July 1863, and the actions at Gettysburg did not really enhance his reputation. He almost takes a half a step back. That might be a little strong, but he certainly doesn't take a step forward. He's principally engaged on the first day, and his division just happened to come in on the right part of the field while A. P. Hill's corps was engaged in a pretty much west to east fight with John Reynolds's First Corps of the Army of the Potomac. Earlier in the day, on July 1, Rodes's division of Ewell's corps came in right on the northern end of the field where they could look down the defensive position of the Union First Corps. It's a perfect place to be on the battlefield, and Rodes launched attacks that didn't go anywhere at first. The two leading brigades happened to be his weakest two brigades of the five in his division, and they were both repulsed. He sort of gathered himself, Rodes did, brought up his stronger brigades in a second round of assaults, led by young officers Dodson Ramseur and George Doles and Junius Daniel, those brigades broke the Federal line on the second round of attacks and pursued the Federals all the way through Gettysburg to the high ground south of town. So, Rodes gets off to a fumbling start on July 1, but manages to gain his equilibrium and his division then plays a key role, these three brigades of his division, in breaking the Union line north of Gettysburg.

Later in the day he joined Richard Ewell and Jubal Early, as we've seen, in recommending that the attacks be continued, but only if they were supported on their right by A. P. Hill, and we know what happened there. There was no help forthcoming from A. P. Hill, and the attacks were not continued and that became a matter of great controversy.

The rest of the battle of Gettysburg Rodes does nothing His behavior on July the 2nd at Gettysburg is especially difficult to figure out. He did have a role on the second day. His division, which was positioned opposite the arch in the northern defensive position opposite Cemetery Hill, he was supposed to be involved in the attacks late in the day. Jubal Early was to his left, he attacked. Allegheny Johnson was to Early's left, he attacked. Everybody in Ewell's corps attacked except Rodes. Rodes and some of his officers went forward, looked at the Union position, and decided on their own that it was too powerful to attack. Just to his left, Jubal Early's attack got all the way to the top of east Cemetery Hill, and there were later suggestions that if Rodes had been doing his job, that breach of the Union lines might have been made much more positive for the Confederates. But, Rodes did not attack, and he never really talked about it and no one else really explained it. He was curiously passive on July the 2nd, that is all we know, curiously passive. One observer said at one point of him, although he had behaved very aggressively at Chancellorsville and elsewhere, this officer said, "General Rodes is always very careful about fighting, and never has been taken by surprise, and during the fight he is efficient, careful and strong, besides quick in his movements, and therefore hard to defeat." Well, that may give us a clue as to what was going on on July the 2nd. Maybe he looked and decided it would be more prudent not to try to attack this high ground. It didn't really hurt him in the army. It is an interesting contrast between Lee's reaction to Ewell's failure to attack on July 1 and Rodes's failure to attack on July 2. Ewell, very much held responsible by Lee; Rodes doesn't seem to register on Lee's radar screen very much here.

On July 3, Rodes was assigned no part. This was a mystery. This has to be Lee's doing or someone else's. Rodes's division, much of it, was in a position, literally, to watch the Pickett-Pedigrew assault unfold. They sat there and watched just a little ways to the north, watched the attack, didn't fire their muskets, absolutely didn't take a part in that battle. They were well within supporting distance and were not used. That's not Rodes's fault.

Rodes forged an enviable record during the campaign in 1864. That is when he really hit his stride as a division commander. He had done well at Chancellorsville, now he did even better. He was someone who looked like a soldier. He's much like John Bell Hood here, only on a smaller scale. He's not as tall as Hood, not 6'2" the way Hood was, but he looked like a soldier. Jubal Early didn't, Robert Rodes did. He was on a smaller frame than Hood, slender, sort of ordinary in height, but he had a military bearing—very erect, clear eyes the soldiers said, and these sweeping moustaches that were quite memorable. He didn't have a beard in a much-bearded army. Various soldiers described him as the "most splendid looking officer of the war." Another man, "One of the finest dashing young officers I ever saw. He was only about twenty-six," he was actually in his mid-thirties, so he must have looked younger than he really was. Another man said, "He's a very young man, not more than twenty-seven years old, a fine officer." And, another soldier said, "He has a very striking appearance, an erect fine figure and martial bearing."

He also did what soldiers demanded their officers do, he was always leading from the front, as we've talked about before. He met that criterion for success in Lee's army, and he got wounded repeatedly because he was leading from the front. As we've seen, wounded twice in 1862, wounded once in 1863. He is leading from the front and he's paying the price.

He did well enough in the battle of the Wilderness, fought on Ewell's end of the line, which was the Confederate left, the northern end of the line along the Orange Turnpike corridor at the Wilderness, but his great day as a division commander, the greatest one he had, came in the Mule Shoe; we talked about that in contrast to Richard Ewell's behavior there in an earlier lecture. While Ewell is falling apart, Robert Rodes is not. Robert Rodes, this enormous break in that salient of the Confederate line, Rodes's division is on the left of the salient, and he orchestrates a very effective effort to stem the hemorrhaging of the Confederates on that end of the line. He handles his brigades very well. He solidifies the left side of that salient, the Mule Shoe salient, and restores the line on up toward what became known as the "Bloody Angle" at Spotsylvania, that little stretch of earthworks there about two hundred yards that became the focus of the bloodiest fighting of this very bloody war. Twenty hours of unremitting combat for control of that northwestern corner of the salient, and Rodes and his division did much to allow Lee's army to hang together in the Mule Shoe, great contrast to his corps chief. Rodes was decisive, he was cool in action, he kept his head, he handled his men well, while Ewell was out of control. An artillerist who saw Rodes and was admiring of him at Spotsylvania, used very vivid language that showed how many men in the army viewed Rodes. This man wrote, "He constantly passed and repassed in the rear of our guns, riding a black horse that champed his bit and tossed his head proudly until his neck and shoulders were flecked with white froth. Rodes's eyes were everywhere, and every now and then he would stop to attend to some detail in the arrangement of his line, and then ride on again, humming to himself, and catching the ends of his long tawny mustache between his lips." He was a man who was in his element in the Mule Shoe, and doing his job very effectively and impressing his army commander and others as well.

He accompanied Jubal Early and the Second Corps to the Shenandoah Valley in June of 1864, and that is where he would play out the final acts of his part of the Confederate drama. He took part in all of the early phases of the campaign, that great successful initial phase in June and July when Early got all the way to the outskirts of Washington, and he's in a company of very able young division commanders that Early has. Early is very fortunate in his division commanders in the Valley. He has Rodes, he had Dodson Ramseur, whom we'll talk about in a later lecture, and he has John Gordon, whom we'll talk about in a later lecture. No one had a better group of young major generals than Jubal Early in the Shenandoah Valley. Rodes fought very well at Third Winchester on September 19. He brought his division to the battlefield where the Federals, under Sheridan, were pushing

Dodson Ramseur very hard. There were three Federal corps on the battlefield. Sheridan had an enormous advantage in manpower at Third Winchester, as he did everywhere in the Valley, we've talked about that. But, Rodes came onto the field, delivered a powerful and timely counterattack that stabilized Early's part of the line after disaster had seemed to be looming for the little Army of the Valley. He helped stop the assault of Sheridan's troops.

He was also wounded, for a fourth time, and this time he wasn't so lucky. A shell burst and a fragment entered behind his ear, and he died a few hours later. Here is his fourth wound in combat, and this one proves to be mortal. It was a very heavy blow to the Army of the Valley. Jubal Early described it precisely that way, as a very heavy blow, and then went on to say that in addition to being a close friend and someone to whom Early could look for counsel, Rodes was "a most accomplished, skillful, and gallant officer upon whom I placed great reliance." Jedediah Hotchkiss, the famous topographical engineer in the Second Corps who fought under Jackson, and then through Ewell, and now under Jubal Early, wrote in his famous journal, the journal that became famous when it was published, he wrote what a great blow the loss of Rodes was to the army. Then he wrote a letter to his wife, Hotchkiss did, in which he made the same point. He wrote the letter immediately after the battle of Third Winchester. He said, "We have never suffered a greater loss, save in the Great Jackson. Rodes was the best division commander in the Army of Northern Virginia, and was worthy of and capable for any position in it." That's Jed Hotchkiss on Robert Rodes.

Rodes typified many successful younger officers in Lee's army. He was atypical of the major generals in some ways in that he didn't have any West Point training, but he was typical in other important ways, and we'll see these ways also applied to the next three young officers we look at. He led by example. He was frequently wounded, wounded three times, as we've seen, before his final mortal wound. He demonstrated initiative and often manifested a predilection for the offensive. The anomaly in that regard being July 2 at Gettysburg, something I'm sure we can't really explain. He wasn't as aggressive there as he often was. And, as with many officers such as himself, he was killed before the end of the conflict, and he was killed largely because of his style of leadership, this style of leadership that ran up and down the ranks in the Army of Northern Virginia, that placed these men, even two-star generals such as Robert Rodes, so close to the front of the action that they were subject to being hit either by artillery fire or by musketry. He wasn't unusual in that regard. It makes us wonder, as we look in retrospect at this, why it didn't occur to someone at the time that maybe it would be a good thing for some of these men perhaps not to be quite as close to the front as they were, that maybe the integrity of the command structure would have remained intact to a greater degree. But what you have to balance is a 19th century understanding of what an officer should do and our 20th century understanding from sort of an academic perspective what would be best for the overall picture of the army. They might have answered in the 19th century it wouldn't make any difference if all these men remained alive if they hadn't inspirited their soldiers by placing themselves at risk on the battlefield. At any rate, Rodes was gone, dead in his thirties, at the battle of Third Winchester.

Next time, we're going to look at another young officer who did not survive the war, Rodes's friend and comrade in the Second Corps, Stephen Dodson Ramseur of North Carolina.

# Lecture Nineteen
# Younger Officers II—Stephen Dodson Ramseur

**Scope:** Stephen Dodson Ramseur, a staunch advocate of the South's slaveholding society and a West Pointer from the class of 1860, first fought under, then alongside Robert Rodes in the Second Corps. He shared a number of characteristics with Rodes and other successful young officers, including aggressiveness on the battlefield, conspicuous bravery—some might say recklessness—that inspired his soldiers, and a habit of getting wounded. His record as a brigadier general included superior days at Chancellorsville, Gettysburg, and Spotsylvania that earned strong commendation from his superiors and brought him promotion to major general on June 1, 1864, just one day past his 27th birthday. He subsequently went to the Shenandoah Valley under Jubal Early, where he fought well at Third Winchester and Cedar Creek. Wounded three times before the Valley campaign, he was shot through the lungs at Cedar Creek and died the day after the battle. A subordinate noted that Ramseur's fearlessness, the trait that cost him his life, had become "conspicuous throughout the army."

## Outline

I. Ramseur brought sound training and strongly held political views to his service as a Confederate officer.

    **A.** He graduated near the top third of his class of 1860 at West Point.
        **1.** He excelled in military topics at West Point.
        **2.** He served as a captain in the battalion of cadets.

    **B.** He held strong proslavery views.
        **1.** He prophesied possible conflict between the North and South.
        **2.** His allegiance to the South was more important than his allegiance to the United States.
        **3.** He resigned from the U.S. Army well before his home state of North Carolina seceded.

    **C.** Like many young Confederates of his class and generation, he developed into a Confederate nationalist.

II. Ramseur proved successful from the outset of the war.

A. He commanded artillery units during the early phase of the Peninsula campaign of 1862.

B. He commanded the 49$^{th}$ North Carolina Infantry at Malvern Hill.
   1. His regiment participated in the Confederate assaults at Malvern Hill.
   2. Ramseur was seriously wounded in the right arm.
   3. He was promoted to brigadier general while convalescing from his wound.

C. His leadership of a brigade of North Carolinians marked him for greater responsibility.
   1. The brigade made a famous and costly attack at Chancellorsville on May 3, 1863. He lost 800 of 1,500 soldiers.
   2. Ramseur was wounded a second time.
   3. His superiors, including Jackson and Stuart, applauded his work.

D. Ramseur's brigade helped break the Union First Corps line on July 1 at Gettysburg.

E. His greatest day as a brigadier came on May 12, 1864, at Spotsylvania.
   1. His soldiers played a crucial role in repairing the break in Lee's lines.
   2. Ramseur was wounded for a third time.
   3. His superiors lavished praise on him.
   4. Promotion to major general followed on June 1, 1864.
      a. Ramseur replaced Jubal Early, who had been raised to corps command.
      b. One day past his 27$^{th}$ birthday, Ramseur was the youngest West Pointer to be made a major general in the Confederate army.

III. Ramseur demonstrated considerable talent as a division commander between June and October 1864.

A. He made a fumbling debut at Bethesda Church but performed competently at Cold Harbor.

B. He accompanied Early and the Second Corps to the Shenandoah Valley in June.

C. His most prominent service came in the second phase of the 1864 Valley campaign.

   1. He was surprised at Stephenson's Depot on July 20.
   2. He anchored Early's defense at Third Winchester on September 19.
   3. He held the Confederate left at Fisher's Hill on September 22.
   4. He distinguished himself at Cedar Creek on October 19.
      a. His were the last of the Confederate infantry to give way.
      b. He received his fourth and final wound and died on October 20.

IV. Ramseur shared key traits with other successful young officers in Lee's army.

   A. He was aggressive.
   B. He led by example and suffered multiple wounds.
   C. He exhibited an especially strong strain of Confederate nationalism.

**Essential Reading:**

Gallagher, *Stephen Dodson Ramseur: Lee's Gallant General*.

**Supplementary Reading:**

Freeman, *Lee's Lieutenants*, vol. 2, chapter 34; vol. 3, chapters 20, 30.

**Question to Consider:**

1. What could explain Ramseur's willingness to continue to exert leadership on the firing line despite being wounded several times?

2. How should we judge the overall effect of aggressive leadership that brought results on the battlefield yet often led to the death of key officers?

# Lecture Nineteen—Transcript
## Younger Officers II—Stephen Dodson Ramseur

Stephen Dodson Ramseur is the second of the four young officers we're going to examine in detail. A staunch advocate of the South's slaveholding society and a West Pointer from the class of 1860, Ramseur first fought under and then alongside Robert Rodes in the Second Corps. He shared a number of characteristics with Rodes and other successful young officers, including aggressiveness on the battlefield, conspicuous bravery—some might say recklessness—that inspired his soldiers, and a habit of getting wounded. His record as a brigadier general included superior days at Chancellorsville, Gettysburg, and Spotsylvania that earned strong commendation from his superiors and brought him promotion to major general on June 1, 1864, just one day past his $27^{th}$ birthday. He subsequently went to the Shenandoah Valley under Jubal Early, where he fought well at Third Winchester and Cedar Creek. Wounded three times before the Valley campaign, he was shot through the lungs at Cedar Creek and died the day after the battle. A subordinate noted that Ramseur's fearlessness, the trait that cost him his life, had "become conspicuous throughout the army."

Ramseur brought sound training and strongly held political views to his service as a Confederate officer. He was born in 1837 in Lincolnton, North Carolina, in the piedmont of North Carolina, again into a slave-holding family of some stature. He had an excellent private education, and then went off to West Point. He graduated $14^{th}$ of 41 in the class of 1860 at West Point. Some of his classmates were Horace Porter, who would be distinguished as a member of U. S. Grant's staff during the war; Wesley Merritt and James Harrison Wilson, both of them became cavalry commanders during the Civil War on the Union's side; George Custer, who was a friend of Ramseur's, was just one class behind. Custer and another fellow gave Ramseur and some others a farewell party at West Point when Ramseur graduated.

He excelled at military topics at West Point. All through his life as a young man in North Carolina he loved to read about famous battles and famous generals in history, and he had his eye on West Point from an early stage in his life. He complained while he was at West Point that there wasn't enough about military subjects and too much math and too much engineering, and so forth. He also lamented the fact that Southern cadets such as he arrived at

West Point at a disadvantage. Northern cadets often had a better educational background. More Southern cadets washed out. More Southern cadets couldn't do as well in the rigorous math and engineering classes, and Ramseur said if the South ever really wanted to be on an equal footing with the North (he was very conscious of sectional tensions and rivalries), he said the education system had to get better in the South. Nonetheless, his qualities of leadership were such that he served as captain in the battalion of cadets, a very high honor, and his ranking allowed him to enter the artillery, again, one of the more exclusive branches of service, when he graduated.

While he was at West Point he was one of the few overtly religious cadets. Religion wasn't big for the most part amongst students at West Point, cadets at West Point. Ramseur was part of a small prayer group that was overseen by a young officer and instructor named Oliver Otis Howard, who would later be a corps commander in the United States army during the Civil War, and would head the Freedmen Bureau. His name is attached to one of the great African-American universities in the United States, Howard University. Well, Howard was an instructor at West Point, and he conducted what was called "Howard's Little Prayer Group" in a dismissive way by many of the candidates. Ramseur was part of that. He was a Presbyterian as his later idol Stonewall Jackson was, of course.

He held very strong pro-slavery views, Ramseur did. He was very interested in politics. He watched the election of 1856 with great interest, an election that pitted the first Republican candidate, John C. Frémont, and the Republican call for barring slavery from the territories, against James Buchanan, the Democrat from Pennsylvania who was, in the parlance of the day, a "doughface," in other words a Northern man of Southern principles, and Ramseur was very distressed by the fact that this sectional party, the Republican party, with no strength in the South, did very well in the election. He was happy that Buchanan won, but he didn't think that this would be a long-term trend. He wrote in 1856, "I believe an awful crisis is approaching." He predicted that there might be a war. He said that the South should get ready to wage a war, that the sectional tensions were such that the slave-holding South, which from Ramseur's point of view was under siege by abolitionists in the North. The South was going to have to go its own way, and it might have to fight to go its own way.

So, he's at West Point with this sort of mixed set of feelings. He loves the United States. He likes to walk around West Point and see the ruins of the old revolutionary era forts there, but at the same time he feels somewhat alienated from the United States, and in this way he's typical of many

Southern slave-holding men of his age, who grew up in the midst of great sectional discord. Ramseur didn't know anything except confrontation between the North and the South over the issue of slavery, different from someone like Lee who was old enough to have known a time when those controversies weren't quite so obvious.

I think his allegiance to the South, on the whole, was more important than his allegiance to the United States. He resigned from the United States Army well before his home state of North Carolina seceded. That's an indication of his Southern as opposed to his North Carolina loyalties. He resigned in April 1861, North Carolina seceded in May. He offered his service to the Confederacy and there he was. He's one of these young guys who, I think, at some level had been feeling that the South certainly should go, didn't feel the old attachments to the Union that many older Americans did, and he very quickly became an ardent Confederate nationalist. That's another trait he shares with these other young slave-holding men. They're ardent Confederate nationalists. They in many ways form the backbone of the Confederate war effort in the Confederate armies. They are not going to give in to the United States. They really believed in a Southern nation. They really are advocates of slavery and a slave-holding south. They don't have the equivocal views about slavery that some older white Southerners did. He is typical of many of these young Confederates in that way.

He proved successful from the very beginning of his career in the Confederate army. His story is almost entirely one of success. He commanded artillery units during the early phase of the war in the Peninsula campaign in 1862. He led a battery, a North Carolina battery, very early on, then, in effect, a battalion of artillery under John Bankhead Magruder on the peninsula in the spring of 1862, when Magruder was in command before Joseph Johnston arrived to replace him.

He was very ambitious, Ramseur was. He knew that you could only go so far in the artillery. There wasn't the opportunity for advancement in the artillery that there was in the infantry. When he heard that a new regiment was being raised in North Carolina, he pulled every string he could, tried to have every family member, every acquaintance do what they could to get him the colonelcy of this new regiment, the 49th North Carolina Infantry, and he was successful. So, he was promoted to colonel, given command of this new regiment, and the regiment reaches Virginia in time to participate in the Seven Days' battles at Malvern Hill. It was part of the final round of assaults at Malvern Hill on July 1, 1862, those final, bloody, failed assaults that Lee launched, not well-considered assaults, attacking a very strong position. It's one of Lee's worst decisions of the war, to launch those attacks at Malvern Hill, and Ramseur and his regiment, they are in on the last phase of this and Ramseur was severely wounded late in the day, shot in his right arm, a wound so serious that the doctors at first thought that he would lose the arm. Instead, they managed to save it, but he had a long convalescence to get back to the point where he would be ready for duty.

While he was convalescing in North Carolina, he learned that he was promoted to brigadier general, and here the story of attrition in the army is what happens. Actually, Ramseur is part of that story of attrition. He's wounded. He has to be replaced in the 49th North Carolina, but while he's convalescing a general named George Burgwyn Anderson was mortally wounded at the battle of Antietam. He fought in the Sunken Road alongside Robert Rodes's Alabama brigade at Antietam. When Anderson died, it left a vacancy at the head of his brigade, which was a brigade of all North Carolina regiments, and they looked for, I think, a North Carolina officer who might replace Anderson, and Dodson Ramseur was the person they settled on. Ramseur never went by Stephen, his name was Stephan Dodson Ramseur, he went by Dodson, his middle name, another example of this, we've talked about it before in the class. Dodson Ramseur would replace George Burgwyn Anderson, but he was too ill to take the field immediately. Ramseur missed all of the fighting of 1862 after the Seven Days because of his wound. He wasn't at Second Manassas, he wasn't at Antietam, he wasn't at Fredericksburg. He rejoined the army in January of 1863, and that is when he took command of his new brigade, new to him, this brigade that already had a distinguished record during the war, this brigade of North Carolinians, and his leadership of that brigade marked him as one who almost certainly should be given greater responsibility.

His first battle was Chancellorsville as a brigadier general, and he took an opportunity there and absolutely made the most of it. His moment came on May the 3rd. He was part of Stonewall Jackson's flank attack, but his brigade didn't take an active role because the brigade in front of him stopped when it shouldn't have and stacked up the brigades behind it, including Ramseur's and Stonewall Jackson's "Old Stonewall" brigade. They didn't get into the fight because of this brigade in front of them. But on the 3rd, when the real fighting took place, Ramseur and his men were in the thick of it. They launched an assault on the morning of May 3 that helped make possible the reuniting of the two wings of Lee's army. It resulted in that scene at the Chancellorsville crossroads that I described in an earlier lecture where Lee rode in the midst of his men and there was this great outpouring of emotion. Ramseur's brigade, through very hard fighting on the morning of May 3, helped set that up.

There were very heavy losses. Ramseur took 1,500 men into the fight and lost eight hundred of them on the morning of May the $3^{rd}$, in a matter of about an hour. Ramseur himself, later in the day, was wounded again. This was his second wound. But everybody took note, everybody who counted took note, of what Ramseur had accomplished. He was fighting in the division that Robert Rodes was commanding on a temporary basis there remember, and Rodes said that Ramseur's brigade "made the most glorious charge of that most glorious day." Stonewall Jackson especially commended Ramseur to Robert E. Lee. A. P. Hill wrote very glowingly about Ramseur. Jeb Stuart wrote very glowingly about Ramseur. So, everybody who counted, his corps commander, Stonewall Jackson, the replacement of his corps commander, Jeb Stuart, A. P. Hill, Robert Rodes—they all said this guy did a great job here, and Lee certainly made a note to keep an eye on this young soldier.

He did well at Gettysburg in the next battle. He's in Robert Rodes's division. Remember, Rodes didn't do especially well at Gettysburg but Ramseur did. Ramseur was one of the reasons that Rodes didn't have a worse July 1 at Gettysburg. Ramseur's brigade was the one that really broke the Federal line out on the northern extension of Cemetery Ridge and then pursued the Federals all the way through Gettysburg and toward the high ground south of town. So, he has two very good battles in a row—Chancellorsville better than Gettysburg, but Gettysburg very strong as well.

His greatest day as a brigadier general came on May 12, 1864. The Mule Shoe played such a key role in the careers of so many officers, either sending them downwards as in the case of Richard Ewell, or sending them upward as in the case of Rodes and Ramseur and, as we'll see in our next lecture, John Brown Gordon. Ramseur was in the Mule Shoe—he'd done well at the Wilderness. He didn't have a big part in the battle of the Wilderness, but on May the $6^{th}$, the second day of the battle of the Wilderness, Ambrose Burnside's corps was sort of stumbling toward a gap in Lee's line, between Ewell's corps on the left and Hill's corps on the right, and just as the Federals were getting near this gap Ramseur's brigade, which was the only reserve brigade in all of Ewell's Second Corps, came into the gap and put up enough of a resistance so that Burnside couldn't make any more progress. So, it's a small role, but a very effective and successful role at the Wilderness for Ramseur, not nearly as important as Spotsylvania on May 12.

May 12—his brigade is the one that does the most to restore the line on the left side of the Mule Shoe salient early in the action. Early, when the Confederates are trying to stem this Northern success, Gordon over on the east side of the salient; Ramseur, under Rodes, on the west side of the salient, plays a key role. He's wounded again, in the same right arm that had been so badly mangled by the wound at Malvern Hill back in 1862. Once again, his superiors take note of what he did here. In fact, Robert E. Lee spoke to him in person to tell him, and to thank him, for the service that he had rendered in the Mule Shoe. Lee, of course, had been there as well. He had been a witness to what was going on with Ramseur.

Ewell said, "Ramseur was the hero of the day." That's saying a lot in a day that includes Rodes's performance and John Gordon's. An officer on Lee's staff named George Burgwyn Anderson after the war wrote about this campaign, and he said that overall, in this great crisis of the army on May the 12th, 1864, that Gordon, Rodes and Ramseur were the heroes of this bloody day. Here was a great crisis and Ramseur had stepped up in the crisis. He had a moment when he might do well, and he did extremely well.

He was promoted to major general temporarily at the end of May 1864. He is a major general. He is just past his 27th birthday. He's the youngest West Pointer to be made a major general in the Confederate army. Attrition, again, is the story here. Ewell is moved out, Early is moved up to replace Ewell at corps command, Ramseur is moved up to replace Early at division command, and so he now commands Jubal Early's old division.

His attributes as a brigadier offer a sort of blueprint for what you want in someone who commands at that level. He was very assiduous at drill. He'd drill the regiments individually, he drilled the brigade as a brigade, so he was able to handle the brigade very effectively as a brigade in combat situations. Jackson commented on that in fighting on the first day at Chancellorsville. He led by example, which the men demanded. He had the wounds to prove it. By the end of his command as a brigadier—three wounds, extremely brave—he had an excellent eye for ground. That might be part of his artillery training or his training at West Point. Whatever the reason, he had a great eye. He could see where the important ground was and he could take advantage of it. He took very good care of his men. He forged an excellent bond with his men. I keep talking about these bonds. Some generals forged them, some generals didn't. Dodson Ramseur did. Even though his men tended to suffer very high levels of casualties, they, in general, wrote very approvingly of him because he was so successful. They were part—they had an espirit in his brigade that made them count their brigade among the very best in the army, and it was among the best in the army. It doesn't get all the attention that Hood's Texas brigade or the Stonewall brigade gets. On the whole, on the basis of its fighting record, it was a better brigade than the Stonewall brigade. It wasn't better than Hood's Texas Brigade, but one of the best brigades in the army, and a lot of credit for that has to go to Dodson Ramseur.

Now he's a division commander, now he's a major general, and he was quite successful at that rank as well. He functioned at that rank from June to October 1964. He didn't have a very good start. He had a kind of rocky start at a little battle at Bethesda Church, which was a prelude to the battle at Cold Harbor. He attacked without taking proper precautions. He's too aggressive at the Bethesda Church. Again, if you're going to err on one side or the other in Lee's army, err on the side of being aggressive rather than being passive. That's what Ramseur did at Bethesda Church. He did fine at Cold Harbor, confidently. He didn't have a big role in it.

He accompanied Jubal Early and the Second Corps in the Shenandoah Valley in June of 1864, just as Robert Rodes did, and as we'll see, just as John Gordon did. His most prominent service came in the second phase of the '64 Valley campaign. He participates in all of the first phase, he's at Lynchburg, and then marches down the Valley with the army. He participates in the battle of the Monocacy on July 9, but doesn't have a key role. Gordon carries almost all of the burden of the fighting there. Neither Robert Rodes nor Stephen Dodson Ramseur really gets into the fight at the Monocacy to a certain degree, but he's with the army and doing fine with the first phase, but it's the second phase where he really has his heaviest service as a division commander.

He was surprised at Stephenson's Depot on July 20 1864. Again, he was too aggressive. It's sort of what he did at Bethesda Church. He did have faulty intelligence from the cavalry that was with him. But he nonetheless was not as careful as he should have been, and he got into a rough little fight in which he was handled by a Federal opponent who wasn't exactly a brilliant general. It's not a great day for Ramseur, and he didn't handle this very well at all. I think it's because he was so young, and because he wasn't used to being a failure at anything. He'd always been successful in his life. Well, here he's not successful, and he doesn't take responsibility himself. He points the finger at other people; he makes all kinds of excuses. His wife was forced, a woman named Ellen Richmond Ramseur, was forced at one point essentially to tell him, "Stop talking to me, stop writing to me about what happened at Stephenson's Depot. Just look to the future, you have a great record, the rest of your record will be good. I don't want to hear any more whining," essentially is what she told him. Just stop it. He didn't handle this reverse very well.

He anchored Early's defense at the battle of Third Winchester on September 19. His division bore the brunt of the early part of the fighting. It was pretty much alone on the battlefield early in the day when Sheridan launched his attacks. Part of his command broke early on and Ramseur rode into the thick of it, he picked up a musket, and actually clubbed a couple of his soldiers who were running away on the head, reestablished a second line, and then absolutely held the Federals back while the rest of Early's army marched to the battlefield—while Robert Rodes's division marched to the battlefield and John Gordon's division marched to the battlefield. Ramseur was rock solid all through the rest of the day at Third Winchester, and his was the division that really covered Early's retreat late in the day after Sheridan's cavalry and powerful infantry had broken the final Confederate line. He did an extremely good job at Third Winchester.

His friend, Robert Rodes, as we saw in our last lecture, was mortally wounded at Third Winchester. Rodes's division had been the division that Ramseur's brigade had been a part of. His North Carolina brigade had been in that division, and after Third Winchester Jubal Early reshuffled the high command in his little Army of the Valley. Once again, attrition forces him to do that, Rodes is gone, what does he do? He shifts Ramseur over to command Robert Rodes's division. So now Ramseur is in charge of the division where he had made his name as a brigadier general, and he will command that division for what little time remained in his life.

There's a battle right after Third Winchester, just three days later, the battle of Fisher's Hill, just a little bit south in the Valley from the battlefield of Third Winchester, and there Jubal Early, as we saw earlier in the course, was routed again. His left flank turned. Ramseur was off on the left flank on that battlefield with some cavalry extending out beyond his left. It was Ramseur's command that broke first at Fisher's Hill. It wouldn't have mattered who was out there, it was an absolutely impossible position. Ramseur didn't add anything to his reputation at Fisher's Hill, but it didn't really hurt him either because the entire army gave way at Fisher's Hill and retreated a good many miles up the Valley.

He distinguished himself at the battle of Cedar Creek on October 19, 1864. That's the last of the major battles in the Valley, as we've seen. It's a time in the war when Ramseur was quite optimistic, even though he was on edge about the upcoming Northern elections and was very unhappy that Atlanta had fallen. He knew that that would help the Republicans, the abolitionists as he always called them, in the United States. But he still thought that if Early's army could manage a victory in the Shenandoah Valley in October that that would hurt the Lincoln administration in the elections. He was also happy about the fact that his wife had given birth to a child just before the battle of Cedar Creek. They had sent news by signal station up to the army, and he and his wife had worked out a code where she would let him know that she was well and the child was well. He got that message just before the battle of Cedar Creek. He didn't know whether he'd had a boy or a girl, but he knew that he and his wife had had their child and that the child was all right. He had a flower in his lapel on the day of the battle to honor his new child, as he put it, and he seemed to be optimistic that morning.

His division was one of those that made that epic flanking march that I talked about earlier across the north fork of the Shenandoah River, around the nose of Massanutten Mountain, around and across the north fork of the Shenandoah River again, and moving into position to attack at dawn on October the 19th. His division helped overrun the initial Federal positions to sweep the Union 8th Corps, and then the Union 19th Corps, away from their positions, and eventually to even push back the Union 6th Corps. All three Federal corps on this battlefield pushed back in the initial phase of the fighting. Ramseur had been moving back and forth, from one part of his line to another in the course of this fight, very much a hands on leader as he always was. By mid afternoon the Confederates were in a defensive position north of Middletown, a little town that was on the battlefield there. As Sheridan gathered his strength for his counterattack, Ramseur's soldiers, together with the other Confederates on the field, became more and more concerned about what was going to happen, and when this heavy blow came from Sheridan, the left of the Confederate position gave way first, down on John Gordon's end of the line. The strongest defense was mounted by Ramseur's division, or a piece of it. Part of his division ran as well. He gathered fragments from other commands, and Jubal Early off to the south pointed up to Ramseur's defense and said, "If only others would emulate what Ramseur was doing, that the day might be saved." In the end, Ramseur couldn't hold on. His horse was shot out from under him; he found another animal, that horse was shot as well. He somehow found a third horse in the midst of all this, he was just in the process of mounting when he was shot again, shot through the lungs this time, and, of course, that was a fatal wound in the mid 19th century context. He was carried, once the Confederate army retreated, he had been carried south a ways, but his ambulance was captured, he was taken to Federal headquarters at a mansion called Belle Grove, and he lingered through the night in terrible pain. Some of his old West Point comrades came and sat with him, including George Custer, Henry Dupont, another man who had been at West Point with him, they kind of sat and talked with him. He lingered through the night and died early the next morning on October the 20th.

He was much praised, again, up and down the ranks for his behavior there. Jubal Early wrote glowingly about him. Robert E. Lee was very upset when he got word that Dodson Ramseur had been wounded. He called him the "gallant General Ramseur." He said that he had been struck in the fighting in the Shenandoah Valley. So, like his friend Rodes, he went to the Valley as a division commander and he did well, he made it longer into the campaign than did Rodes, but here he is, mortally wounded, in the final big battle, in Early's Valley campaign.

Now, Dodson Ramseur, again, shares characteristics, as I said about Rodes, Ramseur shares characteristics with many of these young officers in the Army of Northern Virginia, the ones who were successful. He was even more aggressive than Rodes. When he was a very junior officer in Confederate service, he idolized Stonewall Jackson. He said, "I want to fight under somebody like Stonewall Jackson. I wish I could fight under somebody like Stonewall Jackson." In the end, he ended up fighting under Stonewall Jackson and being precisely the kind of officer that Stonewall Jackson and Robert E. Lee wanted. He fit the culture of the army perfectly. Aggressive, he could show initiative in a fight, he could deliver very powerful attacks, he could also defend well, and he could promote an attitude among his soldiers that made them willing to try to accomplish a great deal on a battlefield. They would follow him. They would fight with him, in a way that would often produce good results on a battlefield. His leading by example, as with Rodes, and as we'll see with Gordon, meant that he was frequently wounded. Terribly wounded in the first wound in his arm, his arm was in a sling for many months after that wound, then the second wound at Chancellorsville, then wounded in the arm again at Spotsylvania—that arm was in really bad shape after that. It's interesting to read his letters, to look at his handwriting. He would write with his left hand after he was wounded in the right hand. At first he doesn't write well with his left hand, but he has to do it so long that it actually gets to be pretty good handwriting. Then his arm comes out of the sling, he starts to write with his right hand again, and then after Spotsylvania he's back to writing with his left hand. You can chart his wounds by what his letters look like in a way. But, his kind of leadership, the model leadership, again, is the kind that is going to end up with your getting shot.

He also is typical in that he exhibited this particularly strong strain of Confederate nationalism, as so many of these young officers did. His letters are belligerent, filled with invective directed against the United States and the North, very much defending slavery, very much attacking abolitionists, a real siege mentality on Ramseur's part, both when he was a cadet at West Point, and then all through the Civil War when he's a Confederate. He says, whatever we do we can't give up, we can't place ourselves at the mercy of the Lincoln administration, we cannot put ourselves in a position where they dictate to us and tell us what kind of a society we will have. This very strong, pro-slavery, pro-South, anti-abolition, anti-North attitude on Ramseur is one that you see on many of these young men who came to maturity in the 1850s in the midst of the virulent sectional struggles of Bleeding Kansas, and the clubbing of Charles Sumner, and the decision of the Supreme Court regarding whether Dredd Scott was still a slave after he went into free territory or not, that is the political background out of which Ramseur and these young men came. They grew up with these hot debates about sectional issues, and they decided very firmly that they were on the Southern side of these debates. He's typical in that regard as well.

So, he's the second of our four young officers. Next time we will turn our attention to John Brown Gordon. Rodes, a V.M.I. graduate; Ramseur a West Point graduate; John Gordon, as we'll see, was a complete amateur who accomplished enormous success in the course of his career in the Army of Northern Virginia.

# Lecture Twenty
## Younger Officers III—John Brown Gordon

**Scope:** John Brown Gordon, a 29-year-old with no formal military training, entered Confederate service as a captain in the 6$^{th}$ Alabama Infantry. Four years later, he commanded Stonewall Jackson's old Second Corps when Lee's army surrendered at Appomattox. In between those dates, he played a noteworthy part as a regimental, brigade, and division commander on numerous battlefields and fit the same mold as Rodes and Ramseur—hard-hitting, oblivious to personal danger, and often wounded. Other nonprofessionals proved to be able officers, but none surpassed Gordon's contributions. He shone at Antietam and Gettysburg and, especially, in the operations of 1864–1865—from the Overland campaign, through the 1864 Valley campaign, to the siege of Petersburg and Richmond. By the last winter of the conflict, he stood alongside James Longstreet among Lee's most trusted subordinates. Although his postwar writings, which proved widely influential among students of Lee's army, often indulged in extravagant claims, Gordon's record compares favorably to those of all but a handful of the most accomplished Confederate generals in the eastern theater.

## Outline

**I.** Gordon's pre-Civil War career included nothing that hinted at his later skill as a Confederate soldier.

    **A.** He was successful at the University of Georgia but did not graduate.

    **B.** He became a lawyer but practiced only a short time.

    **C.** He worked in his father's coal-mining business.

    **D.** He manifested a strong interest in Democratic politics and developed strongly sectional pro-Southern attitudes.

**II.** Gordon rose from captain to brigadier general in rapid fashion.

    **A.** He commanded the 6$^{th}$ Alabama Infantry early in the Peninsula campaign.

    **B.** He temporarily led Robert Rodes's brigade after Rodes was wounded at Seven Pines.

        **1.** The brigade fought at Gaines's Mill and Malvern Hill.

        **2.** Gordon was temporarily blinded from dirt thrown by an artillery explosion at Malvern Hill.

        **3.** His personal bravery and coolness in battle impressed his soldiers and his superiors.

    **C.** He led the 6<sup>th</sup> Alabama at South Mountain and Antietam, receiving five wounds in the Sunken Road on September 17.

    **D.** His reward for excellence was promotion to brigadier general.

**III.** He compiled a good record as a brigadier in Jubal Early's division.

    **A.** He fought at Second Fredericksburg and Salem Church during the Chancellorsville campaign.

    **B.** He assisted in breaking the Union 11<sup>th</sup> Corps line on July 1 at Gettysburg.

    **C.** He orchestrated a successful flank attack on the second day of the battle of the Wilderness.

        **1.** He had to overcome opposition from Jubal Early.

        **2.** Lee noted Gordon's initiative and gave him temporary division command.

    **D.** He distinguished himself, along with Rodes and Ramseur, in the Mule Shoe at Spotsylvania on May 12, 1864, and was promoted to major general.

**IV.** The remainder of Gordon's career highlighted his growth and abilities.

    **A.** He served in the Shenandoah Valley with Jubal Early in 1864.

        **1.** He did well at the battle of the Monocacy on July 9.

        **2.** He was largely responsible for the initial Confederate success at Cedar Creek on October 19.

            **a.** His soldiers were also among the first to give way at Cedar Creek.

            **b.** Gordon and Early quarreled about the battle for many years.

    **B.** Gordon left the Valley to rejoin the Army of Northern Virginia in the trenches at Petersburg.

    **C.** He commanded the Second Corps but never received promotion to lieutenant general.

1. Lee assigned to him numerous important tasks.
2. He led the last major attack mounted by Lee's army—at Fort Stedman on March 25, 1865—and received his seventh wound of the war.
3. He performed well during the retreat to Appomattox.

V. Gordon's widely read and self-serving postwar memoirs should not detract from his unique record as a nonprofessional soldier who reached the highest echelon of Lee's subordinate command.

### Essential Reading:

Eckert, *John Brown Gordon: Soldier, Southerner, American.*

Freeman, *Lee's Lieutenants*, vol. 3, chapters 20, 29–30, 33.

### Supplementary Reading:

Gordon, *Reminiscences of the Civil War.*

### Questions to Consider:

1. Should Gordon's unreliable postwar reminiscences color assessments of his wartime career?
2. Can you imagine any situation on a battlefield in which Gordon's lack of formal military training might be an advantage?

# Lecture Twenty—Transcript
## Younger Officers III—John Brown Gordon

This lecture, the twentieth of our course, will introduce us to our first true nonprofessional. John Brown Gordon, a 29-year-old with no formal military training, entered Confederate service as a captain in the 6th Alabama Infantry. Four years later, he commanded Stonewall Jackson's old Second Corps when Lee's army surrendered at Appomattox. In between those dates, he played a noteworthy part as a regimental, brigade, and division commander on numerous battlefields and fit the same mold as Rodes and Ramseur—hard-hitting, oblivious to personal danger, and often wounded. Other nonprofessionals proved to be able officers, but none surpassed Gordon's contributions. He shone at Antietam and Gettysburg and most especially in the operations of 1864–1865—from the Overland campaign, through the 1864 Valley campaign, to the siege of Petersburg and Richmond. By the last winter of the conflict, he stood alongside James Longstreet among Lee's most trusted subordinates. Although his postwar writings, which proved widely influential among students of Lee's army, often indulged in extravagant claims, Gordon's record compares favorably to those of all but a handful of the most accomplished Confederate generals in the eastern theater.

Gordon's pre-Civil War career included nothing that hinted at his later skill as a Confederate soldier. He was born in Georgia in 1832. He attended but did not graduate from the University of Georgia, and decided to read law. He became a lawyer, but only practiced for a short time. With his intelligence and his gifts as a speaker, and he was truly gifted as a speaker, he likely would have been very effective in the courtroom. But he decided not to pursue law and instead to go into business, into his family business, his father's coal mining business, which included developing sources of coal in northwestern Georgia. He's a successful businessman before the war, and a businessman who manifested a strong interest in politics. He was very much a Democrat, very much a sectional pro-Southern Democrat in his attitudes. He shared this trait with men such as Dodson Ramseur, as I said last time, and he's typical of those types of young Confederates—much attuned to the political situation in the 1850s, very stridently on the side of the South in those political fights of the 1850s, and worried on some level about whether it would be possible to reconcile those differences between a North that seemed to be intent on interfering (from Gordon's point of view) with the slave-holding society of the South, and those on the other side, on the South, who wanted to make sure that they didn't simply become a mirror image of the North. So, he's interested in politics, and it's a very obvious kind of politics for someone from his part of the world and for his age—very pro-Southern and very much sectional.

He joined the Confederate army as soon as the war was eminent. He's there from the very beginning to the very end, from the first scenes to the last scenes he's in a Confederate uniform. His first post was as a captain of a company called the "Raccoon Roughs" in the 6th Alabama Infantry. We talked about how the basic building block of the Civil War armies was the company, on paper one hundred men, ten of those companies, on paper, would make a thousand man regiment, the regiment is the 6th Alabama, and his company is called the Raccoon Roughs. Companies early in the war, North and South, would give themselves what they considered martial names—the Sumter County Yankee Killers or the Central Pennsylvania Rebel Killers or something like that. They loved to come up with those kinds of names. Here he is in the Raccoon Roughs. He commanded this group of men early in the Peninsula campaign.

He really got into action for the first time, as several of the people we've talked about did, at the battle of the Seven Pines at the end of May in 1861. Robert Rodes was wounded at Seven Pines. The 6th Alabama is in Robert Rodes's Alabama brigade. There was a very strong showing for Gordon at Seven Pines, an assault that extracted a very heavy toll on Rodes's brigade, and young Gordon found himself temporarily in charge of Rodes's brigade on this battlefield because the casualties had been so high. As he put it in his memoirs, as Gordon did, he said, "Our losses were appalling. All the field officers except myself had been killed. Of forty-four officers of the line, but thirteen were left for duty. Nearly two-thirds of the entire command were killed or wounded. My young brother, Captain Augustus Gordon, who'd been shot through the lungs, was carried back with the wounded. The disabling of General Rodes left the brigade temporarily without a commander, but movement was succeeding movement and battle following battle so rapidly that someone had to be placed in command at once. That position fell to my lot." Here we have this amateur in command of a brigade here in the second spring of the war.

Gordon was a rank amateur, but he impressed his superiors and he was marked as one on whom they should keep their eye. The brigade fought at Gaines's Mill and Malvern Hill, Rodes's brigade did. Rodes came back to the army too soon really, he came back to lead it at Gaines's Mill, which is only about a month after his wound at Seven Pines. Gordon's part of the brigade did very well; they are in D. H. Hill's division at this stage of the war; Rodes's had to step aside. Because of his wound, he left the army again, so that at the end of the Seven Days campaign Gordon found himself once again in command of the brigade; Rodes still too weak from his wound to continue. At the battle of Malvern Hill on July 1, an artillery round exploded near Gordon and threw dirt in his eyes and temporarily blinded him. He didn't even count this as a wound, although I suspect it would be counted as a wound in many instances, being blinded on the field of battle. His personal bravery and coolness in action had impressed both his soldiers and his superiors. Rodes's brigade had done well on several occasions during the campaigns around Richmond, and Gordon had stood out among Rodes's subordinate officers. A very auspicious start for this young man with no professional training.

He led the 6th Alabama at South Mountain and at Antietam, and he received five wounds in the course of the fighting on September 17 at Antietam. Now, often he indulged in hyperbole in his memoirs, and I along with many others have been skeptical of a lot of the things he said. One of the things he said in his memoirs was that he was wounded five times at Antietam, and I made fun of him for that for many years, and then it turned out that contemporary accounts, newspaper accounts from the time, bear out what he said about the action at Antietam. He fought in the Sunken Road with Robert Rodes's brigade, a very bloody place to be, and this is how he described his succession of wounds. He said,

> A ball passed through my calf on the right leg. Higher up on the same leg I was again shot, but no bone was broken. I was able to walk along the line and give encouragement to my resolute riflemen. Later in the day a third ball pierced my left arm, tearing asunder the tendons and mangling the flesh. The men caught sight of the blood running down my fingers, and these devoted and big-hearted men, while still loading their guns, pleaded with me to leave them and go to safety. A fourth ball ripped through my shoulder. I could still stand and walk, although the shock and loss of blood and left but little of my normal strength. I'd gone but a short distance when I was shot down by a fifth ball, which struck me squarely in the face, and passed out barely missing the jugular vein. I fell forward and lay unconscious with my face in my cap, and it would seem that I might have been smothered by the blood running into my cap from this last wound, but for the act of some

Yankee, who, as if to save my life, had at a previous hour during the battle shot a hole through the cap which let the blood out.

Well, it seems to me, he can't quite leave a good story alone here. I don't believe he was going to drown in his own blood except that a Federal had shot a hole through his cap, although maybe even that is true. It's hard to tell. But he was wounded multiple times, remained in action in the Sunken Road, and added to his reputation as a soldier who led rather than told his men what to do, and would remain in the thick of things even when he had a reason to withdraw. No one would have pointed a finger at John Gordon if he had left the Sunken Road after the first or second or third or fourth of these wounds, but he remained, and his men were impressed, as were his superiors. His men described him again and again as the most martial looking soldier they'd ever seen, even though he was very slight in build. He was rail thin, but absolutely ramrod straight according to everybody who talked about him. He was easy to pick out on a firing line because of this posture that he had. You could always find Gordon because he was near the front and he really did look like a soldier according to his men.

His reward for excellence during the campaigning in the summer and fall was promotion to brigadier general. He was promoted on November 1, 1862. Rodes praised him, as did D. H. Hill, for his action during the Maryland campaign. Rodes, who himself had done so well in that campaign, said that at South Mountain Gordon led the 6th Alabama "in a manner I have never heard or seen equal in this war." Daniel Harvey Hill, talking about Gordon down through Antietam, from the Seven Days to Antietam, said that he'd done a very good job at Seven Pines, a very good job in the Seven Days, but he was even better in Maryland. Then he added, "Our language is not capable of expressing a higher compliment" than to say that he was even better in Maryland than he was earlier in the year.

So, here he was a brigadier general. A brigadier general before the end of 1862, and he did very well at that rank. He's in Jubal Early's division in the Army of Northern Virginia, in the Second Corps, in Jackson's Second Corps in Jubal Early's division. He fought under Early at what was called Second Fredericksburg, that is the fighting at the Fredericksburg end of the line during the Chancellorsville campaign, and also at Salem Church, the action that marked the end of the fighting during the Chancellorsville campaign. He did a good job in both instances. You'll remember our talking about how unhappy Lee was at Salem Church with the behavior of Lafayette McLaws and Richard H. Anderson, that they weren't aggressive as division commanders, that only Jubal A. Early was really aggressive at

Salem Church, well, Gordon was one of the brigades in Early's division that attacked with dash and élan, as they would have said during the Civil War. They loved French military terms and words during the Civil War and that is one they loved to use, and that's what Gordon demonstrated at Salem Church. He stood out in that battle and did very well overall in the Chancellorsville campaign

He did well again at Gettysburg. He came onto the field with the rest of Jubal Early's division on the afternoon of the first day, and his brigade played an important part in breaking the 11th Corps' line north of town. They attacked the high ground, known as Barlow's Knoll. It was Blocher's Knoll until Frances Barlow put his Union command on it; it was Barlow's Knoll after. But that's where Gordon's men fought, out north of town on the afternoon of July 1, and they played an important part there. They pursued the Federals into Gettysburg just as Ramseur's brigade had over in Robert Rodes's division, and had a quite satisfying part in that successful day for the Confederates. He ended up down below the high Cemetery Hill, east Cemetery Hill, late in the day, and John Gordon is right at the front of that group of Confederates who after the war said that Ewell had done badly there, that if only Stonewall Jackson had been there that Jackson would have taken that high ground. It would have been a much grander victory. If only, if only, if only…

This is how he wrote about it in his memoirs. He said, "No soldier in a great crisis every wished more ardently for a deliverer's hand that I wished for one hour of Jackson when I was ordered to halt," that is, ordered not to attack the high ground there. "Had Jackson been there his quick eye would have caught at a glance the entire situation, and instead of halting me he would have urged me forward." Well, there's a me-me-me quality to this statement that is all through the memoirs. If you read Gordon's memoirs, you have the sense about a half a dozen times that if only everybody else present would have done what Gordon wanted to do the war would have been over and there would have been Confederate independence. It's all about Gordon in many ways. This is what he said after the war. At the time he wrote a letter to his wife right after the battle, I mean that night, on July the 1st. He made no mention in that letter that Richard Ewell hadn't done well. There isn't a hint in that letter that Richard Ewell should have done something that he didn't do. But post-facto, he got onboard with those who thought that Jackson would have been the answer and Ewell was the problem. It had been a long days' fighting, as he noted in the letter to his wife on July 1. His brigade suffered losses, the men were tired. So Gordon after the war takes one position. It's a position he didn't take during the war. But he did a good job on the first day at Gettysburg, and that's really the end of his action there. He didn't have much of a role for the rest of the battle.

His next important scene in our drama came during the battle of the Wilderness. We've talked about that in connection with both Ewell and Early. Gordon is still a brigadier general in Early's division, in Ewell's corps, and out on the Confederate left. On May the 6th, he went out and taking the initiative, trying to find out what was going on, way out on the flank, and he came back and said, "Hey, we can get around Grant's right flank. We can launch a flank attack up on this end of the line that will yield great results." Jubal Early said, "No, I don't think that will work." And Ewell deferred to Early. We've talked about this. Gordon pleaded his case more than once. Eventually word came to launch the attack, Lee got onboard. They launched the attack, they destroyed a couple of Union brigades, captured a couple of Union generals, had a very successful attack, but it came so late in the day that the possibility to accomplish much simply wasn't there. But, Gordon had been right. He'd been right, and he had been right because he had been pro-active. He hadn't just sat and wondered what was going on, he had taken the initiative to go out and find out what the situation was, and he had made a good recommendation even though it wasn't picked up by either his immediate superior or his corps chief. But, Lee noted Gordon's initiative.

He already knew about Gordon, this is another example of Gordon's being someone to keep an eye on, and when Jubal Early replaced A. P. Hill temporarily later in the Overland campaign, when Hill was sick and Early temporarily replaced Hill before he permanently replaced Ewell, Lee wanted Gordon to replace Jubal Early, and he did a great deal of shuffling around of officers senior to Gordon in order to make a place for Gordon at the head of Early's division. He didn't demote anybody; he didn't get anybody out of the army. It was a very imaginative piece of structuring on Lee's part. He improved everybody's position who was moved, and that made way for John Gordon to get division command, temporary division command, as a brigadier general, by the time of Spotsylvania. This is right after the Wilderness and Spotsylvania, you're probably tired of hearing about the Mule Shoe at Spotsylvania by this point. We've talked about Rodes there, we've talked about Ramseur there, we've talked about Ewell there, we've talked about Lee there. It's also a place where Gordon had a wonderful opportunity and where he made the most of it. He operated, as I've mentioned once before, on the eastern side of the Mule Shoe salient.

He stabilized the Confederate line on the eastern side while in temporary command of Jubal Early's division, as Rodes and Ramseur worked on the western side of the salient. And as I quoted last time, Charles Venable of Lee's staff included him, Gordon, along with Rodes and Ramseur as the real heroes of that day in the Mule Shoe. Once again, this happened right where Lee was on the battlefield. Lee saw all these young men in action in the Mule Shoe, all of them advanced, including John Brown Gordon. His reward for this action, together with the Wilderness and everything else he'd done, was promotion to permanent division command as a major general.

The remainder of Gordon's career highlighted his growth and abilities. Off he goes to the Shenandoah Valley with Jubal Early, just as Rodes and Ramseur did, in the middle of June in 1864, and he is in the middle of everything in the Valley, to an even greater extent than Rodes and Ramseur. He is the crucial component of Early's little army at the battle of the Monocacy on July 9, the battle that preceded the arrival of Early's little force outside Fort Stephens and the defenses of Washington. Rodes and Ramseur, as I've said before, were essentially observers in that action. Gordon's division is the one that carried almost all of the load in that fighting, and it was an aggressive load to carry. The Federals were driven from the field. They were driven from the field because John Gordon exercised excellent offensive leadership in that fight on July 9. He is the one who carried the fight. He fell back into the lower Shenandoah Valley, of course, with the rest of the army after Early withdrew from Washington. As the armies maneuvered up and down and in and out of the hills and low ground of the lower Shenandoah Valley in August, he was wounded again, wounded in the face again, in August, in skirmishing. His horrible wound from Antietam was such that he was always photographed from one side for the rest of his life. The wound was really a disfiguring wound, just as William Henry Seward, the secretary of state, was always photographed from the same side after the attempt to assassinate him at the time of the Lincoln assassination when one side of his face was slashed. Gordon was the same way. A really bad wound in the face at Antietam, and now another wound in the face in August.

He fought at Third Winchester just as effectively as Rodes, and almost as effectively as Ramseur—Ramseur had the larger role at Winchester, as we've seen, but Gordon marched to the battlefield along with Rodes, he arrived within an hour of when Rodes arrived, and he also was very effective in aggressive fighting, and then in defensive fighting off toward

Jubal Early's left. He was caught up in the retreat, of course, at the end of that fight, but he did an entirely credible job as a division commander there.

He is the star in the battle of Cedar Creek, he more than any other officer, including Jubal Early. It was Gordon who once again, taking the initiative, climbed up to the top of Massanuttan Mountain, to the northern nose of Massanuttan Mountain, and from that perch he could look down on all of the positions of Sheridan's army in the Shenandoah, which was scattered in its camps along Cedar Creek and stretching out toward Middletown. He saw from up there that the Federals were well fortified toward their right, but absolutely not expecting any trouble from their left. No reason why they should, anybody to get at their left would have to cross the Shenandoah River twice, and who in the world could imagine that that might happen? Well, Gordon, he had Jed Hotchkiss up there with him, the topographical officer, they went down the mountain and they told Early, "Listen, we think this will work, we think a flank attack against Sheridan's left will be successful." Early thought about it and said, "Yes, let's do it. Let's do it." And so, it's really Gordon's idea, and Gordon led the flanking call, he was, in effect made corps commander of the Second Corps on this battlefield. He was replaced at the division level. Early had two other divisions with the army as well, so Early is the army commander and John Gordon is in charge of his old division and Dodson Ramseur's division, they're off there in the flanking column that goes around the nose of Massanuttan Mountain, and it, as we've seen, is a fabulously successful attack early in the morning.

John Gordon believed, or at least professed to believe for the rest of his life, that Early should never have stopped the attack, that he should have maintained the momentum. Early did stop the attack. He thought that after they had routed two corps and driven back the third that the battle was essentially won. What neither one of them talked about much was how exhausted Early's soldiers were. They had been up literally all night; they had marched all night to get into place to launch the attack. Then they had attacked and fought for several hours in the morning, and they were completely worn out. They also had been short of supplies and there was an enormous amount of looting that took place after the initial part of the battle. Confederates, thousands of them literally, fell out of the ranks and went back to loot the Federal camps that they had overrun. Gordon always denied that this was the case. He denied that there had been looting, but the evidence from the time from diaries and letters from Early's army makes it absolutely clear that there was enormous looting and falling away from the lines about mid-morning and into the early afternoon. At any rate, the

Confederates ended up in a defensive position in the early afternoon, as we've seen, and when Sheridan launched his counterattack the line collapsed. Gordon's end of the line collapsed first, something that he also had a hard time, I think, coming to terms with. He was very touchy about that and very touchy about the plundering, and he and Early quarreled about the battle for many years. Early blaming the men for falling out of the ranks and implicitly talking about Gordon's giving way first, and Gordon saying, "If only Early would have pushed the issue in the morning, the battle would have been a fabulous victory."

Let me quote one more passage from Gordon's memoir. This is an account, this is his account, of his confrontation with Early when the decision was made not to push the advantage. He said, "In the midst of success in the morning, General Early came upon the field and he said, 'Well Gordon, this is glory enough for one day. This is the 19th, precisely one month ago today we were going the opposite direction,' [to the battle of Third Winchester.] I replied, 'It's very well so far general, but we have one more blow to strike and then there will not be left an organized company of infantry in Sherman's army.' I pointed to the 6th Corps and explained the movements I had ordered. Early said, 'No use in that, they'll all go directly.' 'That's the 6th Corps, general,' I said, 'It will not go unless we drive it from the field.' 'Yes, it will go too, directly,' said Early. My heart went into my boots," wrote Gordon. "Visions of the fatal halt on the first day at Gettysburg, and of the whole day's hesitation to permit an assault on Grant's exposed flank on the 6th of May at the Wilderness rose before me." So here he gets to get in his point about not only Jubal Early at Cedar Creek, but also the fact that Jubal Early had persuaded Ewell not to attack sooner in the Wilderness. Early's version of this is very different, needless to say.

For our purposes, what's most important here is that Gordon was the driving force between the initial success at the battle of Cedar Creek, willing to take this great risk to get around the Federal army and launch this attack, an army about a third the size of Sheridan's army. It's a really remarkable episode in the war. Both he and Early deserve a lot of credit. It's too bad they couldn't get along afterward.

Early left the Army of the Valley to rejoin the Army of Northern Virginia in the trenches at Petersburg shortly after the battle of Cedar Creek, and he was the commander of the Second Corps for the remainder of the war. For a long time viewed as the temporary commander, Early would have still been considered the permanent commander, but it's really Gordon's corps for the rest of the war, during the siege of Petersburg and Richmond, because Early remains in the Valley down to the next march, and then he's out of the army. It's really Gordon in charge all the rest of the war. He was never promoted to lieutenant general, however, because he was really acting commander of the corps this whole time. He remained a major general.

Lee assigned numerous important tasks during the siege of Richmond and Petersburg, and the two became quite close. The most famous historian of the Army of Northern Virginia was Douglas Southall Freeman, whose biography of Robert E. Lee, four volumes, won a Pulitzer Prize in the mid-1930s, and then his follow up trilogy titled *Lee's Lieutenants: A Study in Command*, those are sort of bedrock scholarly works on the Army of Northern Virginia. Freeman described Gordon in the winter of 1864–65 as acting commander of the Second Corps this way, "Gordon's continuance in that position, his temperament and his propinquity to Lee gave him a special place during the winter. Longstreet was across the James River, and not in personal touch with army headquarters. Powell Hill was in bad health and was not of the consultative type. Gordon became Lee's principal confidant as far as any man ever enjoyed that status."

So, it's the young temporary commander of the Second Corps and the army commander who really did get to know each other better, and spend a lot of time with one another, during that long winter and early spring of siege. Gordon led the last major attack mounted by Lee's army, the assault at Fort Stedman on March 25, 1865, a really desperate effort for Lee to make a break in the Federal lines and get to a critical railroad and somehow try to break the death grip that Grant's encircling army had on the Army of Northern Virginia. It was an assault that failed, but it was another imaginative assault. It had initial success. It was Gordon's idea, once again, and Gordon led the attack. He's wounded again. This is his seventh wound in the Civil War. Wounded on March 25, it's a failure in the end.

He performed well in the retreat to Appomattox. He keeps his command intact while much of the army is falling apart, and he led the initial surrender process on April the 12th, when the army actually laid down its arms. Surrender terms worked out on the 9th, the actual surrender parade came on the 12th, and Gordon left a very vivid account from the Confederate point of view on that, very much a reconcilliationist account. Joshua Lewis Chamberlain, who was sort of his opposite member on the Federal side also left a very romantic reconcilliationist account of that dramatic exchange between the two, where Chamberlain salutes Gordon and Gordon salutes Chamberlain, and their soldiers salute each other. Their writings from the time don't describe any of this happening, but their postwar writings, written long after the fact, do describe that very touching scene. It's a scene that's been painted over and over and over again, and a scene that's been used to show how quickly the sectionists put aside their sectional hatreds and came back together as Americans. I think it's a much-exaggerated story, but anyway, it's there for all to read now, both in Gordon's reminiscences and in Joshua Chamberlain's book titled *The Passing of the Armies.*

In general, Gordon's widely read and post-war memoirs should not detract from what I consider his unique record as a nonprofessional soldier who reached the highest echelon of Lee's subordinate command. He becomes the corps commander, even if he didn't get the rank. The only other nonprofessional who can contest in any way to Gordon's claim to the palm as the best of the nonprofessionals in Lee's army would be Wade Hampton, who actually did become a lieutenant general, but a lieutenant general of cavalry rather than of infantry, and he didn't finish the war in Lee's army, but finished the war fighting in the Carolinas. Those are the two who forged the best records without benefit of a degree from West Point and all the training West Point conveyed.

Gordon would be very successful after the war. He was a three-time United States senator from the state of Georgia. He was governor of the state of Georgia. He was a much sought after speaker, very heavily active in Confederate veteran affairs. He showed up at reunion after reunion. He was always at the center of attention, which is right where he loved to be, and then wrote one of the most widely read memoirs of the war, and one that, as I've suggested, never put John Gordon anywhere except center stage, even when, perhaps, he didn't belong there. We shouldn't hold those memoirs against him, his record is that strong.

But, we'll now shift from this very gifted nonprofessional that did so well, to Edward Porter Alexander, who was in every way a thorough professional soldier and who distinguished himself in the artillery rather than the infantry in the Army of Northern Virginia.

# Lecture Twenty-One
## Younger Officers IV—Edward Porter Alexander

**Scope:** Although artillerists made up the smallest of the three branches of Lee's army, behind the infantry and the cavalry, they often occupied central positions on the battlefield. By far the best Confederate artillerist, and the fourth of the young officers we will examine in detail, was Edward Porter Alexander. Alexander graduated third in the West Point class of 1857 and left a promising career in the U.S. Army to join the Confederacy. He quickly came to the attention of ranking Confederate officers, serving in turn, on the staffs of P. G. T. Beauregard, Joseph E. Johnston, and Robert E. Lee. Shifting from staff to line in the autumn of 1862, he took charge of an artillery battalion in James Longstreet's First Corps and immediately distinguished himself as a gunner. His eye for ground, grasp of artillery tactics, and overall brilliance placed him in a position to affect the battles of Fredericksburg, Chancellorsville, and Gettysburg. In the spring of 1864, Joseph E. Johnston requested that Alexander be promoted and transferred to the western theater, but Lee refused to let him go. Jefferson Davis remarked that Alexander was "one of a very few whom Gen. Lee would not give to anybody." Alexander fought for the remainder of the war in Virginia, commanding a good part of the army's artillery during the siege of Richmond and Petersburg and drawing the Army of Northern Virginia's last battle line at Appomattox. His postwar writings set a standard for clarity and scrupulous analysis unmatched by those of any other officer who served under Lee.

## Outline

I. Alexander was a strikingly successful officer from the outset of his career.

   A. From a prominent Georgian family, he graduated third in the class of 1857 at West Point.

   B. He taught engineering at the academy.

   C. He assisted in the development of the wig-wag system of motion telegraphy, sending messages by signal flags.

**II.** He impressed a number of important Confederate officers during the first fifteen months of the war.

    **A.** He served on P. G. T. Beauregard's staff at First Manassas.

    **B.** He served on Joseph E. Johnston's staff during 1861–1862.

    **C.** He served on Robert E. Lee's staff from the Seven Days through the 1862 Maryland campaign.

    **D.** Alexander demonstrated aptitude in several areas.

        **1.** He performed effectively as an ordnance officer.

        **2.** He understood the theory and practical applications of artillery.

        **3.** He excelled at engineering and reconnaissance.

**III.** Alexander took command of a battalion of artillery in Longstreet's command after the battle of Antietam and quickly made his mark in several battles.

    **A.** He helped place the Confederate artillery on Marye's Heights before the battle of Fredericksburg.

    **B.** He commanded the crucial part of the Confederate artillery at Chancellorsville.

        **1.** He recognized the importance of high ground at Hazel Grove.

        **2.** Confederates achieved rare superiority over their opponents during action on May 3.

    **C.** He oversaw the bombardment that preceded the Pickett-Pettigrew assault on the third day at Gettysburg.

        **1.** Alexander was chosen for this duty though he was not the senior artillerist in Longstreet's corps.

        **2.** He bridled at interference from Lee's chief of artillery, William Nelson Pendleton.

    **D.** He participated in the sieges at Chattanooga and Knoxville in the autumn of 1863.

**IV.** Alexander was promoted to brigadier general in March 1864.

    **A.** Joseph E. Johnston had requested that Alexander be made head of all artillery in the Army of Tennessee.

    **B.** But Lee refused to allow Alexander to leave the Army of Northern Virginia.

**V.** Alexander participated in the Overland campaign and the siege of Richmond and Petersburg.

    **A.** He helped lay out defensive works during the siege.

    **B.** He eventually commanded most of the Confederate artillery between the James and Appomattox Rivers.

    **C.** He retreated with the army to Appomattox.

        **1.** He discussed guerrilla warfare with Lee just before the surrender.

        **2.** He drew the last battle line of the Army of Northern Virginia.

**VI.** Alexander provides a singular example of how a bright, multitalented young officer influenced Lee's military operations in numerous ways.

### Essential Reading:

Alexander, *Fighting for the Confederacy: The Personal Recollections of General Edward Porter Alexander.*

### Supplementary Reading:

Alexander, *Military Memoirs of a Confederate: A Critical Narrative.*

Klein, *Edward Porter Alexander.*

### Question to Consider:

1. Should students of the Civil War be surprised that Alexander's two sets of memoirs are the most perceptive by any former Confederate?

2. Did service in the artillery make the best use of Alexander's manifest talents?

# Lecture Twenty-One—Transcript
## Younger Officers IV—Edward Porter Alexander

We'll complete our quartet of lectures on younger officers in Lee's army by moving to the artillery. Although artillerists made up the smallest of the three branches in the army, behind the infantry and the cavalry, they often occupied central positions on the battlefield. By far the best Confederate artillerist, and the last of the young officers, was Edward Porter Alexander. Alexander graduated third in his West Point class of 1857 and left a very promising career in the United States Army to join the Confederacy. He quickly came to the attention of ranking Confederate officers, serving in turn on the staffs of P. G. T. Beauregard, Joseph E. Johnston, and Robert E. Lee—all army commanders. Shifting from staff to line in the autumn of 1862, he took charge of an artillery battalion in James Longstreet's First Corps and immediately distinguished himself as a gunner. His eye for ground, grasp of artillery tactics, and overall brilliance placed him in a position to affect the battles of Fredericksburg, Chancellorsville, and Gettysburg. In the spring of 1864, Joe Johnston requested that Alexander be promoted to brigadier general and transferred to the western theater, but Lee refused to let him go. Jefferson Davis remarked that Alexander was "one of a very few whom Gen. Lee would not give to anybody." Alexander fought for the remainder of the war in Virginia, commanding a good part of the army's artillery during the siege of Richmond and Petersburg and drawing the Army of Northern Virginia's last battle line at Appomattox. His postwar writings set a standard for clarity and scrupulous analysis unmatched by those of any other officer who served in the Confederate army.

Alexander's not a Virginian. We're going to depart from our Virginia pattern in discussing Alexander. He was born in Washington, Georgia, in 1835, into a very prominent family. He had both New England and Southern roots among his ancestors. He was given the very best of private educations as a young man so that he was well prepared when he headed to West Point, and he continued his success at West Point. He was successful as a student at home in Georgia, and he was very successful at West Point, graduating, as I said earlier, third in his class—a ranking high enough to guarantee assignment to the coveted engineers.

He was so good at West Point that he was invited to teach at the academy immediately after he graduated. He went on the faculty at West Point. He taught engineering and other topics. He was also selected to assist in an important project in the late 1850s. Surgeon Albert J. Meyer was working to develop a wig-wag system of motion telegraphy, where you could send messages on a battlefield using flags. They were experimenting with the best ways to do this in the late 1850s, and Porter Alexander (Alexander went by Porter, sometimes by Alex with his friends, but usually by Porter, never by Alexander) assisted Albert J. Meyer, he was one of two. In the course of working on this wig-wag system—it was a system both armies used extensively during the Civil War incidentally—in the course of working on this he came to the attention of Senator Jefferson Davis of Mississippi, who chaired the committee on military affairs in the United States senate. So, Jefferson Davis was first introduced to this bright young officer even before the Civil War, and made a mental note of how promising Alexander seemed to be, and, indeed, Alexander was among the most promising young men in all of the United States Army when the secession crisis came.

He unhesitatingly went with his state. He's another ardent state rights man, as are all of the other officers we've discussed, as were all of the others. He goes very quickly when Georgia goes, and he ends up, he resigned in May of 1861, and he ends up with a commission in the Confederate army as a captain of engineers. He goes from the engineers in the United States army to the engineers in the Confederate army. He got an early posting to Beauregard's staff at First Manassas. He became the chief signal officer for that Confederate army that was being put together to confront the largest United States army, which was just outside Washington D.C. He works on the signal corps of this army. He also does various other things for Beauregard. Whatever Beauregard seemed to need a bright young man to do, he would have Porter Alexander do. At the battle of First Manassas one of Alexander's signal stations detected the United States army's flanking movement that put the Confederate army in such difficult shape early in the battle, signaled news of that, and otherwise Alexander performed well at First Manassas.

When Beauregard was deployed to the west after First Manassas, and Joseph E. Johnston replaced him, he kept Porter Alexander on the staff for the army. Alexander not only operated as the signal officer under Johnston, but also took on the duties of being the chief ordnance officer for the whole army, with the rank of lieutenant colonel. So, he's doing two things, wearing two hats, both his signal officer hat and his ordnance hat here, and he continued to do both of those things after Johnston was wounded at the battle of Seven Pines. After Robert E. Lee took command of the army that

Lee christened the Army of Northern Virginia, we see Porter Alexander on his staff, again, as both signal officer and as ordnance officer, and you have a period of several months here, in June and July, August and September, of 1862, when Alexander is right at Lee's side. He has tremendous opportunity to observe Lee, and Lee has tremendous opportunity to observe this young Alexander in action, and both are very impressed.

Alexander demonstrated aptitude in several areas. The range of things he involved himself in is really quite amazing. He did his ordnance work, of course. That is making sure the army had as much ammunition as it needed, both for the soldiers carrying muskets and for the artillery. But he also did other things. He worked on ciphers and codes to send messages that couldn't be read by the enemy. He conducted reconnaissance missions of various kinds. He interested himself very much in the technical aspects of ordnance, of artillery, of different rounds, the pluses and minuses of different types of ammunition for the artillery. He would go out and watch batteries fire in practice, and would take notes and make suggestions and so forth. He was very interested in the artillery.

He also helped design a plan for a battalion system of organizing the artillery. The artillery in the Confederate army initially was deployed with batteries, which in a Confederate context usually meant four cannons, with batteries assigned to brigades of infantry, and placed under the command of the brigadier generals of the infantry, which meant that the artillery was dispersed and there was no controlling hand that could really bring large numbers of guns together on a battlefield. Alexander and others believed that it would be better to organize the artillery into battalions of artillery, which would group several batteries together, place them under the command of an artillery officer, and enable the army to move larger numbers of cannons on the battlefield in concert and bring much greater artillery power to bear at one point or another in the course of a fight. He prepared a very careful paper regarding this, Alexander did, which impressed William Nelson Pendleton, who was the chief of artillery in Lee's army. He just does this in his spare time while he's operating on Lee's staff. It's something that the Confederate army will actually put into place. It is a reform that they will put into place in the winter of 1862–63. February 1863—this new battalion system of artillery will be put in place, and Alexander had a significant role in developing the plan that was eventually implemented.

He just excelled at everything he did. I cannot stress that too strongly. He was an excellent engineer. He was excellent at reconnaissance. He was very good as a man looking after the ordnance in the army and doing everything else that he would be asked to do. He impressed everyone for whom he worked and with whom he worked in this initial phase of the war. Another staff officer commented on Alexander and how good he was at almost everything. He said, "Let me give a word about this splendid fellow Alexander. He was from Georgia. Leaving West Point with very high honors, he was immediately commissioned into the engineers. His was the happiest and most hopeful nature. He was sure of winning at everything he took up, and never did he open his guns on the enemy but that he knew he should maul them into smithereens. An accomplished engineer, he was often called on by both Lee and Longstreet for technical work and special reconnoitering." Now, that quotation refers to Alexander after he became an artillerist, as we'll see in just a minute. It makes the point that even after he went to the artillery full time, he's called upon by Lee and others to come do other things, again because he's so good at them, because he always carries out his missions with great success.

He got to go into the artillery after the battle of Antietam. There was a group of batteries under the command of an officer named Stephen D. Lee at Antietam, a number of batteries that did well at Antietam, although they were pounded there as most of the Confederate artillery was. Lee was promoted, Stephen Lee was promoted, and sent west and Porter Alexander was given command of this group of batteries, and it was in command of what would become his battalion of artillery in James Longstreet's wing of the army that he quickly made his mark in several battles.

The first was in the battle of Fredericksburg where he helped place the Confederate guns on Marye's Heights, that high ground that James Longstreet defended west of Fredericksburg, that high ground against which Burnside's infantry launched their series of futile attacks on the afternoon of December 13, 1862. There's a question about where the guns should be placed on that high ground. Lee, a brilliant engineer himself, thought the guns should be put on top of that high ground so that they could dual with United States artillery across the Rappahannock River on another series of ridges called Stafford Heights. "Put the guns at the top of the hill," said Lee, "so they'll get a little extra range and can fight those United States pieces of artillery across the river." Alexander, talking to one of the staff officers, a man named Sam Johnston who would actually oversee the placement of the guns, said, "No, Sam, don't put them on the top. Drop them down on the slope of the hill a little ways so that if the Federals attack that high ground, the artillery will be able to hit the Federal infantry coming up. If they're all the way on the top of the hill, the infantry would be masked as it came up the hill, but if you drop the guns down a ways, they would be very effective." The choice is, are we going to use these guns to dual with the Federal guns across the river, or are these guns going to be placed in anticipation of United States attacks against the high ground? Well, Johnston put the guns where Alexander suggested they go, and, of course, the battle played out just as Alexander suggested that it would. The attacks came against those guns, and the guns did very bloody work on the afternoon of December 13. Alexander had been right. Two very smart artillerists looking at the ground in Lee and Alexander, two very smart engineers it would be better to say, they looked at the ground, they thought about the problems, and they came up with different solutions as to what would be the best way to employ the guns.

Alexander was right, and after the battle he couldn't resist making sure Lee knew that he had been right. He wrote after the war, he said, "Well, when the battle came on, Burnside's most powerful effort was made at that exact point, and the cannons never fired a shot at their distant view, but fired thousands of rounds into Union infantry swarming over the short range ground and contributed greatly to the enemy's bloody repulse. A few evenings afterward, visiting General Lee's camp, I took the opportunity, when the general was near enough to hear, to say loudly to Johnston, 'Sam, it was a mighty good thing those guns about Marye's Heights were located on the brows of the hills when the Yankees charged them.' I was half afraid the general might find me impertinent, though I could not resist the temptation to have one little dig at him."

Well, I think Alexander was impertinent here, but I suspect Lee smiled inwardly and didn't care. It was another example of this young officer's being very perceptive about a problem, and being right about something. Alexander was almost always right about something. He knew he was almost always right. He had the arrogance of a really brilliant mind. One of his less attractive qualities is that he had little patience with people who weren't as smart as he was, and that was almost everybody. Hardly anybody was as smart as he was. He was very quick, he was two steps ahead of people, and you can sense that he would just sort of wait patiently while they sort of, in a clumsy way, got to the point he had reached a long time ago in analyzing a problem. At any rate, Lee said nothing to him, and I believe was probably amused to a degree about Alexander's behavior here.

Alexander did an even better job at Chancellorsville, the next major battle of the Army of Northern Virginia. Chancellorsville, Lee's masterpiece as we've seen in many ways, was a battle that hung in the balance, especially on May 3 when Lee had to unite the wings of his army, which were separated, near Chancellorsville. One of the keys to allowing the Confederate infantry to fight its way back together, Lee's part and the part that was commanded by Stonewall Jackson and later was commanded by Jeb Stuart, one of the keys was that for the only time in the entire war in the eastern theater, the Confederate artillery achieved dominance over United States artillery on a battlefield, and it did so because of the importance of a key piece of ground called Hazel Grove. That ground came into Confederate possession early on the morning of May 3. Porter Alexander immediately realized how important it was and using the new battalion system massed more than forty pieces of artillery on Hazel Grove very quickly. That artillery poured fire into Federal artillery near Hooker's headquarters at Chancellorsville, and together with some other Confederate guns, along one of the few road paths through that forested part of Virginia, managed to achieve ascendancy and to help drive the Federals away from that crossroads at Chancellorsville. It was a brilliant piece of work at Chancellorsville, one that not only showed that Alexander had a great eye for ground, but also vindicated his belief that a battalion system of artillery would be infinitely superior to the system where the battery simply followed their brigades around. He was able at Chancellorsville to bring together all of these guns much more rapidly, and in a much more concentrated form, than would have been conceivable had there not been this battalion system of grouping the guns.

Now, he shouldn't even have been at Chancellorsville in many ways because his corps commander and half of the corps he operated in was off at Suffolk under James Longstreet. It's an instance again of Alexander also being, always being, kept near at hand. I believe that it's not an accident that Alexander and his guns remained with Lee and remained part of the army. He fights in every battle of the Army of Northern Virginia from Manassas to Appomattox, all of them, and he is very much present during the battle of Chancellorsville.

Gettysburg is his third big battle in a row, and it's the one he's most famous for really. His actions at Gettysburg are his most famous participation in the Civil War because of his key role in the fighting on July 3 during the Pickett-Pettigrew assault. He participated in the action on July 2 as well when Longstreet launched his assaults against the Union left flank on the afternoon of July 2; Alexander's guns supported that infantry action. In fact, at one point, his artillery made a very unusual artillery charge against the

Emmittsburg Road. They'd been set up at Cemetery Ridge, west of the Emmittsburg Road, and as the Federals retreated from the Peach Orchard, he hooked up his cannons and charged across the Emmittsburg Road and deployed again on the east side of the road. It's one of the few instances of the war where artillery was used that way. His gunners did a good job on July the 2$^{nd}$ in supporting Longstreet's assaults.

But the more famous of Alexander's contributions to the battle of Gettysburg came on July 3 because he was selected to oversee the bombardment that Lee hoped would soften up George Gordon Mead's line on Cemetery Ridge and allow this assault by 12,500 Confederate infantrymen to achieve a breakthrough in the middle of the Union line. Now, on the merits of rank, Alexander should not have overseen this bombardment. He wasn't even the senior artillery officer in Longstreet's corps. A man named James B. Walton was the corps chief of artillery in Longstreet's corps, and, of course, William Nelson Pendleton was the chief of artillery for the whole Army of Northern Virginia. This bombardment was going to include guns from both Longstreet's corps and from A. P. Hill's corps, and it really didn't make sense for Alexander to oversee the bombardment unless you're simply looking for the best artillerist, which, of course, he was. It's not even a close call here. Do you want your best gunner to oversee the bombardment? Then get Alexander, he's the best gunner in the army and put him in charge of it. Alexander worried a little bit about being placed over senior officers, but nonetheless that's the role he was given and that is what he did on July 3 at Gettysburg.

He saw very quickly that it was going to be a difficult proposition because what he was being asked to do is soften up a target that was essentially a very shallow target; it's not a deep target. It's a line of infantry and supporting cannons on Cemetery Ridge, and Alexander's guns are pretty much arrayed to the west of that line of Federal guns and a little bit southwest as well. It's going to be not firing down a long target, but trying to hit a very flat, or shallow, target. Alexander doubted whether he could really accomplish much, and his problem was further complicated by the fact that once the firing began he had more than 150 guns under his command at Gettysburg. This is the biggest artillery bombardment in the western hemisphere up to this point in the military history of the western hemisphere. When the firing began the smoke was such that Alexander really couldn't see what was happening. His instructions were soften up the Federal position. When you perceive that your guns have had an effect, let our infantry know, and then the infantry will go in. It's a lot of responsibility.

The guns begin to fire. He has a plan, Alexander does. He'll soften up the Federal position with the first bombardment. He has carefully put aside a dozen guns that he wants to be able to bring in right behind the infantry to support the attack as it gets to its final, and with any luck successful, portion of the days' work. He's put those aside, he wants to use those. The bombardment gets going. Very quickly he can't tell what's happening, there's too much smoke. He has a sense that the Union fire is slackening, but he can't be absolutely sure, but, worse than that, he gets news in the course of the bombardment that the twelve guns that he wanted to use to support the assault are missing. He found out later that William Nelson Pendleton and a lower officer had moved the guns to what they considered a place of safety, but what they had done is move them to a place Alexander didn't know about. So he'd lost the twelve guns that were going to support this attack, and when Longstreet asked him at one point what the effect of the bombardment was, Porter Alexander had to tell him that he was troubled by the fact that he might not be able to support the attack to the degree that he had hoped that he would because these guns had been moved away.

Longstreet didn't want to make the attack, as we have seen. He doubted that the attack would succeed, and at this point he tried to shift the burden for deciding whether or not there should be an attack onto the shoulders of this colonel of artillery. The lieutenant general is trying to get Porter Alexander to decide whether there should be an attack or not, and Porter Alexander, to his credit, would not take that responsibility. He left a graphic description of this very tense exchange between himself and General Longstreet. He's conveying to Longstreet the news that these guns that he's hoped to have to bring in to support the attack are missing, and he's not sure he can give as much support as he had hoped.

General Longstreet spoke at once and decidedly. "Go and halt Pickett at once where he is and replenish your ammunition." I said, "General, we can't do that. We nearly emptied our ammunition trains last night. Even if we had it, it would take an hour to, and meanwhile the enemy would recover from the pressure he's now under. Our only chance is to follow it up now, to strike while the iron is hot." Longstreet answered, "I don't want to make this attack. I believe it will fail. I do not see how it can succeed. I would not make it even now, but that General Lee has ordered and expects it." He made these statements with slight pauses in between while he is looking at the enemy's position through his field glasses. "I had the feeling he was on the verge of stopping the charge, and that with even slight encouragement he would do it. But that very feeling kept me from saying a word, either of assent or dissent. I would not willingly take any responsibility in so grave a matter, and I had almost a morbid fear of personally causing any loss of time. So I stood by and looked on in silence almost embarrassing." Alexander then went on to say that he was very relieved when the infantry emerged from the woods behind his gunners and marched off on their attack. It is a very compelling moment when he, the colonel of artillery, is confronted with this attempt on the part of his corps commander, this lieutenant general, whose trying to get him to take charge of this very difficult situation.

Alexander went west with James Longstreet and the two divisions of the First Corps. He got to the battle of Chickamauga a little bit too late. His guns didn't get to participate in that battle, but he did participate in the siege of Chattanooga and then went on to Knoxville with Longstreet for that very sad affair later in the year.

He was promoted to brigadier general in March of 1864. Joseph Johnston, who back early in the war had been very happy with everything Alexander did for him, when Joe Johnston was given command of the Army of Tennessee out west, replacing Braxton Bragg, he looked at the Army of Tennessee, he saw a lot of things wrong with it, and one thing he saw a weakness in was the artillery. He thought he needed a first rate officer to whip the artillery in the army into shape, and he wanted Porter Alexander. As he said in his memoirs, Johnston did, he said, "The artillery," this he's quoting a letter that he sent to Jefferson Davis, "the artillery wants organization, and especially a competent commander. I therefore respectfully urge that such a one be sent me. I have applied for Colonel Alexander, but General Lee objects that he is too valuable in his present position to be taken from him. Alexander's value to the country would be more than doubled, I think, by the promotion and assignment I recommend." Well, Jefferson Davis isn't going to go against Lee in this. If Lee wants something and Joe Johnston wants it as well, Davis is going to side with Lee. We'll see in greater detail in our next lecture why that was the case. But in any rate, Lee won't let Alexander go, but since the promise of promotion to brigadier general is in the offing if Alexander were assigned to the west, Lee sees that he's promoted to brigadier general in the Army of Northern Virginia. He is made chief of artillery in the Third Corps.

This is in February of 1864. Alexander would serve in that capacity for the rest of the conflict, and he participated in all the rest of the campaigns of the army down to the end, in the Overland campaign, in the long siege of Richmond and Petersburg, and the retreat to Appomattox. He helped lay out the defense works during the siege of Petersburg and eventually commanded most of the Confederate artillery between the James River and the Appomattox River during that siege. He was wounded, he'd been slightly wounded earlier in the war, slightly wounded at Gettysburg, he was wounded again in the summer of 1864, more seriously in the summer of 1864. He missed a little bit of action because of that in the summer. Otherwise he was on the scene the entire time. It was kind of a funny wound in the summer of '64. A minié ball ricocheted off of the very hard packed ground he was standing on and came up and hit him under the armpit. He wasn't gone long, back to the army soon, and he was with the army right down to the end.

Now, it's worth talking for a minute about why Porter Alexander was such a good artillerist, never mind trying to explain why he was so good at everything else, he's just smart, has a very incisive and quick mind, but as an artillerist a number of factors contributed to his success. One was, of course, that first-rate mind and a mind open to innovation. He was always thinking about different ways to do things, even different ways to put your ammunition together. He was fascinated, as I said earlier, by the technical aspects of being a gunner. He also paid particularly close attention to organization as his work on the battalion system indicated. Very careful attention to logistics as well, I think his work as ordnance officer and staff officer contributed to that. He bent every effort that his guns were in the best shape, his animals were well taken care of, his men were well supplied and outfitted and so forth. In terms of equipment and supply he was excellent as well. He had a remarkable eye for ground. He could take in a battlefield and his artillerist eye would simply say here, here, and here are the places that will serve us best in terms of artillery placement. His work at Fredericksburg, his work at Hazel Grove, and elsewhere underscore that.

He also had the ability to inspire his men. His subordinate commanders, the battery commanders he worked with, almost idolized him and this even though he had a personality that seems to me should have put off a lot of people because he was so smart and so quick and so intolerant, really, of ineptitude. But, he didn't seem to have that effect the way so many bright do on others. He was confident, he was aggressive, he was filled with imagination, he inspired his men—he had almost everything you would want in a commander, and he was vastly successful.

During the retreat to Appomattox he had a famous discussion with Robert E. Lee where Alexander said, "Let's don't surrender, general, let's break the army up. Let's wage guerrilla warfare. We could maintain the army for years if we break up into little groups. It will be very hard for the Yankees to track us down." Lee gave him a very stern lecture about why that would be the most disastrous thing possible for the Confederacy, how it would bring unending misery without bringing victory. Alexander admitted later that Lee had been absolutely right and he had been absolutely wrong.

At the very end, Lee asked Alexander to draw, as I mentioned in my opening for this lecture, the last battle line of the Army of Northern Virginia at Appomattox. There's a famous engraving of Alexander overseeing the drawing of this line of infantry and artillery.

Porter Alexander, I think, provides a singular example of how a bright, multi-talented young officer could influence military operations in the Army of Northern Virginia. Even at a relatively low rank—lieutenant colonel—he still had an effect on operations, and he is singular. There literally is no one else like Edward Porter Alexander in the Army of Northern Virginia, no one who does so many different things so well, and has an effect on so many campaigns because of his various talents. He's a fascinating character, and his two books that he wrote after the war are two of the essential volumes on the Army of Northern Virginia, *Military Memoirs of a Confederate* published in 1907, and a book he actually wrote before *Military Memoirs* but did not intend to publish, but was published much later under the title *Fighting for the Confederacy*. No other person wrote two books remotely as important and influential and incisive as those books.

Well, we're going to turn next time to two of the men Porter Alexander impressed early in the war. The first two army commanders on whose staffs he served, P. G. T. Beauregard and Joseph E. Johnston.

# Lecture Twenty-Two
## Gifted but Flawed—J. E. Johnston and Beauregard

**Scope:** Our next two lectures examine four officers whose careers provide a useful counterpoint to the successes of most of those we have discussed thus far. Joseph E. Johnston and P. G. T. Beauregard considered themselves Lee's peers, if not his superiors, as field commanders, but their records reveal an absence of key attributes that helped fuel Lee's accomplishments. An almost exact contemporary of Lee's, Johnston served with distinction in the war with Mexico, shared command of the Confederate forces at First Manassas with Beauregard, and opposed the Union advance toward Richmond under General George B. McClellan in the spring of 1862. Badly wounded in the battle of Seven Pines (or Fair Oaks) in late May, he watched as Lee took charge of the army outside Richmond and led it to a series of fabled victories. Envious of his old friend, Johnston bitterly insisted that luck, rather than superior talent, explained Lee's triumphs. In fact, Johnston lacked Lee's breadth of vision; usually played it safe rather than taking risks; retreated in almost every campaign he directed; and never understood that in a democratic republic, he must defer to civilian superiors and take into account the expectations of the citizenry.

For his part, Beauregard obliquely criticized Jefferson Davis in print following First Manassas, quarreled with the secretary of war and a variety of other officials in Richmond, and opposed any assignment that left him subordinate to Lee or other generals. In sum, neither man possessed the qualities necessary in a general who led a major field army in the Civil War. Unhappy to the end about their relative lack of fame compared to Lee's, both men wrote long postwar memoirs filled with special pleading (Beauregard's was attributed to Alfred Roman).

## Outline

I. Johnston and Beauregard never worked well with Jefferson Davis.

    **A.** Johnston refused to keep the president informed about his plans.

        **1.** The pattern began during Johnston's service in Virginia in 1861–1862.

      **2.** It reached a climax during the 1864 Atlanta campaign, when Johnston was perceived as giving up too much ground.

  **B.** Johnston fought bitterly with the president about rank.

      **1.** Johnston railed at being ranked fourth in seniority among Confederate generals.

      **2.** Davis adamantly refused to concede anything to Johnston.

  **C.** Beauregard also experienced poisonous relations with the president.

      **1.** His report on the battle of First Manassas cast Davis in a poor light.

      **2.** He and Davis sniped at one another during the siege of Petersburg.

  **D.** Lee's relations with Davis offered another model.

      **1.** Lee scrupulously kept Davis informed about his plans.

      **2.** Lee understood that he must be sensitive to Davis's ego.

      **3.** Lee fully accepted the need to defer to civilian authority in a democracy at war.

**II.** Johnston and Beauregard pursued flawed strategic plans.

  **A.** Johnston engaged in retreats that hurt Confederate national morale.

      **1.** He executed a clumsy withdrawal from Manassas in early 1862.

      **2.** His withdrawal up the peninsula in the spring of 1862 seemed to give up too much ground without a fight.

      **3.** His retreat across north Georgia in the Atlanta campaign similarly upset many Confederates.

  **B.** Beauregard tended to formulate grandiose strategic blueprints with little chance of success.

**III.** Johnston's and Beauregard's weak points offset substantial talents.

  **A.** Both were highly intelligent.

      **1.** Johnston impressed a number of able officers.

      **2.** Beauregard's record at West Point, in the war with Mexico, and in concentrating Confederate forces at Shiloh, for example, was impressive.

  **B.** Johnston won the affection of many of his soldiers.

  **C.** Beauregard rendered useful service at Charleston and at the outset of the siege of Petersburg.

**IV.** Johnston's and Beauregard's Confederate careers underscore the fact that few officers possessed all the requisite skills to achieve sustained success as field commanders.

### Essential Reading:

Freeman, *Lee's Lieutenants*, vol. 1, chapters 1, 4–17; vol. 3, chapters 23–24.

Gallagher, ed., *Lee the Soldier*, essay by Davis.

Woodworth, *Leadership and Command in the American Civil War*, essay by McMurry.

### Supplementary Reading:

Johnston, *Narrative of Military Operations, Directed during the Late War between the States*.

Roman, *The Military Operations of General Beauregard in the War between the States, 1861–1865*.

Symonds, *Joseph E. Johnston: A Civil War Biography*.

Williams, *P. G. T. Beauregard: Napoleon in Gray*.

### Questions to Consider:

1. How do you think the war in the eastern theater would have unfolded if either Beauregard or Johnston had been in Lee's place in 1862–1865?

2. What might explain Johnston's substantial reputation as a field commander?

# Lecture Twenty-Two—Transcript
## Gifted but Flawed—J. E. Johnston and Beauregard

Our next two lectures will examine four officers whose careers provide a counterpoint to the successes of most of those we have discussed thus far. Joseph E. Johnston and P. G. T. Beauregard considered themselves Lee's peers, if not his superiors, as field commanders, but their records reveal an absence of key attributes that helped fuel Lee's accomplishments. An almost exact contemporary of Lee's, Johnston served with distinction in the war with Mexico, shared command with Beauregard during the battle of First Manassas, and opposed the Union advance toward Richmond under General George B. McClellan in the spring of 1862. We've seen that he was badly wounded in the battle of Seven Pines (or Fair Oaks) in late May. He watched as Lee took charge of the army outside Richmond and led it to a series of fabled victories. Envious of his old friend, Johnston bitterly insisted that luck, rather than superior talent, explained Lee's triumphs. In fact, Johnston lacked Lee's breadth of vision, usually played it safe rather than taking risks, retreated in almost every campaign he directed, and never understood that in a democratic republic he must defer to civilian superiors and take into account the expectations of the citizenry. For his part, Beauregard obliquely criticized Jefferson Davis in print following First Manassas, quarreled with the secretary of war and a variety of other officials in Richmond, and opposed any assignment that left him subordinate to Lee or other generals. In sum, neither man possessed the elements necessary in a general who led a major field army in the Civil War. Unhappy to the end about their relative lack of fame compared to Lee's, both men wrote long postwar memoirs filled with special pleading. Beauregard's wasn't published under his own name, it was published under the name of someone else, but was, in fact, his memoirs, it was attributed to a man named Alfred Roman.

Let's talk just for a minute very quickly about each of their backgrounds before the war. Johnston is another Virginian. He was born near Farmville in 1807. He's almost exactly Lee's age. He was born fifteen days later than Lee. He graduated 13th in the West Point class of 1839, the same class Lee was second in. He went into the artillery. He fought in Mexico as a temporary lieutenant colonel of a short-term regiment of light infantry and did very well. He won brevets to major for Cerro Gordo and to lieutenant colonel at Chapultepec. He was made the lieutenant colonel to the First

Cavalry, one of those two cavalry regiments created in the mid-1850s, at the same time that Lee was made lieutenant colonel of the Second Cavalry. Their careers go almost in lock step.

He was made brigadier general of staff and quartermaster of the United States Army in 1860. He resigned in April of 1861, was made a brigadier general in the Confederate army, and very soon a full general. He was one of the two heroes of the battle of First Manassas on the Confederate side together with Pierre Gustave Toutant Beauregard, our other subject in this lecture.

Beauregard was born in St. Bernard Parish in Louisiana in 1818 in a very comfortable family. Johnston's family was comfortable, Beauregard's much more so. Beauregard, whose first language was French, his second language was English, although, of course, his English was excellent. He went to West Point, was distinguished at West Point, graduated second in the class of 1838, and went into the engineers.

He also fought in the war with Mexico. He was on Winfield Scott's staff, alongside Lee. He won two brevets for gallantry in Mexico, as did Joe Johnston; Lee won three, of course. He was brevetted to captain for Contreras and Churubusco, and brevetted to major for Chapultepec. He was promoted to captain of engineers in 1853 and was very briefly, in January of 1861, named superintendent of West Point. So, in that regard he was like Lee, but he had one of the shortest, it may have been the shortest, tenure as superintendent in history. It lasted just a few days. I think that people wondered a little bit about his loyalty. His native state had already seceded by the time he was made superintendent of West Point, and he, in fact, left the United States service in February of 1861, was made a brigadier general in the Confederate army, very shortly thereafter was made general. He was the hero of Sumter. He was the Confederate commander in Charleston who oversaw the bombardment of Fort Sumter that triggered the war, in a sense, or it triggered Lincoln's call for volunteers to suppress the rebellion, which really did trigger the war. And he, along with Joseph Johnston, was one of the two principle Confederate commanders at First Manassas. So both of these men, in other words, took up very important positions in the Confederate army very early, and began their careers with great success— Beauregard with Sumter and First Manassas, Johnston with First Manassas.

Anyone observing their careers at the outset of the war would have said these guys are going to be at the center of Confederate military affairs during the war, or very near the center anyway. And, in fact, they were important throughout the war, but they had major problems that prevented their really contributing in the way that some might have thought they would initially, and one of the big problems was neither could work well with Jefferson Davis. Neither worked well with Davis, in fact, both of them developed very poisonous relationships with Jefferson Davis. They got on his wrong side. If you ever got on Davis's wrong side it was virtually impossible to get back on his right side, so it seemed throughout their dealings with Davis in the war is this constantly plunging, plunging isn't the right word, but constantly deteriorating state of discussion and give and take with their commander-in-chief.

Johnston refused to keep Davis informed about what he was doing. This was a pattern that developed very early in the war and continued down to the very end. He would not tell the commander-in-chief what he planned to do. Davis had to pry things out of him with a crowbar, virtually, and even when Davis tried to do that Johnston would often not be forthcoming. He simply either didn't trust the president, and we'll see one reason why he didn't, it had to do with rank, we'll talk about that in a minute, he either didn't trust him or didn't care. He did not have a good sense of being subordinate to his civilian superiors, that is clear, Joseph Johnston didn't. This pattern began very early. He commanded at Harpers Ferry very early in the war and then retreated from there and commanded at Manassas and retreated from there and then commanded on the peninsula and retreated up to Richmond from there, as we've seen. Throughout these retreats he never really let Davis know fully why he was doing the things he did, and what it is and what it was he hoped to accomplish by doing them, and Jefferson Davis became increasingly frustrated by this. He talked about it in his memoirs concerning Johnston's retreat up the peninsula toward Richmond without fighting. Davis wrote this, "I'd written to Johnston that he knew the defense of Richmond must be made at a distance from the city. Seeing no preparation to keep the enemy at a distance, and kept in ignorance of any plan for such purpose, I sent for General R. E. Lee, then in Richmond in general charge of army operations, and told him why and how I was dissatisfied with the condition of affairs. Lee then said General Johnston should, of course, advise you of what he expects or proposes to do, let me go and see him." This is a frustrated Davis turning to his chief advisor, military advisor at that time, and really saying, "Johnston won't tell me what he's doing, what am I supposed to do here?"

This pattern reached a climax during the 1864 Atlanta campaign. Johnston retreated from north Georgia all the way into the defenses of Atlanta. He didn't fight a offensive battle anywhere during this process of going southward. He did win a victory at Kennesaw Mountain when Sherman attacked him, but the perception on Davis's part, on many other politician's part, and the perception across much of the Confederacy was that Johnston was giving up too much ground without a fight during the Atlanta campaign and Johnston, again, didn't seem to care. He wasn't telling Davis why he was doing what he was doing; he was just pretending, not pretending but acting as if military affairs should be carried out in a vacuum. It was not necessary to keep civilian superiors informed.

Johnston fought bitterly with Davis about rank, and much of the negative aspect of their relationship stems from this. Johnston was obsessed with rank, that's not too hard a word, he was obsessed with rank, and he railed at being listed fourth in seniority among the full generals, the four-star generals. Samuel Cooper, or "Cupper" as he pronounced it, a paper pusher in Richmond, was the ranking general officer in the Confederacy, second was Albert Sydney Johnston, third was R. E. Lee, fourth was Joseph Johnston, and fifth was Beauregard. The law was a little bit murky as to how, precisely, rank would be decided. It was based on rank in the old United States Army, but which rank was unclear. There were different kinds of rank in the United States Army. You had your regular rank in the unit within which you were promoted, for example Joe Johnston was lieutenant colonel of the First Cavalry, Robert E. Lee was lieutenant colonel in the Second Cavalry, and Lee later was made colonel of the cavalry just before he resigned from United States service. There was also brevet rank, we talked about that in Mexico, temporary, honorary rank for service rendered. Lee had been brevetted a colonel all the way back during the Mexican War. His formal appointment to colonel came just on the eve of the Civil War. Then there was staff rank, that is, when you left the line, a line unit, and went to staff, you also had a staff rank. Joseph Johnson was a brigadier general of staff. He was a lieutenant colonel of the line in his cavalry regiment. Robert E. Lee was a colonel of the line, as was Albert Sydney Johnston.

Well, Jefferson Davis paid most attention to the rank within the unit, the line rank, and by that way of looking at it Joe Johnson was behind both Albert Sydney Johnston and Lee. Johnson said, "No, I'm a brigadier general. The staff rank is what you count. I'm the only general. I should be the ranking officer among these were talking about." Davis adamantly refused to concede anything to Johnston; Davis was very legalistic, he hated to be questioned or challenged, and Johnston either didn't understand that or didn't care. He wrote this petulant series of communications to Davis, and as this thing played out Davis became more and more angry with

Johnston; Johnston became paranoid that the president was trying to get him, and it really tainted the rest of their relationship during the war.

This is nothing new for Johnston, he'd been concerned about rank his entire career. He even admitted this in a letter in the 1850s. He wrote in 1851 that he "wanted promotion more than did any other man in the army." That's from his own pen, he said that. He wanted it more than any other man in the army, and even Lee, who was very reluctant to criticize his fellow officers and who was very fond of Joe Johnston, Johnston bitterly envious of Lee, we'll talk a little bit more about that in a minute, but Lee didn't know that, he didn't understand that. He really liked Johnston. They were exact contemporaries; they're Virginians; their fathers fought in the American Revolution together, Johnston's father fought under Lee's father; it is a relationship that Lee believed was very close. But after the war, in a discussion with a former Confederate colonel about the improprieties of an officer, as Lee put it, allowing his own advantage or reputation to come into consideration in defending his country, in discussing that topic, Lee uses this example "General Joe Johnston's sensitiveness on this fore, and how wrong and unwise it was." So Lee, after the war, not during the war in any public way, after the war, says Johnston's obsession with rank, his demand, his prickliness about being higher in rank than he was hurt the Confederate service and reflected poorly on Johnston as a soldier.

Johnston was especially upset that Lee outranked him during the Civil War. His whole career he'd been a half a step behind Lee, behind him in the rankings at West Point; he got two brevets in Mexico, Lee got three brevets in Mexico; Winfield Scott called Lee the best soldier in the United States Army after Mexico, Joe Johnston a good soldier to Lee's the best soldier. At every step he's behind Lee. The one time he got ahead of Lee was when he became a brigadier general of staff, quartermaster general to the United States Army in 1860, Lee was just a colonel of the line, and even there, said Johnston, he was cheated out of what that should have gotten him. He should have ranked Lee during the Civil War, and he didn't. He's very bitter about this, and it's apparent to many people, even if it's not to Lee. An official in the war department evaluated Johnston in early 1863, there were rumors that Johnston, who had recovered from his wounds at Seven Pines by then, was going to be sent out to command along the Mississippi River, the theater that embraced Vicksburg and other parts of the Mississippi theater, and this official wrote at the time, and this is a man who is very much on target, he wrote "Johnston is a very little man," he underlined that, "who has achieved nothing, is full of himself, is eaten up with morbid jealousy of Lee and all his superiors in position, rank, and glory. I apprehend the gravest disasters from his command." Very harsh words, but pretty much on target. Joe Johnston was eaten up with envy of anybody of higher rank than he. He believed that he should have been the ranking officer in the Confederacy.

Beauregard also experienced poisonous relations with the president because he simply didn't know how to handle Davis, although it should have been obvious to anyone that Davis is someone who is so thin-skinned that if you don't go along with him, and especially if you challenge him in any kind of public way, it's going to come back to haunt you. Beauregard wrote this very long report on the battle of First Manassas. It may be, I think I've said this earlier in the course, it may be the longest report filed by any officer on either side during the Civil War, filled with flourishes and grand statements and very much reflecting on Beauregard's greatness. Beauregard went by Gustave Toutant Beauregard for most of his professional life, he dropped the Pierre early in life, he's G. T. Beauregard during the Civil War. Some said that he dropped it because it sounded too foreign, he thought it sounded too foreign, Pierre was too foreign, but Gustave Toutant somehow, I guess, was not too foreign. I don't even know if that's accurate, that's just what some people said. At any rate, his report criticized obliquely Jefferson Davis. Well, even the most oblique criticism of Jefferson Davis is going to rankle the president, and this is a report that became widely known in the public sense. So, Beauregard, in a public way, has challenged Jefferson Davis. Jefferson Davis didn't like it and never forgot it.

The second episode came after the battle of Shiloh. Beauregard is sent out west after the initial stage of the war in Virginia, he fought at Shiloh, and then he was the Confederate commander defending the key rail junction at Corinth, Mississippi, in May and early June 1862. Shortly after the Corinth campaign he took sick leave. Now, he was ill, Beauregard was ill. He had fairly frail health through much of the war, but he went home, he took sick leave, without informing the president. He didn't tell Jefferson Davis. An army commander who's just going home, basically. That upset Jefferson Davis as well. That is not what an army commander does. Again, he didn't keep Davis informed, he didn't let Davis know. This is the same kind of behavior that Joseph Johnston might have engaged in, although, to be fair to Johnston, it's hard to see his leaving an army without being completely incapacitated.

Beauregard and Davis sniped at one another at the siege of Petersburg as well. This was further evidence that Beauregard either didn't understand what it took to work well with Davis, or he didn't care, it's one or the other. Both of these relationships with Davis, Beauregard's and Johnston's, contrast dramatically with how Lee worked with Davis.

Lee and Davis had a model relationship for an army commander and the commander-in-chief. One reason was that Lee scrupulously kept Davis informed about everything he was doing. He would sometimes write a letter a day, even during active campaigning. This is what I'm doing, this is what I hope to accomplish, this is the situation. Read the correspondence during the Maryland campaign of 1862, or the Gettysburg campaign, and Lee is telling Davis everything that Davis needs to know. It's a textbook example of keeping your civilian superior informed. Lee understood, also, how sensitive Davis was. He knew that Davis's ego was critical, a critical component in any kind of relationship between a commander and a commander-in-chief. He'd watch Davis up close during the war, he knew him very well, and he behaved in a way that was careful not to alienate the president. Lee fully understood the need to defer to civilian authority in a democracy at war, fully accepted that position. In that regard he followed his model, his idol George Washington very closely. That's the greatest service George Washington bequeathed to the United States military tradition. The great hero of the American Revolution, the man who could have had almost anything after the war, stepped down, went into private life, always insisted that the military defer to civilian authority. Lee took that model to heart, as did Ulysses S. Grant, incidentally. Grant is also a model in that way. George B. McClellan, like Joseph E. Johnston, wasn't. They seemed to think that their civilian superiors simply got in the way, and the superiors were something to be gotten around whenever possible. Just push them aside, ignore them, do what you want to do. Lee never did that, never did it. Neither did Grant. Both following in George Washington's footsteps in that regard.

It helped that Lee and Davis agreed generally on strategic issues. They almost always agreed. Some have accused Lee of being almost too obsequious of Davis, and when you read some of the correspondence Lee is clearly, clearly trying to courier favor in some ways with Davis, but it worked. Lee generally got his way. He got his way both because he knew how to deal with Davis and, of course, more importantly because he gave Davis victories. That made all the difference. Johnston and Beauregard weren't giving the president a lot of victories either.

So, they didn't get along with Davis. They also both, both Johnston and Beauregard, pursued flawed strategic plans. Joseph Johnston never understood, or again, didn't care if he did understand, about the effects of his operations on the home front. Civilian expectations, civilian morale, these things didn't seem to enter his mind as he planned campaigns. Lee, as we've seen, was very much attuned to those factors. Joseph Johnston didn't seem to be because he pursued a strategy in almost every way that was the antithesis of what the Confederate people generally wanted. Confederate people wanted an aggressive stance, a stance that inflicted damage on the enemy, that showed some sense of movement toward independence; Joseph Johnston retreated, and retreated and retreated and retreated. He executed an early retreat from Harpers Ferry at the outset of the war. Now, Harpers Ferry couldn't be held, it's one of the worst positions in the world to hold. It's down in a bowl with three sets of heights, Maryland Heights across the Potomac River, and Loudon Heights across the Shenandoah River, and Oliver Heights to the west. An investing enemy can always capture Harpers Ferry, as Stonewall Jackson did during the Maryland campaign, but the point for our purposes is he abandoned Harpers Ferry before he needed to, he retreated before it was even necessary. He retreated from Manassas in a very clumsy fashion in early 1862. Then he withdrew up the peninsula. He got to the peninsula in mid-April; he was already retreating within two weeks, already retreating back toward Richmond in two weeks. He always retreated, and the perception was: he's giving up ground too easily. That is the perception behind the lines. His retreat across north Georgia in the Atlanta campaign similarly upset many Confederates. Let me just give you a sampling of the kinds of reactions that Joseph Johnston's retreats provoked.

This is from a young Georgia soldier in the spring of 1862 as Johnston was retreating up the peninsula. "General Joseph Johnston, from whom we were led to expect so much, has done little else than evacuate, and the very mention of the word sickens one," this man wrote. A soldier who fought under Johnston in the Atlanta campaign, and who really liked Johnston, who expressed affection toward Johnston in many ways, but he believed that after Johnston was removed by Jefferson Davis it was probably a good thing. "A good thing because," he said, "the general was removed for not fighting and allowing the Yanks to penetrate so far into Georgia. He is too cautious. He's not willing to risk a battle unless he's satisfied he can whip it." A woman in Georgia was much more harsh in her estimate of Joe Johnston a little bit later in the war. She referred to Johnston as "this arch-retreater. All he ever did," she said, "was retreat." An almost humorous take on this was supplied by a young Virginia soldier who served on the staff of a general named Charles Field. This guy came to Virginia, Johnston had been retreating toward Richmond, and he said, "General Joseph Johnston carried prudence to an excess. It was facetiously said that he intended to establish his base in the Gulf of Mexico and throw pontoons across to Cuba, preparatory to a retrograde movement to the land of fragrant weeds." Others commented also that Johnston seemed to be of a mind that would allow him to retreat first to Richmond, then into the Carolinas and eventually down to Florida.

Davis wrote later about the reaction to Johnston's retreat during the Atlanta campaign. He said, "From many quarters, including such that had most urged Johnston's assignment, came delegations, petitions, and letters urging me to remove him from command of the army, and assign that important trust to some officer who would resolutely hold and defend Atlanta." When he did remove Johnston, this is what Davis telegraphed to him: "You have failed to arrest the advance of the enemy into the vicinity of Atlanta, far into the interior of Georgia, and expressed no confidence that you can defeat or repel him. You are hereby relieved." So, out went Johnston from the Army of Tennessee, and Johnston just didn't get it. The way he dealt with this in his memoirs is very instructive. He said that he hadn't informed Davis of what he was doing. He said, "I supposed that my course would not be disapproved by him, especially as General Lee, by keeping on the defensive and falling back towards Grant's objective point under circumstances like mine, was increasing his great fame." Here he got in another dig at Lee. Lee's getting more famous by retreating and here I'm being persecuted because I'm retreating. The difference was, of course, that Lee was inflicting great damage on the Federals while he retreated, and Johnston was not. It's perceptions that are important.

The other factor in all these retreats that was important was when he retreated, he abandoned immense quantities of materials. He wasn't a good retreater in that regard. He left things in northern Virginia, he left things in Harpers Ferry. Wherever he retreated he wasn't careful in terms of taking all the things with him, the precious material that had been built up by the Confederate government with him. The retreats are disastrous in many ways, in other words.

Beauregard, it wasn't so much that he was a retreater as it was he didn't have his feet on solid ground. He spun these fantastic strategic plans in his mind, things that had nothing to do with the reality of Confederate logistical capabilities. He also wasn't really sensitive to the issue of civilian morale. He, like Johnston, seemed to operate without any understanding of the ties of the home front to the battlefield. He saw things as almost intellectual military problems. These are things we can work out, work out on paper and in discussions around the headquarters campfire without taking into account precisely how these will fit with our logistical capabilities and the impact they will have on civilian morale if we do carry them out. It's a major failing on Beauregard's part.

The weak points that Johnston and Beauregard manifested offset substantial talents. There's no reason to deny that. They were both very talented officers in many ways, highly intelligent, both of them. Johnston impressed a number of very able officers, which we have to take as evidence of a strong military personality and of significant gifts. He even impressed Edward Porter Alexander who, as I've said more than once in this course, I think was the most perceptive of all the Confederate analysts of military operations carried out during the war on the Southern side. Alexander wrote, "I think General Joseph Johnston was more the soldier in looks, carriage and manner than any of our other generals. He was of medium stature, but of extraordinary strength, vigor, and quickness. As long as he lived I never had a warmer or a kinder friend than General Johnston, nor he a more affectionate admirer than I. He was a great soldier. I used to think at the time that his one fault was impatience of detail, but to study his fine campaign in front of Sherman in 1864 would seem to imply that he was especially excellent in detail. At any rate, the enemy considered his marches and retreats as superlatively well planned and conducted." That's very favorable, although it's very interesting that Alexander says "his marches and retreats," he doesn't say Johnston's battles, he says "marches and retreats."

Beauregard's record at West Point was fabulous. He did very well in the Mexican War, as did Johnston, and in other places he did well. He was instrumental in bringing about a really impressive concentration of Confederate resources before the battle of Shiloh, a concentration that brought troops all the way from the Gulf Coast to South Carolina, and from other points, brought them together in an army that advanced and attacked Grant at Pittsburgh Landing on April 6, 1862. He did very well there. He also did well outside Petersburg when Lee was fooled by Grant after the battle of Cold Harbor and Grant disengaged from Lee, crossed the James River, and advanced against Petersburg. Beauregard did a very good job—heavily outnumbered—of holding on to Petersburg until Lee finally figured out what was going on and sent the bulk of the Army of Northern Virginia down to oppose Grant. That was excellent service. He also did well at Charleston when he was commanding that important seacoast city during much of the middle part of the war. So, Beauregard did well in some places, he just didn't do well when he had a chance to be a field commander of first importance. He's sort of in the backwater areas when he does his best. He's in Charleston, he's in Petersburg, he's not leading the Army of Northern Virginia or the Army of Tennessee, or a comparable force in either east or west.

Johnston had the ability to win the affection of his soldiers. He's like McClellan in this regard. McClellan's soldiers loved him, and yet resented on some level the fact that McClellan never trusted them enough to really commit them in a battle, to really push everything into a battle. Johnston is the same way. I quoted the one soldier during the Atlanta campaign. He liked Johnston, but he believed that Johnston's removal was necessary because Johnston had been retreating too much; he had not been putting up a fight.

Johnston's and Beauregard's Confederate careers underscore how few officers possessed all the skills requisite to achieve sustained success as a field commander. Lee's the only one in the course of the war on the Confederate side who shows that. Next time we're going to look at two more officers whose weaknesses outweighed their strengths: John Bankhead Magruder and one of the most famous Confederate generals of all, George Edward Pickett.

# Lecture Twenty-Three
# Drama and Failure—Magruder and Pickett

**Scope:** John Bankhead Magruder graduated in the class of 1830 at West Point, won brevets for gallantry in the war with Mexico, and led Confederate forces to victory early in the war in Virginia. Known as "Prince John" in the antebellum army because of his flair for colorful uniforms and his dramatic personality, he waged an effective defense of the peninsula in April and May 1862. He clashed with Joseph E. Johnston as the contending armies drew closer to Richmond and fought as a division commander under Lee during the Seven Days' battles. Rumors about drunkenness arose after the battle of Malvern Hill, and Lee made no attempt to retain Magruder with the Army of Northern Virginia. The difference in attitude Lee displayed toward Magruder and Stonewall Jackson, neither of whom distinguished himself during the Seven Days, reveals much about what Lee would and would not accept in a subordinate. Magruder spent the remainder of the war in the trans-Mississippi theater, a backwater that offered almost no opportunity to regain his substantial early-war reputation.

Pickett offers a more troubling portrait of an officer woefully incapable of mature leadership. He did well as a brigade commander during the fighting around Richmond in 1862, suffering a wound that kept him out of service for several months. Returning to the army as a major general in October, he and his division played a minor role at Fredericksburg and missed Chancellorsville. At Gettysburg, Pickett enthusiastically mounted his part of the famous assault on July 3 that ever after carried his name. He completely broke down in the immediate aftermath of the attack; subsequently oversaw a bungled operation at New Bern, North Carolina; and played no further part in Lee's operations until May 1864. He won a minor success at Bermuda Hundred but ended his Confederate service with a spectacular failure at Five Forks on April 1, 1865. There is much irony in the fact that Pickett is without question the most famous Confederate major general who never achieved higher rank.

# Outline

**I.** Magruder's early Confederate career included considerable success.

    **A.** He won fame in June 1861 with a victory in the small clash at Big Bethel.

    **B.** He conducted an effective defense of the peninsula in the spring of 1862.

        **1.** He slowed the advance of George B. McClellan's much larger force.

        **2.** He employed his dramatic flair to mask his small army's disadvantage in numbers.

    **C.** He achieved less success when placed under Joseph E. Johnston's command.

        **1.** Magruder clearly operated best in independent command.

        **2.** Johnston criticized Magruder in a way that undermined confidence in "Prince John" among civilian and military leaders.

**II.** The Seven Days' campaign marked the end of Magruder's service in Virginia.

    **A.** He did well at the outset in mounting a diversion south of the Chickahominy River on June 26–27.

    **B.** He failed to meet Lee's expectations at the battles of Savage's Station and Malvern Hill on June 29 and July 1.

        **1.** Lee believed Magruder lacked aggressiveness.

        **2.** Rumors that Magruder had been drunk at Malvern Hill circulated soon after the battle.

    **C.** Lee made no effort to retain Magruder in the army after the Seven Days.

        **1.** Lee's attitude may have stemmed in part from Magruder's reputation as a bon vivant.

        **2.** Lee was far more forgiving of Stonewall Jackson's failures during the Seven Days.

    **D.** Magruder departed for the trans-Mississippi theater in October 1862.

**III.** George E. Pickett's Confederate record contained few triumphs.

**A.** The high points came as a brigade commander at Seven Pines and Gaines's Mill in 1862 and as a division commander at Bermuda Hundred in May 1864.

**B.** His low points were far more numerous.

   **1.** He lost control of his division at Gettysburg.

   **2.** He failed to capture New Bern, North Carolina, in February 1864.

   **3.** He often left his headquarters to carry out romantic liaisons.

   **4.** He was absent from his command when it was routed at the battle of Five Forks on April 1, 1865.

**C.** Pickett's conduct at the time of Five Forks prompted Lee to remove him from command.

**IV.** Pickett nursed a long postwar bitterness toward Lee and likely failed to appreciate how the assault that wrecked his command at Gettysburg also guaranteed his own personal fame.

### Essential Reading:

Freeman, *Lee's Lieutenants*, vol. 1, chapters 2, 13–17, 32–38; vol. 3, chapters 13, 23, 33.

Gallagher, ed., *The 1862 Richmond Campaign*, essay by Carmichael.

———, *Lee and His Generals in War and Memory*, chapter 6.

Woodworth, *Leadership and Command in the American Civil War*, essay by Gordon.

### Supplementary Reading:

Casdorph, *Prince John Magruder: His Life and Campaigns*.

Gordon, *General George E. Pickett in Life and Legend*.

### Questions to Consider:

1. Why was an officer of Pickett's limited ability able to retain relatively important positions for so long?

2. What does Magruder's example reveal about how some officers react differently when operating semi-independently or under the command of superiors?

# Lecture Twenty-Three—Transcript
## Drama and Failure—Magruder and Pickett

In this lecture we continue with our look at less successful Confederate generals, and our focus will be on John Bankhead Magruder and George Edward Pickett. Magruder graduated in the class of 1830 at West Point, won brevets for gallantry in the war with Mexico, and led Confederate forces to victory early in the war in Virginia. Known as "Prince John" in the antebellum army because of his flair for colorful uniforms and his very dramatic personality, he waged an effective defense of the peninsula in April and May 1862. He clashed with Joseph E. Johnston as the contending armies drew closer to Richmond and then fought as a division commander under Lee during the Seven Days' battles. Rumors about drunkenness arose after the battle of Malvern Hill, and Lee made no attempt to retain Magruder with the Army of Northern Virginia. The difference in attitude Lee displayed toward Magruder and Stonewall Jackson, neither of whom distinguished himself during the Seven Days, reveals much about what Lee would and would not accept in a subordinate. Magruder spent the remainder of the war in the trans-Mississippi theater, a backwater that offered almost no opportunity to regain his substantial early-war reputation.

Pickett offers a more troubling portrait of an officer woefully incapable of mature leadership. He did well as a brigade commander during the fighting around Richmond in 1862, suffering a wound that kept him out of service for several months. Returning to the army as a major general in October, he and his division played a minor role at Fredericksburg and missed Chancellorsville altogether. At Gettysburg, Pickett enthusiastically mounted his part of the famous assault on July 3 that ever after carried his name. He completely broke down in the immediate aftermath of the attack, however, and subsequently oversaw a bungled operation at New Bern, North Carolina. He played no further part in Lee's operations until May 1864. He won a minor success at Bermuda Hundred that month, but ended his Confederate service with a spectacular failure at Five Forks on April 1, 1865. There is much irony in the fact that Pickett is without question the most famous Confederate major general who never achieved higher rank.

We'll begin with Magruder, who was born in 1807 at Port Royal, Virginia. He attended the University of Virginia for a while, and then went off to West Point where he graduated 15th in the class of 1830. He was a captain in the battalion of cadets, so he exhibited military leadership, or qualities of military leadership, while he was at West Point. He was a captain of artillery in Mexico, and he won brevets to major for his work at Cerro Gordo and to lieutenant colonel for Chapultepec. He commanded for a time the artillery school of instruction at Fort Leavenworth during the antebellum years.

He resigned in April of 1861, on April 20, and became a brigadier general in the Confederate service on June 17. He was deployed on the peninsula below Richmond, and he won fame in June 1861 with a small victory at Big Bethel. It's a very small battle, really a glorified skirmish, but this is even before First Manassas, so Big Bethel made big headlines across the Confederacy. Magruder didn't even have a really direct role in the victory, but his command won the victory and he reaped the benefits. He became quite famous as a result of the fight at Big Bethel. He then began to put together a defense of the peninsula in the spring of 1862. He'd been promoted to major general in August of 1861, so he's one of the early major generals in the Confederacy. Even though he was largely successful on the peninsula, there was a good deal of whispering about him and about some elements of character that might not be very attractive. Even in the autumn of 1861 a priest, a Louisiana priest, who was with some Louisiana troops there, wrote in his diary, "They talk a great deal around here about General Magruder, and what they say is not always complimentary." The priest left it at that. Another observer, however, commented at the time that Magruder looks like "a man too much given to dissipation, and is incapable of planning a battle, although very vigorous in fighting one."

What he was very good at doing was slowing George B. McClellan down. Now, a pebble in the road would slow George B. McClellan down, of course. I'm sure McClellan got up in the morning trying to think of ways to slow down. He was helped in that regard by John Bankhead Magruder. John Bankhead Magruder, once McClellan got his big army on the peninsula and started his very, very plodding movement toward Richmond, Magruder did his best to throw obstacles in McClellan's path. He employed his dramatic flair to mask his small army's disadvantage at numbers. At Yorktown, for example, he would shift troops back and forth, the same troops, have them march back and forth in front of the Federal lines to give the appearance of higher numbers. He had his soldiers put what were called "Quaker guns" at different parts of the line. That is, tree logs painted to look like cannons to give the appearance of more artillery than actually was in the place. McClellan, of course, fell for all of this and wasted a full month at Yorktown, even though he had an overwhelming advantage of numbers over Magruder. Magruder's pretty effective when he's operating pretty much on his own in front of McClellan. Once Joseph Johnston got to the peninsula in mid-April, and came to command Magruder, Magruder did less well. I think it's pretty clear that Magruder preferred to operate on his own. He and Johnston didn't get along. Johnston immediately criticized all of the defensive preparations that Magruder had put in place. It wasn't really fair; he belittled Magruder's work, he convinced Jefferson Davis that Magruder hadn't done a good job. Well, what's going on here is Johnston wanted to retreat. If he had admitted that Magruder had done a good job he might actually have had to fight behind those lines that Magruder had erected. But, instead, he said Magruder did a bad job, it's necessary for me to retreat, and he began to retreat.

Back in Richmond, Robert E. Lee, who's the advisor to Davis at that stage of the war, and George Wythe Randolph, the Confederate secretary of war, disagreed with Johnston's evaluation. They tended to think that Magruder had done a better job, but Johnston is the field commander on the spot, and he begins his retreat. He and Magruder do not get along very well at all.

The Seven Days' campaign marked the end of Magruder's service in the Virginia theater. Even before fighting began he had quarreled with another superior, Magruder had. He was put under the command of an officer named Gustavas Woodson Smith. He chafed at being under Smith, subject to Smith's instructions, to his oversight. The two really didn't get along. There was really petty quibbling about points on both sides. In the end Magruder said, "I want to be put somewhere else. I can't function this way. This is too much for anyone to stand. I need to be sent to duty somewhere else."

The war department said, "All right, we'll send you to the trans-Mississippi theater. You'll command the whole trans-Mississippi theater," that is the theater west of the Mississippi River, and Magruder said, "That will be fine. I'm willing to command in the trans-Mississippi theater. But, because a showdown battle was looming outside Richmond, Magruder requested permission to remain with the army until the battles around Richmond were resolved. Johnston didn't want him to remain with the army, Johnston wanted him to go, but Magruder won his case in this regard. He sort of forced on Joseph Johnston that he would remain with the army defending Richmond until those battles are resolved. Johnston himself was removed at the end of May, as we've seen and talked about several times in the class. At the battle of Seven Pines he is wounded, he's out of the way, Robert E. Lee comes into command, and one of the division commanders he inherits is John Bankhead Magruder. So, Magruder will finish the Virginia element of his Confederate service under the army command of Robert E. Lee, but still in the background is this transfer to the trans-Mississippi. That hasn't been removed. He's just going to continue fighting outside Richmond until that's resolved and then the expectation is, his expectation is, he will go out to the trans-Mississippi.

Well, he did very well at the outset of the Seven Days' campaign in mounting a diversion south of the Chickahominy River on June 26-27. If you'll remember, the situation when the Seven Days' battles began was this: McClellan had gotten his army into a position where about a third of it was north of the Chickahominy River, commanded by FitzJohn Porter, and about two-thirds of it was south of the Chickahominy River, McClellan was commanding that part. Lee's blueprint called for a major Confederate blow against the one-third of the United States force that was north of the Chickahominy River. Lee was going to mass the bulk of his strength north of the river. That meant that somebody was going to have to keep an eye on McClellan and the bulk of the Army of the Potomac south of the Chickahominy River. John Bankhead Magruder would be the key person in that part of the action. About 25,000 men out of the Confederate's 85,000 or so were left south of the river. The two generals there were John Bankhead Magruder and Benjamin Huger. Magruder is the more important of the two, and this is very difficult duty that he has here. In essence, he is to bluff McClellan into believing that the majority of the Confederate army lies south of the Chickahominy River. "You convince McClellan," Lee is telling Magruder, and to a lesser degree Huger, "you convince McClellan that he has to pay attention to you, which will give me a free hand with the bulk of our strength to smash that exposed third of the Army of the Potomac that's north of the Chickahominy River." Magruder did an excellent job, both on the 26th and on the 27th, and McClellan's report indicates the degree to which he was fooled by John Bankhead Magruder. McClellan wrote, "So threatening were the movements on both banks of the Chickahominy," this is in his official report, "that it was impossible to decide until the afternoon where the real attack would be made." Then McClellan added, "The threatening demonstrations were frequently made along the entire line south of the Chickahominy, and that obliged me to hold a considerable force in position to meet them." Part of this is a self-serving explanation on McClellan's part, but, in fact, he did hold two-thirds of his army south of the Chickahominy, he did believe that what Magruder was doing threatened the Army of the Potomac. So it's excellent work.

While Magruder is doing that, Lee and the bulk of the army are fighting the battles of Mechanicsville and Gaines's Mill, where Stonewall Jackson is not doing what he's supposed to be doing. There's a nice contrast between Magruder and Jackson in this regard. Daniel Harvey Hill wrote of Magruder in this part of the campaign, he said that he thought Magruder's love of show and drama explained his ability to fool McClellan. This is an oft-quoted post-war statement by Hill. Hill didn't like Magruder, so he didn't have a reason to be generous to Magruder, but he wrote this, he said, "No one ever lived who could play off the grand señor with a more lordly air than could Prince John Magruder. He put on naturally all those grand and imposing devices which deceived the military opponent." He certainly did that with George B. McClellan. Now, he was fortunate in that his opponent with McClellan, both down around Yorktown and during the Seven Days during the 26th and the 27th of June, because he had an opponent who was willing, almost eager, to be convinced that there were a lot of Rebels on this front. There were always a lot of Rebels everywhere from George B. McClellan's point of view. He thought there were two hundred thousand of them outside Richmond during the Seven Days, as he kept telling Abraham Lincoln, two hundred thousand Rebels. So, if he believed there were two hundred thousand, I guess he could suppose that Lee had a hundred thousand north of the river and Magruder and a hundred thousand south of the Chickahominy.

At any rate, it's good work by John Bankhead Magruder at this stage of the game, but that's the end. He goes downhill very rapidly after that. The rest of the Seven Days unfold in a disastrous manner for John Bankhead Magruder and seal his fate in the eastern theater. I think that a brilliant performance by Magruder during the Seven Days, or even a very solid one throughout the campaign, would have prompted Lee to try to retain him in command. Here's a man who had won reputation, who had done very well earlier in the war. If he had really followed through during the rest of the Seven Days as he had, in the same manner he had conducted himself on the 26th and 27th, I think he might have remained in Virginia, but he did not do that. He failed to meet Lee's expectation at both the battle of Savage's Station on June 29 and at Malvern Hill on July 1.

In the first instance, Lee believed Magruder lacked aggressiveness. That's a cardinal sin from Lee's point of view; he lacked aggressiveness. McClellan was beginning his retreat. He'd pulled FitzJohn Porter south of the Chickahominy River by then, and had begun the movement of his entire army southward across the peninsula. The change is based from the York River to the James River. The Army of the Potomac is in motion, it is retreating. Lee believes it's therefore vulnerable and what he tries to do at

Savage's Station is deliver a heavy blow against the rear guard of the Army of the Potomac, and he assigns to Magruder a key element of that. He wants Magruder to strike the Federals. He wants him and about 15,000 men to strike the Federals. He even reinforces Magruder with troops from other Confederate commanders in hopes that he'll have enough mass to really inflict a serious wound on McClellan's retreating army, and it doesn't happen. Magruder gets going very late in the day, he mounts a very feeble assault, and Lee is deeply disappointed. In fact, Lee sent him a note after the battle. It's a very strongly worded note for Lee. He said, "I regret much that you made so little progress today in pursuit of the enemy. In order to reap the fruits of our victory the pursuits should be most vigorous. I must urge you again to press on his rear rapidly and steadily. We must lose no more time or he will escape us entirely." Lee is very unhappy with Magruder, and I'm sure Magruder got the message. He's given a very secondary role the next day, on the 30th of June. Basically what his division does is march back and forth. They march about twenty miles and don't do any fighting. They're sent to reinforce one end of the line, and they don't fight. They're brought all the way back to the other end of the line, and they don't fight. It's clear that Lee has decided that Magruder is not the guy to have at the point of whatever effort he's going to make.

But he did participate, Magruder did, at Malvern Hill in the 1st of July, the last of the Seven Days. Now, here, Lee planned one more round of assaults. They're ill considered, as we've seen before in this class. McClellan had a very strong position at Malvern Hill. No weakness—ample artillery, ample infantry, in a beautiful defensive position, but Lee decided to attack, Magruder and his forces were going to be a key part of that, Magruder botched his part of the attacks—at least, he didn't accomplish anything with his part of the attacks. He got going early, there was a lack of coordination all up and down the line, it's certainly not all Magruder's fault, it's partly Magruder's fault, and part of the problem was he seemed to be out of control at Malvern Hill. He'd manifested some of this earlier in the campaign as well. He was physically exhausted. One of his staff officers said he was averaging one hour's sleep a night for several days during the Seven Days, one hour of sleep a night. He also had a physical ailment which prompted his physician to prescribe something that Magruder said really made him feel—he said, "I must have been allergic to this medicine, whatever it was, because it left me completely out of sorts. It completely changed my usual equilibrium." He said it was allergies and the loss of sleep, others said, "Baloney, he was drinking, he was drunk, that's why he was acting the way he was. He would gallop to and fro, he would shout out orders and then change the orders. He seemed to be agitated, he seemed to be perspiring profusely, he seemed simply not to be in control of his troops." One man who saw him, one Confederate officer, said, "The wild expression of his eyes and his excited manner impressed me at once with the belief that he was under the influence of some powerful stimulant, spirits, or perhaps, opium." Others said the same thing; Magruder didn't seem to be in control of himself at the battle of Malvern Hill. Lee had ordered an advance. Magruder did mount, again, a fairly feeble attack.

After the battle he becomes the person that the press really goes after. They blame John Bankhead Magruder. Lee has a confrontation with him right after the battle, but almost immediately there are these two things going on. Lee's judging him and the press and private people who read the press are judging him. A diarist in Richmond wrote that night, that very night, "Today General Magruder led his division into action at Malvern Hill, it is said, contrary to the judgment of other commanders. The enemy's batteries controlled all the approaches in most advantageous position and fearful was the slaughter."

That night Lee went to talk to Magruder, and an officer present recorded their confrontation. The army commander came up and said, "General Magruder, why did you attack?" And Magruder, who was aware of the implications of Lee's question answered without hesitation, "In obedience to your order." Twice repeated. And, in fact, Lee had ordered Magruder to attack. He had expected him to attack with a little more finesse and a little more effect than he did, but he had ordered him to attack.

As I said earlier, Lee made no effort to retain Magruder in the army after the Seven Days, and I think that Lee's attitude may have stemmed in part from Magruder's reputation from the old army. He had a reputation as a bon vivant in the old army. He was a man who loved to drink, a man who entertained lavishly, a man also, in effect, who had abandoned his family. He married a very wealthy woman. He used her money throughout his antebellum career to fund this entertaining and so forth, but she and the children went to Europe very early in the marriage. He only saw them a handful of times the rest of his life. He's married, but many people don't even know that he's married because his wife is never around. Now, the insiders in the old army, of course, know that he's married, and Lee, I think, looked at Magruder, and here I'm—this is my five cent psychoanalysis, I think Lee looks at Magruder and sees a lot of the elements he didn't like in his father: someone who is not good with money, spends money lavishly, doesn't really take care of his family, someone who drinks too much—here is a man who doesn't have the personal characteristics, who does not have the self-control that Robert E. Lee prized above almost everything else. There was talk of a court martial for Magruder after the Seven Days. There was talk not only of drunkenness but also of cowardice on his part at Malvern Hill. Now, that was groundless. I don't think he was drunk or a coward at Malvern Hill, but there were rumors and his transfer to the west was held up while these were examined. He didn't go off to Texas until October in the end.

I think it's a very interesting contrast to evaluate how Lee dealt with Stonewall Jackson and how he dealt with John Bankhead Magruder in the wake of the Seven Days. Neither man performed well, but Magruder on the whole performed better than did Jackson, in my view. At least Magruder did well on the 26th and 27th of June. Jackson didn't really do well anywhere, and while Magruder might have been agitated and excited at Malvern Hill, and perhaps the day before, at least he didn't fall asleep in the middle of a battle as Stonewall Jackson did. But, I think that the type of men they were counted a great deal with Lee. On the one hand he has Jackson who Lee knows means a great deal in terms of the morale of the Confederate people. It would be very destructive, potentially, of the civilian morale to do anything to Jackson. Jackson is also well known as a very pious man, someone who had done great things in the Valley. I think Lee decided to cut Jackson some slack; with John Bankhead Magruder he does not. He wrote a very bland review of Magruder's role in operations, basically saying Magruder tried to do his best, it's too bad he didn't do better during the Seven Days, and off Magruder goes to the trans-Mississippi where he's essentially never heard from again. He's the head of the Department of Texas, New Mexico and Arizona, and we can all take three seconds to name the big battles that occurred in those places. There were, of course, none. He did defend Galveston while he was in Texas, and we've just listed all of the things that he did that were noteworthy while he was out in Texas. He never recovers his reputation, and no one cares that he goes. A woman diarist in Richmond said, "Our people think their whole army might have been captured but for the dilatory action of some of our generals." She's writing this right after the Seven Days. General Magruder is relieved and sent to command in the west, and good riddance is the implication. Off he goes; he doesn't come back. He's a case of a man who began the war very well, and then he's gone when Lee decides that there is no reason to keep him.

George Pickett's Confederate record is very different. Pickett is yet another Virginian, born in Richmond in 1825. He was last in his class at West Point, we've mentioned that before, the famous class of 1846. He went into the infantry, as everyone who is last in his class would. He won brevets for gallantry in Mexico to first lieutenant at Churubusco and Contreras, and then to captain for his fighting at Chapultapec. He was one of the first American officers over the wall at Chapultapec. There are engravings of that. It was a much-noted thing at the time. There's no question about George Pickett's bravery in Mexico or elsewhere. He was a very courageous man and he did well in Mexico. He'd been promoted to captain by the time of the Civil War.

He was made a brigadier general in the Confederate service early in 1862. There's a great word portrait of him left by Moxley Sorrell, whom I have quoted before in this class and whose memoirs are well worth reading because of the really wonderful descriptions of a variety of famous officers in the Confederate army. The title of his book is *Recollections of a Confederate Staff Officer*, well worth reading. It's been reprinted many times. It's readily available. This is how Moxley Sorrell, who's on Longstreet's staff, described George Pickett,

> A singular figure indeed. A medium sized well-built man, straight, erect, and in a well-fitting uniform, an elegant riding whip in hand. His appearance was distinguished and striking, but the head, the hair, were extraordinary. Long ringlets hung loosely over his soldiers, trimmed and highly perfumed. His beard, likewise, was curling and giving out the scents of Aerobe. He had been in Longstreet's old army regiment, and the latter was exceedingly fond of him. Taking Longstreet's orders in emergencies, I could always see how he looked after Pickett, and made us give him things very fully, indeed, sometimes to stay with him to make sure he did not get astray.

James Longstreet took care of Pickett; he looked after Pickett. He knew that Pickett wasn't the brightest bulb in the rack of light bulbs, and that he needed a little help in this regard. I think it's an instance of Longstreet allowing his friendship, perhaps, to intrude on his sound military judgment in pushing George Pickett forward.

The high points in Pickett's career came early. They were as a brigade commander at Seven Pines and at Gaines's Mill in 1862. He was wounded at Gaines's Mill in the shoulder, quite seriously, although even there one man accused him of cowardice at Gaines's Mill. An officer from South Carolina said he wasn't really wounded at Gaines's Mill, just barely wounded at Gaines's Mill, and he made a big thing out of it. In fact, he was wounded quite seriously and he was out for several months. He also had a pretty good day as division commander at Bermuda Hundred during the Richmond-Petersburg campaign in May 1864, but it's a minor part of the broader operation at Richmond and Petersburg, and we've just exhausted the really good days he had.

He lost control of his division at Gettysburg. He missed Fredericksburg. As a major general that's his first battle. I mean he missed it in that his division wasn't really engaged. He did miss Chancellorsville because he was down at Suffolk with James Longstreet and John Bell Hood's division during the Chancellorsville campaign. Gettysburg is his first opportunity. He brought up the rear of the army going toward the battlefield, so he missed the first two days of fighting at Gettysburg, couldn't wait to get into the action on the third day. Very enthusiastic about making the assault, couldn't wait to go in, and then when things went wrong he completely fell apart on the battlefield. After his division was repulsed, Lee rode out, Longstreet went out, both immediately went to work to try to bring together the division, to put up a defense in case the Federals counterattacked right away. Lee saw Pickett and said, "We need to get your command in order, your division in order," and Pickett said, "General, I have no division," and made his way to the rear, a completely broken man. The contrast between the enthusiasm before the assault and his inability to help rally the men after the assault is striking, and I can promise you that did not make a positive impression on R. E. Lee.

In February of 1864, after his division was refitted to a degree (it had left the army because it was so shattered at Gettysburg), he failed in an effort to capture New Burn, North Carolina, which is where he was stationed. He often didn't show good judgment. During the Suffolk campaign he fell in love woman named LaSalle Corbell, and he would leave division headquarters without authorization. This infuriated those who knew what he was doing. He asked Longstreet for permission several times, and Longstreet said, "No, you're leaving too often." Pickett went anyway. He would sneak out, and people commented on the fact that this was very, very bad behavior on the part of a major general, to sneak away from division headquarters to meet the young woman he'd fallen in love with.

His last real battle in the history of the army came at Five Forks on April 1, 1865, when his command was routed by Philip Sheridan, way out on Lee's right flank. He was away from his troops at the time, back at a shad bake with Fitz Lee and Tom Rosser and some other cavalry generals. He rode up to the point of action when he found out that the battle was in progress. He showed admirable personal courage, but presided over a complete disaster at Five Forks that prompted the evacuation of Richmond and Petersburg. During the retreat to Appomattox, Lee removed him from command, and at one point saw Pickett riding along, plodding along, westward with the army, and Lee turned to someone who was with him and said, "Is that man still with this army?" That's very harsh language from Lee. What is Pickett doing with this army?

Pickett nursed a long post-war bitterness toward Lee, and likely failed to appreciate how the assault that wrecked his command at Gettysburg also guaranteed his personal fame. They met after the war, Lee and Pickett did, a very tense and bitter meeting. When Pickett walked out he described Lee as "that old man who had my division massacred at Gettysburg." He died young, he was dissipated, almost certainly an alcoholic. He died in 1875, but he died, as I said at the opening of this lecture, the major general in Lee's army who would be the most famous of all the men who held that rank and didn't get higher rank, and he's famous because of one thing— he's famous because the assault at Gettysburg that carries his name. He's still remembered in many ways as a gallant officer, although that in no way correlates with how he should be remembered really. It's at odds with wartime realities, but much post-war reputation doesn't align well with wartime realty, and one of the reasons it doesn't is because of what different Confederates wrote after the war and how they chose to remember and describe what they and their comrades had done.

That is the topic that we'll take up next time when we look at the writings and the influence of those writings by former Confederates.

# Lecture Twenty-Four
## Before the Bar of History—The Lost Cause

**Scope:** Many of Lee's subordinates wrote memoirs and other postwar accounts that wielded enormous influence over the ways in which subsequent generations would interpret the conflict. A number of ex-Confederates contributed to the Lost Cause canon, which included an enormous literature devoted to the Gettysburg campaign. Jubal Early, John Gordon, and many officers of lower rank had their say. Early orchestrated much of the Lost Cause argument, which celebrated Lee's greatness, emphasized the Union's advantages in men and material, and insisted that James Longstreet had cost Lee a great victory at Gettysburg. Mounting an ineffectual effort to defend himself in his memoirs and other publications, Longstreet, who had embraced the Republican Party and criticized Lee in print soon after the war, proved no match for Early and those who shared his views. The Lost Cause interpretation of the war remained influential for many decades after the war and, though Longstreet's reputation climbed in the late 20th century, continues to be evident in popular conceptions of the war.

## Outline

I. Many ex-Confederates sought to establish a written record of the war that placed the Confederacy and their actions in the best possible light.

    **A.** They hoped to find something honorable in their failed bid for independence.

    **B.** They hoped to influence future generations.

        **1.** They understood that there would be a debate over the meaning of the war.

        **2.** They knew historians and other writers would draw on participants' accounts.

    **C.** Their arguments eventually became known as the *Lost Cause* school of interpretation.

        **1.** There was no formal body of Lost Cause dogma.

        **2.** Most Lost Cause writers did agree on several points.

            **a.** Slavery had not been central to secession or the war.

    **b.** U.S. manpower and material might had been crucial in bringing Confederate defeat.

    **c.** The Confederate people had waged a steadfast effort to win independence.

**II.** Robert E. Lee and his army served as an important focus for the Lost Cause writers.

    **A.** Lee and his army stood as the most attractive element of Confederate experience.

        **1.** Lee had many admirable qualities; he was modest, religious, courtly, restrained.

        **2.** His army won famous victories against long odds.

        **3.** Lee and his army could be discussed without addressing the issue of slavery or divisive Confederate political history.

    **B.** This Lost Cause focus represented a continuation of the wartime importance of Lee and his army in the Confederacy.

**III.** Lost Cause writers engaged in heated debates about Gettysburg.

    **A.** They argued that a victory at Gettysburg would have brought independence.

    **B.** They insisted that Lee had not been responsible for the defeat.

        **1.** They said that Richard Ewell lacked aggressiveness on July 1.

        **2.** They also asserted that Jeb Stuart's absence early in the campaign doomed Lee's effort.

    **C.** They soon settled on James Longstreet as their principal villain.

    **D.** Jubal Early and Longstreet became great antagonists in the 1870s.

        **1.** Early proved far more able as a controversialist.

        **2.** Longstreet's politics and criticisms of Lee hurt his case.

        **3.** Longstreet suffered from invidious comparisons with Stonewall Jackson.

    **E.** John B. Gordon represented a later generation of Lost Cause writers.

        **1.** He also attacked Longstreet.

        **2.** He urged reconciliation with the North on many points.

    **F.** Some former Confederates remained largely aloof from the arguments.

        **1.** E. P. Alexander admired both Lee and Longstreet.

        **2.** He wrote the best critical analysis of Lee's campaigns.

**IV.** The Lost Cause remains influential in popular conceptions of the Civil War.

    **A.** Lee is more popular than Grant.

    **B.** Lee and his army remain the most written-about elements of Confederate history.

    **C.** There is evidence that Lost Cause arguments are losing ground—debates over Confederate flags on license plates and on state flags suggest as much.

## Essential Reading:

Gallagher, *Lee and His Army in Confederate History*, chapter 8.

Gallagher and Nolan, eds., *The Myth of the Lost Cause and Civil War History*, essays by Gallagher, Nolan, Simpson, and Wert.

## Supplementary Reading:

Connelly and Bellows, *God and General Longstreet: The Lost Cause and the Southern Mind.*

Foster, *Ghosts of the Confederacy: Defeat, the Lost Cause, and the Emergence of the New South.*

Piston, *Lee's Tarnished Lieutenant: James Longstreet and His Place in Southern History*, chapters 6–11.

## Questions to Consider:

**1.** Did former Confederates win the war of popular memory regarding the Civil War?

**2.** Is it remarkable that a general and an army that inflicted great damage on the United States have received so much favorable treatment?

# Lecture Twenty-Four—Transcript
## Before the Bar of History—The Lost Cause

We'll finish our consideration of Lee and his generals by looking at the writings and the impact of those writings of the men who served under him in the Army of Northern Virginia. Many of Lee's subordinates wrote memoirs and other postwar accounts that wielded enormous influence over the ways in which subsequent generations would interpret the conflict. A number of ex-Confederates contributed to the Lost Cause canon, which included a huge literature devoted to the Gettysburg campaign. Jubal Early, John B. Gordon, and many officers of lower rank had their say. Early orchestrated much of the Lost Cause argument, which celebrated Lee's greatness, emphasized the United States' advantages in men and material, and insisted that James Longstreet had cost Lee a great victory at Gettysburg. Mounting an ineffectual effort to defend himself in his memoirs and other publications, Longstreet, who had embraced the Republican Party and criticized Lee in print after the war, proved no match for Early and those who shared his views. The Lost Cause interpretation of the war remained influential for many decades after Appomattox, and, though Longstreet's reputation climbed in the late 20th century, the Lost Cause continues to be evident in popular conceptions of the war.

Many ex-Confederates sought to establish a written record of the war that placed the Confederacy and their actions as Confederate soldiers in the best possible light. It's important as a starting point to know just how shattering a defeat this was for the white South. Among white Americans in all of our history, only white Southerners have really known the kind of all-encompassing military defeat that people all over the rest of the world have experienced at one time or another, or virtually all other people. About 25% of the military age white population of the Confederacy was dead at the end of the war. Another 25% had been maimed in some way. If we want to place this within a comparative context, if the United States' dead, military dead, in World War II had been as high as a proportion of the population as Confederate military dead were as a proportion of the white population of the Confederacy, we would have had 6.6 million dead soldiers in World War II. As it was, we had about four hundred thousand; 6.6 million dead, it's a loss on a scale unmatched by any other segment of white society in American history.

There was also enormous material loss. The economic infrastructure was shattered in the Confederacy during the war. Roads and railroads and levees and public installations of all kinds destroyed in the course of the war. An enormous amount of the agricultural machinery had been destroyed. Thousands and thousands of agricultural animals, draft animals and hogs and every other type of farm animal had been killed in the course of the war as well. And, at the end of the war, there was a United States army of occupation in place in the former Confederate States. That's another experience that was not an American experience unless you go all the way back to the British army of occupation, as many of the colonists would have seen it.

So, they're facing this kind of defeat, this kind of bleak, unequivocal defeat. There is no way to dress this up if you're a former Confederate. You didn't kind of lose, you didn't almost lose, you lost completely. You failed abjectly in your effort to establish a slave-holding republic, and along the way you had this enormous loss of both human resources and material resources. The question is: How are you going to come away from this with something positive? How are you going to find a way to make sense of this catastrophic effort, make sense of it in a way that would allow you both to hold your head up and to bequeath something positive to future generations of white Southerners? So, that's one thing they're up to here. How are you going to find something honorable in this failed bid for independence?

Another thing they hoped to do, these post-war writers, is influence future generations, both North and South, by shaping the printed record of the war. They understood that future historians and others that wrote about the war would be interested in what participants wrote. They, in effect, were writing for history. They knew that there was going to be a struggle for the public memory of the war, really. How is this war going to be interpreted down the road? One of the ways that that understanding down the road will be shaped is by what we write now, they said, what we get on paper now will be important. They knew that historians and others would look to their writings, and that is one reason they tried to get their writings into the record quickly.

This process began even before the war ended. There are some books that come out assessing what is going on in the war even before it is over. The most famous of these is a four-volume work called *A Southern History of the War* by a man named E. A. Pollard, a Southern newspaper editor who wrote this massive history of the Confederacy as the war unfolded. It's a very rich source. It's very opinionated. It's wrong in a lot of things, but it's a fascinating way to see what people thought was going on and how Pollard assessed what was going on. The pace of publications picked up very rapidly. More things in the '60s, and then more things in the 1870s, and then more things in the 1880s came out as more and more officers, and then later men in the ranks, wrote their accounts.

The arguments put forward by the former Confederates, many of them, eventually became known as the Lost Cause school of interpretation. Pollard's the one that coined the phrase "Lost Cause," but this became not an official body of ideas, not a body that you could say, "there are four parts to the Lost Cause argument and here they are and everybody agreed on it." There's no central clearinghouse for these writings. There's no firm list of tenants to this interpretation of the war. However, most Lost Cause writers did agree on several important points. Perhaps the most important of them: they agreed that slavery had not been central to secession and the war. They knew that the tide of western civilization was against them in this regard. You can't say after the war, "Yes, it was all about slavery," and then expect to have a favorable hearing from people. You're out of step, you have to finesse the issue of slavery, and so what you do is argue that it wasn't a war about slavery, it was a war about constitutional arguments. It was a war about which side was going to be the true inheritors of the revolutionary tradition. Are you going to say that the United States with it's powerful central government is what the founding generation had in mind or are you going to say a more state rights localist view, the Confederate view, is what the founders had in mind. This is absolutely crucial for them. You've got to distance yourself from slavery, and so post-facto they pretend that slavery wasn't that important.

Of course, in 1861 slavery was everything, and they were very blunt about saying that. It's fascinating to compare the writings and speeches of Jefferson Davis and Alexander Stephens, the president and vice president of the Confederacy in 1861, and what they wrote in their post-war memoirs. In 1861, Stephens gave his famous cornerstone speech when he said slavery was the cornerstone of southern civilization, a positive good, the whole point of everything. Davis, in an early message to congress, said, "We had to secede. We're going to have to fight in order to save our slave-holding society." But, after the war, they both said no, no, no, no—it's not really about slavery, it's really about constitutional principle. Alexander Stephens called his two-volume work *A Constitutional View of the Late War Between the States*, and Jefferson Davis, in his two thick volumes of memoirs, made the point again and again that it was about constitutional principle. Well, they had to make that point after the war if they were going to try to get a favorable hearing, but we should never let that obscure the fact that slavery is absolutely central to why they seceded and why they established, or tried to establish, this slave-holding republic.

So, you've got to get slavery out of the picture if you're a Lost Cause writer. Another thing they agree on is the overwhelming power of the United States is the critical element in bringing Confederate defeat—the United States had too much of everything, they said. Their armies were bigger, far more manufacturing, far more railroads, far more everything you need to fight a mid-19$^{th}$ century war. Of course they won, look at their industrial base, look at their population, look at all of the advantages they had, said the Lost Cause writers. We never had a chance, we never had a chance, but, boy, didn't we wage a gallant defense against this powerful foe. That's the next step. The Confederate people had been steadfast in the face of this United States juggernaut. The Lost Cause writers airbrushed out of their picture all of the internal dissent in the Confederacy, the wrangling about conscription and about a tax in kind, and about impressments, and other policies of the Confederate government that made the Confederate government by far the most powerful and intrusive central government in American history, down until late in the 20$^{th}$ century. This government, ostensibly founded on the notion of state rights, became this government that reached down into the lives of all the Confederate people and dictated all kinds of things. Let's don't write about that; let's don't write about opposition to the draft. Let's write about how loyal and steadfast the women and men of the Confederacy were in the face of this Northern power. We never could win, but boy didn't we put up a strong fight. That is what the Lost Cause writers say—that there's no loss of honor in that. If you can't win anyway because the odds are so great against you, then there's no loss of honor in losing. But there is great honor to be derived from struggling so valiantly and so long against the enormous power of the United States and against officers such as Ulysses S. Grant and William Tecumseh Sherman and Philip Henry Sheridan who applied that power so brutally. Those are all themes in the Lost Cause writings. It isn't about slavery, it's all about the power of the United States, and boy wasn't the white South brave in mounting this defense.

Now, there are large elements of truth in the Northern power element of this argument, of course, because the United States did have a great deal more of almost everything. A far greater population, it did have larger armies, it did have more material and so forth. They're not making all of this up, but they're fitting it together in such a way as to present a picture that in many ways is at odds with what really happened during the war.

Now, Robert E. Lee and his army serve as the absolutely essential focus of much of the Lost Cause writings. They have to play their best cards, these former Confederates. What are their best cards? Their best cards are Robert E. Lee and the Army of Northern Virginia. They don't have a comparable card. If you're going to try to put your best foot forward, put Lee and his army forward. Lee himself is a very attractive figure, even to many in the United States, even during the war, and surely shortly after the war. He's the most important Confederate figure. We've all ready talked about that. They don't have to make up Lee's importance, he is important. They can take their most important figure, and put him front and center, and say here is our cause, it's in Robert E. Lee. Look how modest he is, look how religious he is, look what a brilliant soldier he is against long odds, look how knightly a figure he is, what a courtly figure he is. Look how he doesn't make war against civilians. Look, look, look—they elevate Lee to a position, they take this figure who was a very prominent figure during the war, by far the most celebrated Confederate figure, and make him into a perfect figure retrospectively. They begin with great material, they make it even greater, and then they say this man and his army won these victories, look at these victories they won against the odds, look at Chancellorsville, look at Lee and Stonewall Jackson, this grand partnership, these two Christian soldiers. They say how can this have been a bad cause when it's led by men such as this? Now, they can do all of that, they can talk about Lee and his army, they can talk about Lee and Jackson, without talking about slavery. You don't even have to mention slavery if you're going to focus on the Army of Northern Virginia and its campaigns in Virginia. Let's keep the focus on the military; that is, we don't have to talk, if we're Lost Cause writers, about Jefferson Davis and about conscription, and about disaffection behind the line, and about arguments in politics. You can just forget all that and talk about Lee and his army, the army that's winning victories, the army commanded by this very, very appealing figure in many ways. Slavery is out of the picture.

This Lost Cause focus represented a continuance, of course, of the wartime importance of Lee and his army, and this is very important, too. They're not making all of this up either, the Lost Cause writers. Their not looking around and saying gosh, which leader looked good? We know Joe Johnston's the most important; he's kind of unattractive in some ways. We can't really use Beauregard, how about Lee? Let's build him up into a great figure. They didn't have to do that. Lee was already a great figure within the context of the war. They could go with someone who was already prominent. Scholarship in the late 20th century tended to argue that Lee was almost a complete post-war fabrication. Thomas L. Connelly, a historian who wrote the book *The Marble Man* about Robert E. Lee, has been most influential in this regard, arguing that Lee was just one among many officers during the war. He didn't tower above Joe Johnston, or Albert Sydney Johnson, or Beauregard, or even others, they're all about the same. But, after the war, the crafty Lost Cause writers took Lee and made him superior to the others. The only way you can reach that conclusion is if you don't read anything written during the war. If you want to come at it that way, great, you can come to any conclusion you want, but if you actually read the sources from the war, Lee stands out so starkly as the most important figure that you cannot possibly reach the conclusion that Lost Cause writers just took this one guy from a sort of crowd and arbitrarily made him number one. Lost Cause writers started with good material.

They, however, tended to become bogged down in Gettysburg as the post-war decades unfolded, and they kind of got in their own way, in one regard, in their explanation about the Confederate defeat. On one hand they're saying we never could win, the odds were overwhelming, we did our best in a very difficult situation, and that is admirable. That's one explanation for defeat. They come up with an alternate explanation for defeat, and that is James Longstreet undid Robert E. Lee at Gettysburg and because the Confederates lost the battle of Gettysburg, they lost the war. They could've won the war. They are one of the principle reasons, the Lost Cause writers, why Gettysburg took on such enormous proportion retrospectively. They made Gettysburg the great watershed of the war. They made Gettysburg the moment at which the war turned toward Appomattox and in making Gettysburg the great point in which the war turned, they also could absolve Lee of all blame for Gettysburg. They're going to make Longstreet the villain. Initially they thought others might be the problem. They thought that maybe it was Ewell, we've talked about that, on the first day. Maybe it was Jeb Stuart for not doing what he should do, and we've seen also that Lee actually believed during the war that Ewell and Jeb Stuart didn't do very well at Gettysburg. Lee never said that Gettysburg was the turning point of the war. He did say that he was unhappy with Ewell and Stuart. The Lost Cause writers said that as well, but they very quickly settled on James Longstreet as their principle villain, and James Longstreet, as I've commented before while we were talking about Longstreet, makes a perfect villain.

He is the perfect villain. He sits down, draws a great big bull's-eye on a piece of paper, pins it on his back, and then walks around so the Lost Cause writers can lob shells at him. He, in 1865, published in a New Orleans newspaper a critical piece on Lee, published a critical piece about Lee, saying that Lee had not done well during the Gettysburg campaign. In other writings he said other things like Lee attacked and attacked and attacked at Gettysburg until his blood lust was satisfied, and then he quit. Those aren't the kinds of things that are going to endear James Longstreet to the white South. He also became a Republican, as I have noted before. He accepted office from his old friend, Ulysses S. Grant. He argued for early reconciliation at a time when the white South remained very bitter toward the United States, didn't want to reconcile, wanted to nurture and nourish their hatred of the North. And he finally even became a Catholic—that's just too much. He did all the things the white South didn't want him to do, and so here we have our villain for Gettysburg if we're Lost Cause writers. It's all Longstreet's fault. It's Longstreet's fault, and his principle antagonist became Jubal Early. Jubal Early went after Longstreet no-holds-barred, and Longstreet was absolutely no match for Jubal Early. Jubal Early, the old commonwealth's attorney; Jubal Early, who could make an argument, just made mincemeat of Longstreet, mincemeat in the eyes of most of the white South, and it quickly became accepted widely among former Confederates that Longstreet had cost Lee the battle of Gettysburg, and that by losing the battle of Gettysburg the Confederacy had lost its best chance to win the war.

Along the way there were also innumerable comparisons between Longstreet and Stonewall Jackson, always invidious comparisons. Jackson, Longstreet; Jackson the great lieutenant, Longstreet the plodding marcher Lee had to keep an eye on; Jackson the semi-independent commander, Longstreet the man who bullheadedly disagreed with Lee at Gettysburg; Longstreet never comes out well in those comparative estimates, always Jackson comes out well, and it's hard to come out well against the sainted Jackson who dies at the absolute apogee of his fame at Chancellorsville. If Longstreet had been killed on the Orange Plank Road on May the 6th in the battle of the Wilderness instead of just horribly wounded, his reputation would have been much higher after the war. He would have been right alongside Jackson in the Confederate camp, killed under dramatic circumstances in the midst of a wonderful attack, and so forth, but that wasn't the case. In this debate, Longstreet lost and this notion that he at Gettysburg was the great villain gained more and more currency, especially in the early bitter phase of the Lost Cause writings.

There are kind of two phases to the Lost Cause writings. The ones that Early really dominated are in the late '60s. Early is the first major figure on either side to publish his memoirs. He published a book titled *A Memoir of the Last Year of the War*. He published it in 1866, just one year after the war he'd already published his memoirs. The Early Confederate memoirs are more bitter, much more anger toward the North.

There is a second phase of Lost Cause writings. It's dominated by John Brown Gordon and people who agreed with him. It's a second generation, a second wave, of Lost Cause writings which agrees on many things with the earlier Lost Cause writers. Slavery is not central to the war. Lee is a great leader, an unblemished leader. Longstreet is to blame for Gettysburg, and so forth. But this element of Lost Cause writing was much less bitter toward the North. It pursued a reconcilliationist approach. It said, listen we were all great, we were all Americans; we were all brave together. Let's don't talk about why we went to war; we all had good reasons for going to war, our own good reasons, our own strong beliefs. Let's don't differentiate among those beliefs. Let's don't say the United States was on the side of the angels because it wasn't fighting for slavery. Let's just say that everybody was fighting for what they thought was important, and that the men on both sides showed American virtues of manliness, steadfastness to their cause, and bravery in battle. Let's agree on that. Gordon on the Confederate side and on the Federal side Joshua Lawrence Chamberlain typify this kind of retrospective writing, this reconcilliationist type of writing.

As I said, these guys in the second wave of writing did agree that Longstreet was at fault, however. They did agree on that. Let me quote from Gordon's memoirs. This is at a time when even many of Lee's staff officers had stepped forward to say, "No, Lee didn't order Longstreet to attack at dawn on the 2$^{nd}$. No, Lee didn't order Longstreet to attack at dawn on the 3$^{rd}$. Those charges by Jubal Early and others are wrong," and yet John Gordon, even though the staff officers had said that, wrote this in his memoirs published in the early 20$^{th}$ century, he said, "It now seems certain that impartial military critics, after thorough investigation, will consider the following as established: first, that General Lee distinctly ordered Longstreet to attack early the morning of the second day, and if Longstreet had done so, two of the largest corps of Mead's army would not have been in the fight, but Longstreet delayed the attack until four o'clock in the afternoon, and thus lost his opportunity to occupy Little Round Top, the key to the position, which he might have done in the morning without firing a shot or losing a man. Second, that General Lee ordered Longstreet to attack at daybreak on the morning of the third day, and that Longstreet did not attack until two or three o'clock in the afternoon, the artillery opening at one." And then he went on to say, "The great mistake of the halt on the first day," that is Ewell, "would have been repaired on the second, and even on the third day, if Lee's orders had been vigorously executed, and that General Lee died believing the testimony on this point is overwhelming," said Gordon parenthetically, "that he lost Gettysburg at last by Longstreet's disobedience of orders."

Well, Lee never wrote anything of the kind. In his post-war conversations it's pretty clear that he was harder on Ewell than he was on Longstreet, and harder on Stuart than he was on Longstreet, but Gordon is saying it's Longstreet, it is Longstreet.

Elsewhere, though, Gordon emphasizes that the reconciliation is what counts. He wrote at the end of his memoirs, "It will be a glorious day for our country when all of the children within its borders shall learn that the four years of fratricidal war between the North and South was waged by neither with criminal or unworthy intent," by neither side, that is, "but both to protect what they conceive to be threatened rights and imperiled liberties. The issues which divided the sections were born when the republic was born, and were forever buried in an ocean of fraternal blood. The republic, rising from its baptism of blood, with a national life more robust, a national union more complete, and a national influence ever widening shall go forever forward in its benign mission to humanity." That is classic late Lost Cause rhetoric. Longstreet's still to blame, Lee is still wonderful and gallant, but the war basically shows us how glorious Americans are, white American men in the North, white American men in the South.

The other thing airbrushed out of this reconcilliationist view is black participation in the war, the two hundred thousand African-Americans who fought for the United States, yet virtually no mention in much of the reconcilliationist literature.

Now there are other Confederates who write after the war who really don't have an axe to grind at all, and Porter Alexander is the most obvious of them. His writings are not filled with this kind of Lost Cause argument. He takes a much more aloof, almost academic, analytical approach to what was going on. He admired both Lee and Longstreet. He also criticizes both Lee and Longstreet. The thing about Alexander is that he offers a pointed critique of everyone, plusses and minuses, warts and all, even for Lee, which is very, very unusual. Lee really does become a sort of saint, sort of out after the war. There's a wonderful anecdote, probably apocryphal, about a little girl who comes home from Sunday school to her grandmother's house and she seems upset and her grandmother says, "Well, what's the matter dear, you seem to be troubled by something?" The little girl says, "Well, grandmother, I'm confused about what went on in Sunday school today. I never can keep it straight. Was General Lee in the Old Testament or the New Testament" That is a very common notion, I think, in the white South after the war. Lee becomes this sort of saint, certainly not something he would have countenanced had he lived.

The Lost Cause influence remains quite prominent, I think, even down to today in popular conceptions of the war. Lee is more popular than Grant. One of the great Lost Cause arguments was that Grant was a ham-handed butcher; of course he succeeded in the end. He simply fed his absolutely unending line of soldiers into the meat grinder and eventually wore Lee down. Who couldn't figure out to do that, said the Lost Cause writers, that doesn't take a great general. It just takes a sort of low cunning of some sort that says I've got more and I'll just pound you into submission. Lee was a great general; Grant a ham-handed general in some ways, but a general who had so much of everything that he could win anyway. Well, there's still a lot of that perception. Grant almost never gets a break in the popular imagination. Grant has one of the grandest monuments in all of the United States in Washington D.C., and nobody even knows where it is. It's right in front of the United States capitol, looking right at the Washington Monument and around the monument down to the Lincoln Memorial and nobody even knows that it's there. It's to that degree that Grant has been forgotten in many ways. Grant should be the great figure—he isn't. Lee is more prominent in novels than Grant; Lee is more prominent in recent Civil War art, that is, art created for the Civil War market. There are four or five or six or seven or eight paintings, prints, of Lee for every one of Grant, and often the ones that Grant is in have to do with Appomattox, so Lee's in them too. It's just that Lee is everywhere, and it must be that they sell better or the artists would be painting Grant everywhere. Grant at Shiloh, Grant at Chattanooga, Grant at Fort Donalson, Grant at Fort Henry—there aren't paintings like that, but we have Lee everywhere, Lee everywhere again and again and again, and especially Lee at Gettysburg. Even in recent films Lee is much more dominant. In the movie *Gettysburg*, based on the novel *Killer Angels*, Lee is at the center of that. In the more recent *Gods and Generals*, Lee is an important character in that. Grant is not a central character in any recent film about the Civil War. Lee is a major character in a number of them.

Lee's been on five postage stamps in the United States. For God's sake, why? He's the Rebel general. Why is he on United States postage stamps? I think that must be unprecedented in the history of failed civil wars, that the major Rebel leader would be on the postage stamps. I think the Lost Cause writers have a lot to do with that. They were so successful, so successful, in their portrait of Lee that it is a portrait that continues to resonate, together with the whole underdog element of it, there's a sense that Lee was an underdog, but what a grand underdog.

He and his army, Lee and his army, remain by far the most written about element of Confederate history, by far. Their campaigns in the eastern theater dissected again and again and again, and not just Gettysburg, although the literature on Gettysburg is just grown to such bloated proportions that it's just impossible to keep up with it, even if you try hard. Now, Lee and his army were very important, as I've argued in this course. They are the most important national institution in the Confederacy, but the attention to them in the literature is out of proportion even conceding that they loomed so large on the Confederate landscape, and I think that, again, is partly a function of the effectiveness of the Lost Cause writers.

Now, the Lost Cause is losing ground recently, I think, in the United States. There is evidence. There are debates about Confederate symbols in many places, whether they're flying over the statehouse in South Carolina, or whether they are in the Georgia flag, or whether there are efforts to put Confederate flags on license plates in different states, or to put a picture of Robert E. Lee along the floodwall of Richmond, Virginia. There have been a number of public debates about these Confederate symbols, and it's becoming harder and harder, I think, to employ these Confederate symbols, especially the Confederate battle flag, in ways that they were once employed without any thought at all given to them. But, whatever happens in that regard, I believe that there is still enormous residual influence from these Lost Cause writers. It is really a remarkable element of the war, and whenever anyone takes up the study of Lee and his generals, as we have in this class, it is exceedingly important to begin with the knowledge that part of what we are going to read, part of our understanding of Lee and his army was shaped by these men who fought under Lee, and then after the war wrote with a very distinct agenda about how best to present themselves and their actions before the bar of history.

# Maps

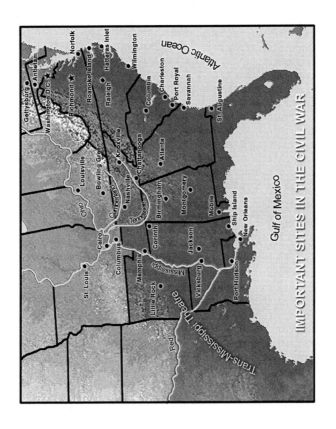

341

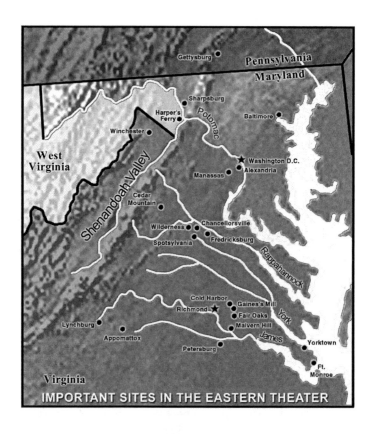

IMPORTANT SITES IN THE EASTERN THEATER

342

# Timeline

1846–1848 ..................................... War between the United States and Mexico gives many Civil War generals their only real experience in field operations.

1859 ............................................... John Brown's raid on Harpers Ferry intensifies sectional tensions; Robert E. Lee and Jeb Stuart both present when Brown and his followers are captured.

Nov. 1860 ...................................... Abraham Lincoln elected as the first Republican president.

Dec. 20, 1860 ................................. South Carolina secedes from the Union.

## 1861

Jan. 9–Feb. 1 .................................. The remaining six states of the Lower South secede (Mississippi, Jan. 9; Florida, Jan. 10; Alabama, Jan. 11; Georgia, Jan. 19; Louisiana, Jan. 26, Texas, Feb. 1).

Feb. 4–March 11 ............................. A convention of delegates from the seven seceded states meeting in Montgomery, Alabama, writes a constitution and selects Jefferson Davis and Alexander H. Stephens as provisional president and vice president of a new slaveholding republic called the Confederate States of America.

March 4 .......................................... Abraham Lincoln inaugurated.

April 12–13 .................................... Confederate bombardment overseen by P. G. T. Beauregard results in the surrender of Fort Sumter.

April 15 .......................................... Lincoln calls for 75,000 volunteers to suppress the rebellion.

April 17–June 8............................Four states of the Upper South secede in response to Lincoln's call for volunteers (Virginia, April 17; Arkansas, May 6; North Carolina, May 20; Tennessee, June 8).

May 20..........................................Confederate Congress votes to move the national government from Montgomery to Richmond.

June 10..........................................Confederates under John Bankhead Magruder win a small engagement at Big Bethel on the Virginia peninsula between Yorktown and Fort Monroe.

July 18..........................................Engagement at Blackburn's Ford serves as a preliminary to First Manassas or Bull Run.

July 21..........................................P. G. T. Beauregard and Joseph E. Johnston share command in the Battle of First Manassas or Bull Run, which yields a flashy Confederate victory that builds confidence in the South and convinces many Northerners that the war will be longer and harder than first thought.

Oct. 21 ..........................................Union forces suffer a debacle at Ball's Bluff, near Leesburg, Virginia.

Nov. 1 ..........................................George B. McClellan replaces Winfield Scott as general-in-chief of the U.S. Army.

**1862**

Feb. 6–16 ......................................Ulysses S. Grant captures Forts Henry and Donelson on the Tennessee and Cumberland Rivers.

March 7–8 .....................................Union victory at Pea Ridge, Arkansas, deals a blow to Confederates in the trans-Mississippi theater.

| | |
|---|---|
| March 9 | The *Monitor* and the *Virginia* fight the first naval engagement between ironclad vessels. |
| March 23 | Stonewall Jackson defeated at the First Battle of Kernstown near Winchester; this action nevertheless aids the Confederacy by persuading Federals to keep strength in the Shenandoah Valley that could have helped McClellan in his drive against Richmond. |
| April 5 | George B. McClellan begins a month-long siege of Yorktown, Virginia, marking the first important event in his Peninsula campaign. |
| April 6–7 | Ulysses S. Grant wins the battle of Shiloh in southwestern Tennessee. |
| April 16 | C.S. Congress passes the first national conscription act in American history; acts passed on Sept. 27, 1862, and Feb. 17, 1864, supplement the original legislation. |
| May 3 | Confederates abandon Yorktown. |
| May 5 | Battle of Williamsburg a delaying action for Confederates retreating up the peninsula toward Richmond. |
| May 8 | Stonewall Jackson wins the battle of McDowell, the first of several victories in his Shenandoah Valley campaign. |
| May 23 | Jackson's advance guard wins a small engagement at Front Royal and captures nearly 1,000 Federal prisoners. |
| May 25 | First Battle of Winchester gives Jackson his third victory of the Valley campaign. |

May 29–30 ..................................... P. G. T. Beauregard withdraws from the vital rail center of Corinth, Mississippi.

May 31–June 1 ............................... The battle of Seven Pines or Fair Oaks is fought near Richmond; Joseph E. Johnston is wounded on the first day of action and command of the Confederate army defending Richmond against George B. McClellan's Army of the Potomac passes to Robert E. Lee.

June 12–15 ..................................... Jeb Stuart's cavalry makes its first "ride around McClellan."

June 25–July 1 .............................. The Seven Days' battles reverse a tide of U.S. military success as Robert E. Lee drives George B. McClellan away from Richmond.

June 26 ........................................... The first big battle of the Seven Days takes place at Mechanicsville.

June 27 ........................................... Gaines's Mill marks the second and bloodiest of the Seven Days' battles.

June 29 ........................................... Confederates fail to inflict serious damage on McClellan's retreating Federals in the battle of Savage's Station.

June 30 ........................................... Confederates launch heavy but indecisive assaults against McClellan in the battle of Glendale or Frayser's Farm.

July 1 .............................................. Lee mounts a final series of attacks against McClellan in the battle of Malvern Hill, the final clash of the Seven Days' campaign.

Aug. 9 ............................................ Stonewall Jackson defeats part of John Pope's Army of Virginia at the battle of Cedar Mountain near Culpeper.

| | |
|---|---|
| Aug. 26–27 | Jackson completes a flanking march around Pope's Army and destroys the Federal supply base at Manassas Junction. |
| Aug. 28 | Battle of Groveton opens fighting at Second Manassas; Richard S. Ewell receives a wound that requires amputation of his leg. |
| Aug. 29–30 | Robert E. Lee wins a victory over Pope's Army at the battle of Second Manassas. |
| Sept. 14 | Battle of South Mountain circumscribes Lee's options during the Maryland campaign. |
| Sept. 15 | Stonewall Jackson captures Harpers Ferry. |
| Sept. 17 | Union victory at the battle of Antietam or Sharpsburg ends Robert E. Lee's first invasion of the North. |
| Sept. 22 | Lincoln issues his preliminary Emancipation Proclamation. |
| Oct. 9–12 | Jeb Stuart rides around McClellan's army a second time. |
| Nov. 5 | Lincoln replaces George B. McClellan with Ambrose E. Burnside as commander of the Army of the Potomac. |
| Dec. 13 | Robert E. Lee defeats Burnside at the battle of Fredericksburg. |
| Dec. 31 | First day of the battle of Murfreesboro or Stones River, Tennessee. |

# 1863

Jan. 1 .............................................. Lincoln issues his Emancipation
Proclamation.

Jan. 2 .............................................. Battle of Stones River concludes with
Braxton Bragg's retreat.

Jan. 25 ............................................ Lincoln replaces Burnside with Joseph
Hooker as commander of the Army of
the Potomac.

April 11–May 4 .............................. James Longstreet conducts his largely
unsuccessful Suffolk campaign and, as
a result, misses the battle of
Chancellorsville.

May 1–4 .......................................... Robert E. Lee defeats Joseph Hooker in
the battle of Chancellorsville; Stonewall
Jackson is badly wounded on May 2
and has his left arm amputated.

May 1–17 ........................................ Ulysses S. Grant wins battles at Port
Gibson (May 1), Raymond (May 12),
Jackson (May 14), Champion Hill (May
16), and the Big Black River (May 17)
en route to bottling up John C.
Pemberton's army in the Vicksburg
defenses.

May 10 ............................................ Stonewall Jackson dies at Guiney's
Station, Virginia.

June 9 .............................................. Jeb Stuart's cavalry wins a hard-fought
victory over Alfred Pleasonton's
Federal cavalry at the battle of Brandy
Station.

June 14–15 ...................................... Richard S. Ewell wins the battle of
Second Winchester en route to
Pennsylvania.

June 20 ............................................ West Virginia joins the Union as a new
state.

**1864**

March 12 . . . . . . . . . . . . . . . . . . . . . . . . . . U. S. Grant named general-in-chief of Union forces; plans simultaneous offensives designed to pressure Confederate military forces on a broad front.

April 8–9 . . . . . . . . . . . . . . . . . . . . . . . . Battles of Mansfield or Sabine Crossroads and Pleasant Hill, fought near Shreveport, Louisiana, mark the climax of Nathaniel P. Banks's unsuccessful Red River campaign.

April 12 . . . . . . . . . . . . . . . . . . . . . . . . . Confederates under Nathan Bedford Forrest capture Fort Pillow, Tennessee, killing a number of black and white Unionist troops who try to surrender.

May 5–6 . . . . . . . . . . . . . . . . . . . . . . . . . Battle of the Wilderness opens the Overland campaign between Robert E. Lee and U. S. Grant; James Longstreet severely wounded during the second day of fighting.

May 7 . . . . . . . . . . . . . . . . . . . . . . . . . . . William Tecumseh Sherman begins his Atlanta campaign against Joseph E. Johnston's Army of Tennessee.

May 8–20 . . . . . . . . . . . . . . . . . . . . . . . . Battles around Spotsylvania Court House continue the struggle between Grant and Lee; heaviest fighting occurs on May 12 in the Confederate salient known as the Mule Shoe.

May 11 . . . . . . . . . . . . . . . . . . . . . . . . . . Jeb Stuart mortally wounded in the battle of Yellow Tavern and dies the following day.

May 15 . . . . . . . . . . . . . . . . . . . . . . . . . . Battle of New Market blunts Franz Sigel's Union campaign in the Shenandoah Valley.

May 16 . . . . . . . . . . . . . . . . . . . . . . . . . . Battle of Drewry's Bluff, with P. G. T. Beauregard and George E. Pickett playing key roles on the Confederate side, stops progress toward Richmond of Benjamin F. Butler's Union Army of the James; Butler retreats to Bermuda Hundred.

May 23–26 ..................................... Lee and Grant face each other at the North Anna River; A. P. Hill launches precipitate attack on May 23; Lee later too ill to take advantage of possible opening.

June 1–3 ........................................ Battles at Cold Harbor between Lee and Grant include massive and unsuccessful Union assaults (the heaviest attacks occurred on June 3).

June 12–18 ..................................... Grant orchestrates a brilliant crossing of the James River but fails to capture Petersburg; his troops begin what will become a nine-month siege.

June 13 .......................................... Jubal Early and the Second Corps leave Lee's army for what will become the 1864 Shenandoah Valley campaign.

June 17–18 ..................................... Early's force turns back a Federal advance under David Hunter at Lynchburg.

June 27 .......................................... Union attacks bloodily repulsed at Kennesaw Mountain, Georgia, after which Sherman resumes his campaign of maneuver.

July 2 ............................................. The Wade-Davis Bill passes the U.S. Senate, presenting an alternative to President Lincoln's 10 Per Cent Plan for Reconstruction; Lincoln kills it with a pocket veto on July 4, and supporters of the bill answer with the "Wade-Davis Manifesto" criticizing the president's actions.

July 9............................................Jubal Early wins the battle of the
Monocacy just south of Frederick,
Maryland, and over the next three days,
advances to the outskirts of Washington
and skirmishes with Federals in the
capital's defensive works.

July 17...........................................Jefferson Davis replaces Joseph E.
Johnston with John Bell Hood as
commander of the Confederate army
defending Atlanta; Hood launches
unsuccessful offensives against
Sherman's invading forces in the battles
of Peachtree Creek (July 20), Atlanta
(July 22), and Ezra Church (July 28)
before the two armies settle into a siege.

July 20...........................................Stephen Dodson Ramseur is defeated in
a small battle at Stephenson's Depot,
just north of Winchester.

July 24...........................................Jubal Early wins a victory in the
Shenandoah Valley at the Second Battle
of Kernstown.

July 30...........................................Lee's victory at the battle of the Crater
costs Grant a good opportunity to break
the stalemate at Petersburg.

Aug. 5 ...........................................David G. Farragut's Union fleet wins
the battle of Mobile Bay, closing the
last major Confederate port on the Gulf
of Mexico.

Aug. 18–19 ....................................Battle of the Weldon Railroad on the
Richmond/Petersburg front.

Aug. 25 ..........................................Battle of Ream's Station on the
Richmond/Petersburg front.

Sept. 2 ...........................................Sherman's Union forces enter Atlanta,
providing a critical Union victory that

virtually guaranteed President Lincoln's reelection in November.

Sept. 19 .......................................... Climactic phase of the 1864 Shenandoah Valley campaign opens with Philip H. Sheridan's victory over Early's Confederate army in the battle of Third Winchester; Robert E. Rodes mortally wounded and dies on the battlefield.

Sept. 22 .......................................... Sheridan defeats Early for a second time in the battle of Fisher's Hill.

Sept. 26–Oct. 7 ............................... Sheridan's army destroys much of the logistical capacity of the Shenandoah Valley between Strasburg and Harrisonburg.

Sept. 29–Oct. 2 ............................... Fighting at Peeble's Farm and Fort Harrison on the Richmond/Petersburg front.

Oct. 10 ........................................... Cavalry battle of Tom's Brook gives Federals in the Shenandoah Valley another victory.

Oct. 19 ........................................... Jubal Early's defeat at the battle of Cedar Creek ends large-scale operations in the Shenandoah Valley; Stephen Dodson Ramseur mortally wounded and dies the next day.

Nov. 1 ............................................ New Maryland state constitution abolishing slavery takes effect.

Nov. 7 ............................................ Jefferson Davis proposes enrolling slaves in the Confederate military and freeing all who serve faithfully; this touches off an acrimonious debate that continues for several months.

Nov. 8 ............................................ Abraham Lincoln reelected, and Republicans gain large majorities in both houses of Congress and do well in Northern state races.

Nov. 16–Dec. 21 ............................. Sherman's army makes its famous "March to the Sea" from Atlanta to Savannah, leaving a wide path of destruction in its wake.

Nov. 30 ........................................... John M. Schofield wins a Union victory over John Bell Hood's Army of Tennessee at the Battle of Franklin, a short distance south of Nashville.

Dec. 15–16 ...................................... George H. Thomas routs Hood's Army of Tennessee in the battle of Nashville, the final significant engagement in Tennessee.

## 1865

Jan. 11 ............................................ Missouri state constitutional convention abolishes slavery.

Jan. 13 ............................................ John Bell Hood resigns as commander of the Army of Tennessee.

Jan. 19 ............................................ William Tecumseh Sherman begins his march from Savannah into the Carolinas.

Jan. 31 ............................................ Robert E. Lee is named general-in-chief of all Confederate armies.

Jan. 31 ............................................ U.S. House of Representatives approves constitutional amendment abolishing slavery.

Feb. 3 .............................................. Peace conference at Hampton Roads leads to no agreement.

Feb. 5–7 .......................................... Fighting at Hatcher's Run on the Richmond/Petersburg front.

Feb. 17 ............................................ Columbia, South Carolina, falls to
Sherman's army; fires sweep through
the city.

Feb. 17 ............................................ Charleston, South Carolina, evacuated
by Confederate military forces.

Feb. 22 ............................................ Joseph E. Johnston receives command
of Confederate forces defending the
Carolinas.

March 2 ........................................... Jubal Early defeated at Waynesboro in
the final engagement in the Shenandoah
Valley; Lee removes him from
command shortly thereafter.

March 4 ........................................... Abraham Lincoln delivers his second
inaugural address.

March 13 ......................................... C.S. Congress authorizes President
Davis to recruit slaves as soldiers (but
not to offer them freedom if they serve).

March 19, 21 ................................... Battle of Bentonville near Raleigh,
North Carolina, marks the end of
significant fighting on Johnston's and
Sherman's front.

March 25 ......................................... John B. Gordon leads Lee's last major
tactical offensive of the war at Fort
Stedman.

March 31 ......................................... Fighting at White Oak Road and
Dinwiddie Court House on the
Richmond/Petersburg front

April 1 ............................................ Union victory in the battle of Five
Forks, where George E. Pickett
performs poorly, sets the stage for the
Union capture of Richmond and
Petersburg.

April 2 ............................................ Confederate government abandons
Richmond; Robert E. Lee's army

evacuates Richmond-Petersburg lines and begins retreat westward; A. P. Hill killed in fighting west of Boydton Plank Road.

April 3 ............................................ U.S. forces occupy Petersburg and Richmond.

April 6 ............................................ Battle of Sailor's Creek a disaster for Lee's retreating army; Richard S. Ewell taken prisoner.

April 9 ............................................ Lee surrenders the Army of Northern Virginia to U. S. Grant at Appomattox Court House.

April 14 .......................................... Abraham Lincoln shot in Ford's Theater; he dies the next morning.

April 26 .......................................... Joseph E. Johnston surrenders his army to Sherman at Durham Station, North Carolina.

May 4 ............................................. Richard Taylor surrenders Confederate forces in the department of Alabama, Mississippi, and East Louisiana to E. R. S. Canby at Citronelle, Alabama.

May 10 ........................................... Jefferson Davis is captured near Irwinville, Georgia.

May 12–13 ..................................... The final land battle of the war takes place at Palmito Ranch, near Brownsville, Texas.

May 26 ........................................... Confederate forces in the trans-Mississippi theater surrender in an agreement signed in New Orleans.

Dec. 18 ........................................... The Thirteenth Amendment is ratified; it abolishes slavery throughout the United States.

# Glossary

**abatis**: A tangle of felled trees or brush in front of an entrenched position, with branches facing the enemy's lines, to retard an attacking force.

**blockade**: A force of naval vessels placed to intercept shipping into or out of an enemy's ports.

**bounty**: A cash payment by the national, state, or local government designed to attract volunteers to the armed forces.

**breastworks**: A barricade of dirt, logs, sandbags, or other materials designed to protect soldiers fighting on the defensive.

**breechloader**: A shoulder weapon that is loaded at the breech, or rear of the barrel.

**brevet rank**: An honorary promotion of a military officer to a rank above his regular rank, given to reward exceptional service but conveying no increase in authority.

**cavalry screen**: A body of cavalrymen charged with protecting the front and flanks of an army from probes by the enemy's cavalry.

**commissary**: The military department dealing with the supply of food.

**company-grade officers**: Those who hold the commissioned ranks of captain or lower.

**contraband**: Material belonging to an enemy subject to seizure by a belligerent power in time of war. During the Civil War, the term most often applied to slaves in the Confederacy who made their way to Union lines.

**demonstration**: A military term for a maneuver intended to hold the enemy's attention while a major assault or movement is made elsewhere.

**earthworks**: Fortifications constructed of dirt, sand, and similar materials (a term often used interchangeably with *breastworks* or *field works*).

**enfilade**: To fire against an enemy's position from the side or flank. Such fire is especially effective because the defenders are unable to bring a large volume of counter-fire to bear.

**entrenchments**: Defensive works prepared either in the field or as part of more permanent fortifications around cities or other crucial positions (also often called, simply, *trenches*).

**envelop**: To move around an enemy's flank, placing troops in position to render a defensive posture untenable.

**feint**: A movement intended to hold the enemy's attention while a larger attack or maneuver is carried out on another part of the field (a term often used interchangeably with *demonstration*).

**field-grade officers**: Those who hold the commissioned ranks of colonel, lieutenant colonel, or major.

**fire-eaters**: Outspoken advocates of Southern rights who took extreme positions regarding the protection of slavery. Many of them played a prominent role in the secession movement.

**flank**: The end of a line of troops on the field of battle or in a fortified position. To *flank* an enemy's position involves placing troops on its side or rear. A *flanking march* is the maneuver designed to give the troops in motion either a tactical or strategic advantage.

**fleet**: A group of naval warships and support vessels operating as a unified force.

**flotilla**: Similar to a fleet but usually consisting of a smaller number of vessels.

**forage**: The feed for horses and mules. As a verb, *to forage* means the procurement of hay, grains, or grass necessary to feed an army's animals. The verb also applied to soldiers' search for food to feed themselves.

**forced march**: A movement made at a rapid pace to meet a dire threat (either real or perceived).

**guerrilla**: A combatant who operates in small units or bands beyond the control of major organized military forces. These men often carried out raids and small attacks behind enemy lines.

**logistics**: Military activity dealing with the physical support, maintenance, and supply of an army.

**martial law**: Temporary government of civilians by military authorities, typically involving the suspension of some civil liberties.

**minié ball**: More properly called a *minié bullet*, this hollow-base lead projectile of cylindro-conoidal shape was the standard round for Union and Confederate infantrymen armed with rifled shoulder weapons.

**mortar**: An artillery piece designed to fire projectiles in a high arc that could strike targets behind fortifications. Mortar boats deployed this type of artillery piece in naval actions.

**muzzleloader**: A shoulder weapon that is loaded at the muzzle, or front of the barrel.

**non-commissioned officers**: Those who hold the ranks of sergeant and corporal.

**ordnance**: The military department responsible for the supply of arms and ammunition.

**parole**: An oath taken by a captured soldier, given in return for release from captivity, not to bear arms again until formally exchanged for one of the captor's soldiers. As a verb, *to parole* means to obtain such an oath from a prisoner as a condition of releasing him.

**partisan**: A combatant operating in small groups beyond the control of major military forces. The term is sometimes used interchangeably with *guerrilla*, but during the Civil War, partisans often were viewed as better disciplined and less likely to commit outrages against civilians or enemy soldiers.

**picket**: A soldier assigned to the perimeter of an army camp or position to give warning of enemy movements.

**prisoner cartel**: An agreement between the warring governments to exchange captured soldiers rather than sending them to prisoner-of-war camps. If one side had a surplus of prisoners, they typically would be paroled until a sufficient number of the enemy's troops were captured to make an exchange.

**quartermaster**: The military department responsible for the supply of clothing, shoes, and other equipment.

**reconnaissance in force**: A probing movement by a large body of troops intended to reveal the enemy's position and likely intentions.

**repeating firearm**: A weapon that can be fired more than once without reloading.

**salient**: A portion of a defensive line that protrudes toward the enemy and is, thus, potentially vulnerable on three sides.

**strategy**: The branch of warfare involving the movement of armies to (a) bring about combat with an enemy under favorable circumstances or (b) force the retreat of an enemy.

**tactics**: The branch of warfare involving actual combat between attackers and defenders.

**trains**: The wagons accompanying armies that carried food, forage, ammunition, and other supplies (not to be confused with railroad rolling stock).

**trooper**: A cavalryman.

**volley**: The simultaneous firing of their weapons by a number of soldiers in one unit.

**works**: A generic term applied to defensive fortifications of all types.

# Biographical Notes

**Alexander, Edward Porter** (1835–1910). One of the most versatile officers in the Confederate army, he served brilliantly on the staffs of P. G. T. Beauregard, Joseph E. Johnston, and Robert E. Lee before transferring to the artillery. He proved himself the most able artillerist in Confederate service, fighting in most of the great battles of the Army of Northern Virginia and writing a pair of classic memoirs after the war.

**Banks, Nathaniel Prentice** (1816–1894). One of the most prominent Union political generals, he served throughout the war without achieving any distinction on the battlefield. No match for Stonewall Jackson in the Shenandoah Valley in 1862, he similarly came to grief during the 1864 Red River campaign.

**Beauregard, Pierre Gustave Toutant** (1818–1893). One of the ranking officers in the Confederacy, he presided over the bombardment of Fort Sumter in April 1861, led the Southern army at the opening of the battle of First Bull Run or Manassas, and later held various commands in Mississippi, at Charleston, and at Petersburg, Virginia.

**Bragg, Braxton** (1817–1876). A controversial military figure who led the Confederate Army of Tennessee at Stones River, Chickamauga, and Chattanooga. Intensely unpopular with many of his soldiers and subordinates, including James Longstreet during the Chattanooga campaign in 1863, he finished the war as an advisor to Jefferson Davis in Richmond.

**Breckinridge, John Cabell** (1821–1875). Vice president of the United States under James Buchanan and the Southern Democratic candidate for president in 1860, he served the Confederacy as a general and secretary of war. He fought in the eastern and western theaters, winning the battle of New Market in May 1864.

**Burnside, Ambrose Everett** (1824–1881). Union general best known for commanding the Army of the Potomac at the battle of Fredericksburg in December 1862. His wartime career also included early service along the North Carolina coast and later action with Grant's army during the Overland campaign. After the war, he served Rhode Island as governor and U.S. senator.

**Butler, Benjamin Franklin** (1818–1893). Union general who coined the term *contraband* for runaway slaves in 1861 and commanded the army that approached Richmond by moving up the James River during U. S. Grant's grand offensive of May 1864. A prewar Democrat who supported John C. Breckinridge in 1860, he became a Radical Republican during the war.

**Davis, Jefferson** (1808–1889). Colonel during the war with Mexico, secretary of war under Franklin Pierce, and prominent senator from Mississippi in the 1840s and 1850s, he served as the Confederacy's only president. He and his nationalist policies triggered great political debate among Confederates.

**Early, Jubal Anderson** (1816–1894). Confederate general who compiled a solid record as an officer in the Army of Northern Virginia between First Manassas and the 1864 Overland campaign. He ended the war a disgraced figure in the Confederacy because of his defeats in the 1864 Shenandoah Valley campaign. After the war, he became one of the leading architects of the Lost Cause interpretation of the conflict.

**Ewell, Richard Stoddert** (1817–1872). Confederate general who made his name as a division commander under Stonewall Jackson in 1862 but never achieved distinction after being promoted to replace Jackson at the head of the Second Corps in the Army of Northern Virginia. He suffered the indignity of being eased out of corps command during the Overland campaign but remained in service to the end of the war.

**Frémont, John Charles** (1813–1890). Famous as an antebellum western explorer, he ran as the first Republican candidate for president in 1856 and served as a Union general in Missouri and Virginia during the war. While commanding in Missouri in 1861, he attempted to free the state's slaves by issuing a proclamation that abolitionists applauded, but Lincoln ordered him to rescind. He was among the U.S. generals who opposed Stonewall Jackson in the 1862 Shenandoah Valley campaign.

**Gordon, John Brown** (1832–1904). Although lacking formal military training, Gordon rose to become a Confederate corps commander on the basis of hard fighting between 1862 and 1864. He participated in most of the battles of the Army of Northern Virginia, playing important roles at Spotsylvania, in the Shenandoah Valley campaign of 1864, and during the siege of Petersburg. A prominent politician after the war in his native Georgia, he also ranked among the most influential Lost Cause writers.

**Grant, Ulysses S.** (1822–1885). The most successful Union military commander, serving as general-in-chief for the last 14 months of the war and twice winning election as president during the postwar years.

**Hill, Ambrose Powell** (1825–1865). Confederate general whose record in 1862–1863 as the head of the "Light Division" in Lee's army was impressive. He struggled after being promoted to corps command just before the Gettysburg campaign, was frequently ill, and was killed in battle just before the retreat to Appomattox.

**Hood, John Bell** (1831–1879). Confederate commander who fought effectively in the Army of Northern Virginia in 1862–1863 but is best known for his unsuccessful defense of Atlanta against Sherman's army and the disastrous campaign in Tennessee that culminated in the battle of Nashville in mid-December 1864.

**Hooker, Joseph** (1814–1879). Union general nicknamed "Fighting Joe" who commanded the Army of the Potomac at the battle of Chancellorsville. Replaced by George G. Meade during the Gettysburg campaign, he later fought at Chattanooga and in the opening phase of the 1864 Atlanta campaign.

**Hunter, David** (1802–1886). A Union general who, as commander along the south Atlantic coast in May 1862, tried to free all slaves in his department, only to see Lincoln revoke his order. He later led an army in the Shenandoah Valley in 1864 and was defeated by Jubal Early at Lynchburg.

**Jackson, Thomas Jonathan** (1824–1863). Nicknamed "Stonewall" and second only to Lee as a popular Confederate hero, he was celebrated for his 1862 Shenandoah Valley campaign and his achievements as Lee's trusted subordinate. He died at the peak of his fame, succumbing to pneumonia after being wounded at the battle of Chancellorsville.

**Johnston, Albert Sidney** (1803–1862). A prominent antebellum military figure from whom much was expected as a Confederate general. He compiled a mixed record in the western theater before being mortally wounded on April 6, 1862, at the battle of Shiloh.

**Johnston, Joseph Eggleston** (1807–1891). A Confederate army commander who served in both Virginia and the western theater. Notoriously prickly about rank and privileges, he feuded with Jefferson Davis and compiled a record demonstrating his preference for defensive over offensive operations. His wound at the battle of Seven Pines in May 1862 opened the way for R. E. Lee to assume field command. (He and A. S. Johnston were not related.)

**Lee, Robert Edward** (1807–1870). Southern military officer who commanded the Army of Northern Virginia for most of the war. His successes in 1862–1863 made him the most admired Confederate public figure and his army, the most important national institution in the Confederacy.

**Lincoln, Abraham** (1809–1865). Elected in 1860 as the first Republican to hold the presidency, he provided superior leadership for the Northern war effort and was reelected in 1864 before being assassinated at Ford's Theater on the eve of complete Union victory.

**Longstreet, James** (1821–1904). Lee's senior subordinate from 1862 until the end of the war, he compiled a generally excellent record while under Lee's eye but proved unequal to the demands of independent command during the East Tennessee campaign of 1863–1864. He became a controversial figure in the South after the war because he refused to embrace Lost Cause ideas.

**Magruder, John Bankhead** (1807–1871). Confederate military officer who achieved considerable success defending the Virginia peninsula in early 1862 but suffered a loss of reputation during the Seven Days' battles. Transferred to the trans-Mississippi theater, he spent the remainder of the war far removed from the arenas of important military campaigning.

**McClellan, George Brinton** (1826–1885). One of the most important military figures of the war, he built the Army of the Potomac into a formidable force and led it during the Peninsula campaign, the Seven Days' battles, and at Antietam. Often at odds with Lincoln because of his unwillingness to press the enemy, he was relieved of command in November 1862 and ran as the Democratic candidate for president in 1864.

**McDowell, Irvin** (1818–1885). Military officer who commanded the Union army at the battle of First Bull Run or Manassas. The remainder of his wartime career, which included roles during the 1862 Shenandoah Valley campaign and the battle of Second Manassas, was anticlimactic.

**Meade, George Gordon** (1815–1872). Union general who fought throughout the war in the eastern theater, commanding the Army of the

Potomac at Gettysburg and for the rest of the war. U. S. Grant's presence with the army after April 1864 placed Meade in a difficult position.

**Pickett, George Edward** (1825–1875). Perhaps the most famous of the Confederacy's major generals because of the grand attack on the third day at Gettysburg that bears his name, Pickett compiled a spotty record at best during the Civil War. He was relieved of command shortly after his defeat at the battle of Five Forks but remained with the army until the surrender at Appomattox shortly thereafter.

**Pope, John** (1822–1892). Union general who won several small successes in the western theater before being transferred to the eastern theater in the summer of 1862 to command the Army of Virginia. His defeat at the battle of Second Bull Run or Manassas in August 1862 ended his important service during the war.

**Ramseur, Stephen Dodson** (1837–1864). A talented young officer who fit the aggressive mold of successful combat leaders in the Army of Northern Virginia. After a sterling record as the head of a brigade at Chancellorsville, Gettysburg, and Spotsylvania, he commanded a division under Jubal Early in the 1864 Shenandoah Valley campaign. He was mortally wounded trying to rally Confederate soldiers at the battle of Cedar Creek.

**Rodes, Robert Emmett** (1829–1864). One of the best young generals in the Army of Northern Virginia, Rodes did well as a brigade commander before taking charge of a division at Chancellorsville. He rendered his best service at Spotsylvania and during the 1864 Shenandoah Valley campaign, falling mortally wounded at the battle of Third Winchester.

**Scott, Winfield** (1786–1866). One of the great soldiers in U.S. history, he performed brilliantly in the war with Mexico, influenced nearly all the men who held major U.S. or Confederate commands during the Civil War, and remained the ranking officer in the army until the autumn of 1861. He devised the "Anaconda Plan" in the spring of 1861, a strategy that anticipated the way the United States would win the conflict.

**Sheridan, Philip Henry** (1831–1888). Ranked behind only Grant and Sherman as a Union war hero, Sheridan fought in both the western and eastern theaters. His most famous victories came in the 1864 Shenandoah Valley campaign; at the battle of Five Forks on April 1, 1865; and during the Appomattox campaign.

**Sherman, William Tecumseh** (1820–1891). Union military officer who overcame early-war difficulties to become Grant's primary subordinate. An advocate of "hard" war, he is best known for his capture of Atlanta and "March to the Sea" in 1864.

**Sigel, Franz** (1824–1902). German-born Union general who was popular among German-speaking troops but ineffective as a field commander. His most famous service came in the Shenandoah Valley in 1864, ending in defeat at the battle of New Market on May 15.

**Stephens, Alexander Hamilton** (1812–1883). A moderate Democrat from Georgia who supported Stephen A. Douglas in the 1860 presidential campaign and embraced secession reluctantly, he served throughout the war as vice president of the Confederacy. Increasingly at odds with Jefferson Davis over issues related to growing central power, he became an embittered public critic of the president and his policies.

**Stuart, James Ewell Brown** (1833–1864). Known as "Jeb," he commanded the cavalry in the Army of Northern Virginia from June 1862 until his death following the battle of Yellow Tavern in May 1864. His role in the Gettysburg campaign generated a great deal of controversy, but overall, he compiled a superb record as the "eyes and ears" of Lee's army.

# Bibliography

**Essential Reading:**

Alexander, Edward Porter. *Fighting for the Confederacy: The Personal Recollections of General Edward Porter Alexander*. Gary W. Gallagher, ed. Chapel Hill: University of North Carolina Press, 1989. Reprinted in paperback. The most perceptive memoir written by any officer who served in the Army of Northern Virginia, this work traces in detail Alexander's remarkable Confederate career.

Connelly, Thomas L., and Jones, Archer. *The Politics of Command: Factions and Ideas in Confederate Strategy*. Baton Rouge: Louisiana State University Press, 1973. An overview of Confederate strategy that reaches generally negative conclusions about Robert E. Lee.

Eckert, Ralph L. *John Brown Gordon: Soldier, Southerner, American.* Baton Rouge: Louisiana State University Press, 1989. This excellent biography provides a case study of a young, nonprofessional soldier who earned a solid reputation and rose to the rank of corps commander.

Freeman, Douglas Southall. *Lee's Lieutenants: A Study in Command*. 3 vols. New York: Scribner's, 1942–1945. Reprinted in paperback. These compellingly written volumes are the classic treatment of the Army of Northern Virginia's high command. Few studies have exerted as much influence on the military history of the Civil War. (Note: This set is also recommended as supplementary reading.)

———. *R. E. Lee: A Biography*. 4 vols. New York: Scribner's, 1934–1935. Easily the most famous biography of Lee, which won a Pulitzer Prize and has influenced all subsequent work on the topic. (Note: This set is also recommended as supplementary reading.)

Gallagher, Gary W. *The Confederate War*. Cambridge, Mass.: Harvard University Press, 1997. Reprinted in paperback. A concise treatment that devotes considerable attention to Lee and his army as the Confederacy's most important national institution.

———. *Lee and His Army in Confederate History*. Chapel Hill: University of North Carolina Press, 2001. Includes essays on the ties between the battlefield and the home front and on the Lost Cause interpretation of Lee's operations.

———. *Lee and His Generals in War and Memory*. Baton Rouge: Louisiana State University Press, 1998. Reprinted in paperback. Includes essays on Lee, several of his principal lieutenants, and Jubal A. Early's Lost Cause advocacy.

―――, ed. *Lee the Soldier*. Lincoln: University of Nebraska Press, 1995. Reprinted in paperback. Includes a selection of interpretive essays by Confederate officers and later historians regarding Lee as a Confederate general. The roster of authors includes E. P. Alexander, Jubal A. Early, Albert Castel, Thomas L. Connelly, William C. Davis, Douglas Southall Freeman (two essays), Gary W. Gallagher (two essays), D. Scott Hartwig, Robert K. Krick, James Longstreet, Alan T. Nolan (two essays), Carol Reardon, Charles P. Roland, and Noah Andre Trudeau.

―――, ed. *The Richmond Campaign of 1862: The Peninsula and the Seven Days*. Chapel Hill, University of North Carolina Press, 2000. The essays by Peter S. Carmichael on John Bankhead Magruder and by Gallagher on the campaign as a military watershed are most useful for this course.

―――. *Stephen Dodson Ramseur: Lee's Gallant General*. Chapel Hill: University of North Carolina Press, 1985. Reprinted in paperback. A useful case study of the development of a young officer in the Army of Northern Virginia, this biography examines elements of Ramseur's military character that were typical of other officers of his generation.

―――, and Nolan, Alan T., eds. *The Myth of the Lost Cause and Civil War History*. Bloomington: Indiana University Press, 2000. A collection of essays on different aspects of the Lost Cause, including contributions by Gary W. Gallagher, Lesley J. Gordon, Alan T. Nolan, Brooks D. Simpson, and Jeffry D. Wert that are most useful for this course.

Krick, Robert K. *The Smoothbore Volley That Doomed the Confederacy: The Death of Stonewall Jackson and Other Chapters on the Army of Northern Virginia*. Baton Rouge: Louisiana State University Press, 2002. A learned and strongly opinionated collection that includes two highly critical essays on James Longstreet.

McMurry, Richard M. *John Bell Hood and the War for Southern Independence*. Lexington: University Press of Kentucky, 1982. Reprinted in paperback. The best biography of the hard-fighting soldier who performed well under Lee but found himself promoted beyond his abilities during the last two years of the war.

―――. *Two Great Rebel Armies: An Essay on Confederate Military History*. Chapel Hill: University of North Carolina Press, 1987. Reprinted in paperback. A perceptive comparative study of the Army of Northern

Virginia and the Army of Tennessee that highlights the strengths of Lee and his soldiers.

Thomas, Emory M. *Robert E. Lee: A Biography*. New York: Norton, 1995. Reprinted in paperback. This excellent one-volume treatment allocates a good deal of attention to Lee the man, as well as to Lee the soldier. (Note: This is also recommended as supplementary reading.)

Woodworth, Steven E., ed. *Leadership and Command in the American Civil War*. Campbell, Calif.: SavasWoodbury, 1995. The essays by Lesley J. Gordon on George E. Pickett and by Richard M. McMurry on Joseph E. Johnston are most pertinent to this course.

**Supplementary Reading:**

Alexander, Edward Porter. *Military Memoirs of a Confederate: A Critical Narrative*. New York: Scribner's, 1907. Reprinted in paperback. Less personal and more of a scholarly history than Alexander's *Fighting for the Confederacy*, this book has been an essential title on Lee's army for nearly a century.

Casdorph, Paul D. *Prince John Magruder: His Life and Campaigns*. New York: Wiley, 1996. This straightforward biography is the only full-scale treatment of the mercurial Magruder.

Connelly, Thomas L., and Bellows, Barbara L. *God and General Longstreet: The Lost Cause and the Southern Mind*. Baton Rouge: Louisiana State University Press, 1982. Reprinted in paperback. This influential series of essays traces the continuing influence of Lost Cause arguments.

Early, Jubal A. *Autobiographical Sketch and Narrative of the War between the States*. Philadelphia: Lippincott, 1912. Reprinted in paperback. This detailed, posthumously published account is far more restrained than might be expected from a leading Lost Cause warrior such as Early.

Ewell, Richard S. *The Making of a Soldier: Letters of General R. S. Ewell*. Percy G. Hamlin, ed. Richmond, Va.: Whittet and Shepperson, 1935. These wonderfully quotable letters offer numerous insights into Ewell's personality and conduct.

Foster, Gaines M. *Ghosts of the Confederacy: Defeat, the Lost Cause, and the Emergence of the New South, 1865–1913*. New York: Oxford University Press, 1987. Reprinted in paperback. The best examination of the development of Lost Cause arguments about the causes and conduct of the Civil War.

Gordon, John B. *Reminiscences of the Civil War*. New York: Scribner's, 1903. Reprinted in paperback. A much quoted Lost Cause classic, this account always places its author in a positive, and often in a heroic, light.

Gordon, Lesley J. *General George E. Pickett in Life and Legend*. Chapel Hill: University of North Carolina Press, 1998. Reprinted in paperback. Easily the best study of Pickett, this biography thoroughly explores both positive and negative elements of his career.

Harsh, Joseph L. *Confederate Tide Rising: Robert E. Lee and the Making of Southern Strategy, 1861-1862*. Kent, Ohio: Kent State University Press, 1998.

————. *Taken at the Flood: Robert E. Lee and Confederate Strategy in the Maryland Campaign of 1862*. Kent, Ohio: Kent State University Press, 1999.

Hassler, William W. *A. P. Hill: Lee's Forgotten General*. Richmond: Garrett and Massie, 1957. A straightforward, careful biography that makes the most of a limited array of sources on Hill.

Hood, John Bell. *Advance and Retreat: Personal Experiences in the United States and Confederate States Armies*. New Orleans: Hood Orphan Memorial Fund, 1880. Reprinted in paperback. The early chapters on Hood's service in Virginia offer a rich lode of quotable material, while the later chapters, which deal with his mostly unhappy service in the western theater, attempt to even scores with Joseph Johnston and place Hood's own actions in the best possible light.

Johnston, Joseph E. *Narrative of Military Operations, Directed during the Late War between the States*. New York: Appleton, 1874. Reprinted in paperback. A contentious, often inaccurate book that unintentionally illuminates the problematical side of Johnston's character.

Klein, Maury. *Edward Porter Alexander*. Athens: University of Georgia Press, 1971. More interested in Alexander's postwar career than in his Confederate service, this remains the only biography of the brilliant young Georgian.

Longstreet, James. *From Manassas to Appomattox: Memoirs of the Civil War in America*. Philadelphia: Lippincott, 1896. Reprinted in paperback. An essential title on Confederate military history, Longstreet's memoirs show their author at both his best and his worst.

McWhiney, Grady and Perry D. Jamieson. *Attack and Die: Civil War Military Tactics and the Southern Heritage.* University, Alabama: University of Alabama Press, 1982.

Nolan, Alan T. *Lee Considered: General Robert E. Lee and Civil War History.* Chapel Hill: University of North Carolina Press, 1991. Reprinted in paperback. A revisionist look at Lee that portrays him as a general whose penchant for the offensive likely shortened the life of the Confederacy.

Osborne, Charles C. *Jubal: The Life and Times of General Jubal A. Early, C.S.A.* Chapel Hill: Algonquin, 1992. Reprinted in paperback. A well-written narrative of Early's career, this biography is better at description than at analysis.

Pfanz, Donald. *Richard S. Ewell: A Soldier's Life.* Chapel Hill: University of North Carolina Press, 1998. This deeply researched volume offers a detailed and generally favorable estimate of Ewell's Confederate career.

Piston, William Garrett. *Lee's Tarnished Lieutenant: James Longstreet and His Place in Southern History.* Athens: University of Georgia Press, 1987. Reprinted in paperback. Brief in its treatment of Longstreet's Confederate service, this volume concentrates on Lost Cause controversies regarding the conduct of "Old Pete" at Gettysburg and elsewhere.

Robertson, James I., Jr. *General A. P. Hill: The Story of a Confederate Warrior.* New York: Random House, 1987. Reprinted in paperback. The most detailed discussion of Hill's life and career, this biography draws on some materials Hassler's earlier study did not use.

————. *Stonewall Jackson: The Man, the Soldier, the Legend.* New York: Macmillan, 1997. Reprinted in paperback. Exhaustive and well-written, this biography concludes that Jackson was a great soldier.

Roman, Alfred. *The Military Operations of General Beauregard in the War between the States, 1861–1865.* 2 vols. New York: Harper, 1883. Reprinted in paperback. Extremely detailed and sometimes tedious, this set, though attributed to Alfred Roman, should be considered Beauregard's personal memoirs.

Symonds, Craig L. *Joseph E. Johnston: A Civil War Biography.* New York: Norton, 1992. The best modern biography of Johnston, this volume presents its subject in a largely favorable light.

Thomas, Emory M. *Bold Dragoon: The Life of J. E. B. Stuart.* New York: Harper and Row, 1986. Reprinted in paperback. A sound scholarly biography that, like its author's book on Lee, gives the man, as well as the soldier, full attention.

Thomason, John W. *Jeb Stuart*. New York: Scribner's, 1930. A classic biography that captures the spirit of Stuart and his troopers but glosses over "Jeb's" failures while lavishing attention on his more successful exploits.

Vandiver, Frank E. *Mighty Stonewall*. New York: McGraw-Hill, 1957. Reprinted in paperback. This careful, splendidly written biography remains valuable for anyone interested in Jackson.

Welsh, Jack D. *Medical Histories of Confederate Generals*. Kent, Ohio: Kent State University Press, 1995. This useful reference work includes detailed information about the wounds—in many cases the multiple wounds—and illnesses of all the men who served as Confederate generals.

Wert, Jeffry D. *General James Longstreet: The Confederacy's Most Controversial Soldier*. New York: Simon and Schuster, 1993. Reprinted in paperback. Well researched, well written, and very favorable to its subject, this is the best modern biography of Longstreet.

Williams, T. Harry. *P. G. T. Beauregard: Napoleon in Gray*. Baton Rouge: Louisiana State University Press, 1955. Reprinted in paperback. The standard biography of Beauregard, which points out the "Great Creole's" flaws, as well as his gifts as a commander.

# Notes

# Notes

# Notes

# Notes

# Notes